DOPE MENACE

ILLUSTRATION BY ALEXANDER KING FROM *BLACK OPIUM* • AND/OR PRESS • 1974

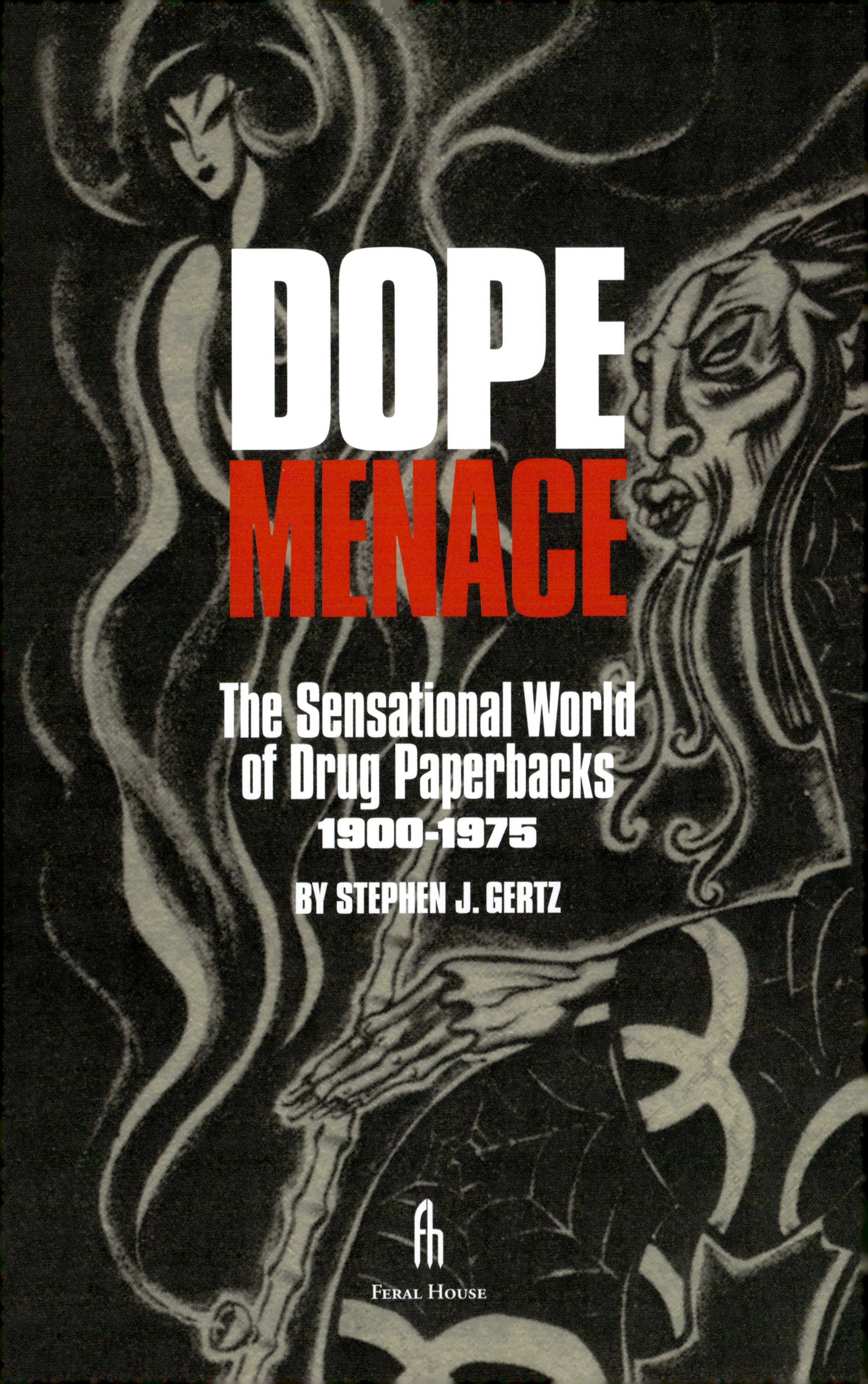

DOPE MENACE

The Sensational World of Drug Paperbacks 1900–1975

BY STEPHEN J. GERTZ

FERAL HOUSE

ISBN: 978-1-932595-34-5

10 9 8 7 6 5 4 3 2 1

FERAL HOUSE
1240 W. Sims Way, Suite 124
Port Townsend, WA 98368

To browse our selection of visually rich titles, please log on to *www.FeralHouse.com* or send us an SASE for a free catalogue.

DESIGN BY BILL SMITH

PRINTED IN CHINA

"...the mind-opening substances...are available for the first time in limitless, mass-produced quantities. What a threat! What a challenge! What a widespread menace!"

Timothy Leary
Richard Alpert [Ram Dass]
The Politics of Consciousness Expansion

This Book Is for "Adults of Low Ethical Standards."[1]

In 1952, Congressman Ezekiel C. Gathings (D-Arkansas) convened a House Select Committee to investigate the proliferation of literature he considered a pox on contemporary American society, taking particular aim at paperback books which he believed were specifically marketed to the above demographic group.

Attacking "the so-called pocket-size books, which originally started out as cheap reprints of standard works, [but which] have largely degenerated into media for the dissemination of appeals to sensuality, immorality, filth, perversion, and degeneracy,"[2] the Committee devoted much of its attention to paperbacks that contained the use of illegal drugs as thematic material.

Welcome to that world, a universe of paperback books — mass-market-sized, larger digest and trade-paper format — that because of their dramatically high print runs and broad distribution into multi-various retail outlets, exposed Americans to drugs and drug use in a far more influential manner than hardcover volumes, which were released in small print runs and distributed through bookstores only. And paperbacks were the only medium to do so in a lasting, material way: Film depictions of drug use and trafficking[3] had been banned by Hollywood's Production Code (a.k.a. The Hays Code) in 1930,[4] radio was by nature evanescent, and newspapers generally disposed of within 24 hours. As such, drug-themed paperback books provide the richest, most direct record of American pop culture's fascination, repulsion, fears, realities, perceptions, fantasies, paranoia, facts, hopes, follies and fallacies regarding psychoactive drugs during the beginning, rise and crest of what has been characterized as "America's Second Drug Epidemic."[5]

This did not occur in a vacuum. In the immediate aftermath of World War II, when drug smuggling routes had been re-established — having been completely disrupted during the war with narcotics distribution and use in the U.S. declining to their lowest levels in the century — and addiction to heroin and use of marijuana began to return with slow, steady drive, another phenomenon became manifest: the saturation of the marketplace with mass-market paperbacks, which began in 1939 with a hugely successful experiment by Pocket Books that yielded over 1.5 million copies sold of 34 reprint titles at 25 cents each.[6]

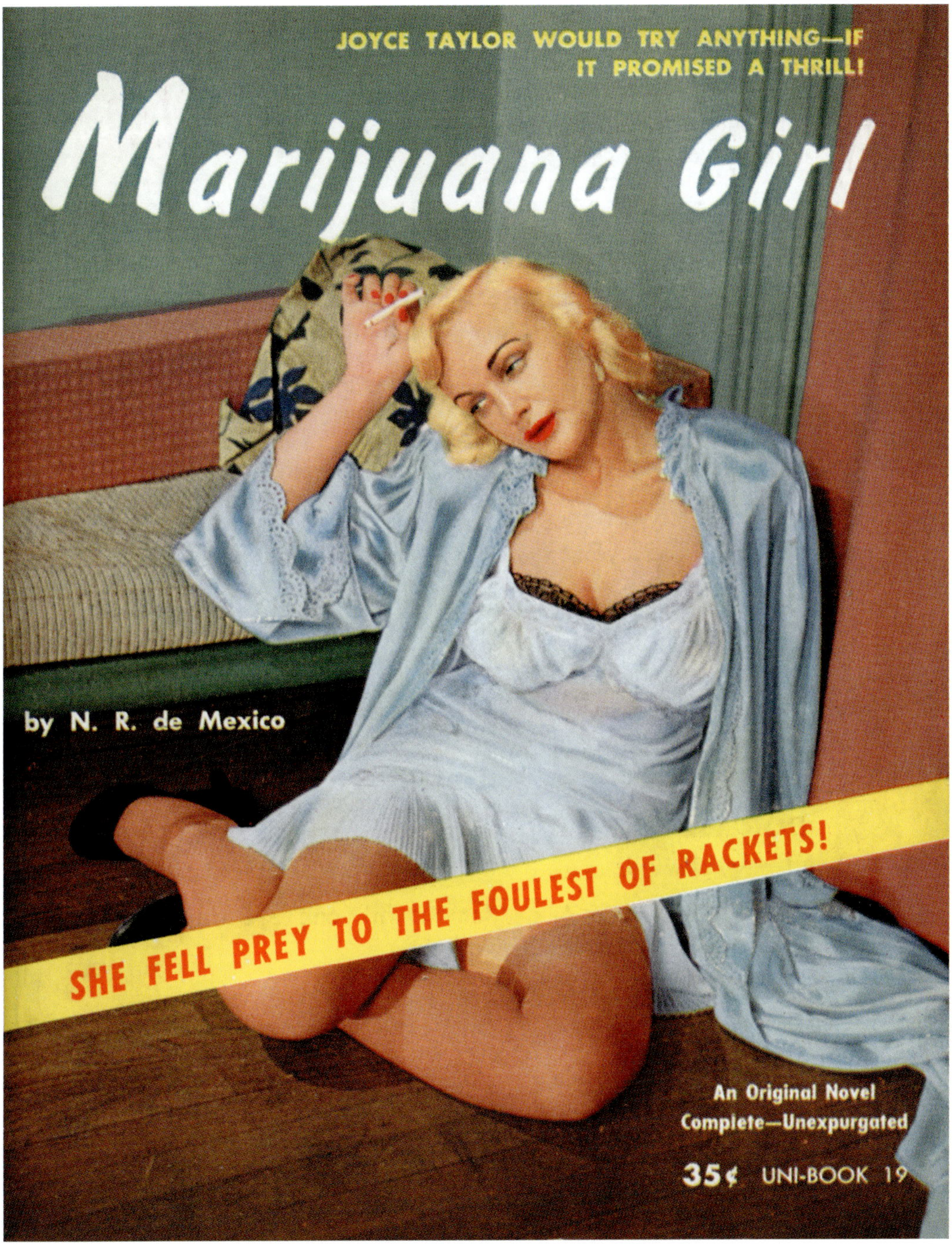

Gathings Committee Exhibit A: "A Manual of Instruction for Potential Narcotic Addicts."

N.R. De Mexico [Dallas McCord Reynolds or Lawrence Taylor Shaw] • ***Marijuana Girl*** • UNI BOOK 19
1951 • PBO • REPRINTED AS STALLION 204 (1954) AND BEACON 328 (1960)

By the early 1950s many social critics and latter-day Catos were becoming alarmed. Other publishers had entered the field, and many reprints and new, original paperbacks were not of the finest literary quality. "Some of these books [are] filled with sordid, filthy statements based upon sexual deviations and perversions..." Gathings reported.[7]

Further, the Gathings Committee stated, "other paper-bound books dwell at length on narcotics and in such a way as to present inducements for susceptible readers to become addicts out of sheer curiosity. As an example of how this subject is handled by current books, one need only read *Marijuana Girl* by N.R. de Mexico (Universal Publishing & Distributing Corp.). A more appropriate title would be: 'A Manual of Instructions for Potential Drug Addicts.' It even has a glossary of the jargon used by dope peddlers and their customers.[8] The noble motives ascribed to the author on the back cover, and quoted below, are not manifest in the book he wrote.

"Quotes below are on the back cover of *Marijuana Girl*, the book in question:

'This extraordinarily valid book does more than reaffirm the reputation of the author as a literary stylist and a shrewd, blunt commentator on our social scene. It tells the real story behind the lurid newspaper headlines — the crime investigations — the reports, official and unofficial — all screaming of the spread of dope addiction among children today!'

"Even the evil effects of drug addiction are made to appear not so very unattractive by artful manipulation of the imagination. While the analysis of this book has been directed chiefly to its narcotic phase, that should not be construed as implying that it is not replete with lewdness and vulgarity."[9]

Uh oh. Sex and drugs, the marriage of which has traditionally aroused the ire and righteous indignation of concerned citizen-moralists. And aroused the fascination and curiosity, if not fetishistic fervor, of the general public. Popular culture is Dionysian in nature: of the appetites, instincts and senses. The public bought these books in numbers that will astound.

What prompted Congressman Gathings to approach then Speaker of the House, Sam Rayburn, to approve $25,000 of our taxes for his wacky witch hunt?

"Every time I went into the drugstore to get cigars there would be a long line at the bookstand looking at the lewd covers...I thought, what is this country coming to if we are distributing this type of thing to the youth of the land?"[10] the Congressman declared.

The books were not, of course, aimed at the youth of our fair nation. They were, to the contrary, directed to a group "made up mostly of people who used to read only magazines, who [were] intimidated by the forbidding air of a bookstore, and [could] afford perhaps a small fraction of the price of most new hard-cover books. They [bought] and read on the move, picking books off a rack or newsstand to read while commuting or traveling or during a frenzied day of changing diapers and making meals. They [were] impulse buyers who [picked] books at the point of sale, and after reading them [threw] them away or [passed] them on to someone else."[11]

That said, while Gathings may have been another in a long line of congressional gasbags and something of a crackpot, he wasn't crazy. At a time when there only an estimated 1500 bookstores scattered throughout the United States,[12] paperbacks were distributed into 80,000–100,000[13] retail outlets nationwide including drugstores, newsstands, bus depots, train stations, airports, grocery stores, supermarkets, corner candy store/luncheonettes — in short, any place that sold magazines (paperback publishers had a completely different business model than hardcover publishing; it was the periodicals business); paperbacks of any nature, including those dealing with drugs, were most certainly seen by youngsters. I was surely not the only kid during the 1950s who would wander into the neighborhood candy store/lunch counter and peruse the comics and paperbacks rack, and I was certainly not the only one who was soon chased out with the admonition: "Whad'ya think this is, a library? Scram!" And, too, many drug paperbacks did in fact contain mixed messages, indeed some so mixed that the writers appear to have been typing within Cuisinarts.™

Gathings' fears about drug-themed paperbacks and their influence upon culture were not without substance, and though insinuations toward censorship were most certainly misguided, the democratization of drug use in paperback literature did pose challenges. The paperback was the Internet of its time. "The inexpensive book, more than any other modern instruments of mass communication, is today an outpost of freedom in our democratic culture," a contemporary observer wrote.[14] And, when you add drugs — and sex — to the equation, like the Internet the paperback becomes a satanic tool, opening a biblical sinkhole into which society will inevitably fall. "The nature of any censorship...is often a function of the anxieties generated by the medium or the milieu which the medium serves," Harper's magazine noted at the time.[15]

The books were quite threatening to sober-minded, solid citizens. "The volume of their sales, the manner of their distribution, their modest price and ready accessibility to the public, the provocative nature of some of their jackets and blurbs, and the existence of a national organization that had already sharpened its teeth on comic books and magazines [Citizens For Decent Literature — led by that paragon of moral and ethical virtue, Charles H. Keating, Jr., who, though famed at the time for his moral zeal, would win greater fame in the late 1980s for his role as Public Enemy #1, the top free-booting buccaneer in the U.S. savings and loan industry debacle] all these contributed to the outbreak of censorship aimed at literature in this form," wrote Lockhart and McClure.[16]

While we can now enjoy many of these books for their camp, kitschy quality, writing that is often gloriously lousy, and with postmodern irony be amused by their outlandish assertions and misinformation, at the time high-lit. paperbacks were a dangerous, transgressive medium. There is no denying the perversely seductive quality to so many of them.

In 1953, an unknown writer just shy of his fortieth birthday had his first book published. Issued by a new, small paperback publisher, it sold 113,170 copies in its first year. The book was *Junkie*, written by William S. Burroughs under the pseudonym "William Lee." Given the sales figure,[17] one might reasonably conclude that this was a fabulous success, a best-seller, an amazing accomplishment for a first-time novelist. It was, to the contrary, merely a respectable number, in fact somewhat below average, many if not most paperbacks selling in the 200,000-copy range.[18]

Junkie was published by Ace Books, a paperback house established in 1952 to surf the huge wave of paperback's popularity to the bank. Ace was owned by A.A. Wyn who,

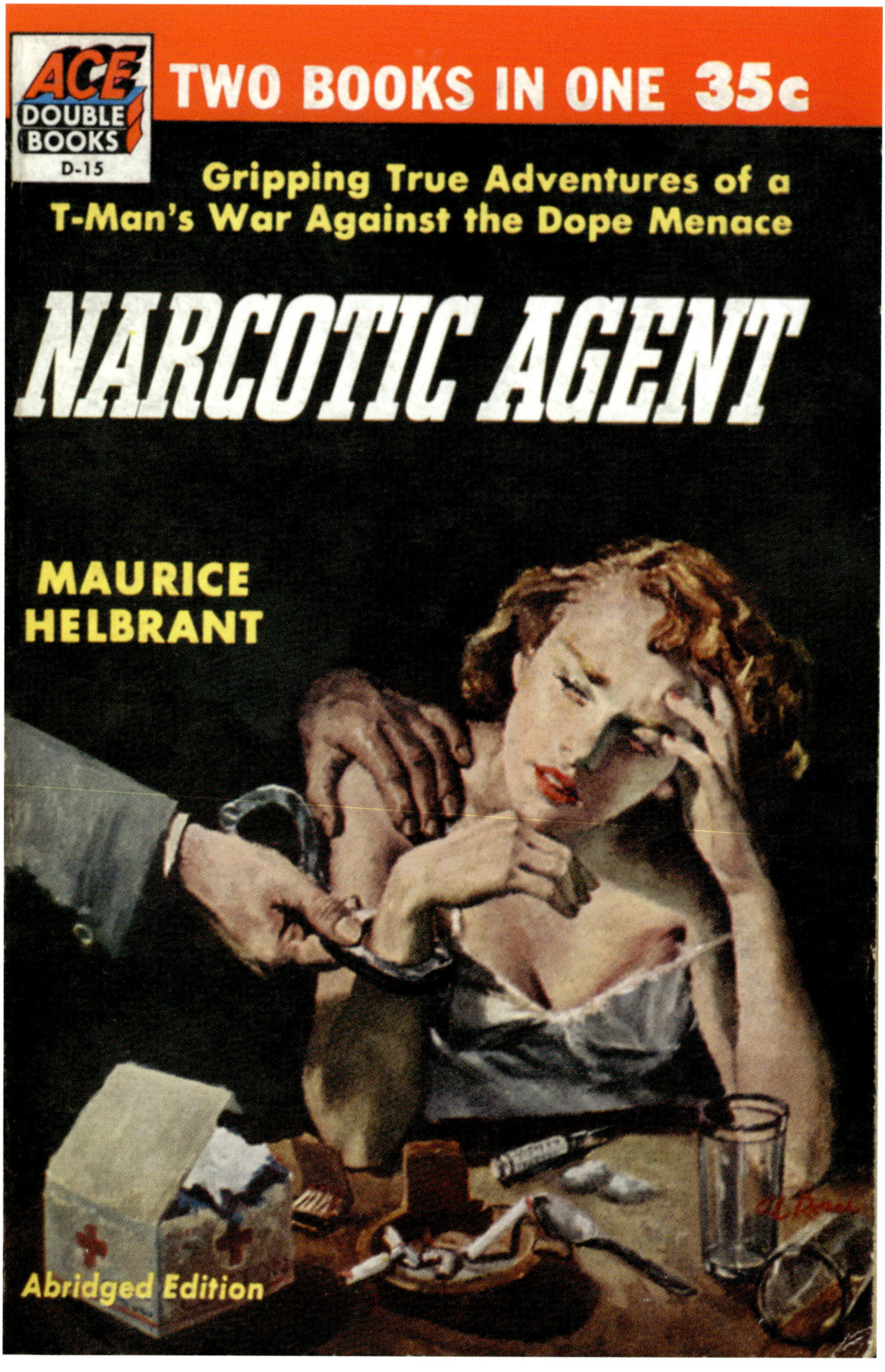

William Lee [William S. Burroughs] • ***Junkie: Confessions of an Unredeemed Drug Addict*** • PBO • BOUND WITH: Maurice Helbrant • ***Narcotic Agent*** • REPRINT • ACE D-15 • 1953 • COVERS BY AL ROSSI

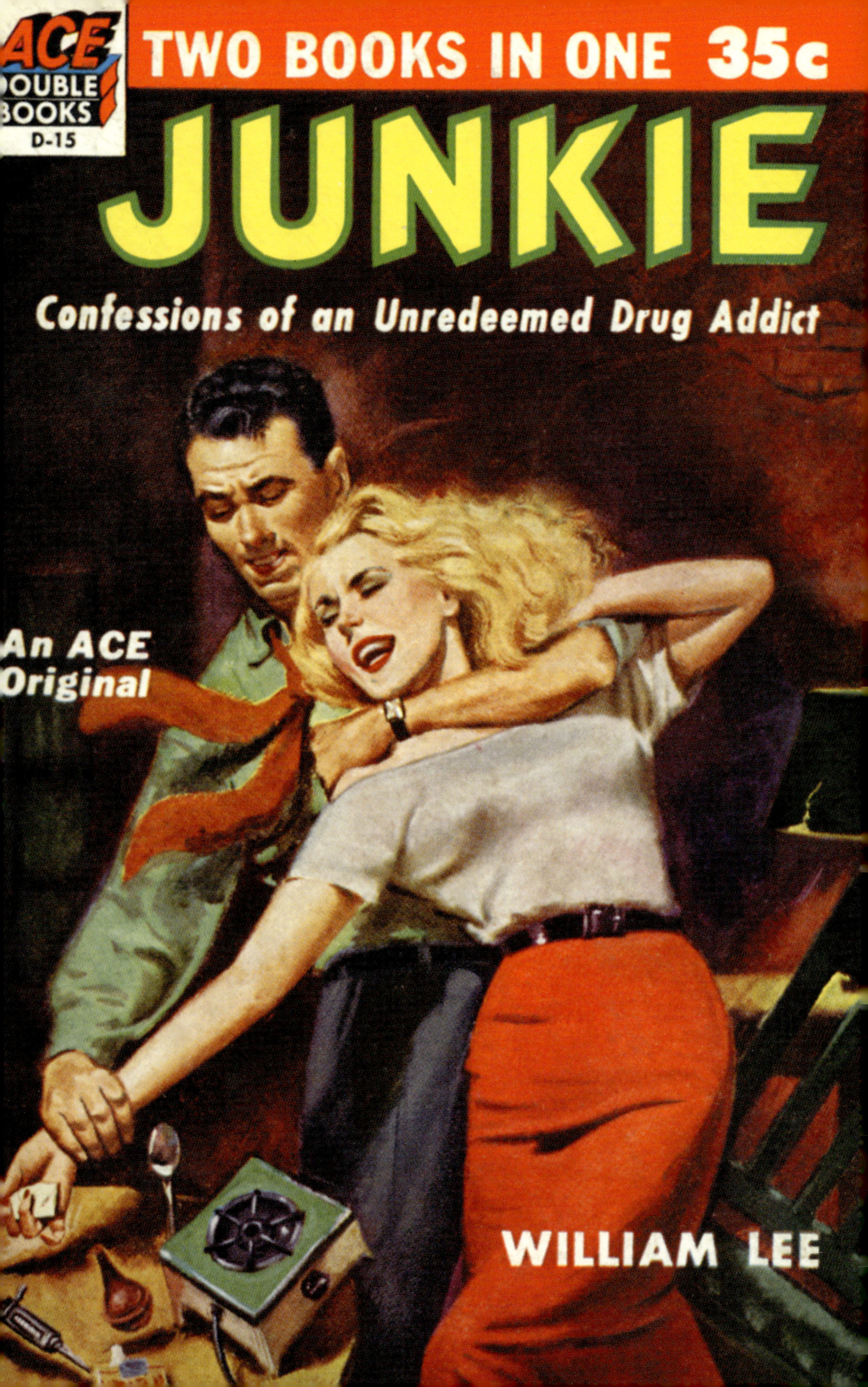

ACE DOUBLE BOOKS D-15
TWO BOOKS IN ONE 35c
JUNKIE
Confessions of an Unredeemed Drug Addict
An ACE Original
WILLIAM LEE

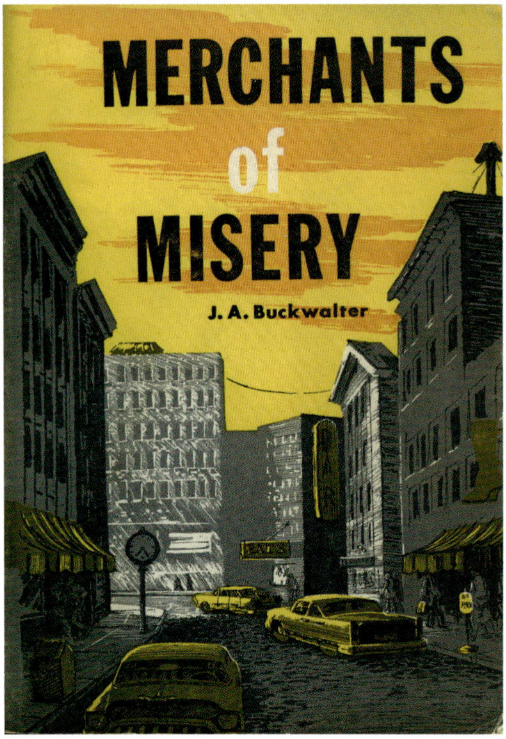

"Slimey Pete was a notorious habitué of the jive joint and bawdy houses of the town. His oily face provided a unique study of life's sinister shadows, and his soul had shriveled into meanness in the most debasing racket of the underworld. Pete was a dope peddler. Helen, his overpainted mistress, was repulsive to any decent man. Pete, well versed in the tricks of seduction and addiction, had caused her downfall and had made her his slave. He had changed her name from Ellen to Helen — 'H' for heroin. She was to be known in the shadowy world as the 'swing man's' contact girl.

"Pete and Helen had a way with teen-agers, particularly in the underprivileged areas. They could always suggest a new false thrill to youthful gangs: first, a few free puffs on a marijuana cigarette, then the reefer binges of the marijuana parties, and finally the bigger 'lift' of the white powders, and addiction's ultimate slavery. Local delinquent youth always knew that this degraded pair had a place for them to go, sordid though it might be."

J.A. Buckwalter • ***Merchants of Misery*** • PACIFIC PRESS PUBLISHING ASSOCIATION • 1956 • PBO
FROM THE AUTHOR'S COLLECTION

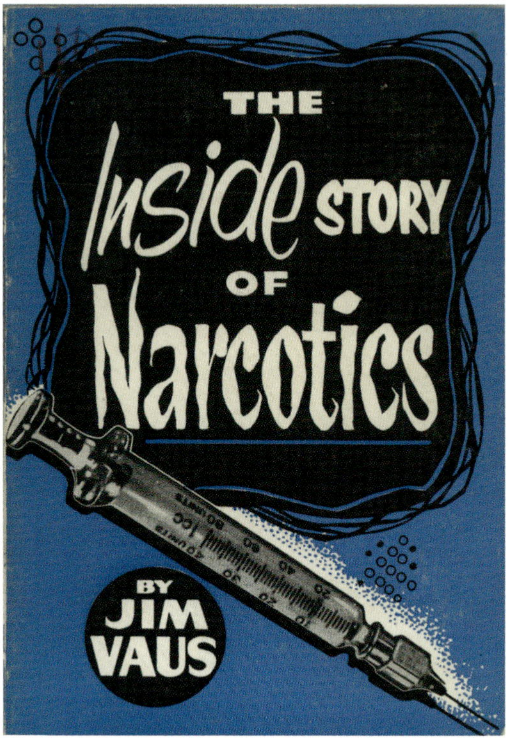

"Every trade has a technical language. Even Christians have a language of their own. They speak of being 'saved,' of a 'Christian worker,' or of 'putting out fleece.' The person not used to their jargon doesn't understand what the Christians are talking about. Addicts, too, have a language of their own, a language which must be understood if this book is to be understood. Some of the words most used are: bad go — too small an amount for the money paid; bang — an injection of heroin; blast party — get together to smoke marihuana."

Jim Vaus • ***The Inside Story of Narcotics***
ZONDERVAN • 1953 • PBO

as most paperback publishers of the era, had strong credentials in the pulp magazine business before launching the imprint. His nephew, Carl Solomon, recently a patient at New York State Psychiatric Institute, was a staff editor (along with writer Donald A. Wollheim). Soon, a friend and fellow patient of Solomon's from the mental hospital, Beat poet Allen Ginsberg,[19] approached him with a few manuscripts written by friends who couldn't get the time of day from mainstream publishers. Acting as Burroughs' "secret literary agent,"[20] Ginsberg negotiated a contract granting Burroughs an $800 advance against an initial printing of 100,000 copies,[21] 100,000–250,000-copy print runs typical at the time for all paperbacks. Burroughs likely received the industry standard for royalties: 1¢ per book for the first 150,000 copies sold, 1.5¢ over 150,000[22], though this figure was for 25¢ books; at 35¢, *Junkie* may have earned Burroughs a small fraction more.

Burroughs shared royalties with Maurice Helbrant, an ex-Federal Bureau of Narcotics agent whose 1941 book *Narcotics Agent* was reprinted with Burroughs' *Junkie* as an Ace Double-Book, the two inversely bound together, each with its own lurid cover. Publisher Wyn took no chances: Burroughs' harsh, uncompromising and unapologetic, outlaw romantic, almost positive viewpoint on heroin would be mitigated by Helbrant's tough anti-dope stance.

Why did Ace — as well as a host of other paperback publishers — issue paperback titles with drug themes?

They sold. Big time. Is was estimated that 243,000,000 copies of 830 titles were sold in 1952,[23] and yet while of those 830 titles only a small percentage were drug-themed, their sales could not be ignored. In 1965, a paperback publisher, noting what would seem to be the obvious, commented: "We have noticed a consistent sales trend...the public's readiness to buy books on the same subject,"[24] no matter what the subject. A large number of Americans loved reading about drugs. This was commented upon earlier in 1958, when it was observed that while in the 20th century a great number of people, dulled, exasperated or frustrated by modern life, were drawn to drug use, "even greater numbers of people who lack the courage [or interest] to take them enjoy reading books about people who do."[25] Thus the large body of work within this "curious branch of literature."[26]

Reprints and paperback originals had, since the end of WWII, often featured marijuana, invariably as a demonic drug that drove its users to mayhem and murder; numerous dope noir crime novels with marijuana as the culprit were released. But after the Kevauver Crime Committee Hearings of 1950–51 and the O'Conor Committee Crime Hearings exposed organized crime's illegal narcotics trafficking "as a frightening menace to the youth of America,"[27] the media went into a frenzy. Immediately, newspapers and magazines were all over the issue. Oh, it was bad news indeed! "*Life* magazine ran a twelve-page picture story, giving great prominence to slink-eyed, hopped-up hoodlums leaning against corner telephone poles, or killing time between heroin shots by shootings craps in dark alleyways," it was reported.[28] *Newsweek* ran a story in its November 20, 1950 issue on "Narcotics And Youth;" in its January 29, 1951 issue *Newsweek* followed up with "New York Wakes Up To Find 15,000 Teen-Age Dope Addicts," its cover heralding the tale with the banner headline: "New York's Teen-Age Dope Fiends." In its August 13, 1951 issue, *Newsweek* further reported on "Heroin And Adolescents." The July 14, 1951 issue of *Science News Letter* discussed “Child Dope Addicts.” In September 1951, *Reader’s Digest* got into the act by reprinting a dope-terror story, “A Short — and Horrible — Life.” The very next month, *Reader’s Digest* ran “Facts About Our Teen-Age Drug Addicts.”

These are but a few; 1951 was one hell of a year for heroin in general and high school junkies in particular. “Murder, rape and kidnapping speedily went out of style as first-choice plot material,” a contemporary journalist reported.[29] From the early through late 1950s there was no shortage of paperback books featuring thrill-seeking juvenile delinquents on dope or teen-aged innocents lured onto the needle or marijuana by criminal low-lifes or bad-news boyfriends. And oh, the consequences! In 1953, religious publishing house Zondervan would issue the paperback *The Inside Story of Narcotics* by Jim Vaus. Hell was just around the corner, Lucifer furtively leaning against a lamppost, passing out free samples.

The teenage drug problem of the 1950s was utter nonsense. “It simply doesn’t exist,” wrote John Gerrity in the February 1952 issue of *Harper’s*. “The Federal Narcotics Bureau, which knew the true facts, abandoned an earlier effort to quell the frenetic alarms, fearful that — as one official put it — ‘we’d get our brains beaten out.’”[30] The gross distortion of reality was so egregious — were these people on drugs? — that Federal Bureau of Narcotics Commissioner, Henry J. Anslinger (a man not known for understatements in public pronouncements on illegal drugs) felt compelled to speak up and set the record straight, as it were.

“Why would a business man — and drug peddlers are business men — desert a proven market for the hazards of an unproven one, like teen-age high school students?” he told an interviewer at the time.[31] “Shortly after the Kefauver expose,” he continued, “the New York City Mayor’s office announced that there were 90,000 addicts in the metropolitan area, with many of these being in high schools.

“Another source claimed that among 15,000 parochial and Yeshiva school students they found not one addict. The city authorities began to revise their estimates when we asked them to explain why peddlers have singled out public school students and ignored parochial school students,” Anslinger said.[32]

The simple reality at the time was that “if the average high school student, or anyone else for that matter, wants a marijuana cigarette or a shot of heroin, he will have to prowl the dens of the city for months before he can make a contact. The chances are he won’t succeed at all,” Gerrity reported, based upon his discussions with FBN officials.

The facts did not dissuade paperback publishers from issuing sensationalistic volumes on teen dopers, nor did the reality break through the public’s belief in the legend, nor Congress’. In 1956, *Merchants of Misery* would be published, a wild teens-on-dope/anti-dope peddler non-fiction paperback from Pacific Press Publishing Association, a Seventh-Day Adventist venture dating back to the Thirties whose entire raison d’etre appears to have been issuing anti-dope educational titles.[33] Here, the evil peddlers are thinly disguised Italians so stereotyped it’s all the author can do to restrain himself from using the phrase “wop-greaseballs.” Anti-drug laws, with penalties that had been increasing in severity since the 1930s, reached a draconian apogee in the same year with the passage of the Boggs Act which mandated the death penalty for selling heroin to minors.[34] In the same year, renowned drug researcher Lawrence Kolb would write

Nelson Algren • ***The Man with the Golden Arm***
CARDINAL C-31 • 1951 • COVER BY STANLEY MELTZOFF
COURTESY OF MICHAEL ALDRICH

Reprint. The true first paperback edition is Pocket Books 757 (Jan. 1951), issued with a dust jacket (a failed experiment for paperbacks that was discontinued) featuring Meltzoff's illustration; exceedingly scarce thus.

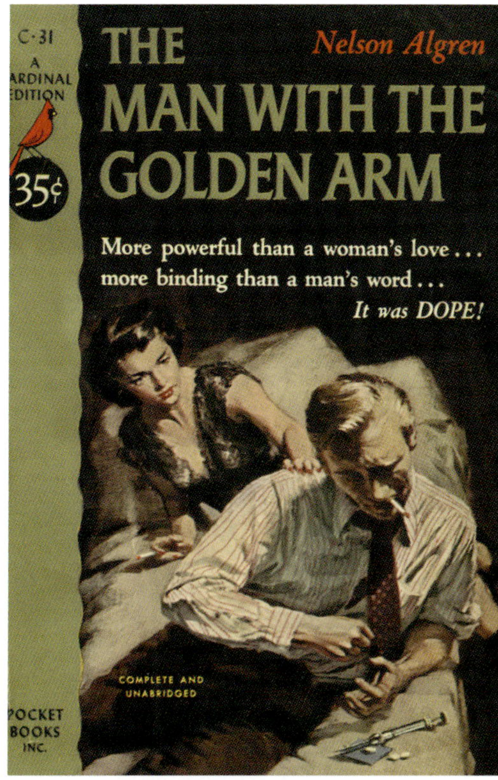

"The Panic had come.

"The period of no dope.

"The time when junkies lined the counters of drugstores to buy paregoric, to take it and boil its sweetness into a brownness for its opium content, to shoot eye-dropperfuls into their veins until their arms swelled, red and stinging, and the sickness was abated momentarily."

Clarence L. Cooper • ***The Scene*** • CREST D-453
1961 • COVER BY TOM O'SULLIVAN • REPRINT

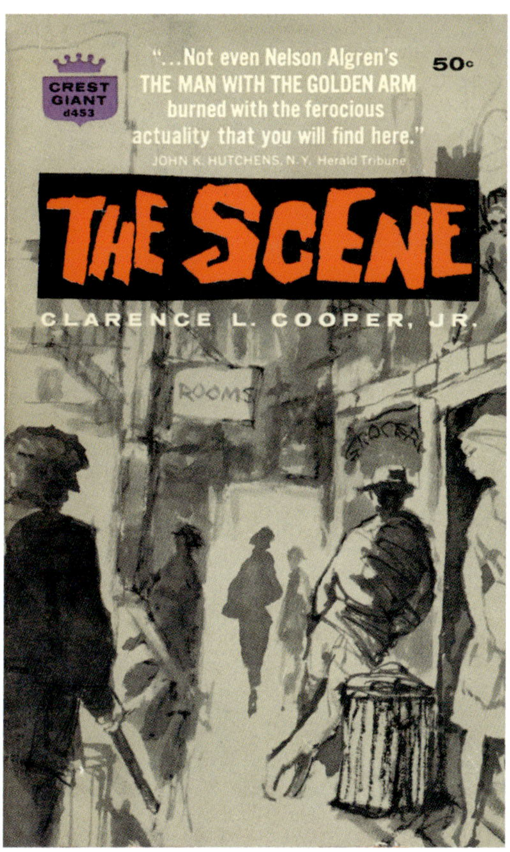

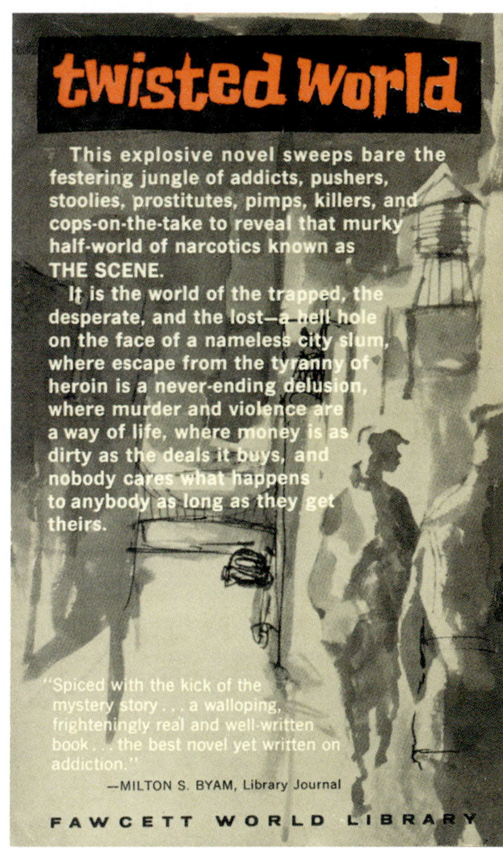

"Let's Stop This Narcotics Hysteria!" in the July 28th issue of *The Saturday Evening Post*, and the July 8th issue of the *New York Times Magazine* would run "To Dispel the Nightmare of Narcotics," to no avail. Once accepted into popular culture, a myth has stubborn staying power against which reason wages a Don Quixote–like struggle. That said, "the first stirrings of a renewed heroin wave in the United States"[35] began to become manifest, though it would be, for the most part, confined to the ghettos and barrios of the major cities, not yet in middle-class white communities. The finest novel on the contemporary black inner-city drug experience remains ex-junkie/convict Clarence L. Cooper's gritty *The Scene*.

The movie industry's self-censorship on drug-themed films would end in 1955 with the release of Otto Preminger's film adaptation of Nelson Algren's *The Man With The Golden Arm* (1955). A paperback reprint of the 1949 first edition appeared in 1951 with a stylishly lurid cover by the renowned Stanley Melztoff with his wife, Alice, as model for Molly-O, the sympathetic woman in junkie card dealer/drummer Frankie Machine's life.[36] With the release of the film, the book was reprinted in paperback again but with a cover reproducing the film's opening title motif by the great film-title designer, Saul Bass.

Competition within the paperbacks business was fierce; all these imprints — there were close to one hundred paperback publishers by 1958[37] — jockeying for retail rack space. It was imperative to "capture the darting eye and interest of the man in motion."[38] How to do it? Jacket illustration and "skyline," the blurb above the title.

Drug paperbacks, in addition to their value as touchstones of attitudes about drugs in American popular culture, also provide a vivid history of pop graphic design during the period under review and, significantly, provide us with the pop-kulch iconography of the American drug experience. Until the late 1950s, when paperback cover illustration began to shift with the times and publishers and distributors felt pressure to tone down appearances, many if not most paperback covers were sensationally — deliciously — lurid. With a "girl on the jacket but no jacket on the girl,"[39] illustrations were invariably characterized as a mix of sex and sadism, and there were so many drug paperbacks with gorgeous babes on their stylish covers that one might conclude that drug use was almost exclusive to women, which it was most certainly not; males have always been the prime consumers of illegal substances. Many paperbacks from the 1940s and 1950s, including those drug-themed, are now avidly collected by connoisseurs of "Good Girl Art," a genre dripping with postmodern irony as the girls depicted are anything but, thumbing their noses at conventional mores and standards of female behavior.

Yet for all the contemporary hue and cry over paperback book-cover design, the illustrations were, and remain, quite artful. "Our sexy covers are given a fine-arts treatment," publishers declared at the time.[40] And so they were, with a hip, lurid-chic panache by commercial artists of great skill and verve. Illustrators Rudolph Belarski and Tom Dunn were graduates of Pratt Art Institute; Raphael M. Desoto, Lou Marchetti, Rudolph Nappi and Robert Maguire studied at the Art Students League of New York; the great Stanley Meltzoff studied art and art history at the National Academy, the Art Students League and the Institute of Fine Arts in New York and elsewhere, and was an in-demand illustrator for many popular magazines before beginning his career as a book illustrator;[41] examples of their covers are found within this volume. Some

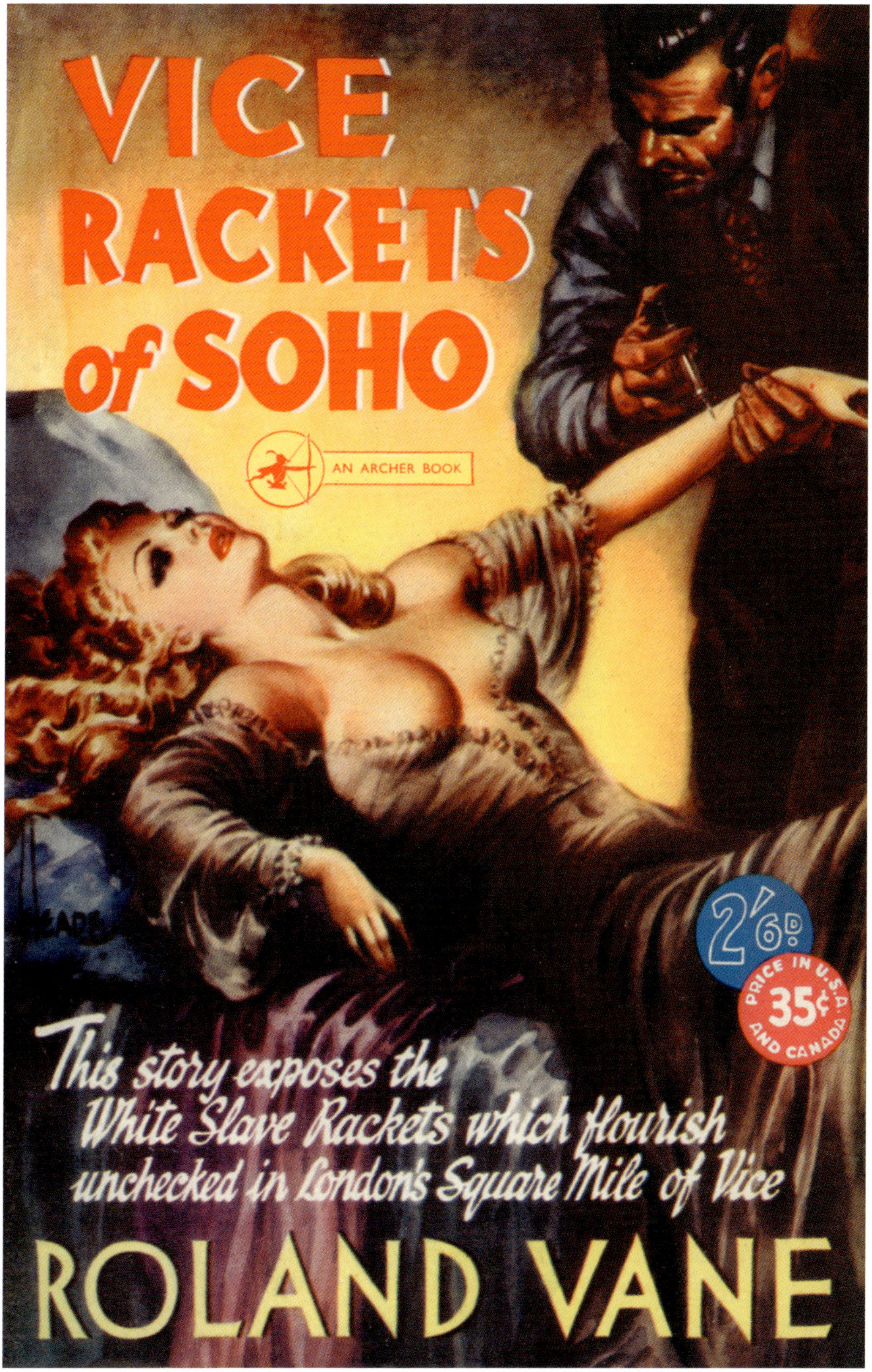

Roland Vane [Ernest McKeag] • ***Vice Rackets of Soho*** • ARCHER 35 • 1951 • COVER BY REGINALD HEADE
FIRST AMERICAN EDITION • REPRINT OF THE ARCHER U.K. PBO FIRST EDITION

were on staff on salary, others were busy freelancers earning an average of $200–$300 per cover illustration.[42] Their work and that of many other talents, formally trained or autodidactic, had to grab eyeballs and mindshare in a crowded marketplace. Once picked up by reason of their compelling artwork, the books had to glue to the emotional centers of the brain and stick to the hands so the volumes would not be returned to the display rack, unsold.

So wild were the covers that the U.S. Army, a huge buyer of paperbacks distributed by its Special Services division facilities to troops through soldier reading programs, became alarmed. In a letter to John O'Conner of the American Book Publisher's Council, Major General William E. Bergin stated that "in searching for books for this purpose, a sincere effort is made to find books which meet public library standards, standards which are satisfactory to the families of young men in service and to all authorities charged with the welfare of those men."[43] Many paperbacks were being rejected simply because of the "growing tendency of publishers to use cover pictures and descriptive material which have a distinctly lurid and sensationalistic character," the General complained.[44] The Army wanted its troops to be all that they could be but not become sex-crazed dope fiends. Bad for morale, Sir, yes Sir.

There were also complaints that many paperback covers promised more than they delivered, and the drug genre was no exception. The illustration by Reginald Heade for *Vice Rackets of Soho* by Roland Vane (Ernest L. McKeag[45]) with its glorious scene of drug eroticism — a half-naked woman lying supine on a bed in a sheer gown that appears to have been spray-painted on, her head thrown back in ecstasy as she's shot up with junk by a leering miscreant — is a prime example. Though the image suggests artist Heade as a sort of twisted Bernini — the Ecstasy of St. Teresa of Avila as sultry babe meets criminal Christ who plunges His flaming scepter of drug-love deep within her — there is virtually no mention of drugs within the text, nor much sex, for that matter. By 1961, the practice of paperback publishers to tease, bait and switch had become so serious that the Federal Trade Commission intervened.[46]

As the Fifties moved into the Sixties, many of the smaller paperback publishers had fallen by the wayside or had been absorbed by larger houses and the remaining publishers turned their back on cover illustration styles of the past. "The reason for this," explained New American Library's Art Director William Gregory in 1963, was that all publishers' covers began to "look pretty much alike…the books just began to blend into the output from other publishers."[47] There were two other reasons that paperback cover art began to change. Paperback books were now being distributed beyond the traditional newsstand, etc. model into…bookstores! The last places you'd go to find a paperback book now began stocking them, slowly devoting more and more space for their sale. And they required covers to appeal to a different class of buyer. And, significantly, sales to schools had become a growing part of the paperback business. The sensational covers had to go. They would not return until Sixties porn publishers took up the lurid look of love.

The most accomplished of these later book illustrators was Robert Bonfils. A student of Thomas Hart Benton at Kansas City Art Institute along with Jackson

"She was afraid of the H at first but Nat had a soothing way of easing her along. He gave her a spike, a syringe, and he showed her how to open the little capsule of white powder and cook it with matches in a spoon, to dissolve it, and then to fill up the syringe and find a vein in her leg and shoot the liquid into the vein. It blew the top of her head off. She came back for more, and learned the little refinements, shooting it into the vein and drawing it back into the syringe to mix it with blood, and ramming it in again, doubling the kick. The horse didn't send her way up high the way M [marijuana] did; it eased off, making her loose and dreamy, taking away all the troubles of the world."

"He looked at her, huddled miserably against the pillow, and told himself that he had never seen anyone suffering so visibly before. If only every teenager in the country could be brought into the bedroom of an addict suffering withdrawal symptoms, there wouldn't be any narcotics problem in America. Round up every kid on his fourteenth birthday and bring him to see a hophead writhe. Kids don't see what lies at the far side of kicks. All they know is that the H takes away all the troubles..."

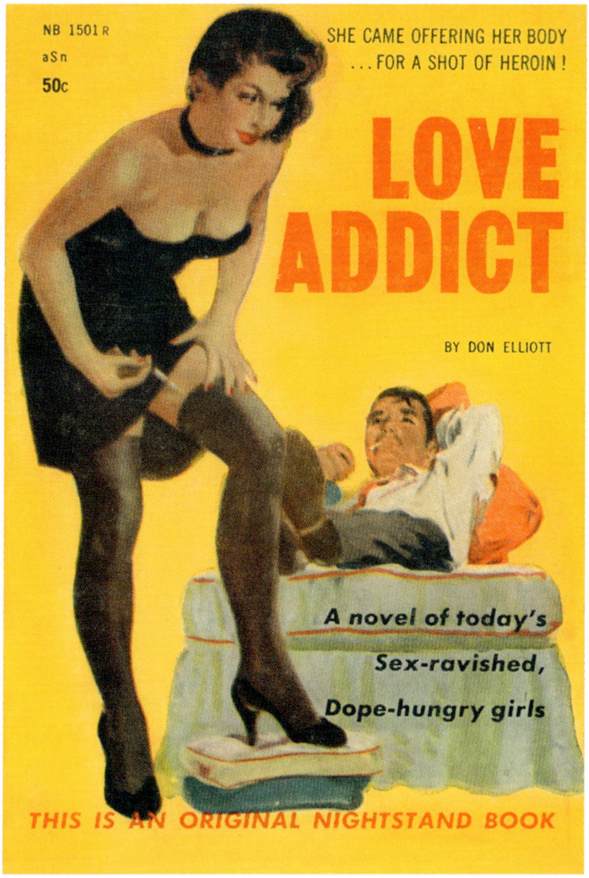

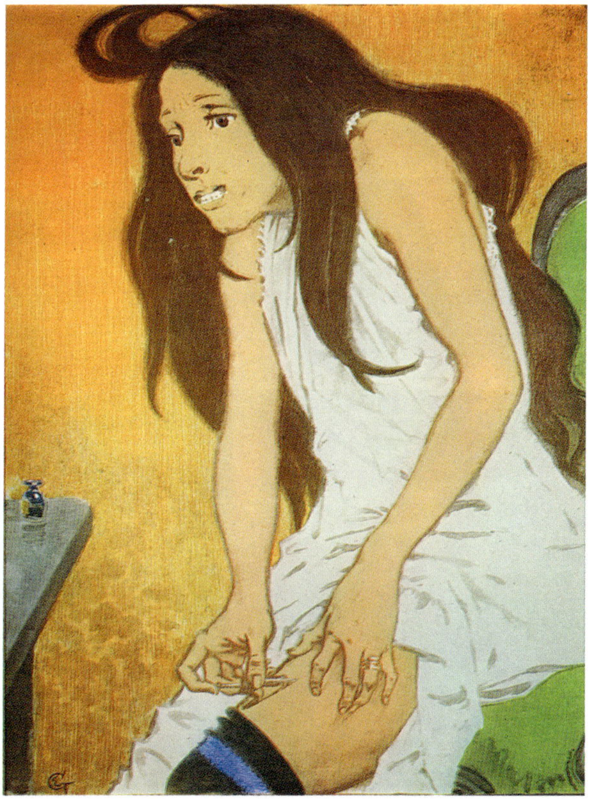

Don Elliott [Robert Silverberg]
Love Addict • NIGHTSTAND 1501 • 1959
PBO • COVER BY HAROLD W. McCAULEY

Eugène Grasset • ***La Morphinomane***
1897 • BIBLIOTHÈQUE D'ART ET D'ARCHÉOLOGIE
JACQUES DOUCET, PARIS

Pollock, after WWII he continued his studies at Chicago Art Institute. Soon, he became a busy commercial artist in advertising, eventually branching out as a freelance paperback book illustrator. Shortly thereafter, he was hired by William Hamling of Greenleaf Publications, the nation's leading publisher of soft-porn, as Art Director, replacing Harold W. McCauley. Supervising and/or creating up to 50 cover illustrations a month, Bonfils was certainly amongst the most prolific book illustrators of his generation, assuredly its most stylishly talented, designing many unforgettable covers that remain without peer.[48]

The U.S. Supreme Court's 1957 Roth decision, which, though attempting to legally curb so-called obscene literature, was worded such that it ironically opened the door to soft-core sex-lit., ushered in a flood of titles issued by soft-core publishers that continued the lurid sexy cover tradition. The drug-addled protagonists had also changed; no longer high high-schoolers and corrupt dames, the focus was now on that dreaded of all subcultures, the Beatniks, as well as jazz musicians, the latter prime fodder for exploitation throughout the 1940s and 1950s secondary to the popular notion that jazz hounds were dopers, an *idée fixe* (pardon me) not without a degree of truth. Of these publishers, Beacon and Greenleaf with its many imprints were leaders. Greenleaf/Nightstand's *Love Addict* by Don Elliott (science-fiction writer Robert Silverberg) is a notable example. The story of a straight guy who falls for a sultry junkie songbird, its cover by Harold W. McCauley is a minor masterpiece — shoot-from-the-hip broad shoots in the thigh, skirt provocatively hiked up — that hearkens back to French La Belle Epoque illustrator Eugène Grasset's 1897 lithograph *La Morphinomane*.

As the baton was passed from the Beat Generation to the youth culture of the Sixties and jazz had been overshadowed by rock 'n roll, so was the character of the dope paperback. In the past it had been axiomatic that writers of these had little if any experience with drugs; indeed, all they seemed to know was what they had learned from newspapers and magazines, then as now rarely reliable sources of information on the subject. This would continue until 1966–1967, when younger writers with first-hand experience and attitudes toward drugs highly influenced by, and rejecting, traditional scare tactics and common misinformation, and questioning authority in all its guises, supplanted the older generation of scribes. The content of the drug paperback, whether novel or nonfiction, had once been cautionary; now, it often became celebratory. Marijuana, now being experimented with on a mass scale by youth (and, to a lesser degree, by adults) was discovered to be not the evil weed it had been advertised as since the 1930s.

With the passage of the Marijuana Tax Act of 1937, born of the Southwestern states' fear of Mexican immigration — those dark-skinned migrants who brought their enjoyment of weed with them — came an avalanche of sensational propaganda ascribing to grass the darkest of consequences to its users and society. FBN Commissioner Anslinger — though not the first to demonize pot — got the ball rolling to a mass audience with his "Marijuana: Assassin of Youth!" article in the July 1937 issue of *The American* magazine ("If the hideous MONSTER FRANKENSTEIN came face to face with the MONSTER MARIHUANA, he would DROP DEAD OF FRIGHT!"), based upon a gross and absurd misinterpretation of the true story of

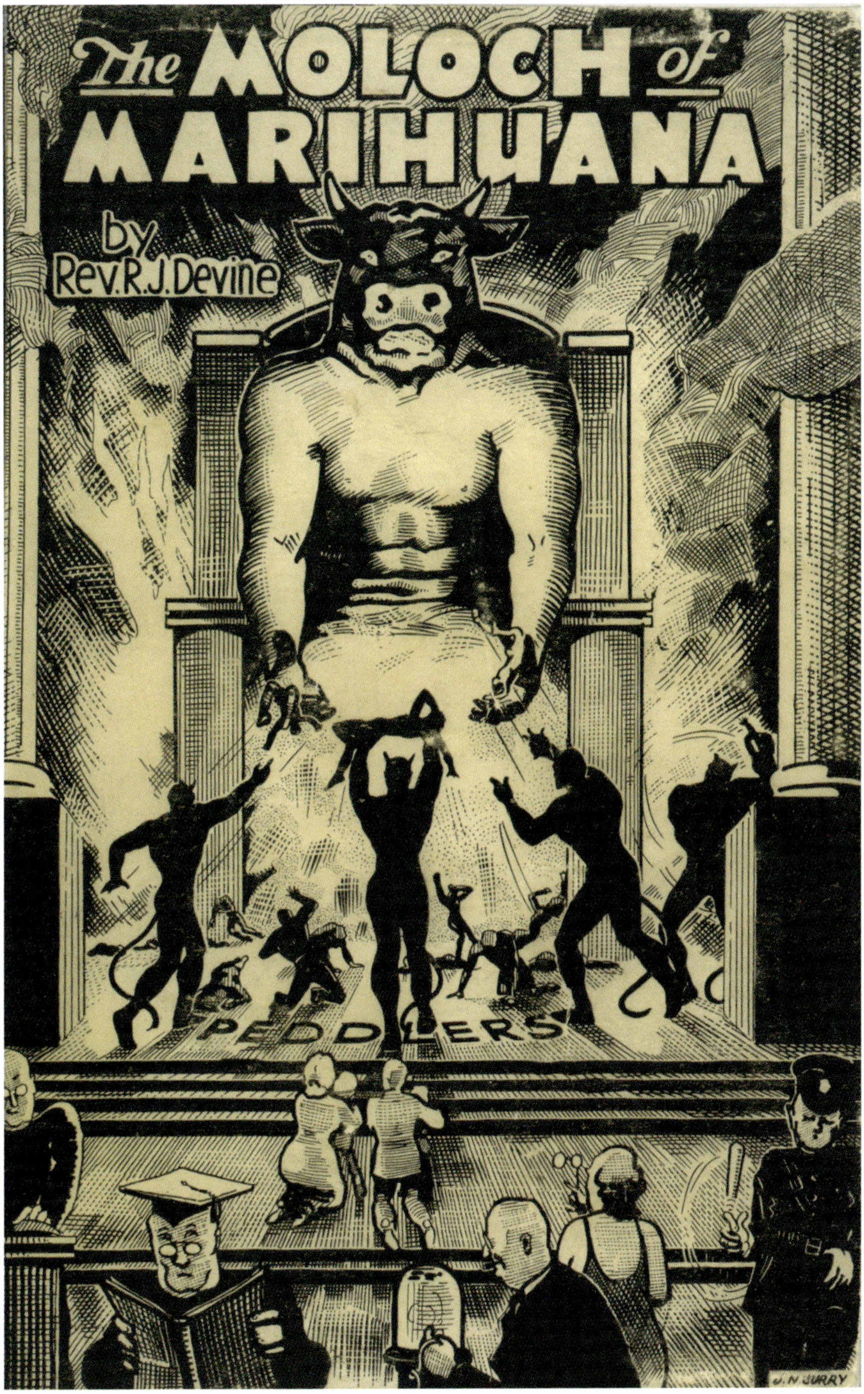

"An ordinary man or woman becomes in the eyes of the Marijuana addict, beautiful beyond compare. Marijuana, grown by trusties, on prison farms unknown to prison officials, has been taken to the inmates. Under its influence the prisoners fall desperately in love with each other; as they would with members of the opposite sex outside prison walls. One can understand the debaucheries that take place."

Later: "...Over in a corner, one child begins to disrobe his or her companion. In a few minutes this becomes general, until clothes are scattered over the floor and the naked youngsters give themselves over, with wild abandon, to every imaginable perversion prompted by their drug-crazed minds."

Rev. R.J. Devine • ***The Moloch of Marijuana*** • FUNDAMENTAL TRUTH PUBLISHERS • 1943 • PBO • COVER BY W.N. JURRY

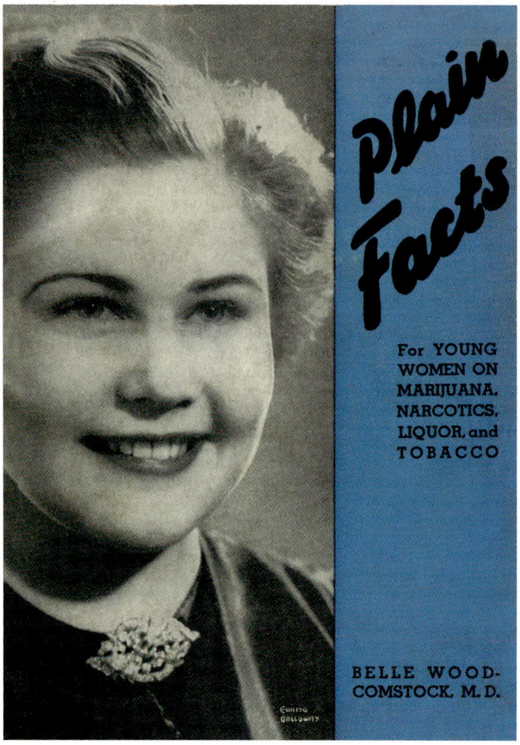

M.D. Comstock, Belle Wood • ***Plain Facts***
PACIFIC PRESS PUBLISHING ASSOCIATION • 1938
COURTESY OF WILLIAM DAILEY

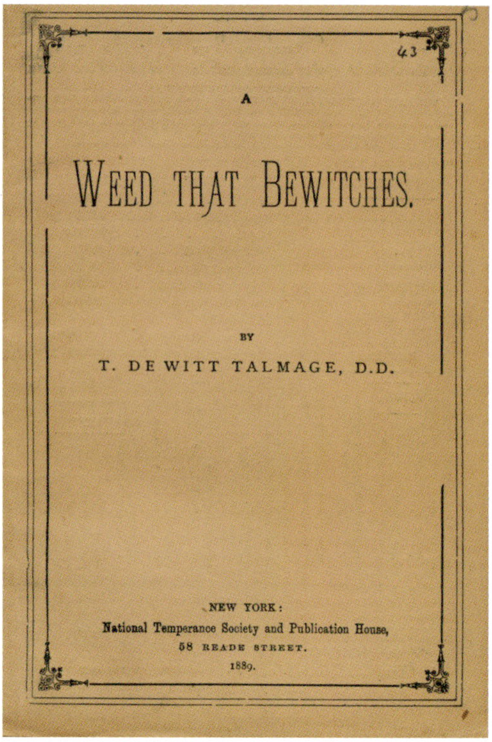

T. De Witt Talmage • ***A Weed That Bewitches***
NEW YORK: NATIONAL TEMPERANCE SOCIETY • 1889
COURTESY OF RONALD K. SIEGEL, PH.D.

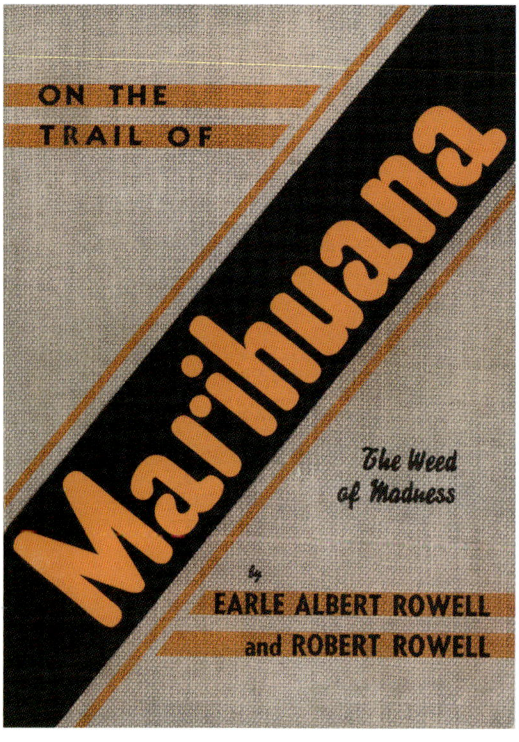

Earle Albert Rowell and Robert Rowell ***On the Trail of Marihuana: The Weed of Madness*** • MOUNTAIN VIEW: PACIFIC PRESS PUBLISHING • ASSOCIATION • 1939 • PBO

"The marihuana user, freed from the restraint of gravitation, bumps his head against the sky. Street lights become orangoutangs [sic] with eyes of fire. Huge slimy snakes crawl through small cracks in the sidewalk, and prehistoric monsters, intent on his destruction, emerge from keyholes, and pursue him down the street. He feels squirrels walking over his back, while he is being pelted by some unseen enemy with lightning bolts. He will thrill you with the most plausible accounts of desperadoes who lurk in the doorway ahead, waiting with long, sharp knives to pounce on him and carve him to pieces."

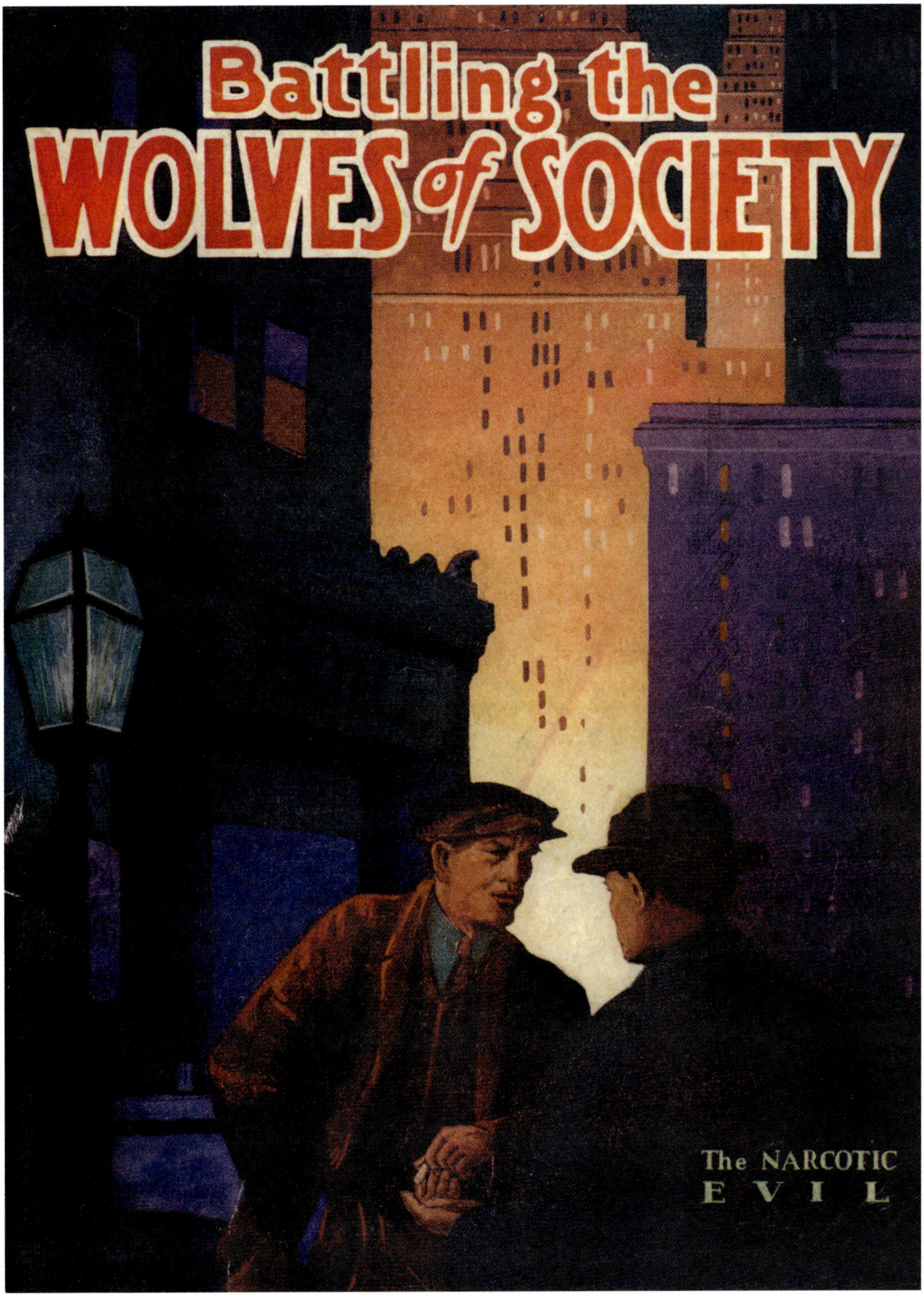

Earle Albert Rowell • ***Battling the Wolves of Society: The Narcotic Evil*** • MOUNTAIN VIEW: PACIFIC PRESS PUBLISHING COMPANY • 1929 • COURTESY OF RONALD K. SIEGEL, PH.D.

Persian Hasan-I Sabbah, the Old Man of the Mountain, the Islamic revolutionary of the late 11th century whose fanatical, murderous followers were known as Hashisheens (whence "assassins"). "They were not fed hashish [the resin exuded by cannabis] in order to carry out their murders; it was used on them without their knowledge in order to encourage fanatical obedience,"[49] such obeisance inspired by the promise of the joys of paradise, i.e. that which they had experienced while under the influence of a hashish-infused beverage; never while on the job. Marco Polo reported the realities of the Hashisheens in his "Travels." The generation of the Sixties would learn that the last thing one wanted to do while under its influence was kill or do much of anything; lassitude is a hallmark of the drug's psychotropic action. Make love, yes. Make war? Hey man, no hostility!

No matter. Paperback pamphlets such as *The Moloch of Marijuana* by Rev. Robert J. Devine (1943), and evangelist Earle Albert Rowell's *Battling The Wolves of Society: The Narcotics Evil* (1929) and *On the Trail of Marijuana: The Weed of Madness* (1939) fanned the flames of pot paranoia. So outlandish and over the top were the sensationalistic claims of these "educational" books that "the bureau attacked such apostles of fear;"[50] Anslinger wished the FBN to be sole source of publicity and educational materials. A few of the Rowell softcovers were issued by — guess who? — Pacific Press Publishing Association, a great thorn in the side of anyone trying to rationally educate the public on drugs.

Pacific Press Publishing Association also issued *Plain Facts for Young Women on Narcotics, Marijuana, Liquor and Tobacco* by Dr. Belle Wood Comstock (1938). Notice that in the title narcotics and marijuana assume top priority despite the fact that young women were certainly more likely to be exposed to alcohol and cigarettes than illegal drugs. So it is within the text.

These paperback drug educational titles were by no means the first. As early as 1889, pamphlets were in circulation warning of the dangers of psychotropics. Though *A Weed That Bewitches* is primarily about tobacco, the author, a theologian, discusses the evils of marijuana, hashish, opium and alcohol.

The antecedent to the mass-market paperback was the paperbound dime novel, a genre that began to flourish in the mid-19th century with the growth of mechanized printing, more efficient distribution, and increased literacy amongst the young working class. Huge print runs and distribution through newsstands and dry goods stores assured that they would reach the masses who eagerly consumed these early pulps' tales of outlaws, detectives, romance and adventure. The subject of drugs rarely if ever appeared within their pages simply because until the turn of the 20th century, drugs now illicit in the U.S were legal. Over-the-counter patent medicines and nostrums for all manner of medical complaint commonly contained opium, later heroin, and to a lesser extent cocaine, and were consumed on a large scale. Injectable morphine had become one of medicine's great panaceas, greatly over-prescribed. Many, many Americans became addicted to narcotics in this manner. The last quarter of the 19th century through the turn of the 20th century was the period of America's first drug epidemic, the typical addict middle-aged and, as often as not, female. The

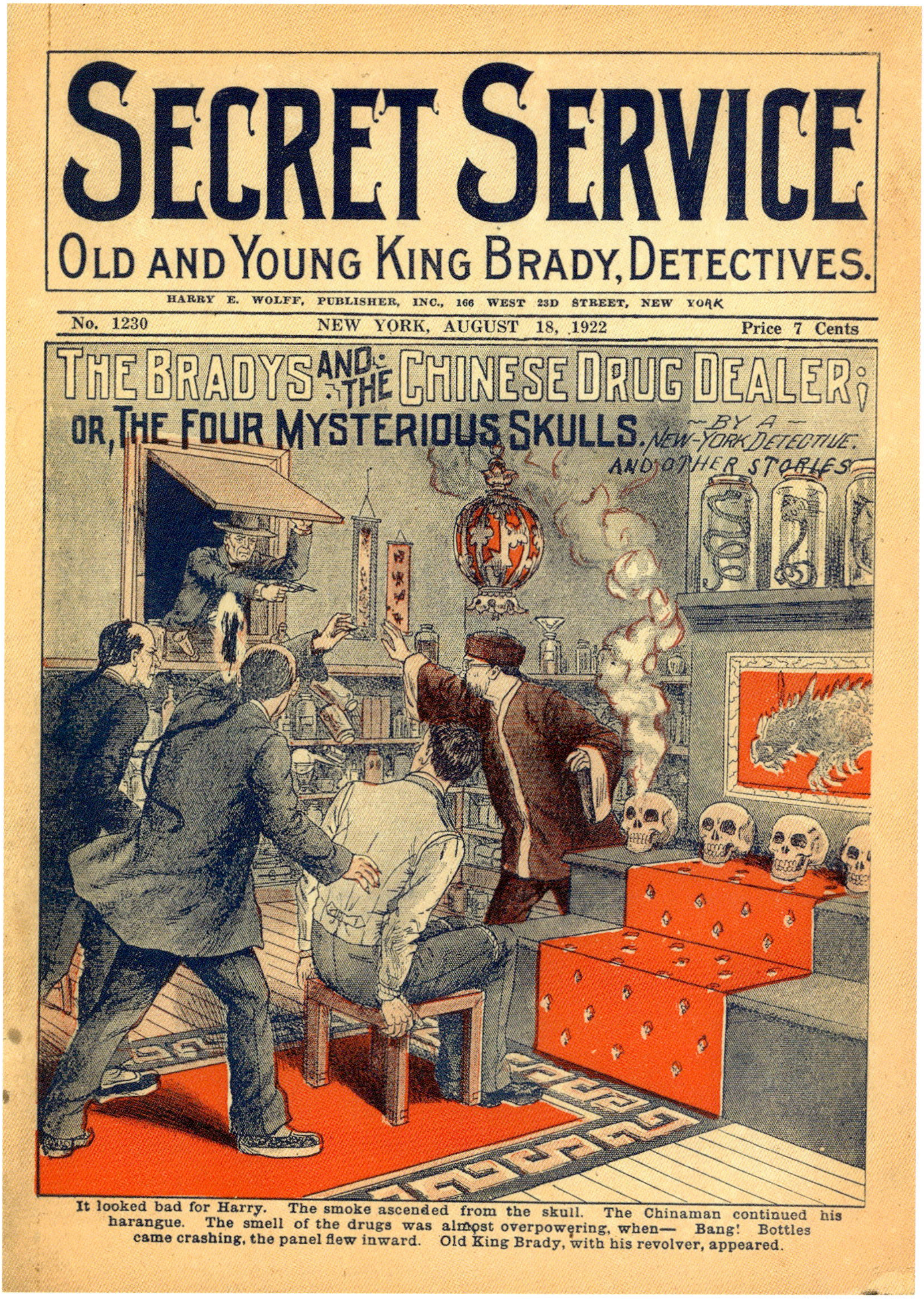

Secret Service #1230: The Bradys and the Chinese Drug Dealer • Harry E. Wolff • 1922
Courtesy of the Ludlow-Santo Domingo (LSD) Library

primary literary example of this phenomenon is Mary Tyrone, the matriarch in Eugene O'Neill's *Long Day's Journey Into Night*, whom O'Neill patterned after his mother, a long-term morphine addict whose initial illness had long since passed, her sequela disease addiction itself. Then, as now, everyone knew someone who had a problem with drugs.

There was an early alert to what would eventually befall upon O'Neill's mother and countless other middle-class Americans and it occurred in popular American literature.

"It will soon be discovered that the modern opium or morphia habit has a large place in this volume. While I have tried to avoid the style of a medical treatise, which would be in poor taste in a work of fiction, I have carefully consulted the best medical works and authorities on the subject, and I have conversed with many opium slaves in all stages of the habit. I am sure I am right in fearing that in the morphia hunger and consumption one of the greatest evils of the future is looming darkly above the horizon of society. Warnings against this poison of body and soul cannot be too solemn or too strong."

That clarion call occurs within the preface to the first full-length American novel to feature drug use, *Without A Home* (1881) by E[dward] P[ayson] Roe. The book was the tenth of 18 best-selling novels written by Roe, who was a clergyman before becoming the most popular novelist of his generation (he outsold Twain) yet is a writer now all but forgotten. His novels were characterized by social/moral purpose and largely based upon real incidents of topical interest drawn from observation or newspapers, then spiced to public taste with romance and pious sentiment. In *Without A Home*, we gain a view into contemporary attitudes about the middle class' emerging drug use. While containing chapters specific to the use of opium/morphine ("A Secret Vice Revealed," "The Beatitudes of Opium," "An Opium-Maniac's Christmas," "The Last Consolation of Opium") the author's moral outrage is focused not on Martin Jocelyn, a Southern businessman addicted to morphine as a result of medical treatment but, rather, upon the "barbarous practice of compelling women, often but growing girls, to stand from morning until evening..." referring to the new phenomenon and plight of the working shopgirl which, alas, daughter Mildred Jocelyn has become to help support the family. Roe treats Mr. Jocelyn's addiction realistically and sympathetically and without judgment. Looking backward, that is the book's big story: Opium/morphine use so new to mainstream American society that its usage was not yet distorted or morally stigmatized. *Without A Home* was a literary fanfare heralding the dawn of the 19th-century drug epidemic in America. Alas, the novel (and every other book by Roe) has never been reprinted in paperback.

As the noxious consequences of opiate use became manifest, regulatory laws were enacted, doctors became less casual in their prescriptions, and nostrum manufacturers were enjoined from including opiates and cocaine (used in many energizing — you bet! — beverages. Vin Mariani, a popular tonic wine, was infused with cocaine, as was Coca-Cola). The scandal of middle-aged matrons strung out on medical dope would not be the subject of dime novels. That honor would lie with Chinese immigrants who'd brought their opium smoking habit with them. Since opium smoking was considered a recreational pleasure rather than a medical necessity, moral opprobrium

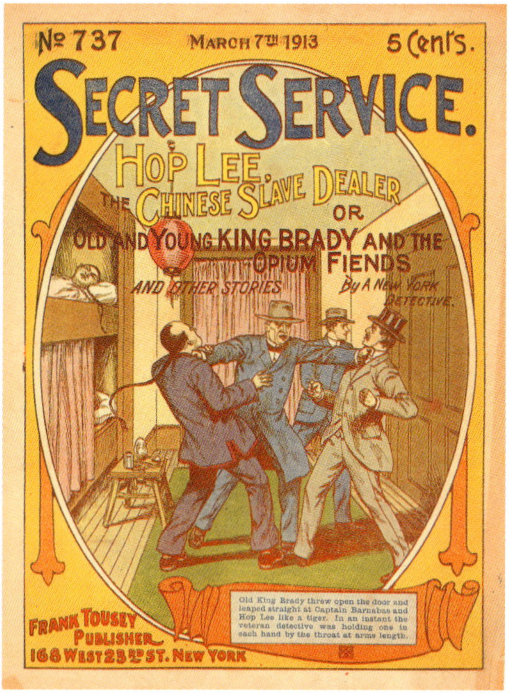

Secret Service #737: Hop Lee, The Chinese Slave Dealer or, Old and Young King Brady and the Opium Fiends • FRANK TOUSEY • 1913 • COURTESY OF THE LUDLOW-SANTO DOMINGO (LSD) LIBRARY

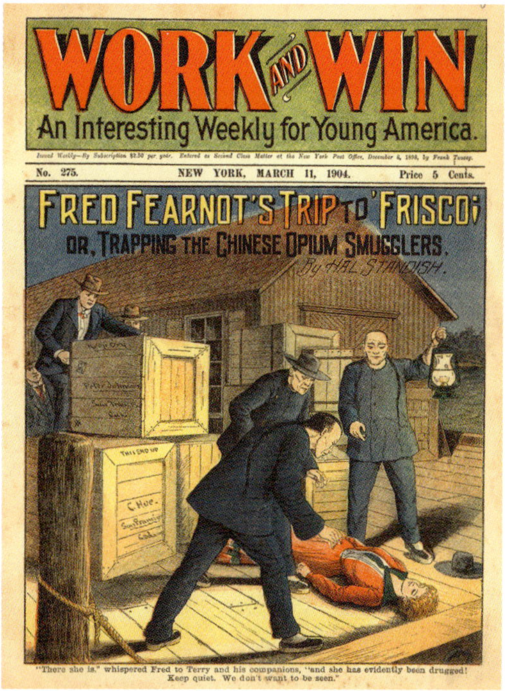

Work and Win No. 275: An Interesting Weekly For Young America: Fred Fearnot's Trip to Frisco or, Trapping the Chinese Opium Smugglers • NEW YORK: FRANK TOUSEY • 1904 • COURTESY OF THE LUDLOW-SANTO DOMINGO LIBRARY

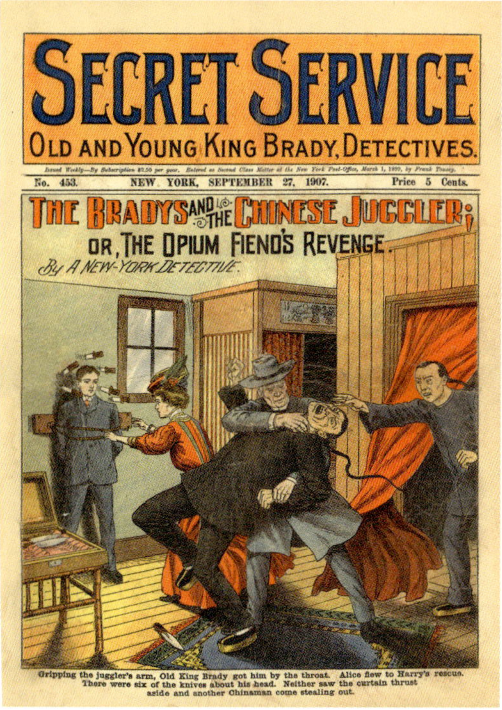

Secret Service #453: The Bradys and the Chinese Juggler or, The Opium Fiend's Revenge NEW YORK: FRANK TOUSEY • 1907 • COURTESY OF THE LUDLOW-SANTO DOMINGO (LSD) LIBRARY

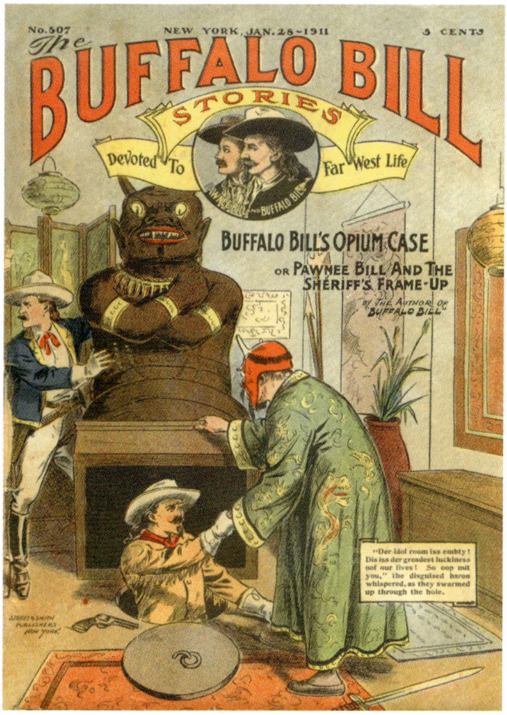

Buffalo Bill Stories #507: Buffalo Bill's Opium Case NEW YORK: STREET & SMITH • 1911 • COURTESY OF RONALD K. SIEGEL, PH.D.

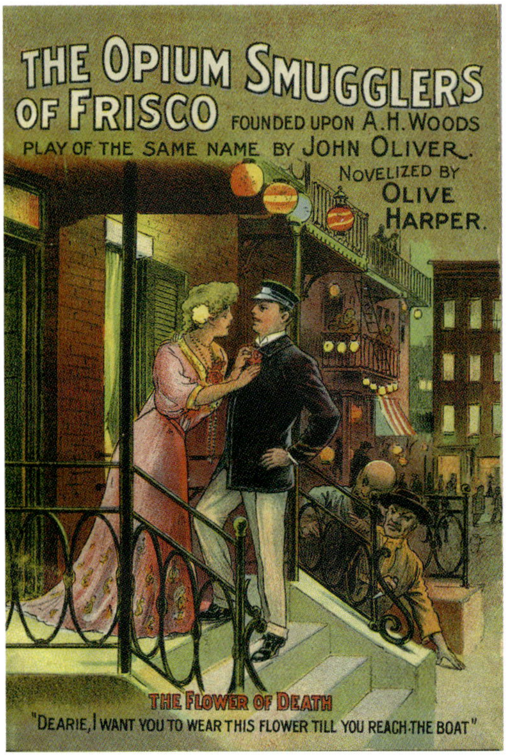

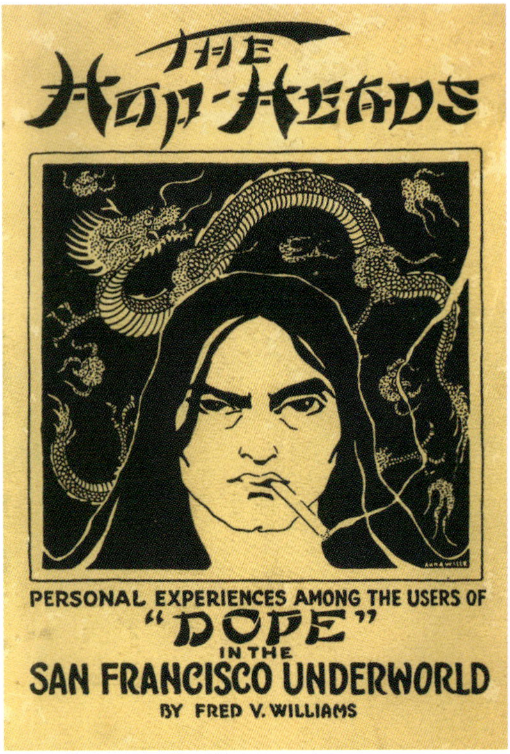

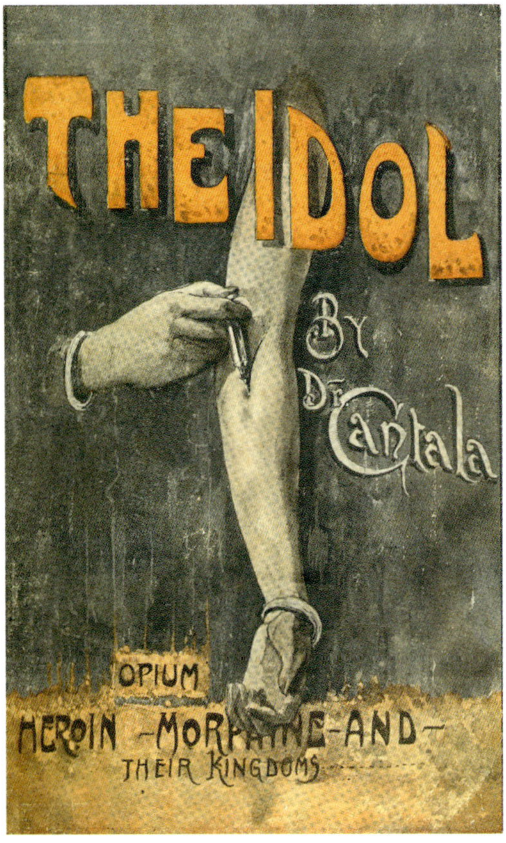

Olive Harper • ***The Opium Smugglers of 'Frisco: or, The Crimes of A Beautiful Opium Fiend*** • NEW YORK: J.S. OGILVIE • 1908 • COURTESY OF RONALD K. SIEGEL, PH.D.

Fred V. Williams • ***The Hop-Heads: Personal Experiences Among Users of "Dope" in the San Francisco Underworld*** • WALTER N. BRUNT • 1920 COVER BY ANNA WILLE • COURTESY OF THE LUDLOW-SANTO DOMINGO (LSD) LIBRARY

Dr. Cantala [Julius] • ***The Idol: Opium, Heroin, Morphine, and Their Kingdoms*** BOTWEN PRINTING • 1924 • COURTESY OF THE LUDLOW-SANTO DOMINGO LIBRARY

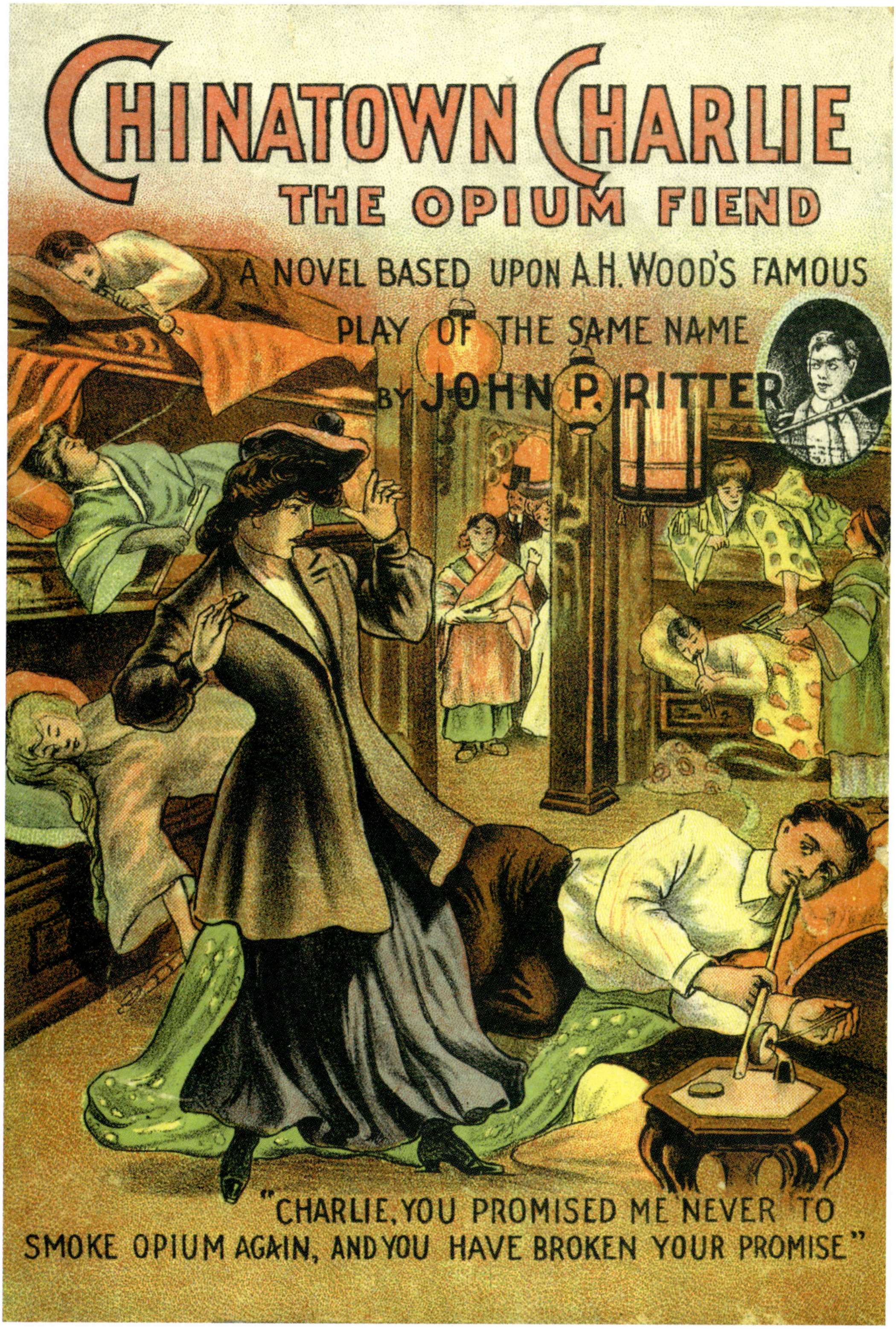

John P. Ritter • ***Chinatown Charlie, the Opium Fiend*** • NEW YORK: J.S. OGILVIE • 1906
COURTESY OF RONALD K. SIEGEL, PH.D.

and scorn were laid upon its habitués, which included those in the sporting life, i.e., gamblers, prostitutes, pimps and their criminal companions including smugglers. As the aging population of iatrogenic, middle-class solid-citizen addicts began to die off, drug use submerged into the underworld and the stage was set for exploitation of the subject by publishers of dime novels. Lurid covers had always been a staple of the dimer, a tradition that continued with the introduction of drug themes into their content. White girls enslaved to the drug by evil Chinese and All-American detectives on the trail of Yellow Peril opium smugglers became ripe subjects. *Secret Service* was a popular series for boys, many issues over the years featuring the derring-do of its protagonists against the opium-soaked heathen Chinee. Even Buffalo Bill was on their trail.

In the first decade of the 20th century, publisher J.S. Ogilvie issued a series of drug-themed dime novels, a handful of them novelizations of plays; drug-soaked melodramas had become popular fare in the theater. These dime novels actually sold for 25 cents which, adjusted for inflation, cost $5.22, quite expensive for the average citizen at the time of their issue.

Not a dime novel, one of two of the most extraordinary drug paperbacks issued during the 1920s is *The Hop-Heads, Personal Experiences Among the Users of "Dope" in the San Francisco Underworld* (1920), which originally appeared as a serial in the *San Francisco Daily News*; it is now a legendary rarity. Journalist Fred V. Williams went in disguise "among the pitiful slaves of cocaine and heroin and morphine, and for the first time told the real facts concerning these outcasts of the night."[51] Note the word "Dope" in quotes within the title, an underworld slang locution beginning to emerge into the popular lexicon.[52] Further note the extraordinary cover illustration by Anna Wille, so modern it looks as if it could have been done by a Sixties counterculture artist.

Scarcer still is *The Idol. Opium, Heroin, Morphine and Their Kingdoms* by Dr. [Julius] Cantala (1924),[53] a softcover volume "devoted to the medical and social uses of opiates, including sections on opium dens, needlemania, the psychology of the addict, the nature of opiate intoxication, love among addicts, etc. There are chapters on cocaine and hashish, and another on Dr. Cantala's method of cure."[54] With its erotic overtones, the cover illustration is the very definition of lurid sensationalism. The good doctor appears to have written only one other volume, *El Insipido* (1941), dealing with diet and syphilis.

By the mid-1920s, the dime novel was a dying if not dead medium, replaced by the emergence of the pulp magazine, which, of course, could not ignore drug use. By the early 1960s, though, the mass-market paperback had by far supplanted the pulp 'zines in popularity.

Despite a paperback publishing recession in 1953, the number of titles issued bounced back and continued to grow. By 1966, the number of paperback titles issued, fiction and nonfiction in all price ranges, original and reprint mass-market and trade format included, had risen from 830 issued in 1952 to 9346,[55] a figure that would continue to grow but ultimately level off to an estimated 9500 annually by 1970. Though all paperback publishers complained of too many titles being issued, it did not stop them from continuing to release new, original titles and reprints at a furious pace. Within these pages, only 72 drug-themed paperbacks from the 1960s are featured, but if we allow for only three percent of an average annual 9500 titles issued over the decade that saw the use of drugs and attendant publicity explode, we arrive at 2850 titles that likely contained references, or were devoted to drug use. With print runs

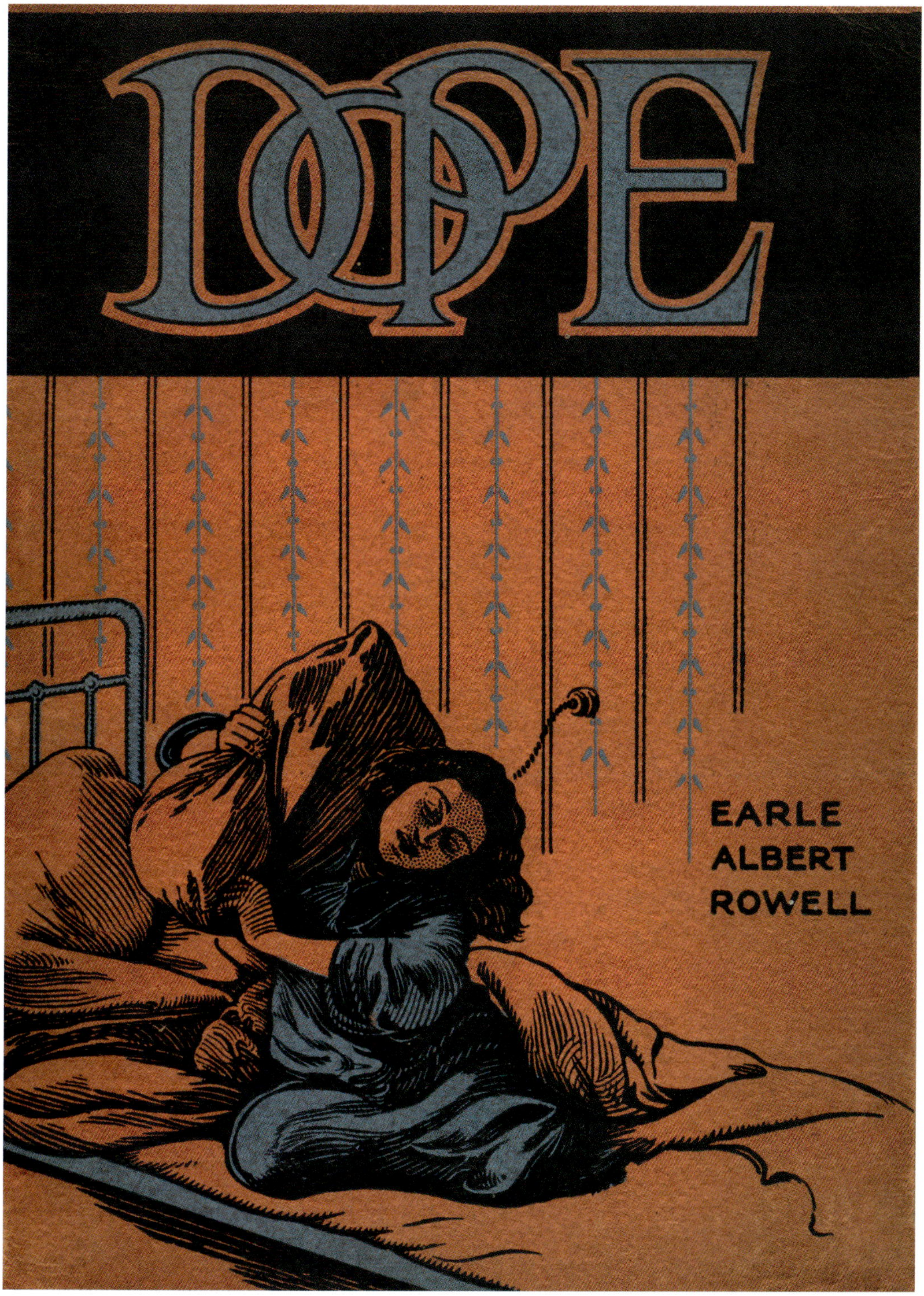

Earle Albert Rowell • ***Dope Adventures Of David Dare*** • NASHVILLE: SOUTHERN PUBLISHING ASSOCIATION 1937 • COURTESY OF RONALD K. SIEGEL, PH.D.

modestly figured at 75K per title, a total of 213,750,000 copies were in circulation. And that figure does not include the avalanche of soft and hardcore porn titles that were published in the wake of the Supreme Court's 1957 and 1966 obscenity decisions. It has been estimated that 12,500 pulp-porn titles were published between 1966–1973, with print runs averaging 20–40 K and higher.[56] If we conservatively allow for three percent of those to contain drug use, we arrive at a respectable 375 titles, 15,000,000 copies in American hands; in truth the figure was much higher, conservatively twice that amount. A total of 228,750,000 copies of drug paperbacks in circulation; these are modest figures that, even taking into consideration the large number of unsold copies, are staggering, inebriating, if you will. And, remember, most paperbacks, then as now, were passed along to friends, resold as remainders, or wound up in used bookshops; total readership was ultimately higher.

The 1960s heralded an unprecedented increase in the use of illegal drugs. Heroin and particularly marijuana use — both drugs thought to be things of the past — dramatically rose. This was coupled with the introduction of LSD and the natural hallucinogens to a new generation coming of age in an era of affluence and disaffection with the material and philosophical status quo. And, too, a generation that because of the over-the-top anti-drug propaganda of the '50s, was not inclined to believe a single word on the subject uttered by authority figures.

There was a revolution in consciousness in books, poetry, theater, films, politics, sex, religion — well, everything! New attitudes crossed the spectrum of American culture. President Kennedy declared his administration The New Frontier. The new attitudes brought new headaches for the authorities. And more scare stories in the press, although this time there was a basis in reality for concern. The emergence of drug use from the inner cities and the bohemian underground to white middle-class youth and drugs on campus were the focus of many articles in newspapers and magazines. Ranging from thoughtful articles found in limited-circulation magazines like *The Atlantic*'s report on The College Drug Scene, popular newsstand and subscription favorites such as *Look*'s August 8, 1967 story "Drugs On The Campus," *Esquire*'s September 1967 article "Confessions Of a Campus Pot Dealer," and *Life*'s July 1967 piece "Marijuana: Millions of Turned-On Users" to wild hand-wringers riddled with well-meaning yet inaccurate information in articles which appeared in *The Saturday Evening Post*'s April 4, 1964 issue, "Dope Invades The Suburbs," and in its December 4, 1965 issue, "The Thrill-Pill Menace." It was a measure of just how large the problem had grown and how it was perceived that in amongst its recipes and household hints, that staple of down-home Middle American traditions *The Ladies Home Journal* would run in its January 1968 issue a feature article, "My Son Is On LSD."

In 1943, a Swiss chemist, Dr. Albert Hofmann, while working on a new drug synthesized from ergot, a grain fungus, accidentally came into contact with the substance, absorbed it through his skin, and soon experienced strange fantasies and hallucinations. He had discovered LSD. A colleague, Dr. Max Rinkel, brought a small quantity of the stuff to the United States and with a partner began experiments at Boston Psychopathic Institute, a pioneering mental health clinic affiliated with Harvard University.

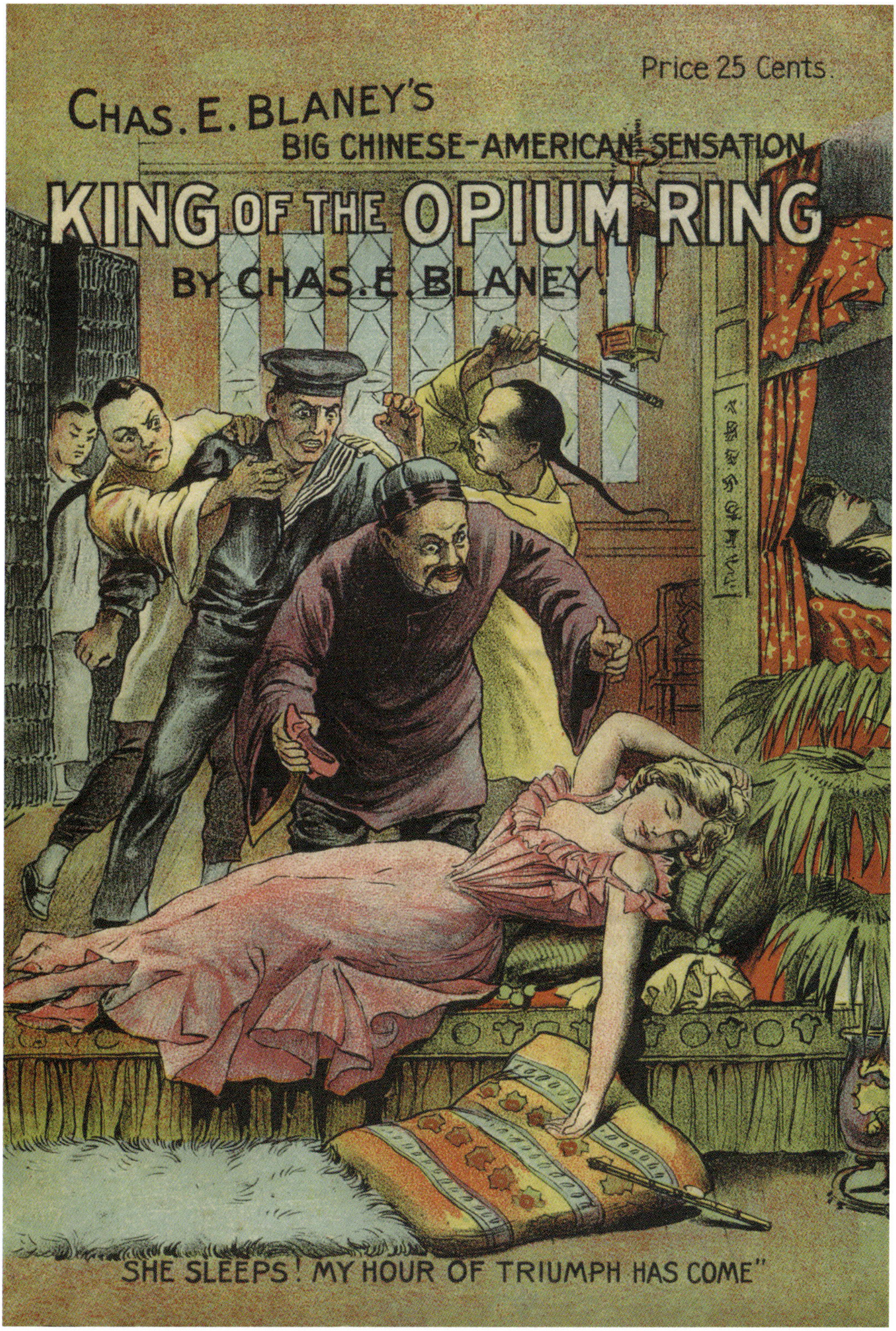

Chas. E. Blaney • ***King of the Opium Ring*** • NEW YORK: J.S. OGILVIE • 1905 • COURTESY OF RONALD K. SIEGEL, PH.D.

The next major step in LSD research was made by Dr. Franz Oderbruch in Communist East Berlin under the Soviet Union's auspices. Few people today are aware of Dr. Oderbruch's groundbreaking work in the field. That's because it only occurred in fiction.

In 1955, a curious, in retrospect astonishing, novel was issued. Published at the height of Cold War anti-Soviet hysteria, it's the action-packed tale of of Milo March, an insurance company private eye who works part-time for the CIA as America's toughest secret agent, and who, posing as a defector to East Germany but soon captured by East German Stassi and Soviet KGB agents, is brainwash-tortured by Dr. Oderbruch, whose highly secret work involved LSD as a mind-control agent. *The Splintered Man* by M.E. Chaber [Kendall Foster Crossen[57]] is the first novel in any language to feature LSD, the drug's dramatic ability to alter consciousness early recognized as a potential boon to psychiatry and psychotherapy, as well as a pathway to mystical experience.

Whence this bizarre book's scenario? In the early 1950s, the CIA began experiments with the drug under its MKULTRA program, the code name for the agency's secret experiments to probe the effects of mind-altering substances as mind-control weapons. "Fearful of LSD falling into Soviet hands, [the CIA] had cornered the market on the drug [or so they thought!], which in minute doses could produce overwhelming sensations ranging from kaleidoscopic acuity to temporary insanity."[58] What is astonishing about *The Splintered Man* is that when it was published the CIA's experiments were strictly Top Secret. In an Author's Note, Chaber/Crossen declares that he has accurately portrayed the effects of LSD (papers on the drug had been published, much early psychiatric research secretly funded by the CIA; the author cites Hofmann and Rinkel's work) but that the rest is a product of his imagination. That's some imagination! The novel was issued in paperback in 1957 with wild cover art by Robert Schultz illustrating a scene that never occurs in the book: Milo ("JEW ZIONIST-BOURGEOIS-IMPERIALIST-AGENT IN BERLIN" as he's characterized in an East Berlin newspaper; Milo the Jewish James Bond) is restrained by a team of East German and Soviet soldiers while menaced by the unseen Dr. Odenbruch wielding a syringe containing a whopping dose of LSD that if administered would have rendered America's toughest, wisecracking-est Secret Agent an incoherent, terrified, raving psychotic incapable of revealing his name or planet of residence, much less classified information.

The cover of the paperback edition of *The Splintered Man* was ludicrous in content, but absurdity would be common in LSD-themed paperbacks written by authors knowing little if anything about the true nature of the drug. Pulp porn novel *Rubber Goddess* by Lana Preston (one of the many pseudonyms of Paul Hugo Little, whose career as a hack porn writer would span the late 1930s through the early 1970s) presents the tender tale of a lesbian dominatrix fetish fashion designer who permeates her latexwear with LSD, the better to render the comely, heterosexual lasses she lures into her den for modeling work into pliant subjects for her dastardly erotic desires! Not a drug to give to unwitting seductees under any circumstances, suffice it to say an entire garment suffused with acid would in reality serve as an one-way ticket to straightjacket city for the drugged subject of this demented scheme.

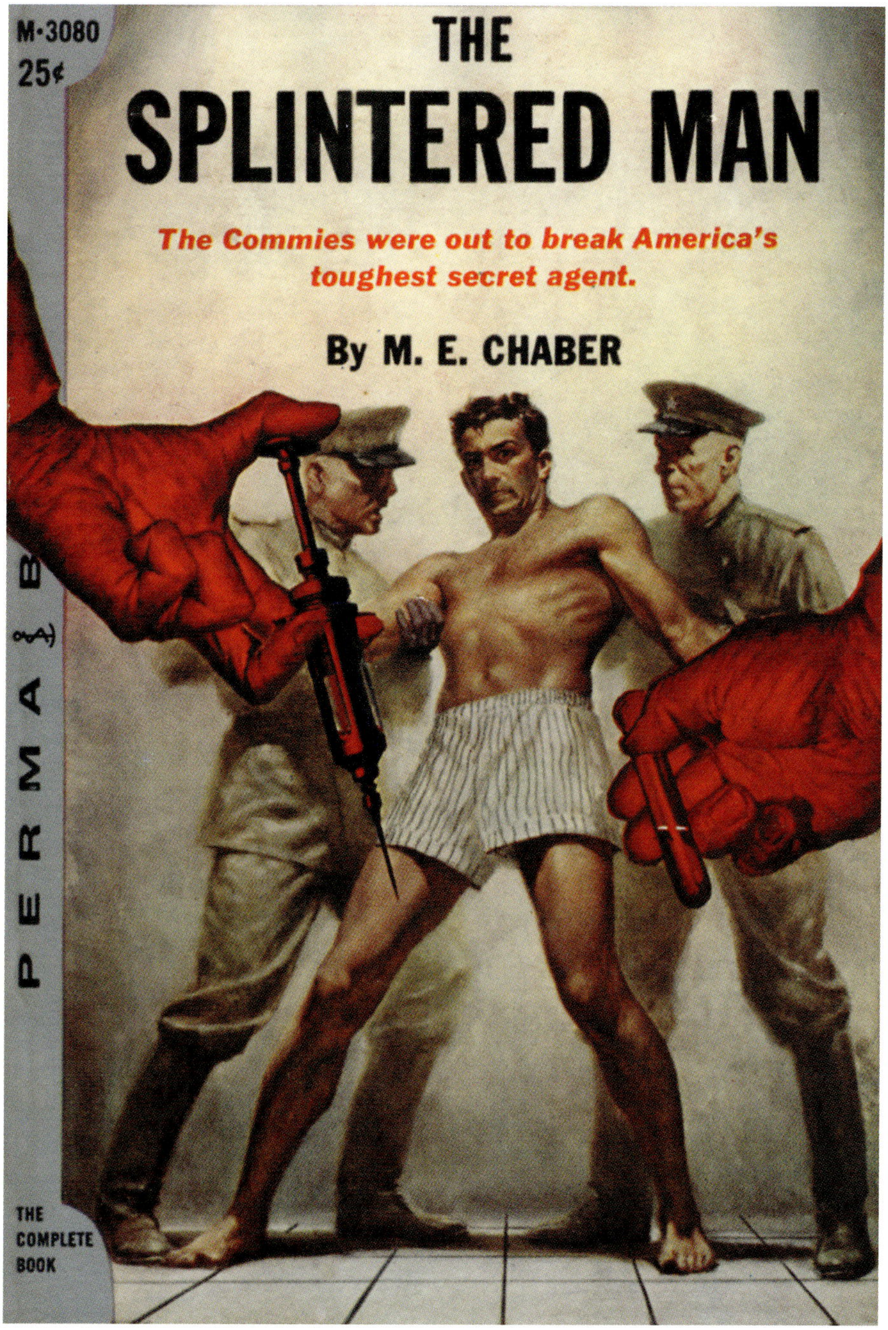

The Oderbruch Method of Brainwashing:
"'Now, Major Marsh, I intend to give you a small quantity of a drug. You may have it in a glass of water, if you like, which will be tasteless. Or if you insist on being stubborn, I will merely call in attendants and have them hold you while I give it to you intravenously. Which do you prefer?'

"'What is it?' I asked. 'Lysergic acid diethylamide?'

"'Exactly. Which method do you prefer?'
"There wasn't much point in arguing about it...

"'I'll drink it,' I said."

M.E. Chaber [Kendall Foster Crossen, 1910–1981] • ***The Splintered Man*** • PERMA 3080
1957 • COVER BY ROBERT SCHULZ • REPRINT

"A muffled moan was faintly heard and Ruth shuddered, arched back to avoid that pressure — for the latex whorls compressed her bare skin with all their torturing potency...as the perspiration of her bare skin moistened those appendages inside the body sheath, a chemical compound was released, odorless as to stain, but devastating in effect...for the hidden whorls and spirals in these bikini-tights had been impregnated with the LSD chemicals which, once naked intimate flesh was moist with perspiration, catalytically spread their aphrodisical [sic] drug into the wearer's nervous system through the pores of the skin.

"...'This Morley dame feeds LSD and other powerful drugs to men and women she wants to get a hold on, so they'll act like sex fiends,'" our slow-on-the-uptake hero, Ken realizes.

LSD-dominatrix Debra Morley's "House of Eros is closed to special clients these days. But Ken drew up a legal contract which will protect her secret formulas for LSD adaptation for many years to come. Several legitimate industries have shown great interest in her ideas of saturating garments with chemicals that accentuate certain reactions. They may even have their place in our work to lead the world in outer-space achievements."

Acid-trippin' sex-fiend astronauts on Mars! Houston, we have a problem.

As a note of interest to bibliophiles, speculative-fiction/fantasy author Louis Charbonneau's *Psychedelic-40* — the story of an ominous cartel's dictatorship of the U.S. through addicting the population to a hallucinogenic drug with powerfully erotic qualities — is the first novel, a paperback original, to use the Humphry Osmond-coined neologism "psychedelic" in its title.

During the 1950s, the CIA feared what would happen if the Soviets got hold of LSD and polluted U.S. water supplies.[59] In 1968, the FBI's worst counterculture-terrorism nightmare came true: the spiking of the nation's water supply with LSD. Fortunately, it only occurred in print in *The Polluters* by R[obert]. L. Seiffert. One typically hungover morning, Chicagoan Stan discovers that that the entire city has gone psychotic, chaos and destruction everywhere, otherwise sensible citizens reduced to slobbering incoherence or depraved sex-crazed rut. Only a street wino and juicer Stan remain unaffected. Seems a local group of Mao- and Che-inspired speed-freaks have, in conspiracy with fellow travelers in every major U.S. city, commandeered urban water plants and mixed huge quantities of acid into the water, which Stan and the wino never, on principle, allow to cross their lips. It's up to Stan and a roving band of flower children — who, led astray by the speed-freaks, assisted in the acidification but now, thanks to Stan, have seen the true light — to retake the plants with — flower-power horrors! — violence. Having saved the day, Stan and the now straightened-out hippies all kick back with bottles of high-end distilled spirits they've kyped from zombified liquor store owners. Supposedly a comic satire, the book possesses all one expects from a comic satire except the comedy and the satire; it's all pretty much a condescending view of the counterculture and misguided youth, 100 proof, the triumph of booze reflecting the contemporary dueling-highs conflict, yet another in the generational divide. Originally commissioned for the famed 1960s original erotica imprint Essex House, it didn't live up to the hopes of Brian Kirby, the imprint's editor, who consigned it to his lesser line, Brandon House Library Editions. Of the 42 Essex House titles released before the imprint's demise,[60] many featured drug use, not the least of which was *Stoned* by "Lady Jane" Gallion (1938–2003), an extremely well-respected speculative-fiction/fantasy novelist.

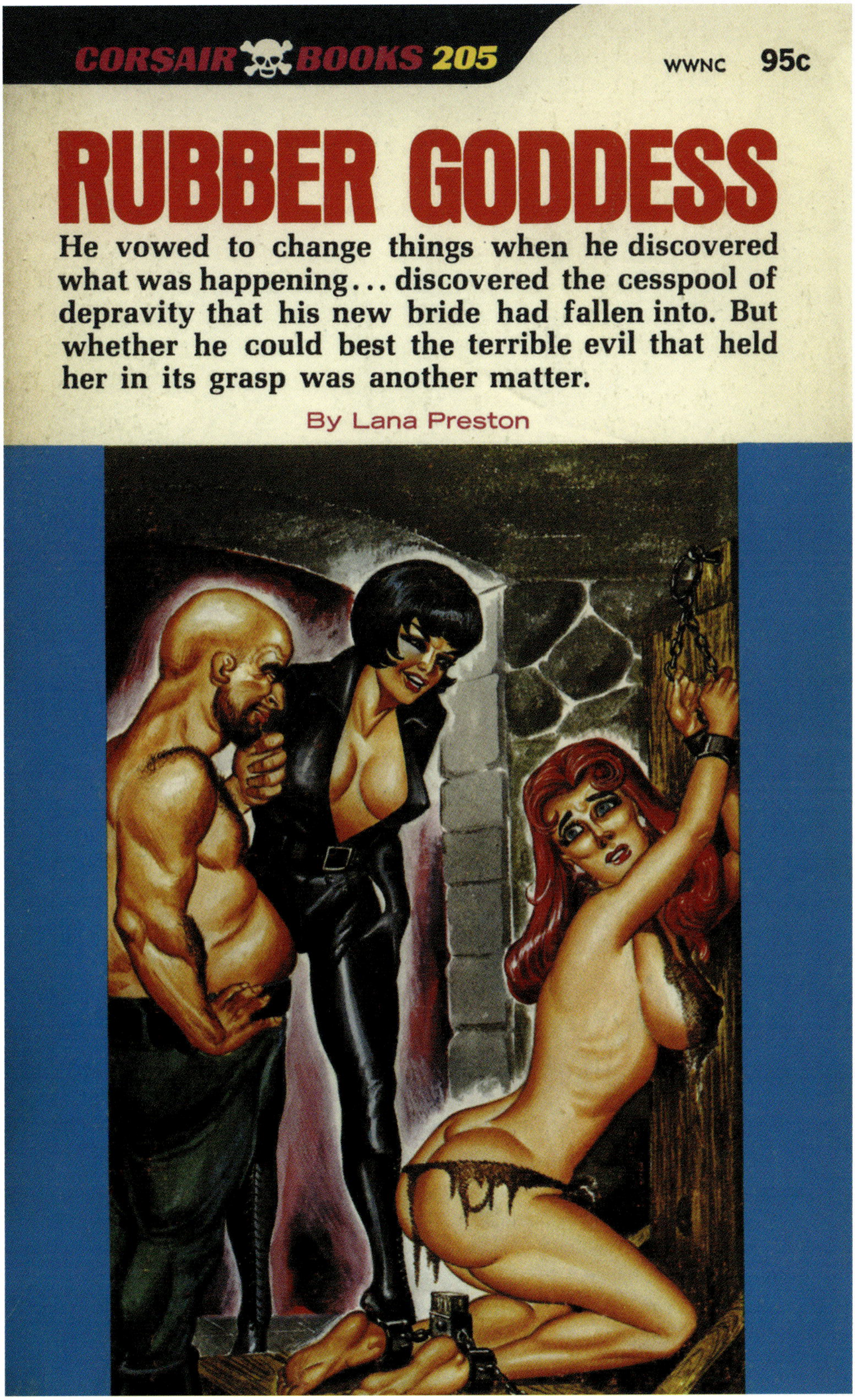

Lana Preston [Paul Hugo Little] • ***Rubber Goddess*** • CORSAIR 205 • 1967 • COVER BY GENE BILBREW
PBO • COURTESY OF MICHAEL HOROWITZ

Under Kirby's close direction and editorial guidance, Marsha Alexander would write what would become and remain one of the finest of the sex & drugs nonfiction titles, *The Sexual Paradise of LSD*, a "sexumentary" in case-history format. Alexander, who ran a head-shop on Fairfax Avenue in Los Angeles, was experienced in the subject but was reluctant to have the book released under her real name. Impressed with her writing talent and feeling that she should be recognized, Kirby insisted otherwise. Marsha Alexander would write other well-done porn books for Brandon House before embarking on a successful career as a romance novelist for Harlequin Books. Later a respected literary agent, she ultimately left the field to pursue a new interest: becoming a renowned designer of fashions for big and beautiful women and opening a thriving retail shop for her work in the L.A. suburb Woodland Hills.

Considering that drug literature is commonly suffused with the erotic, it's surprising that in erotic literature the inclusion of drugs is a relatively recent phenomenon. From the 17th century through the 1930s, there is a record of only one erotic novel concerned with sex and drugs, *Seduction By Chloroform*.[61] In the United States, drugs play virtually no role in erotic literature until the appearance of Robert Sewall's pseudonymously written 1942 clandestine masterpiece, *The Devil's Advocate* by Wood C. Lamont.[62] An erotic novel in the guise of a mystery story, it contains an extremely evocative 30-page scene that takes place at an opium party/sex orgy. It was openly published in its only uncut edition by paperback publisher Holloway House in 1969 under the title *The Devil's Brand*.[63]

Charles Beadle's *Dark Refuge* (1938) was issued in Paris by Jack Kahane's softbound imprint for the English-speaking tourist trade, Obelisk Press, which gained notoriety as the publishing house that boldly issued Henry Miller's early books, including *Tropic of Cancer*. As fulsomely described in Obelisk's catalogue, it is about "The effect of hashish on the individual, its annihilation of all conventional taboos, social and sexual. A symphony of lusts and hates, fears and loves. A memorable novel,"[64] despite which few are aware of; it is quite rare. We begin to see drugs featured in many books published by Kahane's son, Maurice Girodias, through his Paris-based erotica imprint Olympia Press, during the 1950s–early 1960s, most of which were reprinted in the U.S. by pulp porn publishers post-1965. Many of Alexander Trocchi's pseudonymously[65] written novels for Olympia contained drug use. A dedicated heroin addict, Trocchi would later write *Cain's Book*, his autobiographical novel recounting his days and nights as a struggling writer in late-Fifties New York City while working as a scow pilot on the docks and scoring junk; it was, naturally, reissued in a paperback edition. With the emergence of the counterculture in the U.S during the early/mid-1960s, the number of erotic paperback titles featuring drug use exploded.

Many drug-related paperbacks issued during the 1960s were erotic in nature, "drug-porn" emerging as a new sub-genre of erotic literature. The Ludlow-Santo Domingo (LSD) Library — more on which later — has over 600 drug porn titles within its vast holdings; a dealer/collector of erotic literature on the East Coast reports to have considerably more in his collection. Indeed, there appear to have been more drug-porn paperbacks issued during the 1960s–early-1970s than in all drug literature issued prior. Greenleaf, a major porn house during the era, at one time ranked number

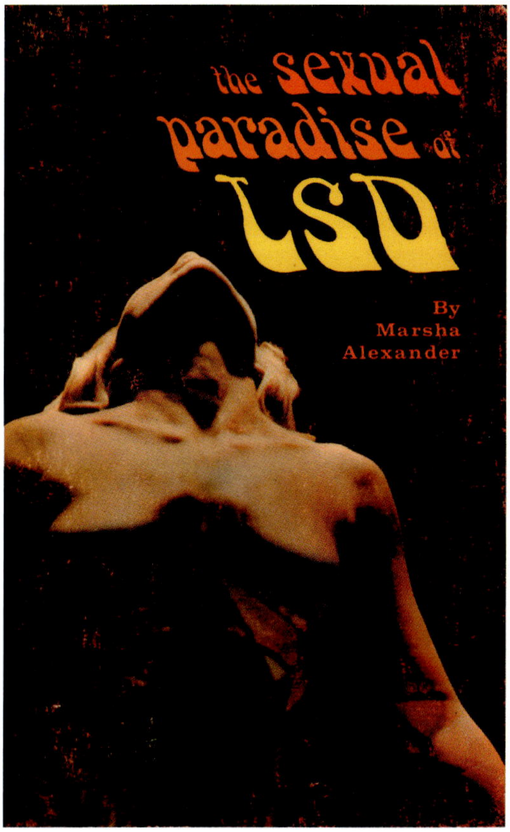

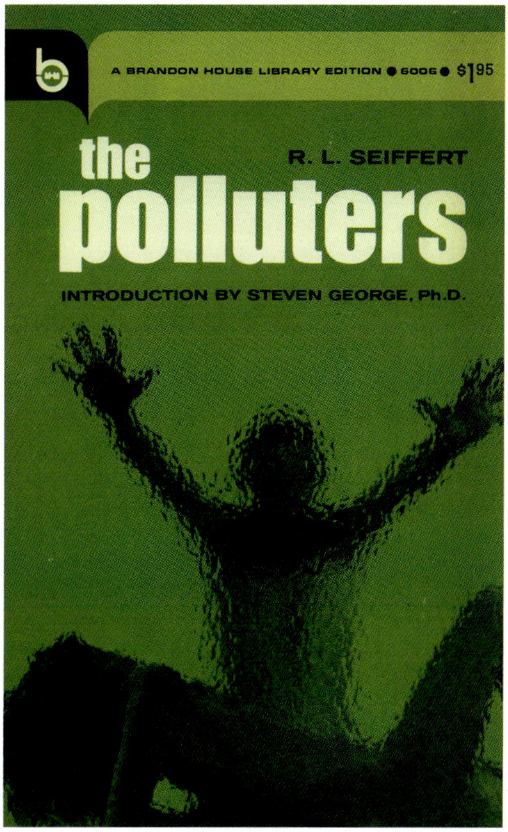

"I remember seeing vapor-like veils passing over Paula's body, altering it with the oiled slickness of rain discoloring the reflection of a rainbow. Her skin was first very white like translucent china, then she darkened until I had an Oriental goddess in my arms. The vapors thickened. My wife became an exotic creature straight out of the Arabian Nights. Paula was a jungle princess next, with flesh that gleamed like a black jewel against the white sheets."

"'We decided,' the boy ran on, 'that the only thing to do to get this society back to reality was to shock it into a sense of awareness of the now...We've expanded their minds...We got together with others who knew the score...We got the chemistry students...the engineering drop-outs... We picked out the biggest centers of the establishment in the country...We found a way to get into the public waterworks in each city...'

"He grinned at Stan. 'Acid!'

"'Acid?' asked Stan.

"'LSD, man, the greatest boon to mankind!'"

Marsha Alexander • ***The Sexual Paradise of LSD***
BRANDON HOUSE BH1067 • 1967 • PBO

R[obert]. L. Seiffert • ***The Polluters*** • BRANDON HOUSE
LIBRARY EDITIONS 6006 • 1968 • PBO
FROM THE AUTHOR'S COLLECTION

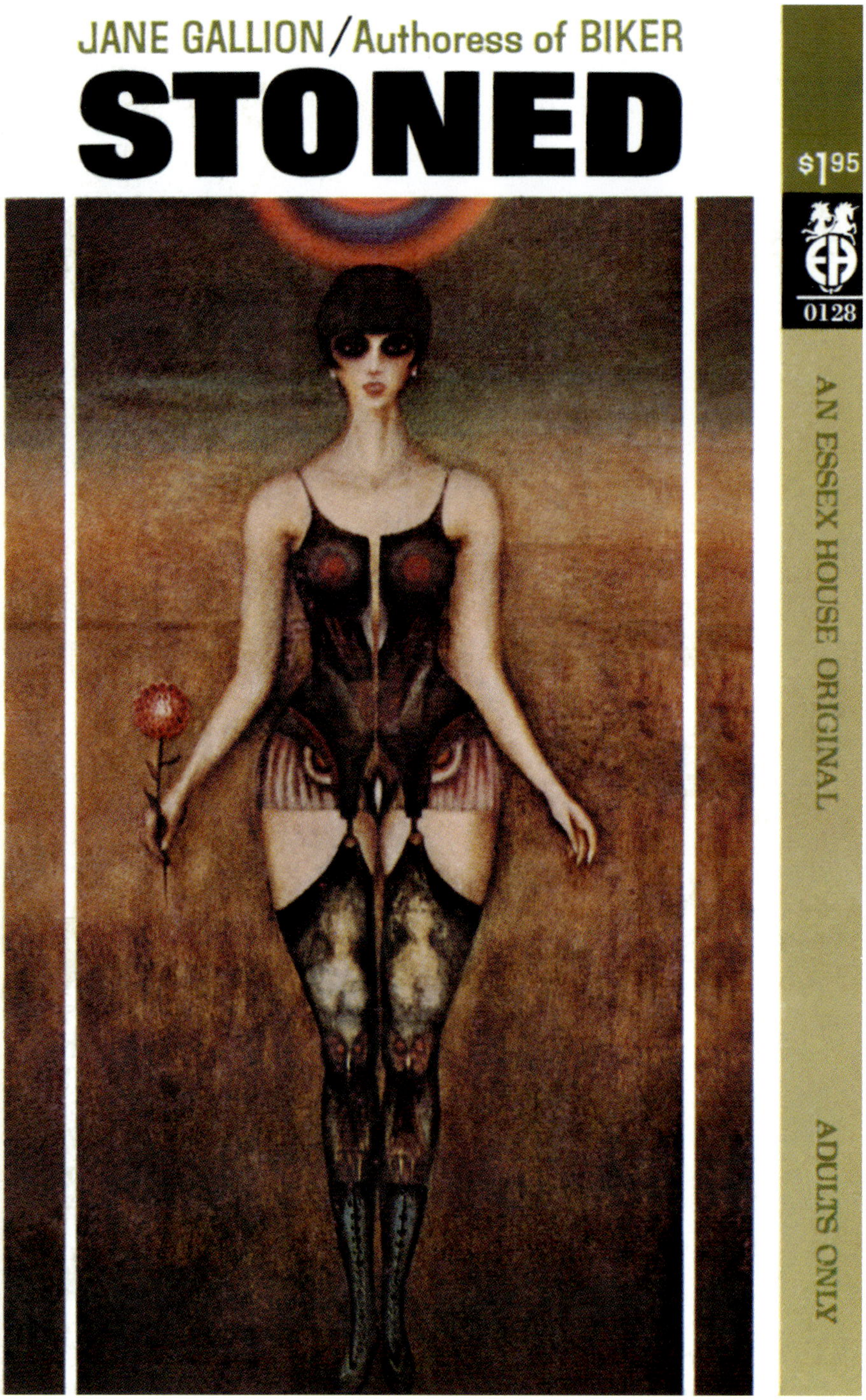

"Dope, Sex, and Cheap Thrills . What was the real world of Elaine Stuart? A boring husband to whom she was stupidly faithful, two screaming kids, a houseful of debts, and long nights of sexual frustration and loneliness...There had to be a way out of this endless nightmare...and where to find it? Then — FREAKOUT! The sweet pungency of pot filled her house night and day, and Elaine found a sudden, new perspective on her old life...Kids be damned! Husband go to hell! Elaine Stuart was free, alive and STONED"

Jane Gallion • ***Stoned*** • ESSEX HOUSE 128 • 1969 • COVER BY LEONOR FINI • PBO

Louis Charbonneau • ***Psychedelic-40*** • BANTAM, F-2929 • 1965 • PBO

F2929 * 50¢ * A BANTAM FIFTY

PSYCHEDELIC-40

LOUIS CHARBONNEAU

1993—A FRIGHTENINGLY PROPHETIC NOVEL OF THE U.S.A. RULED BY THE SYNDICATE—MEN WITH SUPER-MINDS WHO CAN PROBE THE ORDINARY CITIZEN'S THOUGHTS AT WILL.

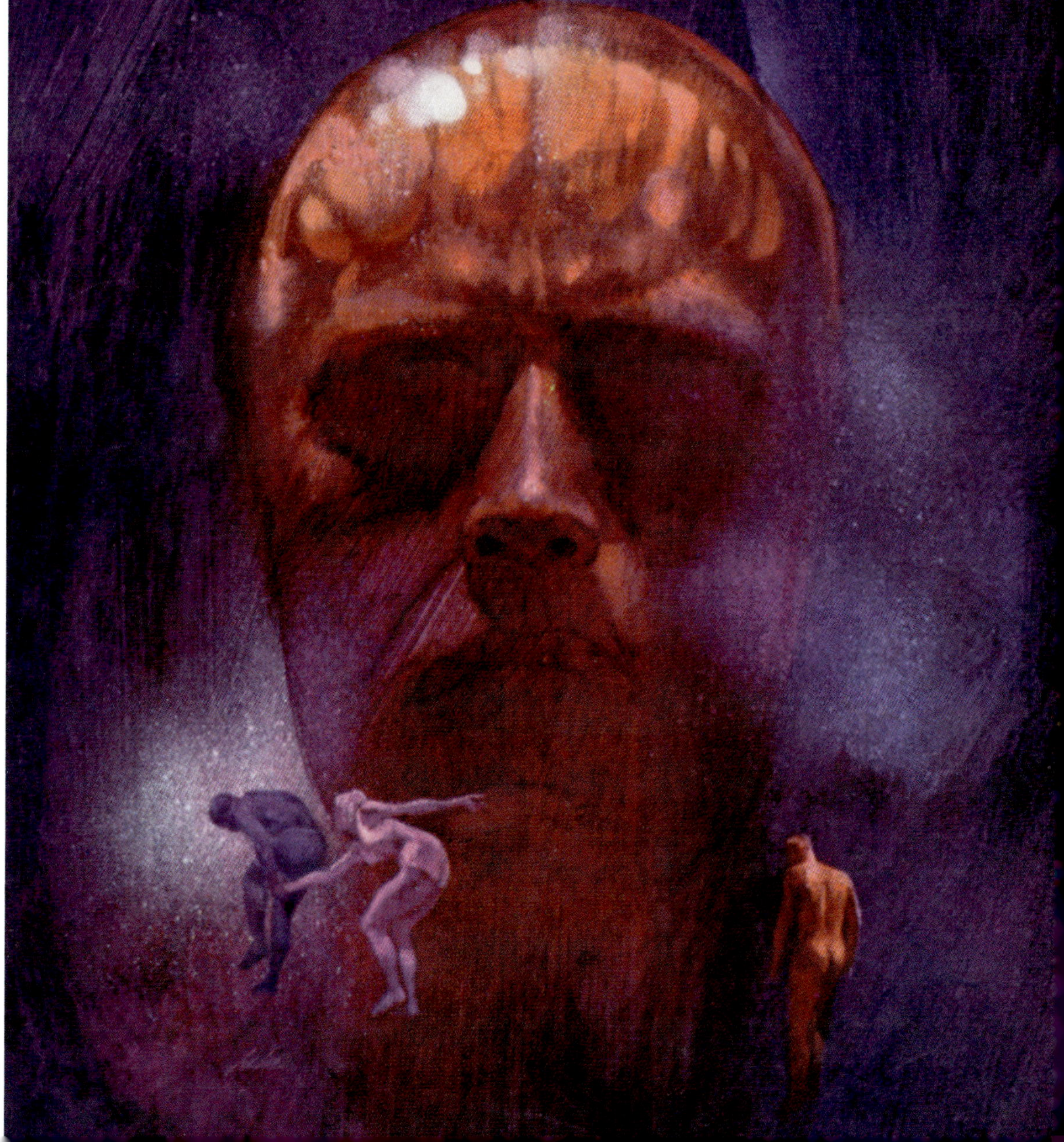

five in titles issued, just behind mainstream paperback house, Bantam,[66] was releasing upwards of 500 titles a year through its many imprints, and while no records were kept on those drug-themed, a large number included drug use. As previously mentioned, many if not most of the earliest drug-porn titles were written by those whose knowledge of the drug experience was tenuous at best. That would change as counterculture writers begin to express themselves in the genre.

Sharon Rudahl's pseudonymously written *Acid Temple Ball* by Mary Sativa, issued by Maurice Girodias when he transplanted Olympia Press to New York, was then and remains now one of the finest drug-porn titles ever written, "a tour de force of psychedelic erotica,"[67] a year in the life of an art student whence she experiences sex under the influence of approximately eight different drugs and drug blendings. (Kids, don't try this at home.) A cult classic, Rudahl wrote the book for that most prosaic of reasons: she desperately needed the money. At the time a starving art student at Cooper-Union College in New York City, she was working as a file clerk to support herself but that barely paid the bills much less tuition. She had read a couple of Girodias' pulp erotica titles and, like many, experienced the eureka epiphany, "I can do better than that!"[68]

Submitting a chapter and outline, she was called by Girodias almost immediately afterward. "He loved the idea," she recalls. She received a $3000 advance with royalties, a cut of the foreign rights, and retained copyright, an extraordinary deal: at the time, the overwhelming majority of pulp erotic writers earned three to three and a half times less that amount, ceding all rights, outright, to the publishers. "I hacked it out in six weeks, working nights, very disciplined. Maurice adored the book." So much so that he ordered a 100,000-copy initial print run,[69] most unusual at a time when most pulp-porn titles were issued in 35K–50K printings. Selling out, it went into a second edition. She wrote it under the pseudomononym Sativa, but Girodias insisted upon adding "Mary"to the name, rounding out the marijuana allusion. Girodias also gave the book its title (he had a gift for titles, in his Olympia Press-Paris years often coming up with a title and commissioning a book to match), an evocative summation of the psychedelic sexual trip as experienced by the book's heroine, whose East Village apartment in Manhattan becomes, under the influence of LSD, a Hindu temple of sexual worship à la Khajurahu and Konarak where " a pageant of the Eastern Gods…unfold[s]," she and her lover as Shakti and Shiva, their sexual union a profoundly spiritual, universal prayer, "Ball" serving as a delightful double entendre for a lavish dance /copulation.

Though the book reads as a memoir, it is almost entirely fiction, the author and heroine sharing only basics of age, art student status, emotional point of view, locations, and enjoyment of acid, grass and hashish, the long menu of drugs the heroine enjoys strictly fictional. "It was more like, 'what drug will I write about tonight!'" Rudahl admits. This is quite remarkable as Sharon writes of these other drugs — speed, heroin, cocaine, DMT, opium, etc.—with extraordinary empathic understanding of their psychotropic effects. As for the number of sexual encounters the heroine has, these were almost entirely the product of Rudahl's inner life. "They were imaginary guys, or guys I knew and wanted to have sex with but didn't." She was married at the time of the book's writing, a precocious, barely–20-year-old. "Maurice insisted that the character's age be upped to 21," for reasons that remain unclear but perhaps the idea of a ripe, underage hippie girl gorging on sex and drugs was too legally provocative for Girodias to risk.

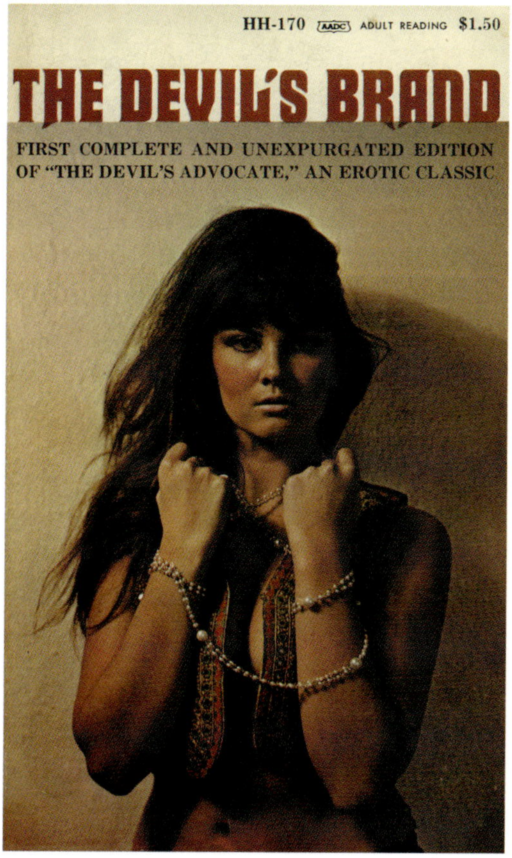

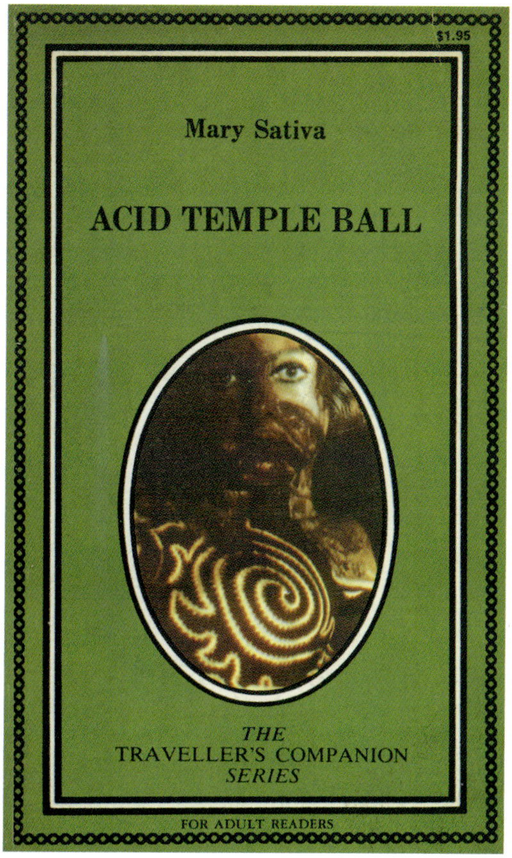

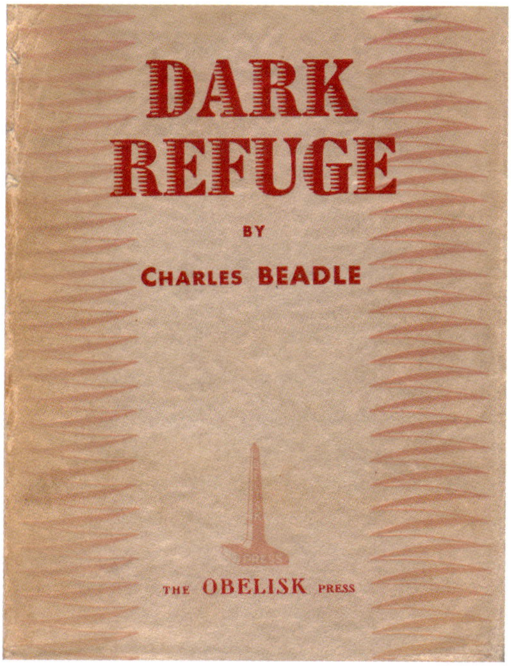

First (only) published edition of the complete clandestine manuscript of *The Devil's Advocate.*

"'And how long have you been kicking the gong [smoking opium] around?'"

[Robert Sewall] • ***The Devil's Brand*** • HOLLOWAY HOUSE HH-170 • 1969 • FROM THE AUTHOR'S COLLECTION

Mary Sativa [Sharon Rudahl] • ***Acid Temple Ball*** • OLYMPIA PRESS-NY TRAVELLER'S COMPANION TC2228 • 1969 • PBO • FIRST EDITION

Charles Beadle • ***Dark Refuge*** • PARIS: OBELISK PRESS • 1938 • COURTESY OF MICHAEL HOROWITZ

Acid Temple Ball was translated into French, German, and Italian, the title of the French edition, *Une Saison dans Paradis*, a play on Rimbaud's classic that at the time Rudahl preferred to the English title. Sharon recalls getting another $3000 for the foreign rights. And though Girodias, in standard operating procedure, ultimately screwed her out of contracted royalties for the second edition, the total $6000 she did earn was a king's ransom, most pulp-porn writers' wet dream. Having written one of the great psychedelic wet dreams, afterward Sharon Rudahl became a renowned artist/writer of underground comix of strong socio-political content and wit. True to her counterculture/anarchist roots, as of this writing she is working on a graphic biography of Emma Goldman.

Marco Vassi [Ferdinand William Vasquez-d'Acugno, 1941–1989] was, by common consent and mainstream critical acclaim (Norman Mailer, Saul Bellow and Gore Vidal were fans), the finest writer of erotica of his generation. Vassi wrote nine such novels, his first four written for Girodias in New York. A sighted Tiresias, Vassi was a prophet who traveled the mystic highway at its intersection of the erotic and psychotropic, "the Siddhartha of sex, the Buddha of the boudoir,"[70] one whose literary (and personal) immersion into sex and drugs was a means to a (hoped-for) illuminated end, not an escape from reality but a fervent rush toward a heightened one.

As with most literature, the vast majority of drug-porn titles were average in quality, and some were just plain lousy. Some were quite amusing — it would not be until the early 1970s that humor would be banned from pornography as the readership declined to strictly the jerk-off brigade, uninterested in serious or otherwise literary exploration.[71]

One of the more comical, if unintentionally so, drug-porn novels of the era was — Gangway! — *Here Come The Hippies* by William Charles Spatari. The author clearly distains the counterculture, pits booze against pot but provides literary documentation to one of the most curious, if now largely forgotten, episodes in hippie lore: smoking dried banana peels as a means to getting high.

"Bananadine? Urban legend? I smoked it once, at a Be-In in Central Park in 1967, the summer Donovan's "Mellow Yellow" came out, and thought I got a buzz. So did we all. The placebo effect at work," drug historian and bibliographer Michael Horowitz remembers. With the social/moral order — bent by the growing popularity of marijuana use amongst the younger generation — seemingly in favor of banning anything possessing redeeming euphoric value, the myth began at the street level, literally a grassroots effort. "Politically, the idea was to make the point that the government would have to ban bananas too!" Horowitz recalls.

One drug-porn novel presents a delightful surprise. William Kalinich's *The Bike Freaks* (Ophelia Press OHP-233, 1967), written under the pseudonym Art Derfall, is, to all appearances, an homage to acclaimed photographer Danny Lyon, whose classic photo-essay *The Bikeriders* (1968) is considered to be one of the seminal photography books of the 20th century. As Lyon did in *The Bikeriders*, the protagonist in *The Bike Freaks*, Danny Lyons [sic], joins a rowdy, party-hardy but essentially benign motorcycle club comprised mostly of college grads and dropouts seeking a fuller, fun-filled life than that which the straight world offers. What's positively spooky about the book, however, is that the connection with Danny Lyon and *The Bikeriders* was purely coincidental.

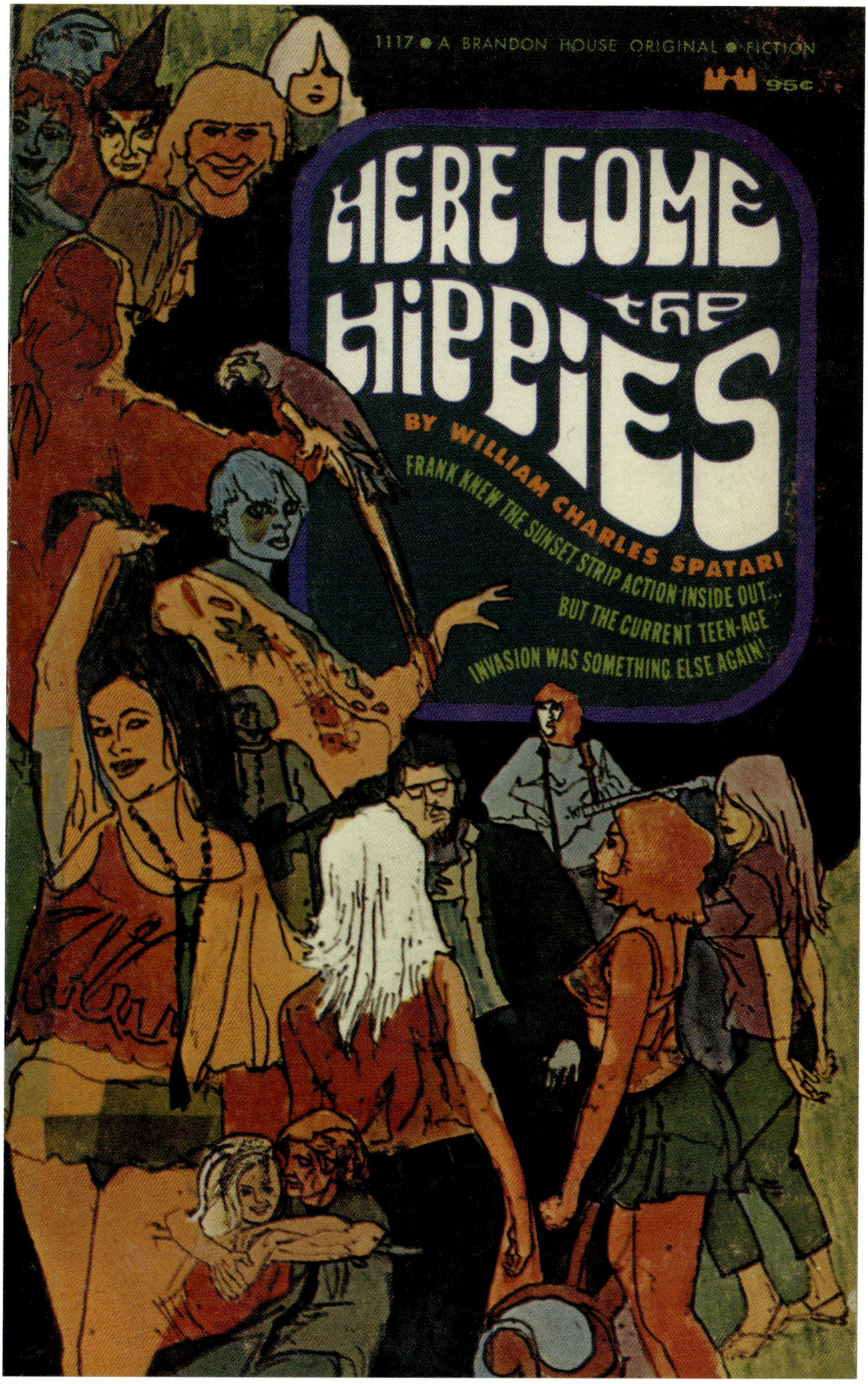

"'Want a banana, Frank?' Hippy asked, holding out a crude hand-rolled cigarette.... 'Brainstorm two!' a girl said as she sucked on a banana butt and exhaled smoke."

William Charles Spatari • ***Here Come the Hippies*** • BRANDON HOUSE 1117 • 1967 • PBO

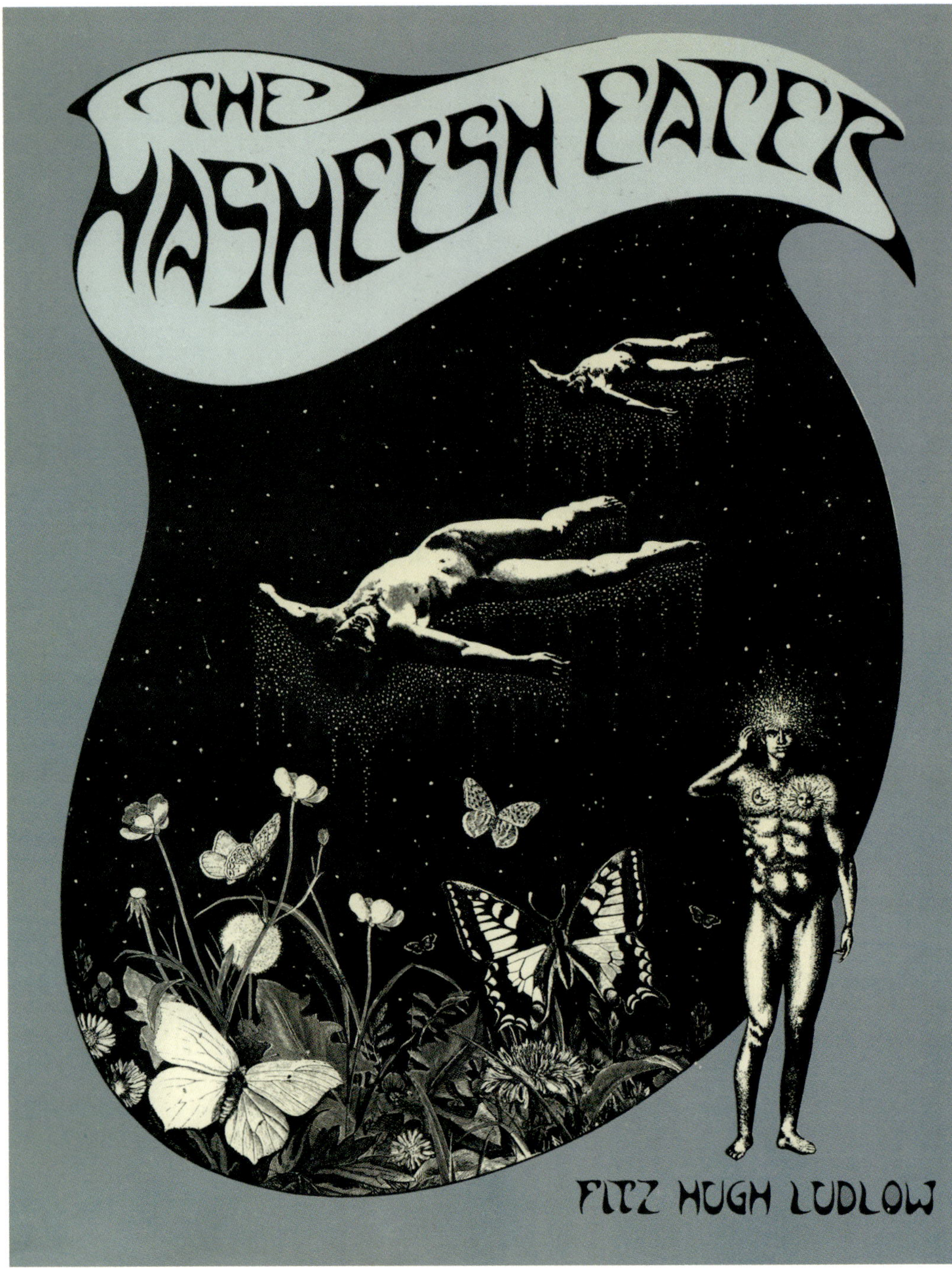

Fitz Hugh Ludlow • ***The Hasheesh Eater*** • LEVEL PRESS • 1975 • COVER ART BY DAVID SINGER AND SÄTTY
FIRST COMPLETE EDITION IN PAPERBACK • A FACSIMILE REPRINT OF THE 1857 FIRST EDITION • FROM THE AUTHOR'S COLLECTION

Fitz Hugh Ludlow • ***The Hasheesh Eater*** • CITY LIGHTS • 1979 • COVER ART BY AUBREY BEARDSLEY, ONE OF THE PLATES USED FOR THE 1903 REPRINT OF THE BOOK

**Second Complete Edition in paperback, a facsimile reprint of the 1857 first edition.
The image by Beardsley was one of a handful used in the 1903 edition.**

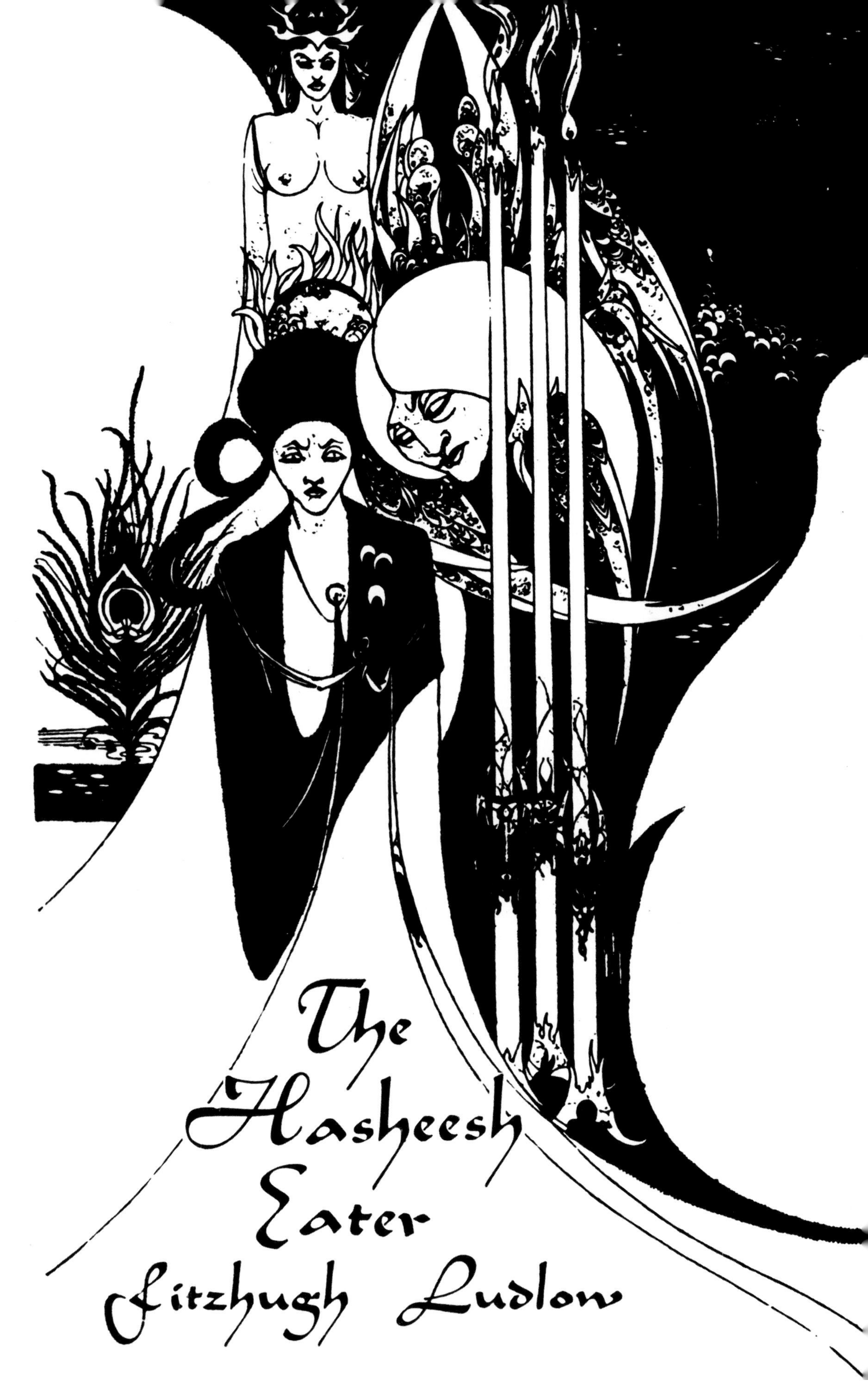
The Hasheesh Eater
Fitzhugh Ludlow

"Not an homage at all," Kalinich asserts. "The characters were just loosely based upon a few friends of mine and all fiction; what we *wished* for, really — the free-love. But the drug stuff, all true."[72]

The drug confessional has become a popular staple of the post-Sixties marketplace[73] yet these volumes, however important as cautionary tales, tell us much about what we are already are aware of: drug use in the postmodern world. To discover the world of the user in the American past, we need only look to contemporary accounts reprinted in paperback.

The granddaddy of all American drug confessionals is Fitz Hugh Ludlow's *The Hasheesh Eater* (1857), published in facsimile in its first paperback edition in 1975 by Level Press. This issue, published under the auspices of the Fitz Hugh Ludlow Memorial Library, with a learned introduction, chronology, bibliography, and bio-critical data, remains the best edition to date. Ludlow (1836–1870), at the time a 20-year-old college student,[74] was experimenting in the U.S. just a short time after the personal investigations of Gautier, Baudelaire, Moreau, Dumas, Balzac, de Nerval, and others in their Club des Hachichins in Paris. Writing pseudonymously as "A Pythagorean," he wrote the book as a therapeutic effort to quit the drug, which he had been ingesting in massive doses — four grams at a time over an 18-month period — that produced mystic, psychedelic highs rarely experienced at lower, smoked doses. His model for the book was Thomas De Quincey's *Confessions of an English Opium Eater* (1822) which had had an enormous influence upon Romantic literature; indeed, Ludlow was then as now considered the American De Quincey. He became a critically recognized writer, and in the early 1860s was one of the first to bestow critical praise upon the work of up-and-coming Mark Twain, who would write, "If Fitz Hugh Ludlow, author of *The Hasheesh Eater*, comes your way, treat him well."[75]

Born in 1894 and raised in Greenwich Village, Millard Fillmore Hopper spent much of his youth playing checkers at the local recreation center while his friend from around the block, Gene Tunney, learned boxing at the local gym. He was 15 when he first tried heroin early in 1910. Hanging out with his friends, he was introduced to the drug by an young man from the neighborhood, a local member of the sporting class whose personal, worldly manner, and style of dress were fascinating to these impressionable kids; he was "the King of the Greenwich Village addicts of my day." Soon addicted, Hopper began to lie and steal to get enough money to support his habit; though legal, the price of heroin had been rising steadily since government regulations had made it increasingly difficult to import. Arrested numerous times for theft, he spent much of his late adolescence in reformatories, unable to kick the habit. This gives lie to the popular notion that the Harrison Act of 1914, which strictly regulated the prescribing of opiates but did not ban them,[76] made criminals out of otherwise innocent junkies; the middle-aged medically addicted population was by then dead or dying out, leaving only the crimester-addicts and those in the "sporting life" of gamblers, sportsmen, pimps, and prostitutes who used drugs for recreation.

In 1915, while a penniless hobo fighter with a prostitute wife and intimately aware of "the demi-monde of pugs and madams, whores and hustlers, in which they knew characters by the score,"[77] future heavyweight champion Jack Dempsey would often

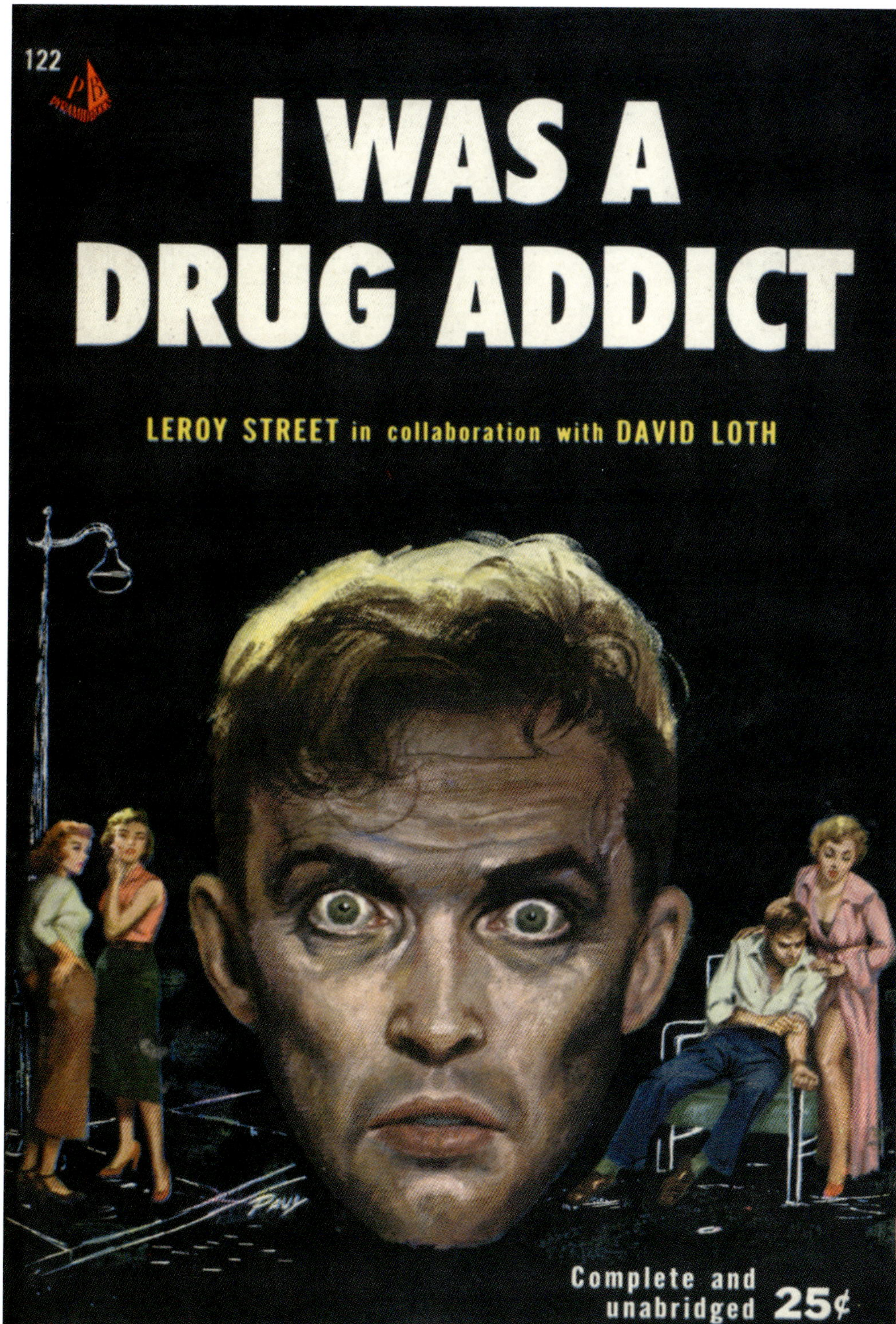

"From the time I was fifteen until I was twenty-eight I was a slave to heroin and morphine. I also experimented with cocaine, marijuana and opium. I became a liar and a thief, an inmate of a reformatory and several jails. I plumbed the depths of degradation, going through cure after cure but invariably slipping back..."

Leroy Street (Millard Hopper) in collaboration with David Loth • ***I Was a Drug Addict*** • PYRAMID 122
1954 • COVER BY JULIAN PAUL • REPRINT

sing a verse from a ditty popular amongst the sporting crowd to keep his spirits up while riding the boxcars to his next fight:

If I was a millionaire and had a lot of coin,
I'd plant a row of coke and grow heroyn.
I'd have forty-thousand hop layouts,
Each one inlaid with pearl,
I'd invite each old-time fighter to bring along his girl.
Down at the fighter's jubilee
We'll build castles in the air
And all feel like millionaires
Down at the fighter's jubilee.[78]

Later, describing the right to the jaw that dropped challenger Gene Tunney into the arms of Morpheus during the infamous "Long Count" heavyweight-title fight of 1927, Dempsey noted, "I had plenty of hop on it,"[79] "hop" sporting life slang for opium, originating circa 1905–1910, that may have been taken from a fusion of the word's original meanings — a journey, especially an airplane flight; a fanciful story; excitement; a state of confusion — that refers to an opium-smoking "pipe dream."[80] Dempsey's punch was loaded with metaphorical dope, his goal to put Tunney on Dreamstreet, Palookaville's avenue for the out-of-this-world.

But before that fight, in the post-WWI years while Tunney and Dempsey were on their ascent to boxing greatness, Millard Hopper continued his heroin use, remaining a stone junkie until 1923, when he was twenty-eight and fed up and rock bottom with the heroin life. Under the pseudonym "Leroy Street" — taken from the narrow thoroughfare he grew up on in Greenwich Village — he provides us with the best glimpse of immediate pre- and post-Harrison Act drug addiction with his 1953 memoir, *I Was A Drug Addict* reprinted in paperback in 1954. After his cure — and far beyond the book's end — Millard Hopper became the greatest American checker-player of the 20th century, winning the U.S. championship at the New York World's Fair of 1939 and writing a series of checkers How-To volumes during the 1940s[81] that remain the best instructionals on the subject, two of which were reprinted in the 1970s. Curiously, on May 24, 1953, in the same year *I Was A Drug Addict* was published, he appeared on Ed Sullivan's early television show *Toast of The Town* as the King of Checkers, the viewing audience (and Ed Sullivan, to be sure) completely unaware of his secret, checkered past. An advertising executive, he died in 1976.

Though British and only semi-autobiographical, occultist Aleister Crowley's 1922 novel *Diary of A Drug Fiend* presents us with love, heroin and cocaine amongst the English post-WWI Lost Generation smart set and the consequences when jaded escapists and drugs meet. The book was released in its first American paperback edition by Samuel Weiser in 1970, a facsimile of the London first edition. There is, alas, no literary work reflecting similar players and circumstances in the contemporary United States.

Milton "Mezz" Mezzrow (né Mesirow), was a jazz clarinetist of some renown; for a brief period, he managed Louis Armstrong. But his real claim to fame was as a popular

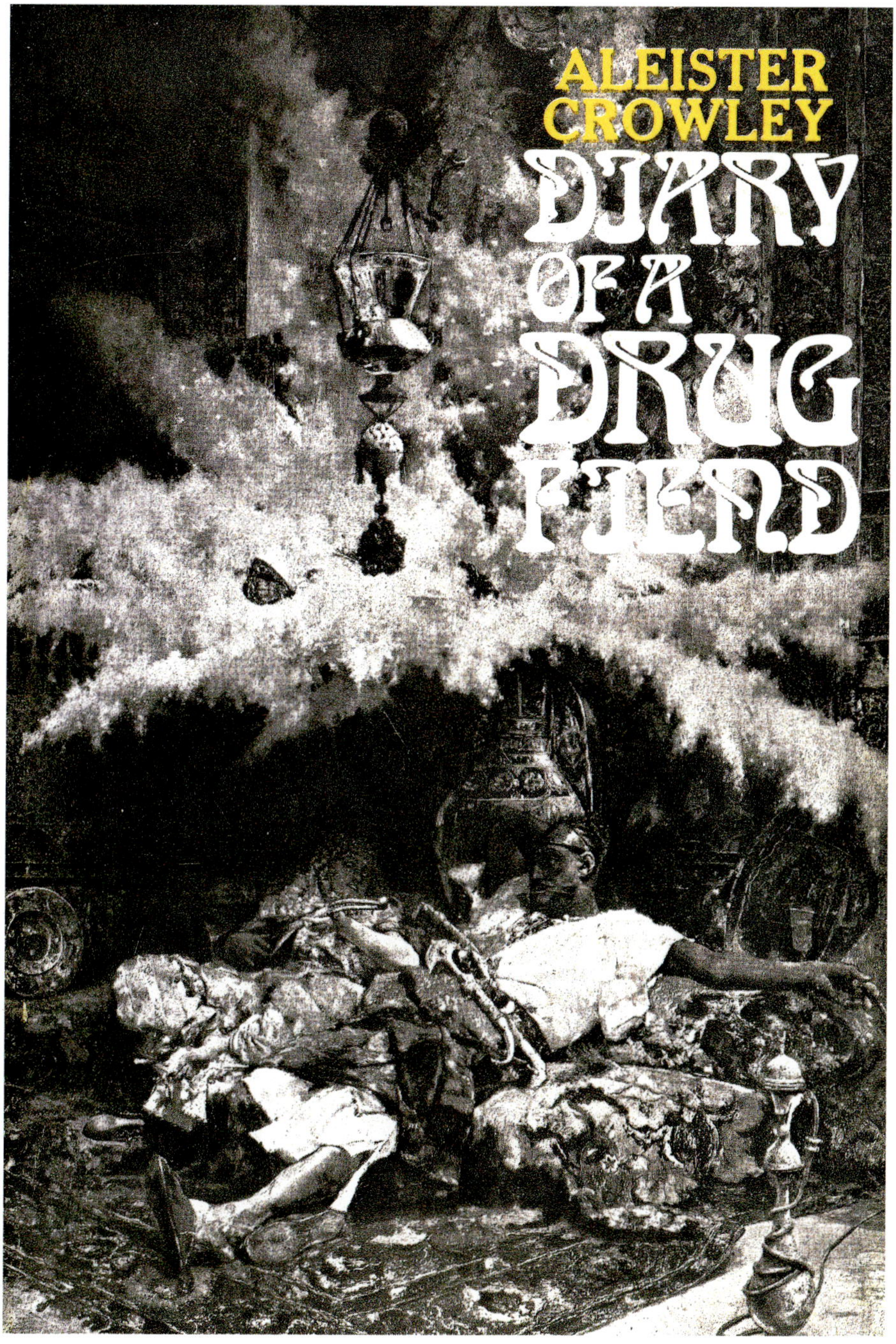

"'I've forgotten what love means, except for a faint sense of nausea when it comes under my notice. I hardly eat at all — it's only brutes that want to wallow in action that need three meals a day. I hardly ever talk — words seem such a waste, and they are none of them true...Human life or the heroin life? I've tried them both, and I don't regret having chosen as I did...Before I started heroin, year followed year, and nothing worthwhile happened. It was like a child scribbling in a ledger. Now that I've gotten into the heroin life, a minute or an hour — I don't know which and I don't care — contains more real life than any five years' period in my unregenerate days...You animals have to die, and you know it. But I am very far from sure that I shall ever die, and I'm as indifferent to the idea as I am to any other of your monkey ideas.'"

Aleister Crowley • ***Diary of a Drug Fiend*** • SAMUEL WEISER • 1970 • FIRST AMERICAN PAPERBACK EDITION
A REPRINT OF THE LONDON 1922 1ST EDITION • FROM THE AUTHOR'S COLLECTION

"To us a muggle wasn't any more dangerous or habit-forming than those other great American vices, the five-cent Coke and the ice-cream cone, only it gave you more kicks for your money.

"Us vipers began to know that we had a gang of things in common: we ate like starved cannibals who finally latch on to a missionary, and we laughed a whole lot and lazed around in an easygoing way, and we all decided that the muta had some aphrodisiac qualities too...All the puffed-up strutting little people we saw around, jogging their self-important way along so chesty and chumpy, plotting and scheming and getting more wrinkled and jumpy all the time, made us howl...We were on another plane in another sphere compared to the musicians who were bottle-babies, always hitting the jug and then coming up brawling after they got loaded. We liked things to be easy and relaxed, mellow and mild, not loud or loutish, and the scowling chin-out tension of the lushhounds with their false courage didn't appeal to us."

Mezz Mezzrow [Mezz Milton] and Bernard Wolfe • ***Really the Blues*** • DELL D118 • 1953
COVER BY WALTER BROOKS • REPRINT, NEW REVISED EDITION, FIRST PAPERBACK EDITION

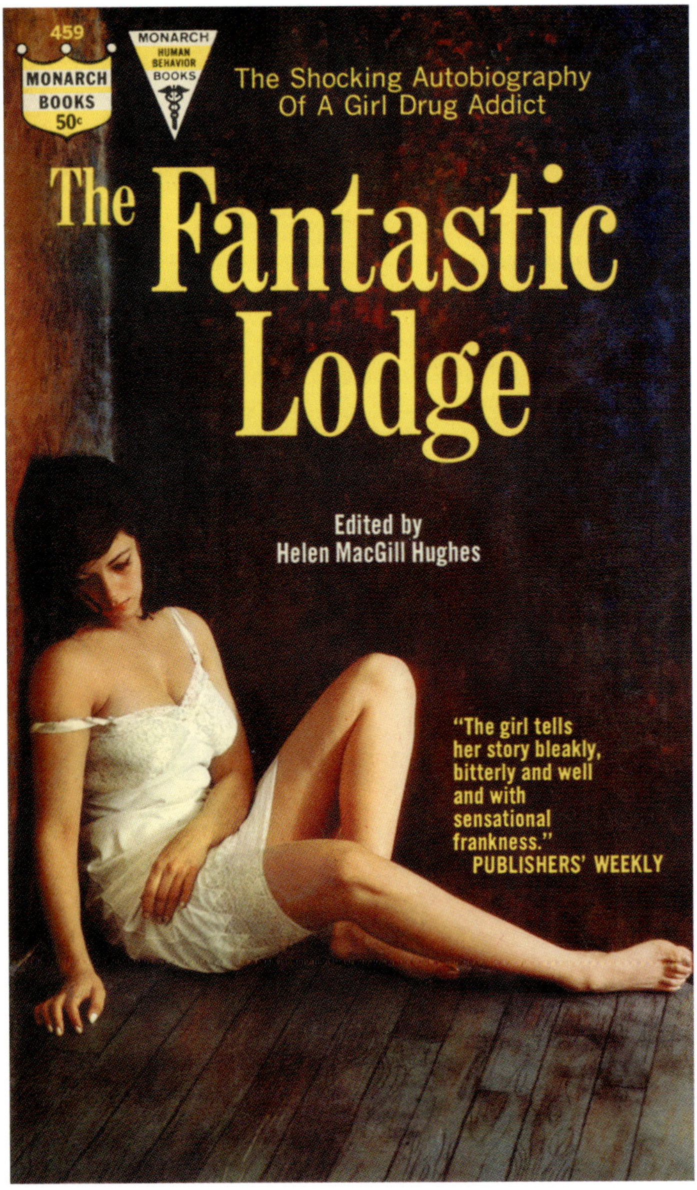

"...it's difficult to define the feeling. The best way I can state it is to say that it's like having warm milk flowing through your veins, instead of blood — and cold blood. But, really, it changes things so little and yet so much, you know, it's such a delicate thing to pin down.

"After you make it, first there's a flash. That's the sudden onrush of the horse feeling. It starts usually the third time you jag it off. There's a term in the jargon that Bob always used a lot and this is the best, the only word I can think of to describe a flash, and that's 'getting a buzz.' I never use that with pot. I always use it referring to horse because that's exactly what it is, you know, that first flash. Flash!...It's a feeling as though, all of a sudden, something good and easy and fine has happened."

Janet Clark (1924–1958), as told to Howard Becker
Edited by Helen McGill
The Fantastic Lodge
MONARCH 459 • 1964 • REPRINT

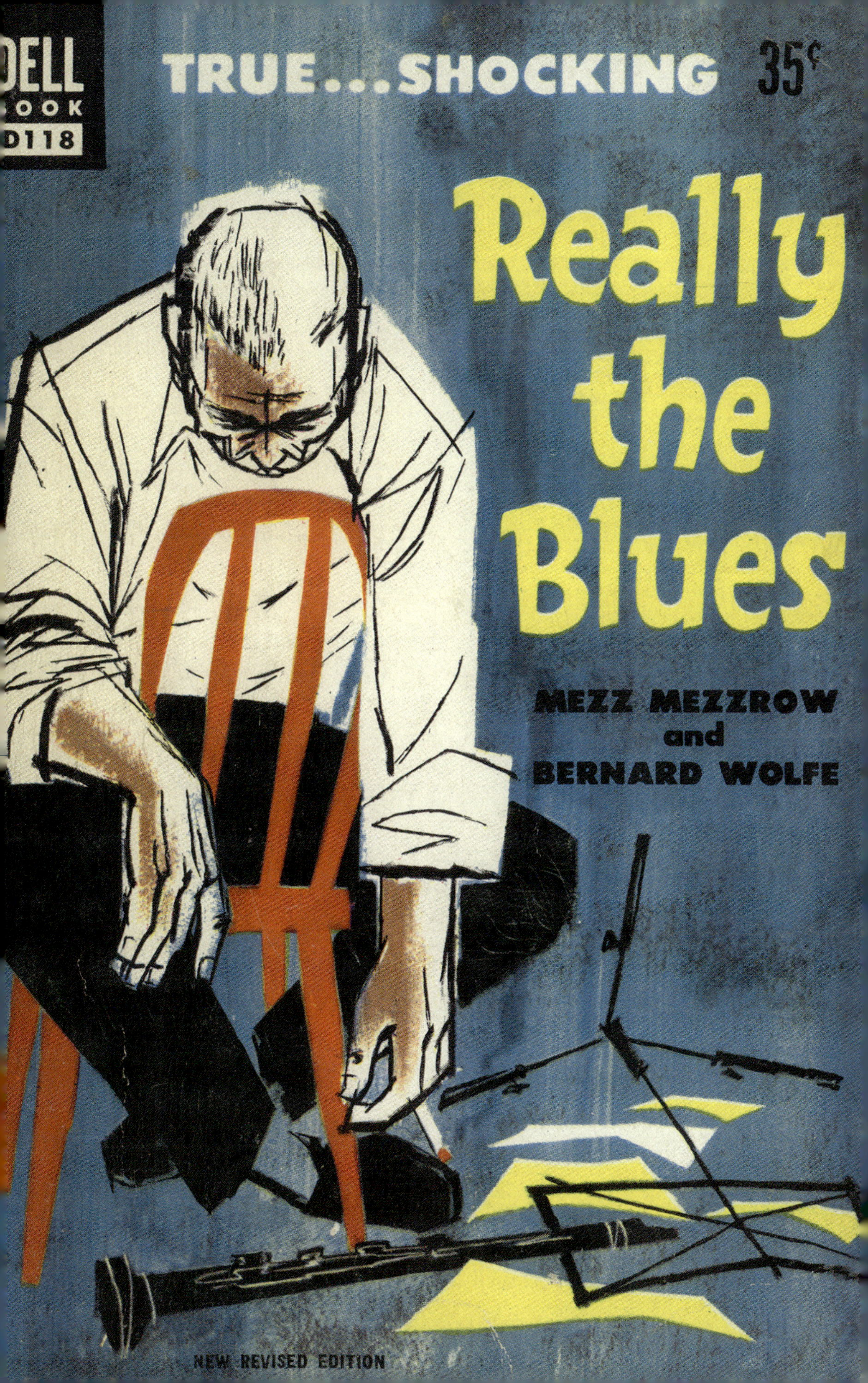
D118
TRUE...SHOCKING
35¢
Really the Blues
MEZZ MEZZROW
and
BERNARD WOLFE
NEW REVISED EDITION

marijuana dealer to his friends in the jazz world. He idolized black culture, absorbed it, assimilated it, lived it: the Eminem of his time. For awhile "mezz" and "the mighty mezz" became hip slang for grass. His memoir, *Really The Blues* (1946, reprinted in paperback 1953), is our best view of the marijuana underground of the '20s–'40s. And, significantly, the book, with its revelation of subterranean hip culture and concomitant drug use, was a major influence on the Beats and their acolytes.

If Charlie Parker had lived long enough and had been able to kick his habit, perhaps he would have written a memoir of junkiedom in the late '40s–50s. Tragically, he died before redemption came to him in his erratic personal life; his incalculable contribution to jazz and American music in general will stand, however, in its stead. To learn about the heroin scene during that period, however, we have the extraordinary *The Fantastic Lodge: The Autobiography of A Girl Drug Addict* by the pseudonymous Janet Clark (1924–1958). A too-hip-for-the-room white chick who devoured Mezzrow's *Really The Blues,* married a black musician, got thoroughly into the bebop scene and more thoroughly into heroin, she provides the keenest sense of the heroin subculture of the late 1940s through the Fifties. In these edited transcriptions of her talk therapy with hipster sociologist Howard Becker while in search of a cure for her addiction, hers is a voice clear, definite and truthful, rich in the slang and jargon of the hip underground and dope universe. She died of a barbiturate overdose in an attempt to alleviate withdrawal sickness.

Enough has been written about Burroughs' *Junkie*; nothing more need be added here beyond the fact that it tells us more about heroin use during the wartime and immediate postwar 1940s than any other volume; millions have read it since its original publication.

Diane Di Prima's original paperback *Memoirs of a Beatnik* is still the best book to capture the spirit and hopes of the Beats, initially a rather small group based in New York City and San Francisco experimenting with alternatives in the arts, morality and consciousness that greatly influenced a new generation of young, white middle-class Americans dissatisfied with and disaffected by the postwar status quo. Psychotropic drug use as an innate, individual freedom, one that might possibly facilitate mystic experience and open the mind to new perspectives in the creation of art, lay at the heart of the Beats' philosophical thesis, and no one has surpassed DiPrima in setting it forth.

Barbara Quinn's *Cookie,* reprinted in paperback as *Junkie,* is the sine qua non record of girl-gang juvenile delinquency, addiction, subsequent prostitution and thievery in the mid-Fifties through the Sixties that we have. She threw herself into addiction with unabashed joy; despair shortly followed. A brave woman, a brave book, she became one of the founders of Phoenix House, one of the more successful drug-rehab programs in the U.S.

We have few literary records of the plight of the medically morphine-addicted in the 20th century. Thirties boxing champion Barney Ross, who became dependent upon morphine while being treated for serious wounds incurred during heroic action in the battle for Guadalcanal in WWII, wrote a fine memoir in 1957 of his addiction, *No Man Stands Alone,* but it is exceedingly scarce in its hardcover edition and was, to the best of my investigation, never issued in a paperback reprint. Radio and television sportscaster Bill Stern's 1959 *A Taste of Ashes,* issued in paperback in 1961,[82] relating the reporter's opiate addiction subsequent to a car crash and resulting chronic pain, is good but our

"'Harry,' I said, 'I feel really weird.' I described my symptoms. 'Is it a habit? Does it mean I have a habit?'

"Harriet took it philosophically. 'Yeah, baby. You got a habit. Ain't that what you wanted?'

"I was thrilled. A real habit. An honest-to-goodness, high flying, down-to-earth, real McCoy habit. Wow, man! I was a junkie. Jay-you-en-kay-eye-ee junkie. Junkie was something special, something big and important and heroic. Real wild. A name that meant something powerful and gutsy like Annie Oakley or Wild Bill Hickok. I was excited..."

Barbara Quinn • ***Junkie***

BELMONT TOWER B5085 • 1971 • REPRINT

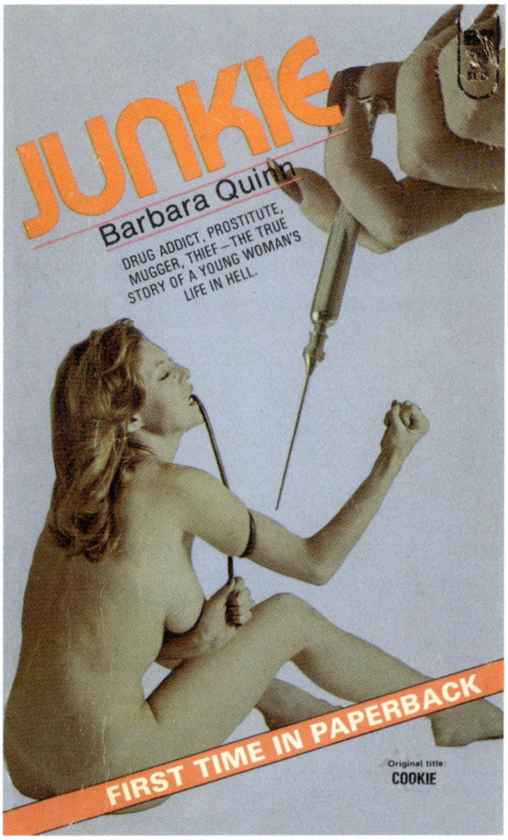

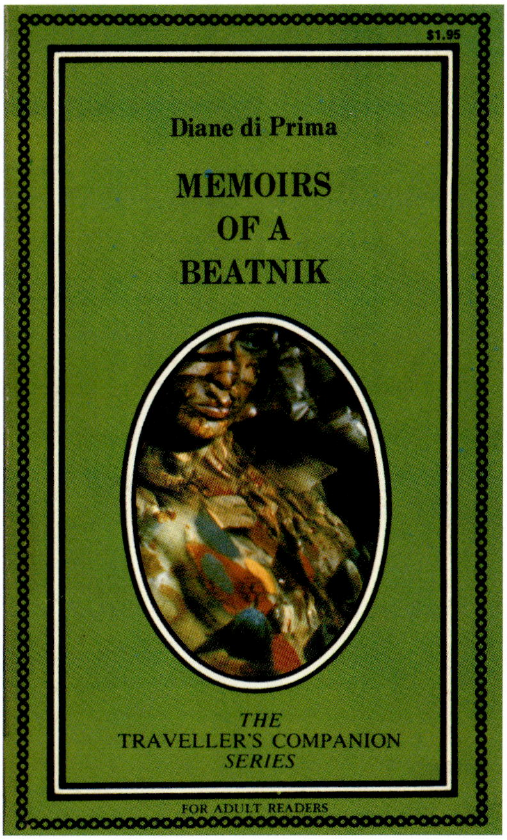

Diane Di Prima • ***Memoirs of a Beatnik***

OLYMPIA PRESS-NY • TRAVELER'S COMPANION 451

1969 • PBO

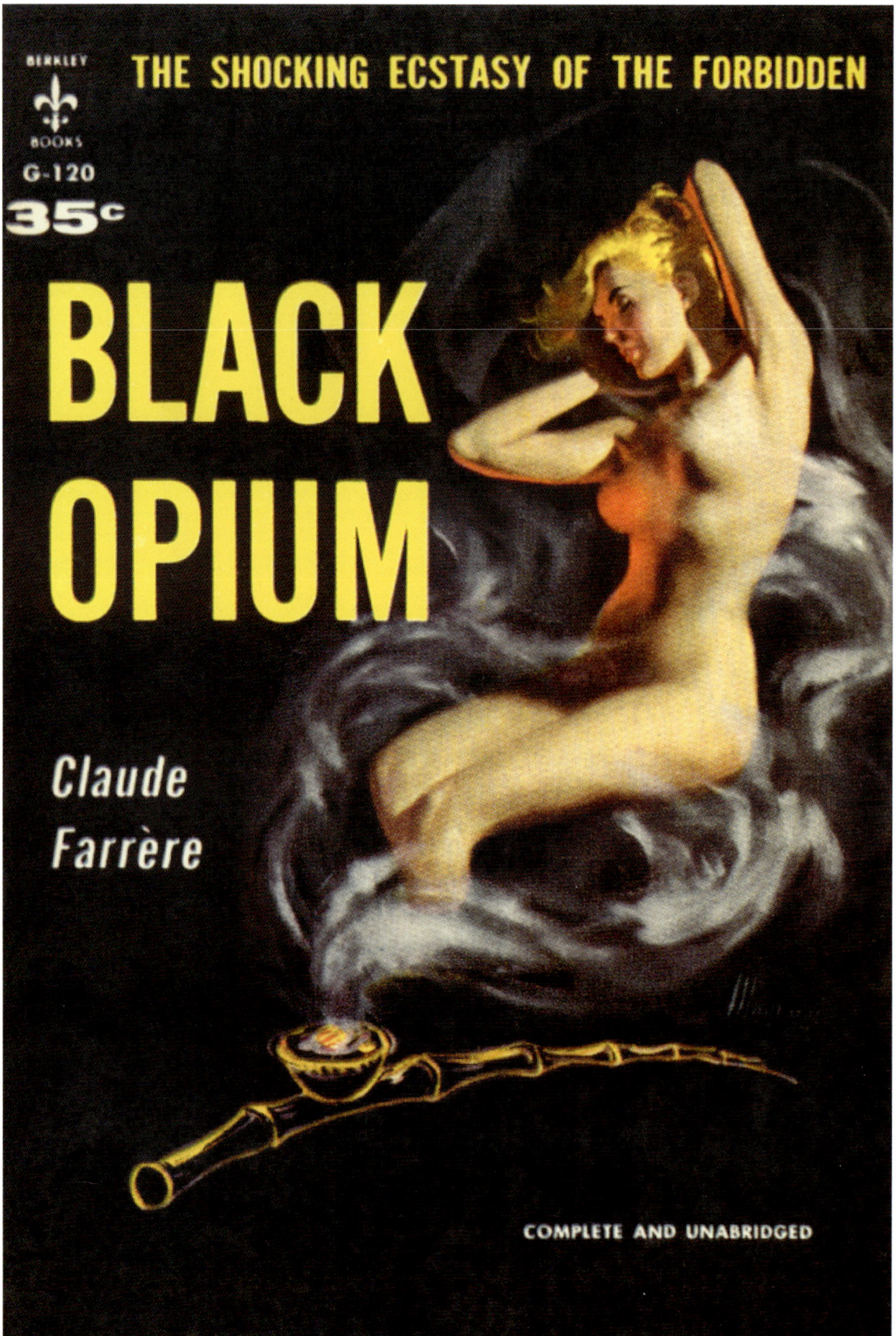

Claude Farrère [Edouard Bargone] • ***Black Opium*** • BERKELEY G120 • 1958 • COVER BY ROBERT MAGUIRE • REPRINT

"The opium has gradually stripped me of my virility, has delivered me from that sexual obsession which is such a weight for proud spirits and those truly eager for liberty. At first, fool that I was, I was afflicted; and I rebelled, like a slave whose chains are broken, and who basely regret his master's bread and roof. I blasphemed the opium's wise law, calling it absurd and unjust. I could not understand how reasonable it was for desire to cease to inhabit my man's flesh at the same time that it passed over into the feminine flesh of my comrade. Stupidly, comically, I wanted to go back upstream; I declined to abdicate my lover's role — until that wiser day when opium unsealed my eyes — unsealed her eyes — until the day when our bodies became divorced in order to permit our souls to share a more amorous marriage — in opium...

"...More, more opium. I wish, today, to go all the way to that frontier which separates drunkenness from death."

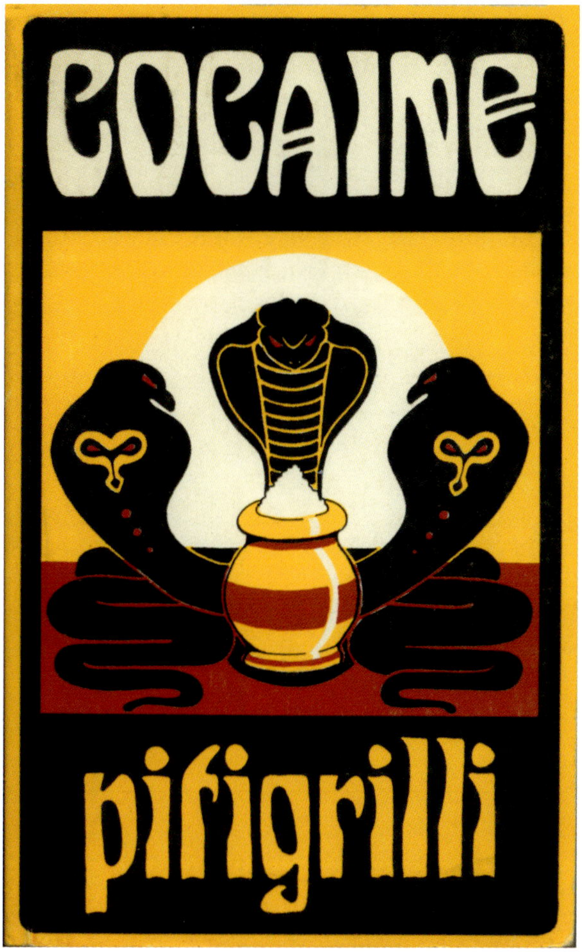

"'You're still in time,' said Kalantan to him. 'I know the workings of that dreadful and deadly powder. You have not yet reached the stage of frightful depressions, the period of brooding and destructive melancholy. You still can smile though your blood be filled with venom. You are in the first stages yet...'

"'Kalantan, you who said that I am still in the merry stage of my poisoning. You think I can still laugh. But it's long since I stopped laughing, Kalantan. I am sad most of the time...Cocaine does not only weaken the lungs and disturb your heart, as all hygienists seem to believe. Its real damage is mainly a psychical one. There is no escape from it. Cocaine literally uncouples and splits your individuality in twain; it accomplishes the almost electrolytic destruction of one's own conscience...Through cocaine, the splitting of individuality occurs like an explosion of long-repressed aversions; the two individualities within myself criticize each other and wage a continual warfare which is bound to create, within myself, hatred against myself.'"

Pitigrilli [Dino Segré] • ***Cocaine*** • AND/OR PRESS — LUDLOW HIP POCKET 7404 • 1974 • COVER AND ILLUSTRATIONS BY JIM OSBORNE • FIRST (ONLY) EDITION IN PAPERBACK, A FACSIMILE REPRINT OF THE 1933 FIRST EDITION IN ENGLISH
FROM THE AUTHOR'S COLLECTION

best view of iatrogenic junkiedom in the mid-20th century rests with *Mine Enemy Grows Older* (Signet D-1753, 1960), the memoir of Alexander King.

King (1900–1965) is perhaps best remembered as the colorful raconteur often a guest on Jack Paar's *Tonight Show* in the early Sixties. A highly respected magazine editor (assistant to Frank Crowninshield at *Vanity Fair*; editor of *Americana; Life; and Stage*) and playwright-collaborator (with Clare Booth Luce and Chester Erskin), in 1945 he became addicted to morphine while being treated for a liver ailment. In 1951, he was arrested on drug charges and sent to Lexington Hospital, the Federal government's rehab facility in Kentucky. In 1954, after relapsing, he was arrested for violation of parole and returned to Lexington for further treatment before finally kicking for good. His early claim to professional fame was as one of the nation's finest book illustrators during the mid-Twenties through mid-Thirties. His illustrated editions of O'Neill's *The Emperor Jones*, *Anna Christie* and *The Hairy Ape*; Smollett's *Peregrine Pickle*; Swift's *Gulliver*; Bulliet's *Venus Castina*; DeFoe's *Moll Flanders*, Fielding's *Tom Jones*, and others, remain highly collectable. But none more so, perhaps, than American literateur Samuel Putnam's English translation of Claude Farrère's [Charles Bargone, 1876–1957] *Black Opium* (1929) featuring striking, exotic and evocative illustrations by King. Originally published in Paris by Paul Ollendorff circa 1900,[83] this collection of 17 short stories in six sections is, as Michael Horowitz would write, "a tour de force of 20th-century drug literature. In narrative art and range the stories bear comparison with James Joyce's early *Dubliners*, published seven years earlier, but their tortured yet graceful exoticism harks back to the prose of the Late Romantics and Decadents."[84] The book would be issued in its first paperback edition without King's sensual illustrations in 1958 yet possess a cover by Robert Maguire that remains one of the most stunning opium-dream images ever conceived, a masterwork of drug eroticism that would inspire Oriental opium-den fantasies in many who were exposed to the book at an impressionable age or otherwise, this author included. I glommed onto it, saucer-eyed, before old man Sol chased me out of his corner luncheonette. I would return to steal peeks at the book for weeks afterward before its time on the paperback rack expired.[85] I was seven years old.[86]

In 1974, *Black Opium* would be reissued complete with King's illustrations in a trade paperback format facsimile reprint of the first edition by And/Or Press, a publishing house founded by Sebastian Orfali in San Francisco.[87] And/Or's first book would be *Laughing Gas*, a trade paperback issued in 1973 co-edited by David Wallechinsky, son of novelist Irving Wallace, and to date the best (and certainly most amusing) volume on the innocuous if used safely, deadly if not, anesthetic inebriant, nitrous oxide.[88] In the same year, And/Or Press would issue the first edition in paperback of the greatest novel of drug-soaked decadent society yet written, *Cocaine*. Penned by Italian journalist Dino Segrè under the pseudomononym Pitigrilli just a year before Crowley's *Diary of a Drug Fiend*, it provides, as William Dailey would write in his Introduction to this edition, "a vivid picture of the cocaine-crazed demimonde of the Parisian 1920s," an understatement in the extreme. This is not a fun-with-coke saga. As seductive as the drug itself, the story grips the reader and pulls us into the downward spiral of the protagonist, whose obsession with the drug draws him into the inevitable pit that awaits virtually all who stay at the "white orgy" too long.

The And/Or editions of *Cocaine* and *Black Opium* were co-ventures with the Fitz

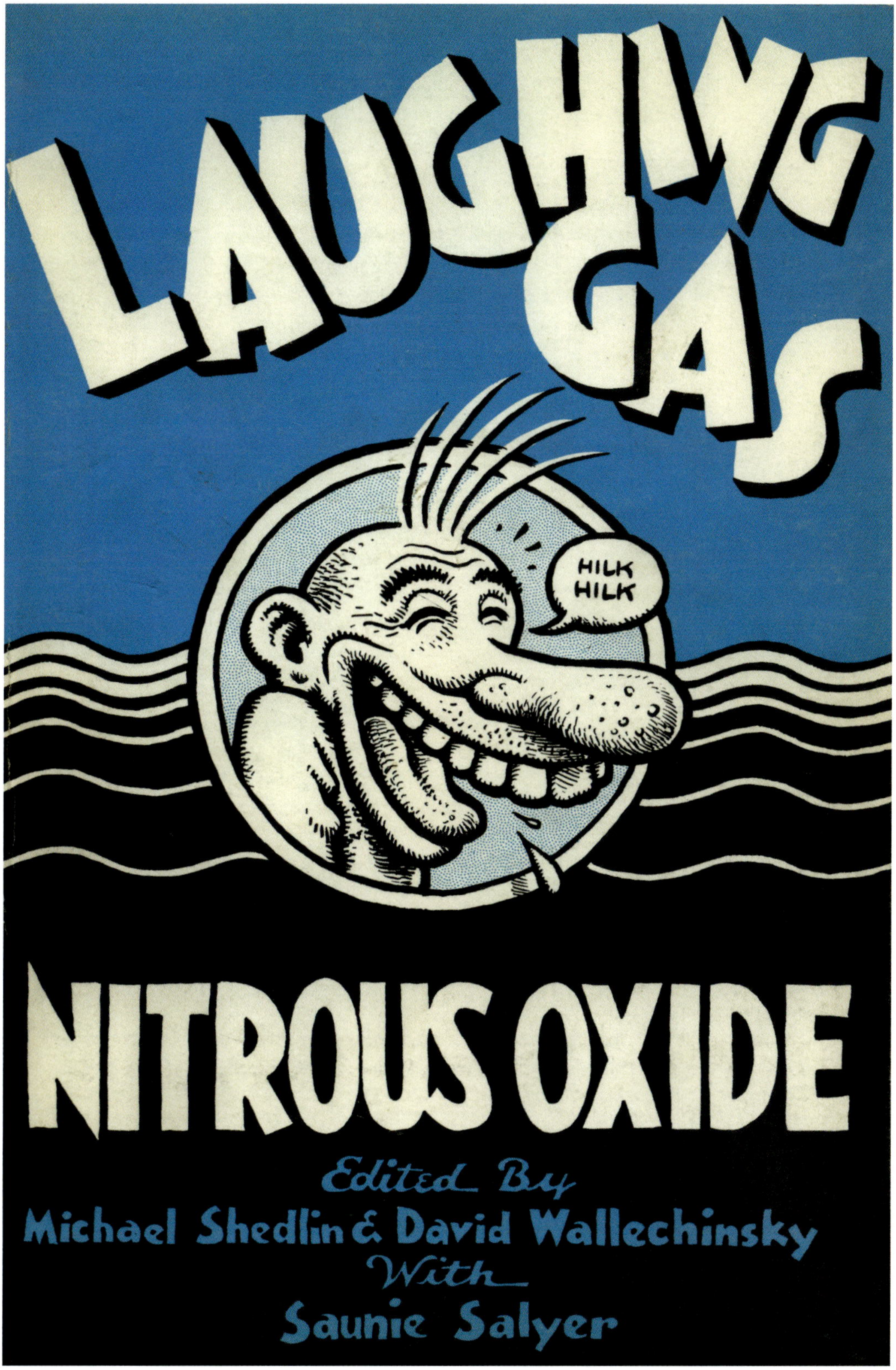

Michael Shedlin & David Wallechinsky with Saunie Salyer • ***Laughing Gas (Nitrous Oxide)***
AND/OR PRESS • 1973 • COVER BY R. CRUMB. ILLUSTRATIONS BY LARRY TODD AND "SIG." • PBO

Hugh Ludlow Memorial Library,[89] which was established in the early 1970s by rare book dealers Michael Horowitz of San Francisco and William Dailey of Los Angeles,[90] along with Michael Aldrich and Robert Barker, to fill what at the time was a massive void: the need of scholars for a research collection of the literature of drugs at a time when it was needed most; there was near complete ignorance of the rich history of psychotropic drug use in this country dating back to the mid-19th century at a time when drug use had become more widespread than ever and alarms rang loud. This body of literature had never been collected by anyone, anywhere and the volumes had been forgotten, scattered, and become scarce.

In the late 1960s, when cocaine — then rare and expensive; the caviar of drugs — began to emerge from the shadows and little was known about it, it was commonly considered to be an innocuous drug with few, if any, consequences to its use. With the establishment of the Ludlow Library, social scientists, now equipped with contrary evidence, knew better. To its shame, the medical community dismissed the late 19th-century medical literature buried in old medical journals and the personal stories that told the truth, dismissing them as unscientific and anecdotal: why take seriously, for instance, *Eight Years In Cocaine Hell* (1902),[91] the memoir of Midwestern society matron Annie Meyers (1851–19??), who fell from lofty, financially comfortable, well-fed status to that of an emaciated hag reduced to performing a pathetic jig (which she called her "cocaine dance") on street corners to solicit coke-change from passersby after becoming a self-described "cocaine fiend," the result of escalating self-medication for a severe cold with Birney's Catarrh Remedy, a popular 19th-century nostrum loaded with coke.

When the population of addicts at the turn of the 20th century eventually died out and within two generations had been forgotten, "our lack of public memory for the earlier waves of opiates and cocaine… unintentionally created an experiment with nature," drug policy historian David Musto observed.[92] That experiment with nature began with these paperbacks, which introduced the post-WWII American general public, after 50 years innocent and ignorant of the subject, to drugs and drug use on a mass scale. As the primary medium for exposure, their influence upon American culture cannot be underestimated. Now, drug paperbacks constitute America's public memory bank of the American drug experience as viewed through the lens of 20th-century popular culture: the mind-altering substance of words and images on mind-altering substances, available for the first time in limitless, mass-produced quantities. What a threat it was. What a challenge. What a widespread menace. ■

"Marijuana turns weak King Turner into a deadly weapon, a conscienceless killer with no more human feeling than a hooded cobra or a mad dog. Turner is the novice taken along to a 'ranch' to blaze weed; his reactions to the drug were intended to provide comedy for his veteran-smoker companions. Then Turner gets his hands on a knife — and a gun!"

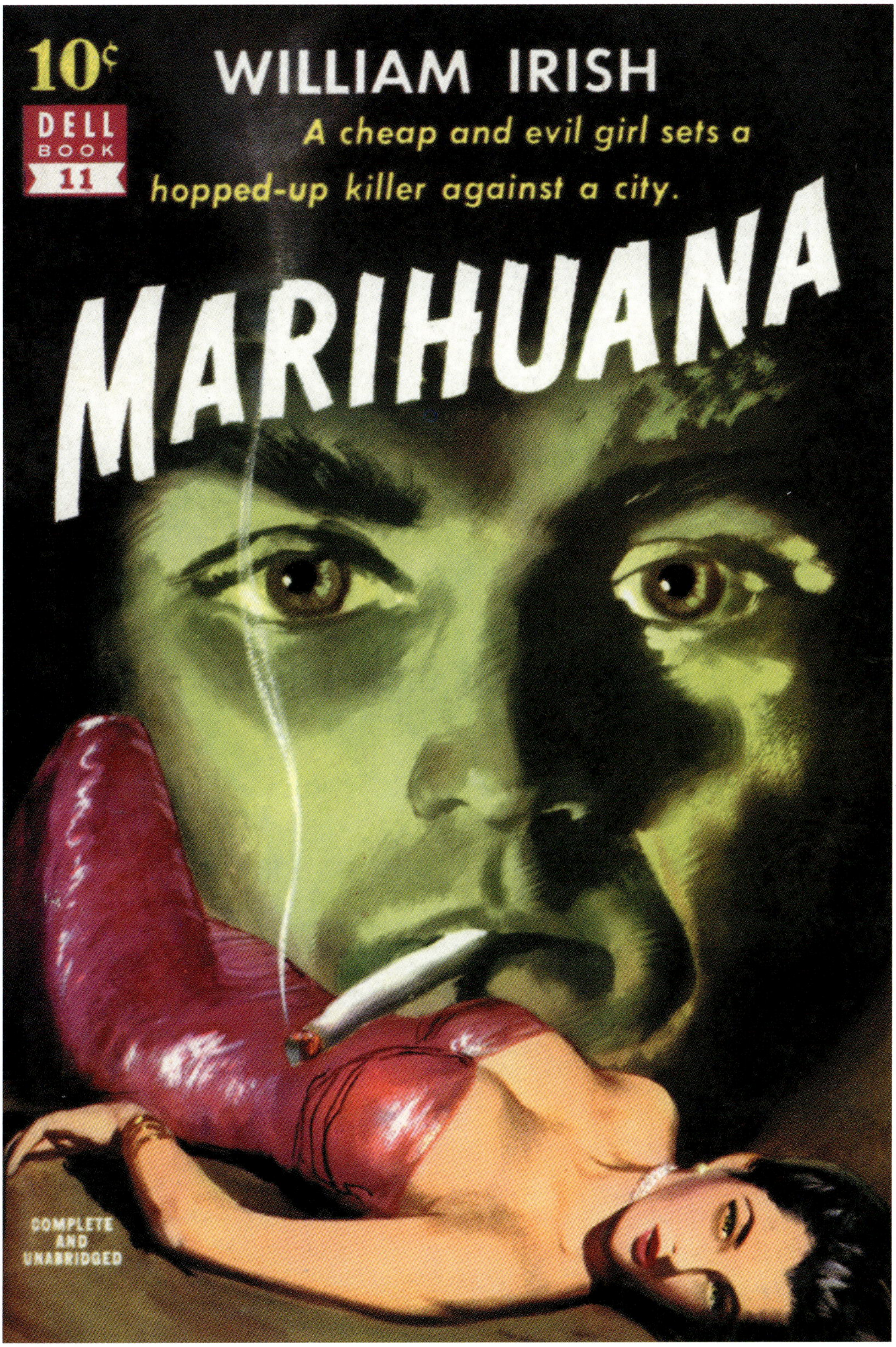

William Irish [Cornell Hopley Woolrich] • ***Marihuana*** • DELL 10¢ NO.11 • 1951 • COVER BY BILL FLEMING • PBO

1. Gathings, Ezekiel C. House Select Committee on Current Pornographic Materials, Investigation of Literature Allegedly Containing Objectionable Material, 82d Congress, 2d Session, 1953, House Report 2510, p. 2.

2. Ibid. p. 3.

3. See: Stark, Michael, Cocaine Fiends and Reefer Madness: An Illustrated History of Drugs in the Movies (1982).

4. Though not rigorously enforced until 1934.

5. Jonnes, Jill. Hep-Cats, Narcs, and Pipe Dreams, Baltimore: Johns Hopkins University Press, 1999 (1st edition, 1996, Scribner's), p. 117.

6. Gertz. Stephen J. (contrib.) Sin-A-Rama: Sleaze Sex Paperbacks of the Sixties, Feral House, 2005, p. 27.

7. Op cit. Gathings, p. 14.

8. The definitive dictionary, through its year of publication, of dope jargon remains M.D./author/lexicographer J.E. Schmidt's Narcotics Lingo and Lore (Springfield: Charles C. Thomas, 1959) containing 2,333 entries.

9. Op cit. Gathings, p. 16.

10. "No Witch Hunt," Newsweek, July 7, 1952, p. 80.

11. "The Boom In Paperback Books," Fortune, September 1953, p. 124.

12. Hutchinson, E.R. Tropic of Cancer on Trial. New York: Grove Press, 1968, p. 78.

13. "Trends In Paper Books Raise Many Questions," Publishers Weekly, Feb. 21, 1953, p. 981.

14. Rorty, James. "The Harassed Pocket-Book Publishers," Antioch Review, XV, Dec. 1955, p. 427.

15. Larrabee, Eric. "Pornography Is Not Enough," Harper's, CCXXI, November 1960, pp. 88-89.

16. Lockhart, William B., and Robert C. McClure. "Literature, The Law of Obscenity, and the Constitution," Minnesota Law Review, XXXVIII, March 1954, p. 302.

17. Op cit. Jonnes, p. 212.

18. Cooney, Thomas E. "The Booming Bust of The Paperbacks," Saturday Review, Nov. 6, 1954, p. 16.

19. Ginsberg's classic poem Howl is dedicated to Solomon.

20. Ginsberg, Allen. "'Junky' Restored," New York Times, Feb. 6, 1977.

21. Ginsberg, ibid.

22. Op cit. Gathings, p. 98.

23. Op cit. Fortune, p. 144.

24. "Sales Trends In Paperback Publishing," Publishers Weekly, Jan. 18. 1965, p. 77.

25. Crosland, Margaret and Sinclair Road. Translator's Introduction to Jean Cocteau's Opium: The Diary of a Cure. New York: Grove Press/Evergreen Editions E771, 1958, p. 11.

26. Ibid.

27. Gerrity, John. "The Truth About The 'Drug Menace.'" Harper's, February 1952, p. 27.

28. Ibid., p. 28.

29. Ibid., p. 28.

30. Ibid., p. 28.

31. Ibid., p. 29.

32. Ibid., p. 29.

33. To be fair, Pacific Press also issued many health titles.

34. Musto, David F. The American Disease: Origins of Narcotic Control, 3rd edition, New York, 1999, p. 246.

35. Ibid., p. 246.

36. Meltzoff's wife was his favorite model; her face can be seen on many of his cover illustrations.

37. New York Times Book Review, June 1, 1958.

38. Op cit. Fortune, p. 124.

39. "Hard Times for Soft Covers," Harper's, February 1955, p. 82.

40. Op cit. Cooney, p. 15.

41. Schreuders, Piet. Paperbacks U.S.A.: A Graphic History 1939-1959, San Diego, 1981, pp. 197-227. This volume contains the most complete survey of paperback cover artists.

42. New York Times Book Review, June 1, 1958, p.8.

43. "Lurid Paper Reprint Covers Cuts Down On Army Buying," Publishers Weekly, December 22, 1951, p. 2315.

44. Ibid.

45. Ernest Lionel McKeag (1896-1974) was an exceedingly prolific British pulp novelist who wrote under many pseudonyms. In addition to his nom de pulp Roland Vane, he wrote as Griff, a pseudonym he established but that soon became a house pseudonym for his publisher.

46. "How To Get On Newsstands," Publishers Weekly, July 24, 1961, p. 50.

47. "Design In Paperbacks: A Report From NAL," Publishers Weekly, April 8, 1963, p. 77.

48. Kemp, Earl (contr.), Sin-A-Rama: Sleaze Sex Paperbacks of the Sixties, pp. 45-46 (Feral House, 2005).

49. Kimmens, Andrew C. (ed.), Tales of Hashish, New York, 1977, p. 25.

50. Op cit. Musto, p. 228.

51. From the Introduction.

52. The etymology of the word is somewhat obscure. According to Schmidt (Narcotics Lingo and Lore, 1959), "the term 'dope' is probably derived from the Dutch 'doopen,' to dip or baptize," and refers to the practice of dipping a long needle into a small canister containing refined opium to gather a small measure of the drug for smoking in the pipe. In reference to the molasses-like density of opium refined for smoking purposes, Luc Sante (Low Life, 1991) writes that "the goo itself was called 'dope,' a term that, according to the boulevardier James L. Ford, derived from daub, the axle grease applied to the prairie schooners, which resembled cooked opium in color and texture." In his footnote to that observation, Sante further writes that "In the nineteenth century 'dope' tended to mean any heavy, viscous solution, and in this connection may have derived from the Dutch 'doop,' meaning sauce." The word's origin is then clear by the street corruption of the Dutch root: cooked opium = a thick dipping sauce = dope.

53. Only four copies are known to exist: in the Library of Congress, two in the Ludlow-Santo Domingo Library, and in a private collection. Those in the Ludlow-Santo Domingo Library have the cover illustration onlaid to cloth boards.

54. I am thankful to William Dailey for allowing me use his inventory catalogue description of this book.

55. Publishers Weekly, January 30, 1967, p. 35.

56. As I have estimated in my unpublished manuscript, An Amazing Kingdom of Thrills: American Pulp Erotica 1966-1973 (2000), based upon the Laven study commissioned by The President's Commission on Obscenity and Pornography (1971) and extensive interviews with industry insiders.

57. Contemporary Authors Online, Gale's, 2003. Crossen (1910-1981), an editor and writer for pulp magazine Detective Fiction Weekly also wrote under the pseudonyms Christopher Monig and Bennett Barlay. He actually was an insurance investigator and during the Depression worked for the WPA Writers Project.

58. "Gottlieb Ran LSD Mind Control Testing," Los Angeles Times obituary, April 4, 1999.

59. Declassified CIA memo, September 4, 1952. Posted on levity.com/acid-dreams/docs/ego.html.

60. Kirby had contracts for 85 Essex House books, only a handful of the remaining volumes issued after his departure as Brandon House Library Editions and Brandon Books. Prior to his exit, he had been in negotiations with The Doors' lead singer and lyricist, Jim Morrison, for the rocker's first book, an erotic novel which would have undoubtedly been freely laced with drug use. With Kirby's exit, the project died.

61. Seduction By Chloroform, Ashby III, p. xxxiii, note. Though Ashby provides no date or identifying information whatsoever, it was likely published in London circa 1846 in the wake of a series of scandalous trials concerning M.D.s and dentists who were accused of raping patients under the influence of the newly introduced drug. No copies are extant. There exists an earlier title, 1739's The Surprize: or The Gentleman Turned Apothecary [The Private Case #1849] that suggests a pharmaceutical-erotic theme, but is, rather, the story of a high-born lady's receipt of a clyster-in-der-keister by a secret admirer who surreptitiously substitutes himself for his lady's usual enema-tech, her personal maid. Though Sade's Juliette used opium, it was only to ease the rigors of travel by coach, not for sexual purposes.

62. "Wood C. Lamont" was Sewell's pointed barb aimed at American litterateur, poet, and author of the still-in-print The Rhyming Dictionary, Clement Wood, who penned many anonymously written works of clandestine erotica from the 1920s-1940s. Another edition of Sewell's manuscript appeared under the pseudonym "Bob DeMexico," a lighthearted jab to his friend, Robert Bragg, who used the pseudonym when writing clandestine erotica during the late 1930s-early 1940s on commission for Oklahoma oil millionaire Roy M. Johnson; one of many writers, including Henry Miller, Anaïs Nin, Caresse Crosby, Jack Hanley, Bernard Wolfe, Paul Hugo Little, and Robert DeNiro Sr., who did so to earn much-needed money. Bragg is not to be confused with the pseudonymous N.R. De Mexico, author of Marijuana Girl.

63. Erotica scholar G. Legman edited a version entitled The Sign of the Scorpion that cut all the sado-masochistic and drug material out. It was issued by Grove Press during the 1960s.

64. From Obelisk's 1938 catalogue, the list reprinted in its entirety within Donald Thomas' A Long Time Burning, New York, 1969, pp. 523-524.

65. "Frances Lengel," "Carmencita de las Lunas."

66. According to Greenleaf Vice President and Editorial Director, Earl Kemp.

67. Palmer, Cynthia and Michael Horowitz, Shaman Woman, Mainline Lady: Women's Writings On The Drug Experience. New York: Morrow, 1982, p. 240. This book remains the key volume on the subject and a cornerstone reference to drug literature.

68. Interview with the author, 12/01/05.

69. Interview with the author, 1/08/06.

70. From my catalogue note to The Stoned Apocalypse, Vassi's autobiography. Thanks to Wm. Dailey for permission to quote.

71. Op cit. Gertz, p. 35.

72. Phone interview with the author, 11/07/05.

73. Linda Yablonsky's semi-autobiographical novel The Story of Junk (1997) with its insider's view of heroin and the New York art scene of the early '80s; Anne Marlowe's startling memoir of her obsession with heroin How To Stop Time: Heroin From A to Z (1999); Jerry Stahl's tragicomic Permanent Midnight (1995); Julia Phillips' chronicle of her love affair with cocaine You'll Never Eat Lunch In This Town Again; and Jim Carroll's The Basketball Diaries (1978) immediately come to mind.

74. Biographical material from the Introduction by Michael Horowitz to this edition.

75. Letter from Samuel L. Clemens to his mother, January 1864, as cited in the Appendix to the Level Press edition, and in Duchinos, Pioneer of Inner Space: The Life of Fitz Hugh Ludlow (1998).

76. That would come very soon with Supreme Court decisions interpreting the Harrison Act that rendered narcotics de facto, if not actually, illegal.

77. Kahn, Roger. A Flame of Pure Fire: Jack Dempsey and the Roaring '20s. New York: Harcourt Brace, p. 124.

78. Ibid. p. 14-15. The best memoir of drugs and the hobo life remains Jack Black's You Can't Win (1926), a book that influenced Wm. S. Burroughs and subsequently the rest of the Beat Generation. It was not released in a paperback edition until Amok Press in 1988.

79. Pacheco, Ferdie. The 12 Greatest Rounds of Boxing: The Untold Stories. Toronto: Sports Media Publishing, p. 27.

80. Wentworth and Flexner. A Dictionary of American Slang.

81. See Time magazine January 29, 1940 book review, How To Play Winning Checkers.

82. Hillman Publications #194.

83. The bibliographical history of this book is quite convoluted. Though the first edition is generally accepted as 1904, a search of the OCLC and KVK reveals a 1902 issue from Ollendorff noted 31st edition, located at Ohio State University (PQ2611.A78 F8 1902). The volume was, however, issued by other publishers in multiple printings 1904-1910, including E. Flammarion and Société d'éditions littéraires et artistiques, and the true first edition remains something of a mystery. Suffice it to say, it was a very popular novel in France.

84. Introduction to the And/Or Press edition of 1974.

85. The average shelf-life for a paperback was 30 days.

86. My next step on the road to hell was paved by listening to Stravinsky's Le Sacre du Printemps at age 12.

87. And/Or would enter bankruptcy in the late '70s-early '80s but ultimately reorganize as Ronin Press, currently active and reissuing many of Timothy Leary's books, amongst other new alternative titles.

88. In the 1970s, And/Or would distribute a reprint series of How-To instructionals from the late '60s on marijuana cultivation by Mary Jane Superweed, and LSD home-synthesis pamphlets by Adam Gottlieb — both the pseudonyms of one man, specifically John Mann, who, after his forays into psychotropic agronomy and chemistry, would write under his own name respected volumes on life extension.

89. Now the Ludlow-Santo Domingo (LSD) Library and located in Geneva, Switzerland.

90. In 1979, Dailey would issue the first rare book catalogue in the world exclusively devoted to the literature of drugs: Phantastica. Named after Lewin's classic volume classifying psychoactive substances, it remains a key reference on the subject and has become a rare collector's item.

91. The first drug confession written by a woman; alas, an exceedingly scarce volume as yet, and unfortunately, never released in a paperback edition.

92. Op cit. Musto, p. ix.

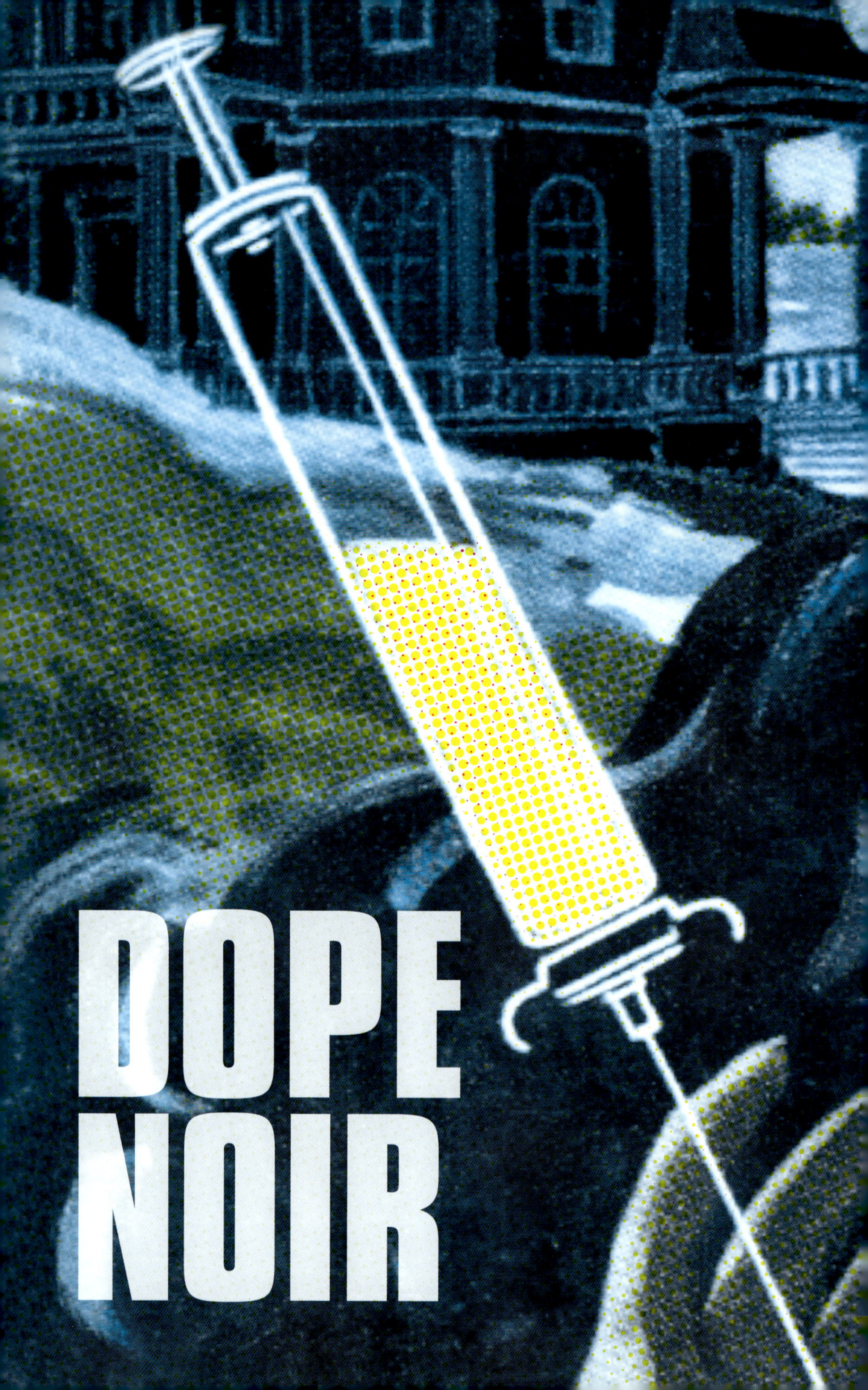
DOPE
NOIR

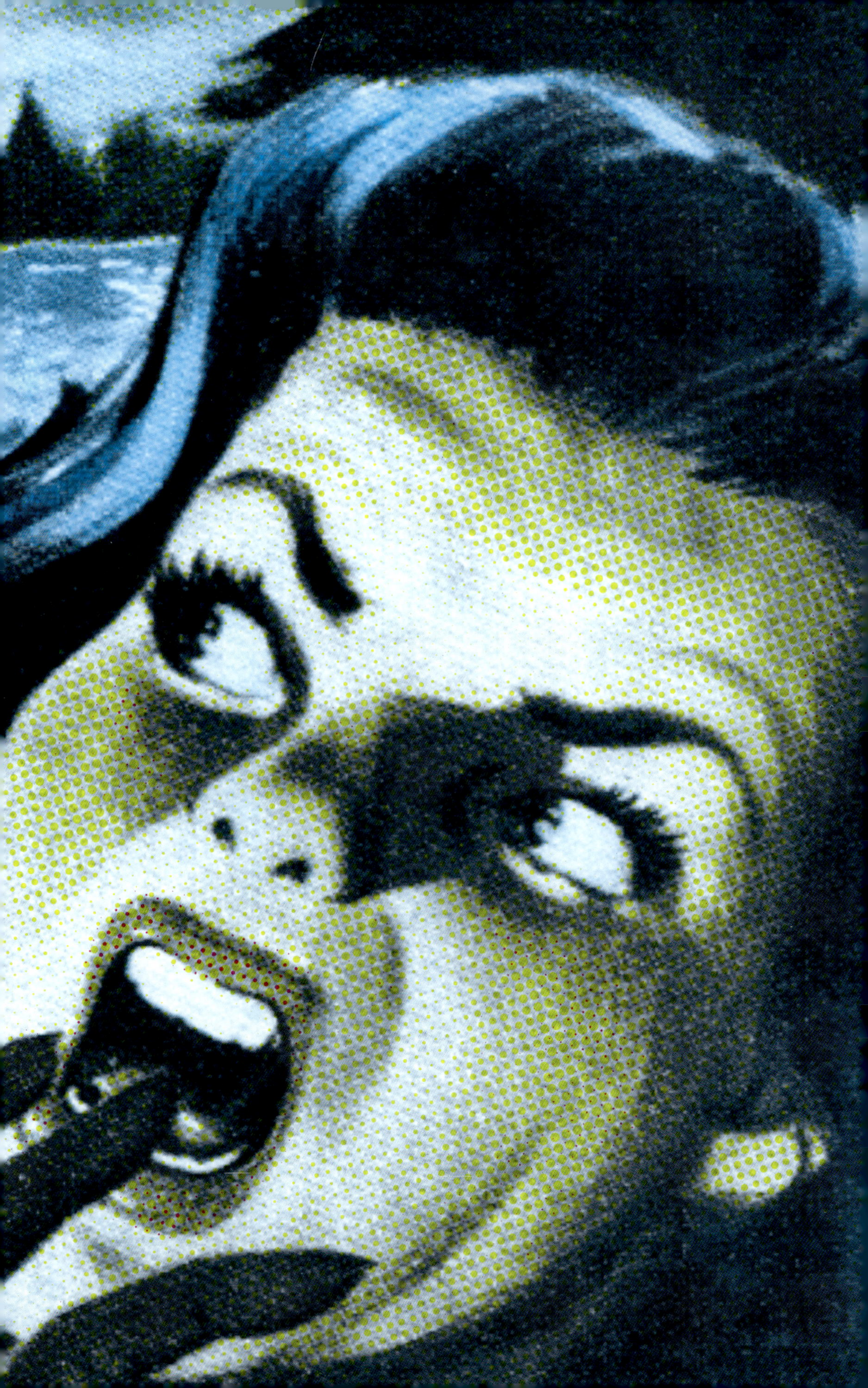

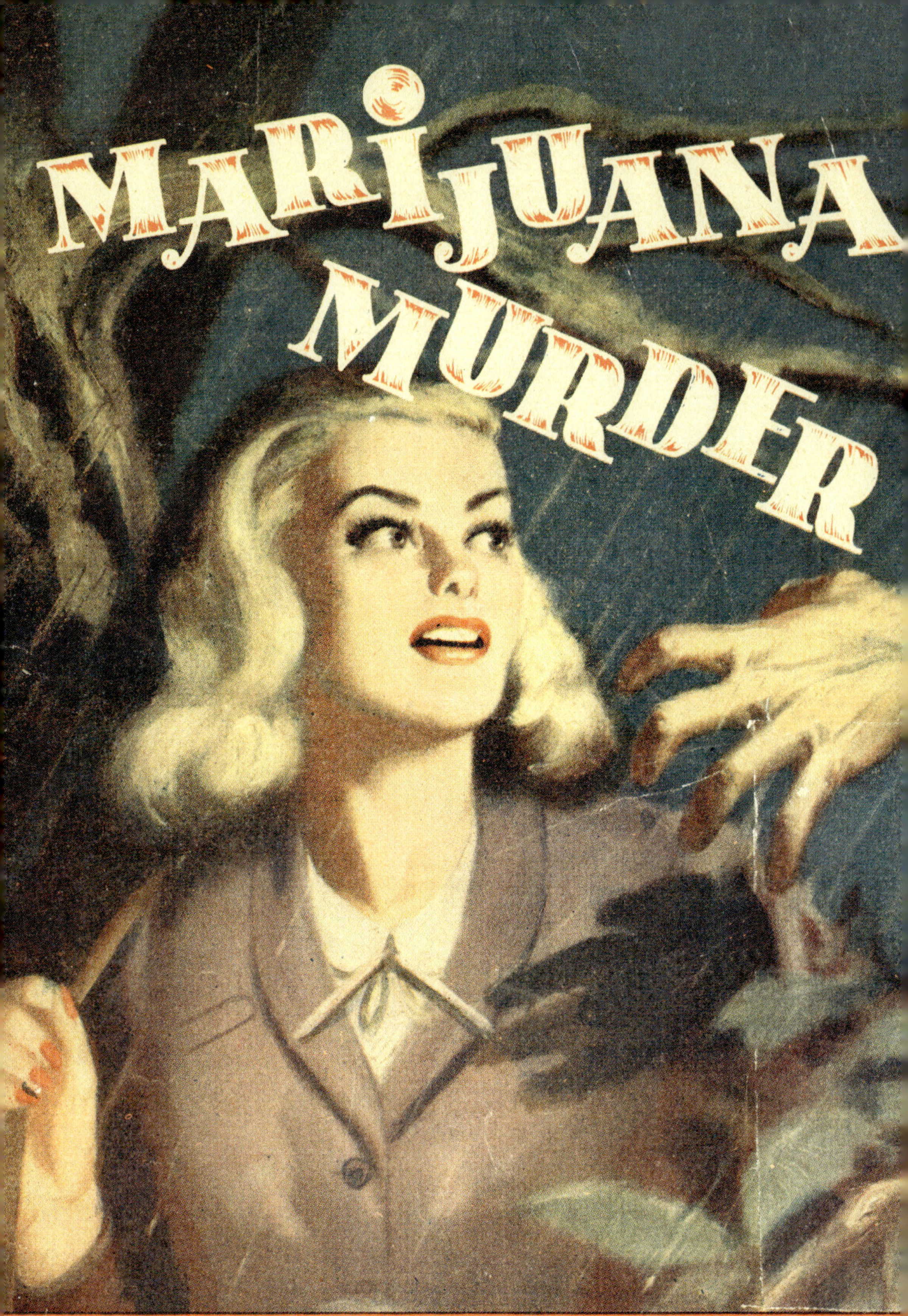

A SUPERIOR BOOK

AUTHENTIC POLICE CASES
EVERY STORY TRUE

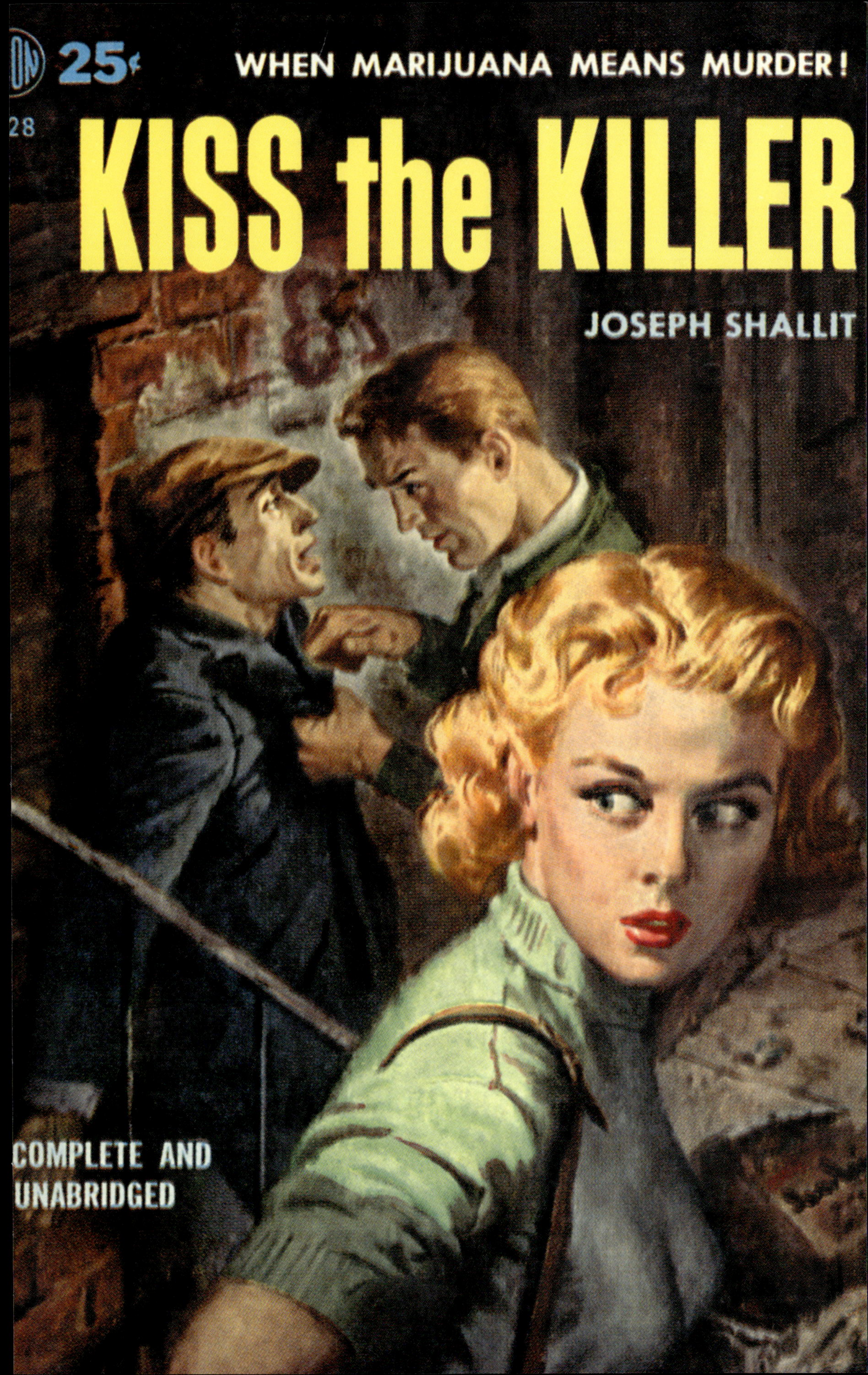
25¢
WHEN MARIJUANA MEANS MURDER!
KISS the KILLER
JOSEPH SHALLIT
COMPLETE AND
UNABRIDGED

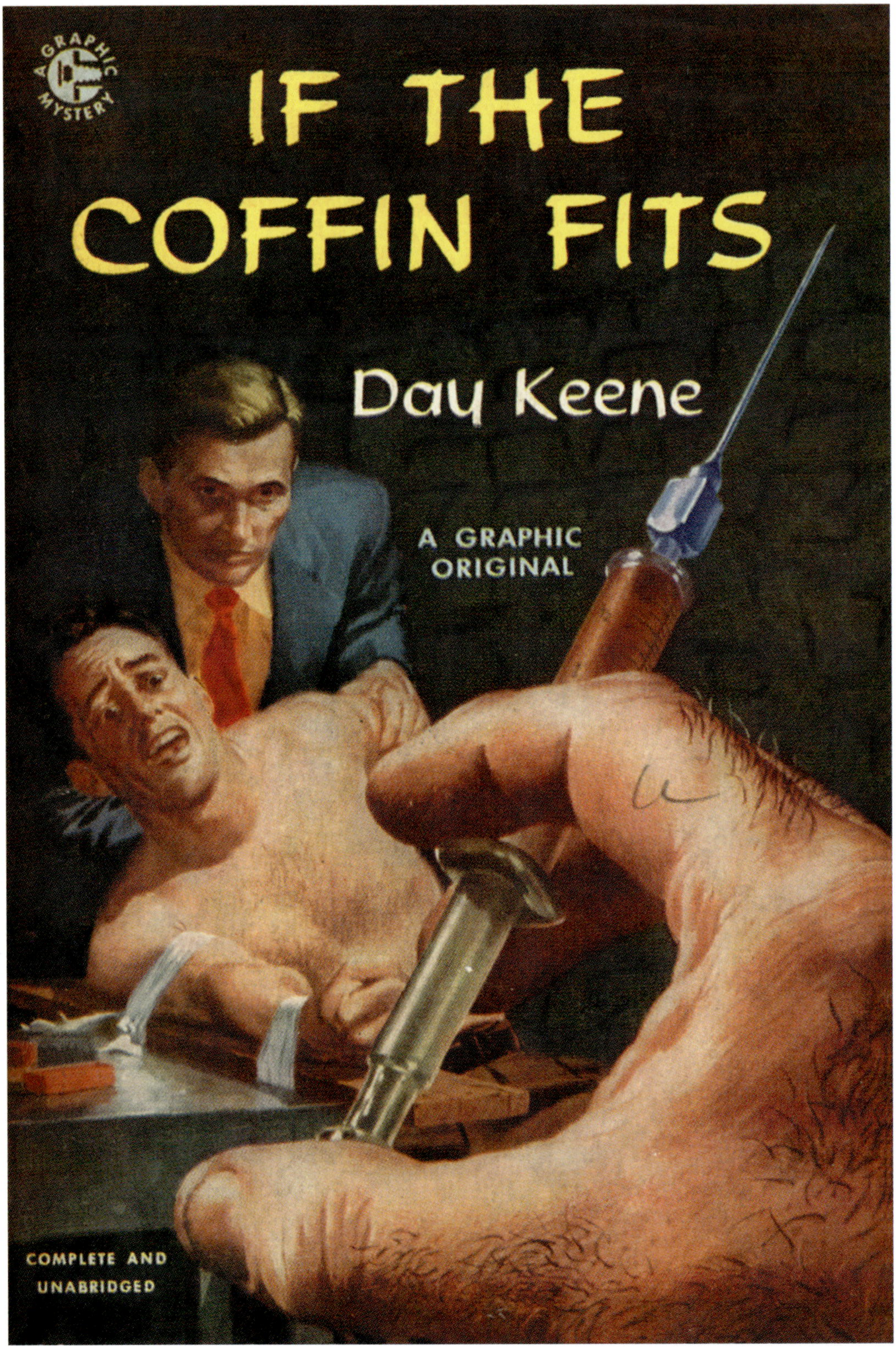

Day Keene • ***If the Coffin Fits*** • GRAPHIC BOOKS 43 • 1952 • PBO DIGEST

(PREVIOUS PAGE) ***Marijuana Murder*** • DUCHESS/SUPERIOR NN-1 • N.D. • 1945 • PBO

(PREVIOUS PAGE) Joseph Shallit • ***Kiss the Killer*** • AVON 528 • 1953

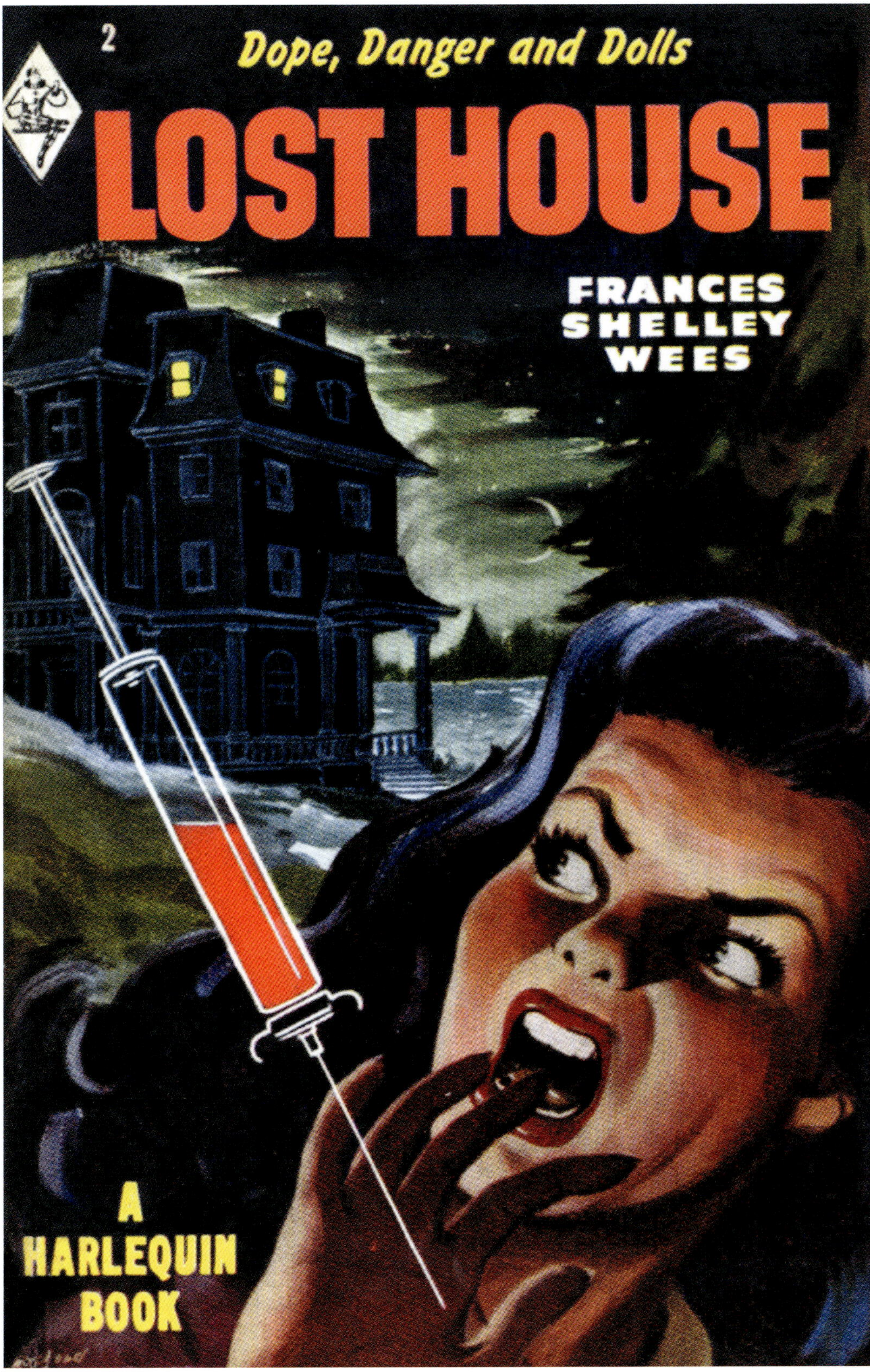

Francis Shelley Wees • ***Lost House*** • HARLEQUIN 2 • 1949 • COVER BY RICKARD • PBO

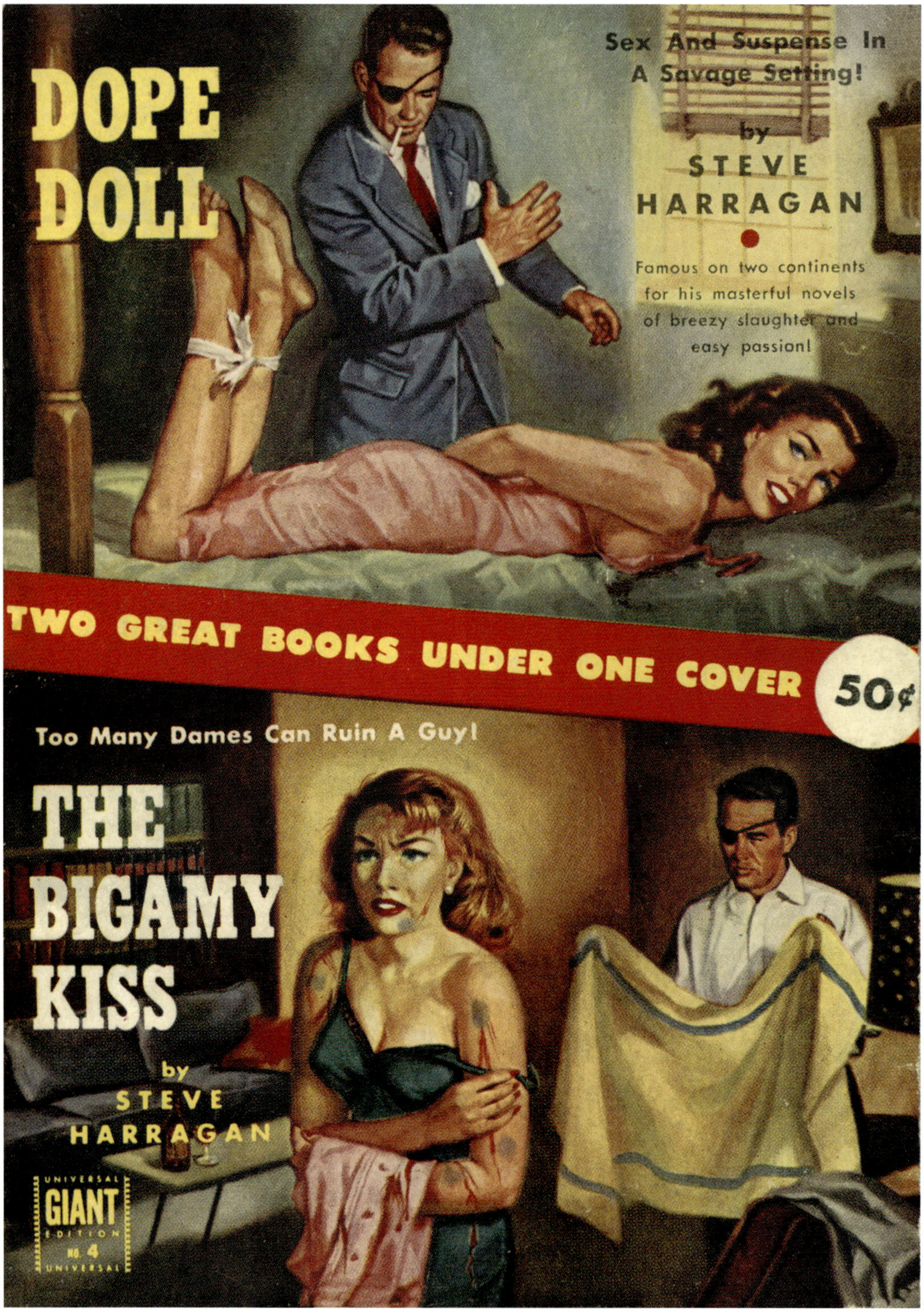

"When that second cigarette girl showed up in my nightclub, I really knew something was wrong! Okay, so her legs were terrific. Her figure was the best in town. She had at least two other highly visible attractions. But I had never hired her!...So I tried to fire the gorgeous gal — and got practically murdered by a couple of her boy friends. She wasn't selling cigarettes in my place. She was there to push the white stuff. Drugs!"

Louis Berg • ***Prison Nurse*** • BANTAM 427 • 1949 • COVER BY WILLIAM SHOYER • REPRINT

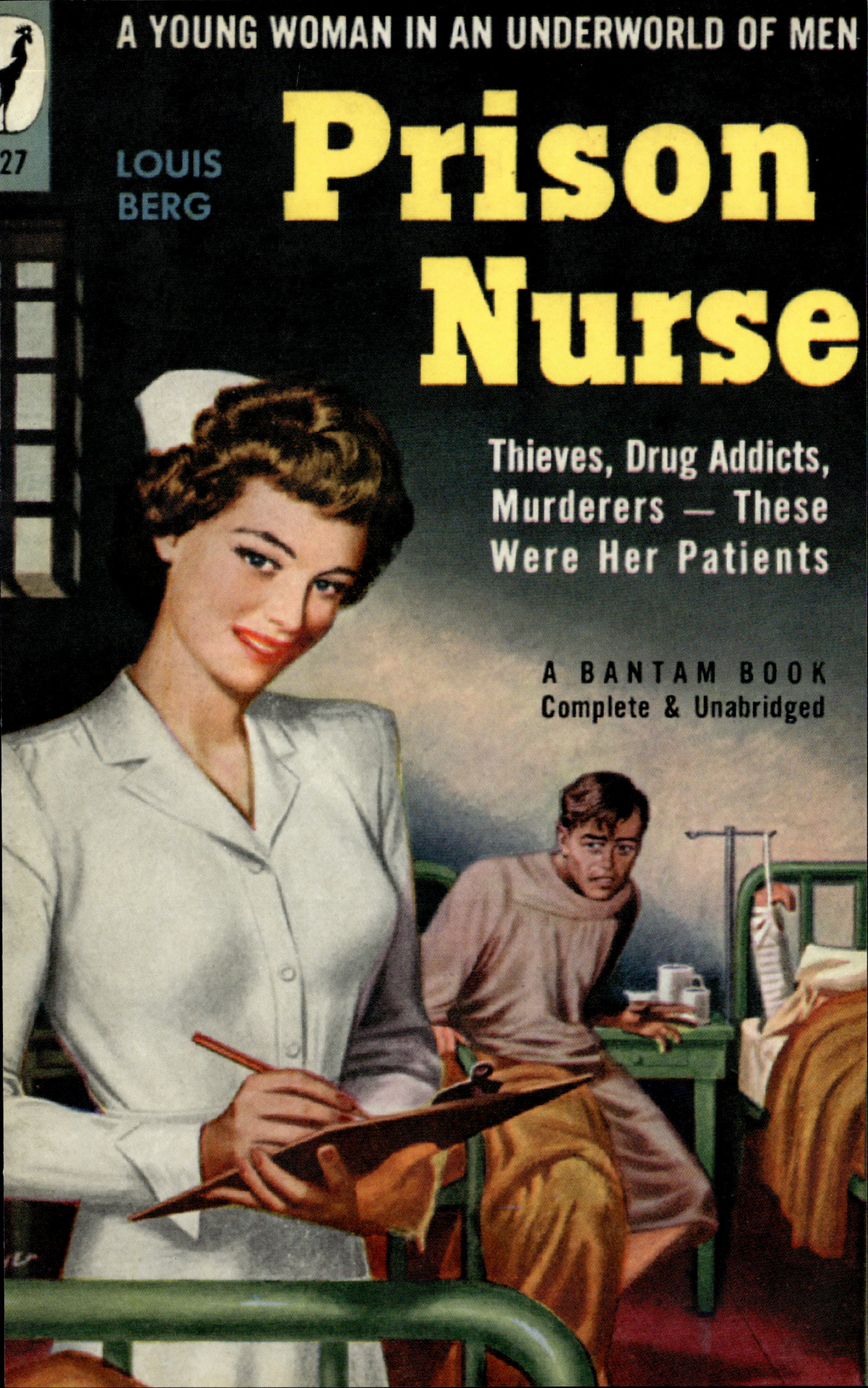
27
A YOUNG WOMAN IN AN UNDERWORLD OF MEN
LOUIS BERG
Prison Nurse
Thieves, Drug Addicts, Murderers — These Were Her Patients
A BANTAM BOOK
Complete & Unabridged

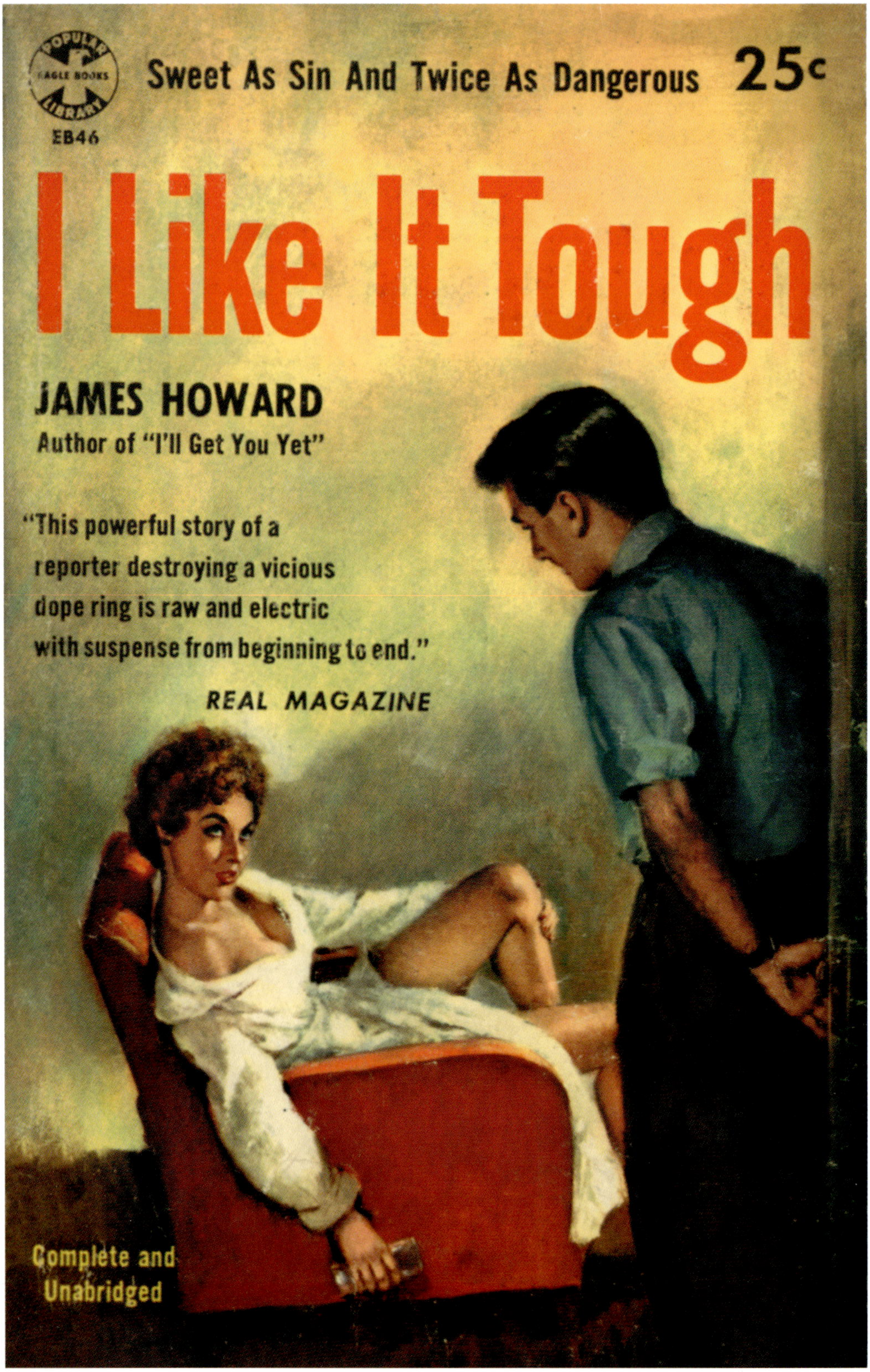

James Howard • ***I Like It Tough*** • POPULAR LIBRARY EAGLE BOOKS EB-46 • 1955 • REPRINT

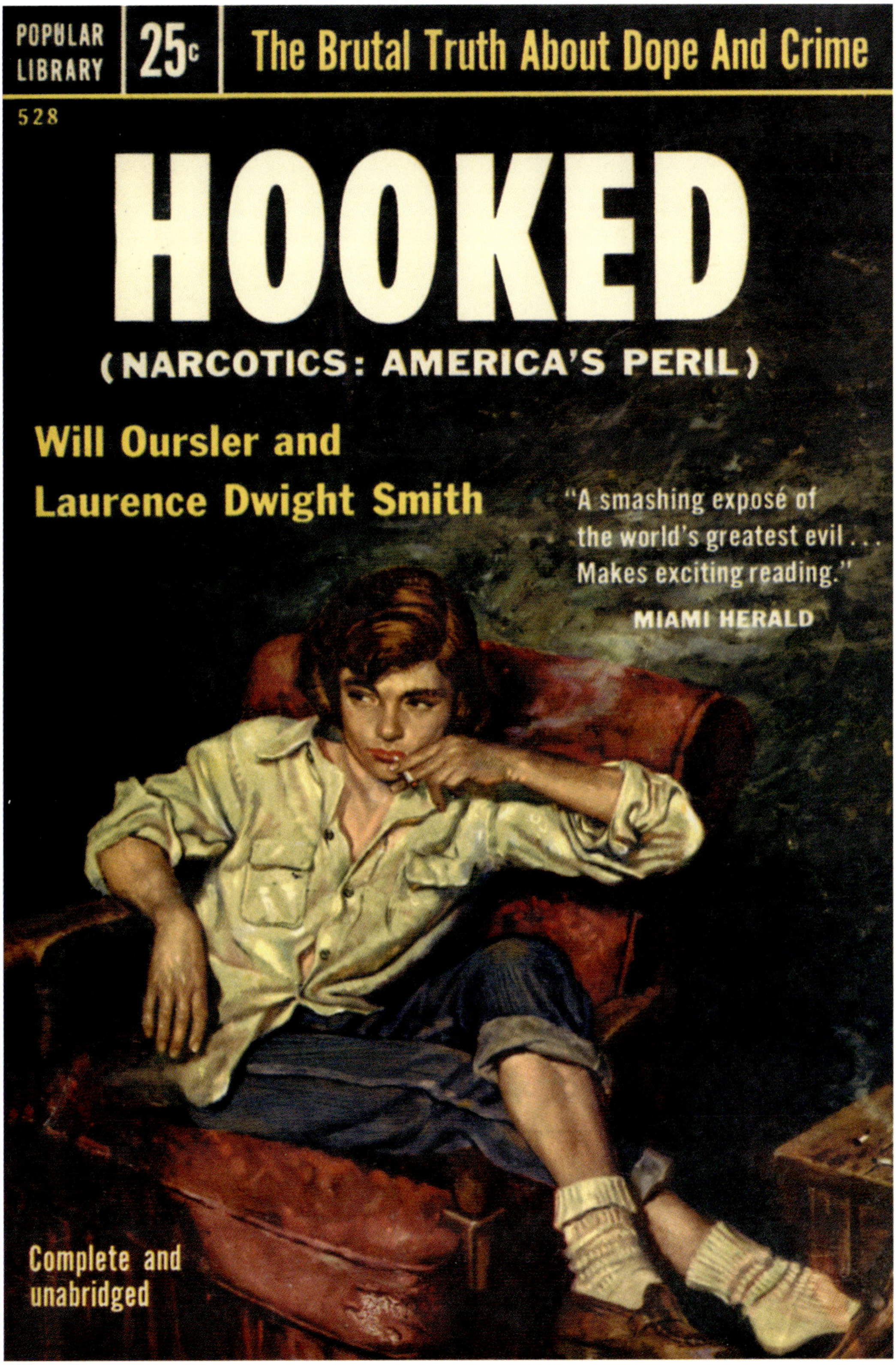

Will Oursler and Laurence Dwight Smith • ***Hooked (Narcotics: America's Peril)***
POPULAR LIBRARY 528 • 1953 • COVER BY RAFAEL DESOTO • REPRINT

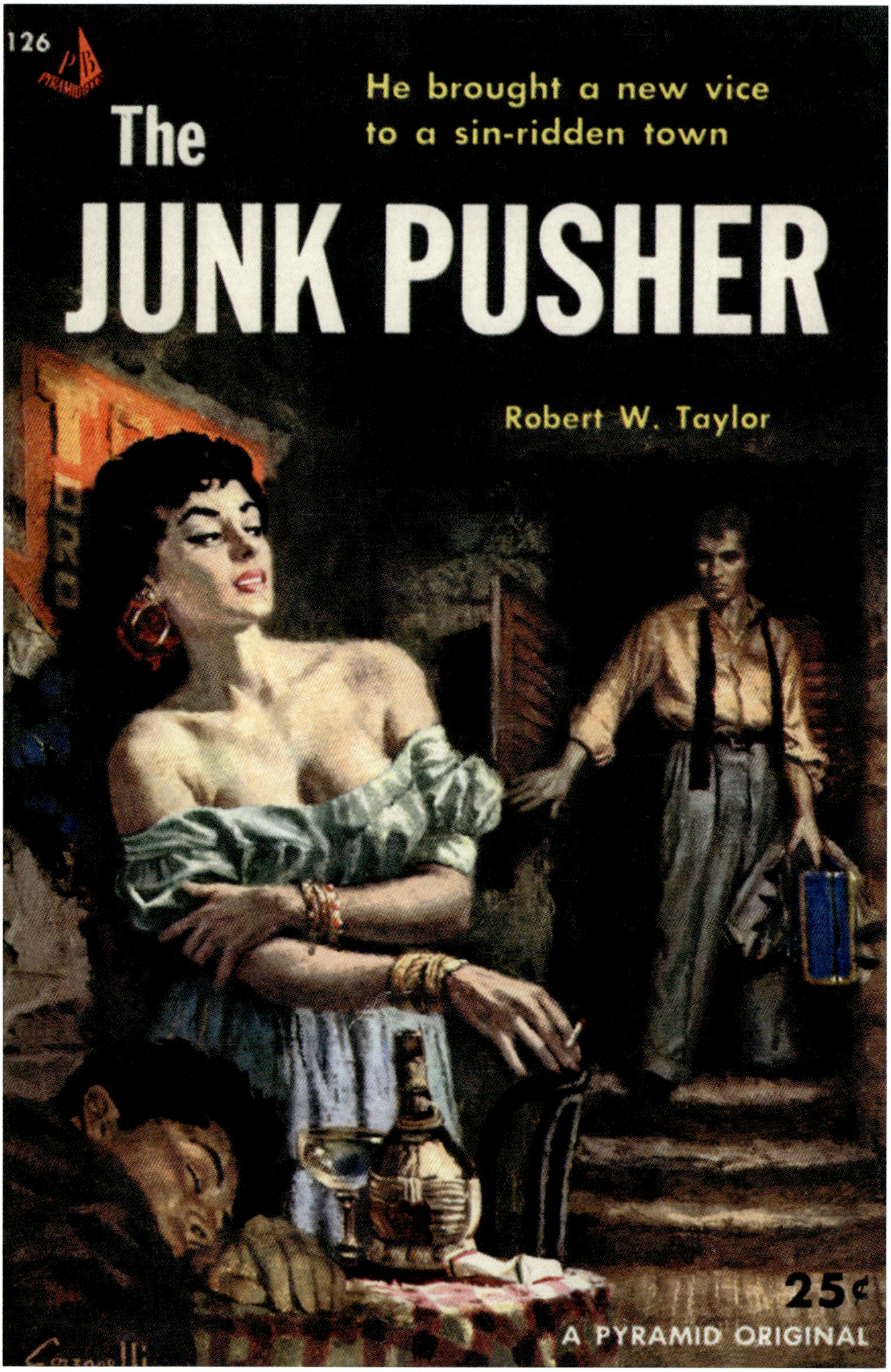

"Rick Hunt was a salesman. His product was depravity."

Robert W. Taylor • ***The Junk Pusher*** • PYRAMID 126 • 1954 • COVER BY FRANK COZZARELLI • PBO

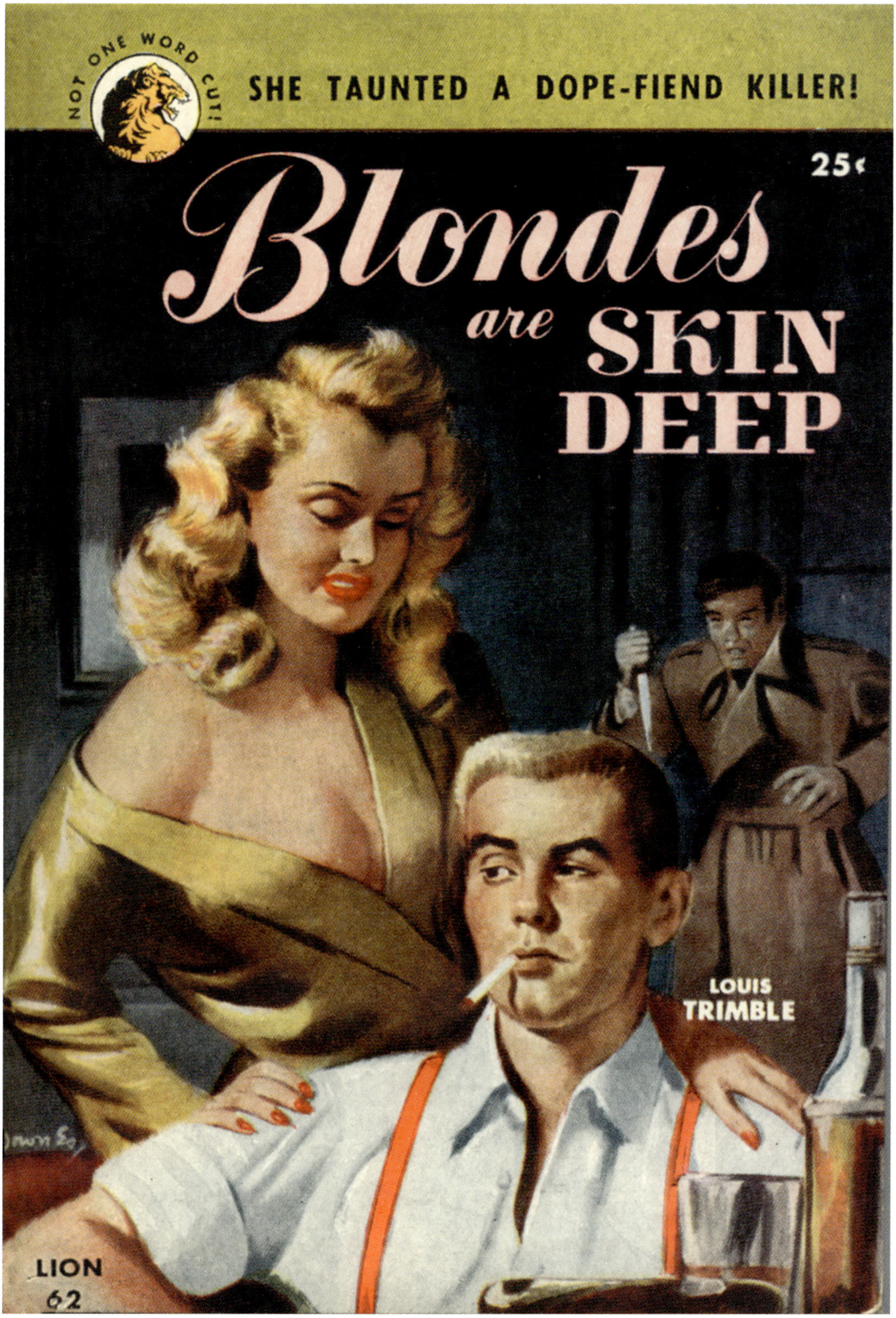

"Fat with cocaine! His name was Peone, of the drugged eyes and the slender knife. Edna Loomis was a beautiful ambitious woman. Peone was a coked-up killer!"

Louis Trimble • ***Blondes Are Skin Deep*** • LION 62 • 1951 • PBO

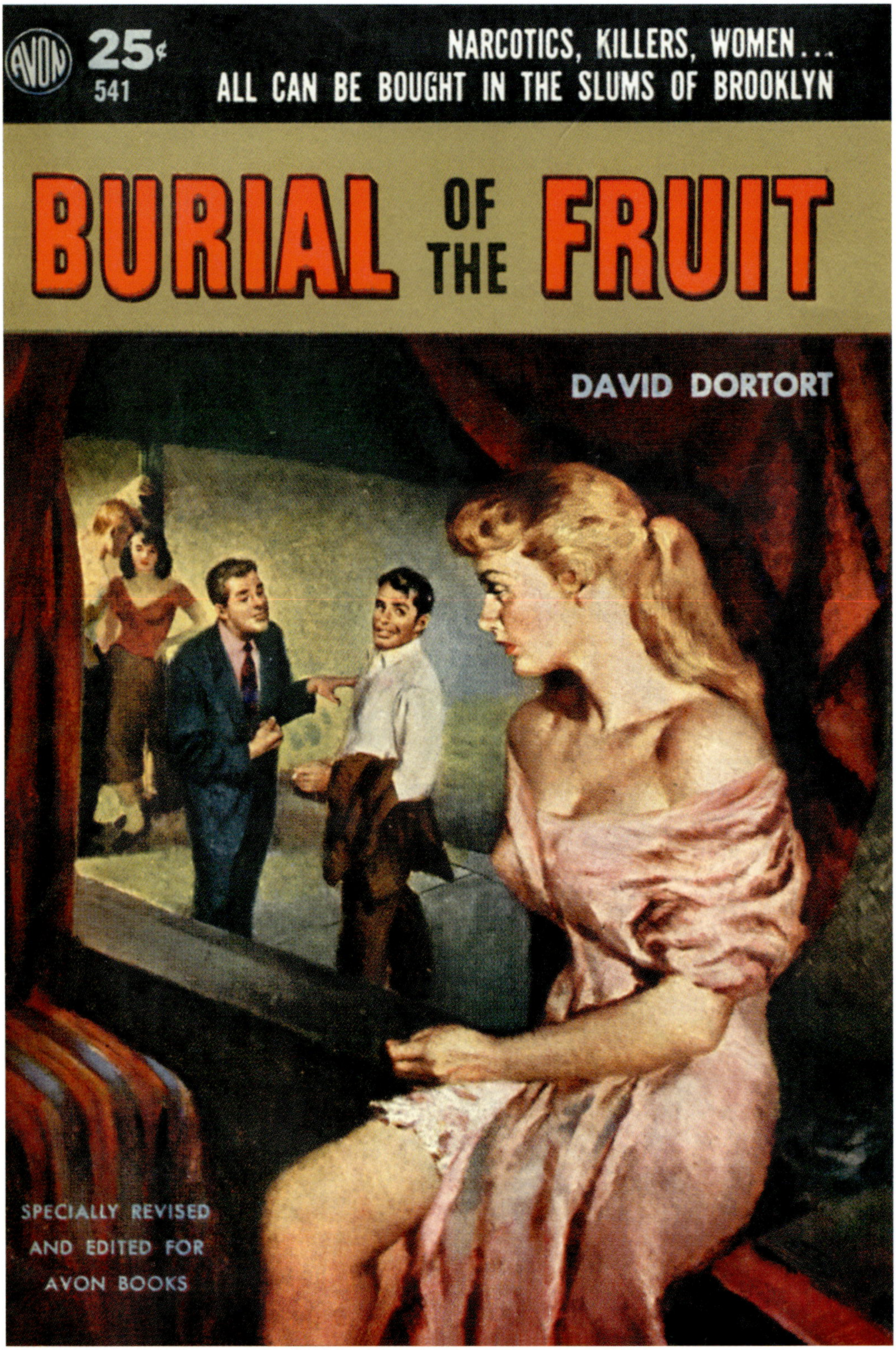

David Dortort • ***Burial of the Fruit*** • AVON 541 • 1953 • REPRINT

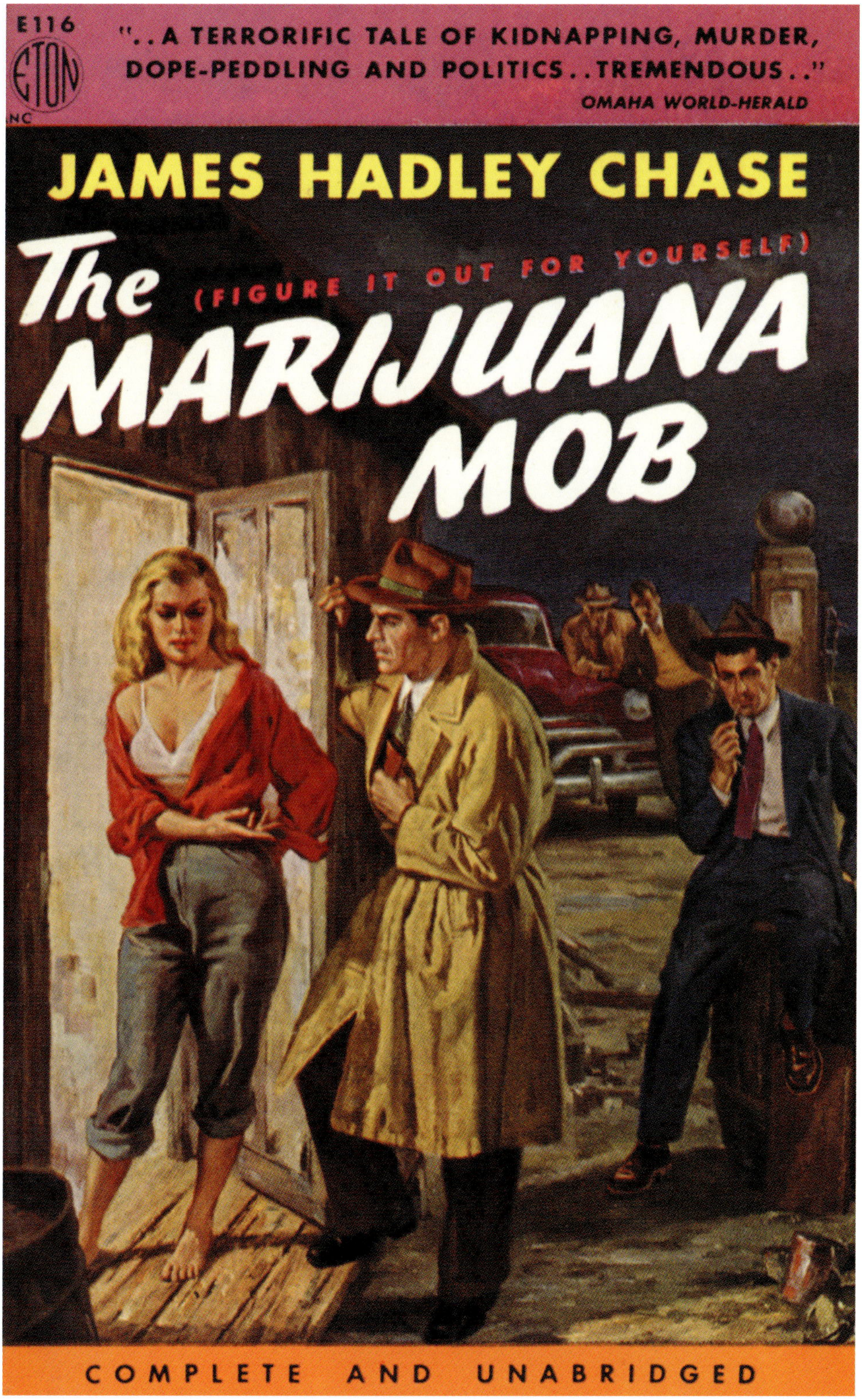

"She was in one of those soft, clingy blue nightgowns. I walked towards her and took her hand. It was cold and the room stank from marijuana smoke."

James Hadley Chase [René Raymond] • ***The Marijuana Mob*** • ETON 116 • 1952
COVER BY VICTOR OLSON • REPRINT OF *FIGURE IT OUT FOR YOURSELF* (1951)

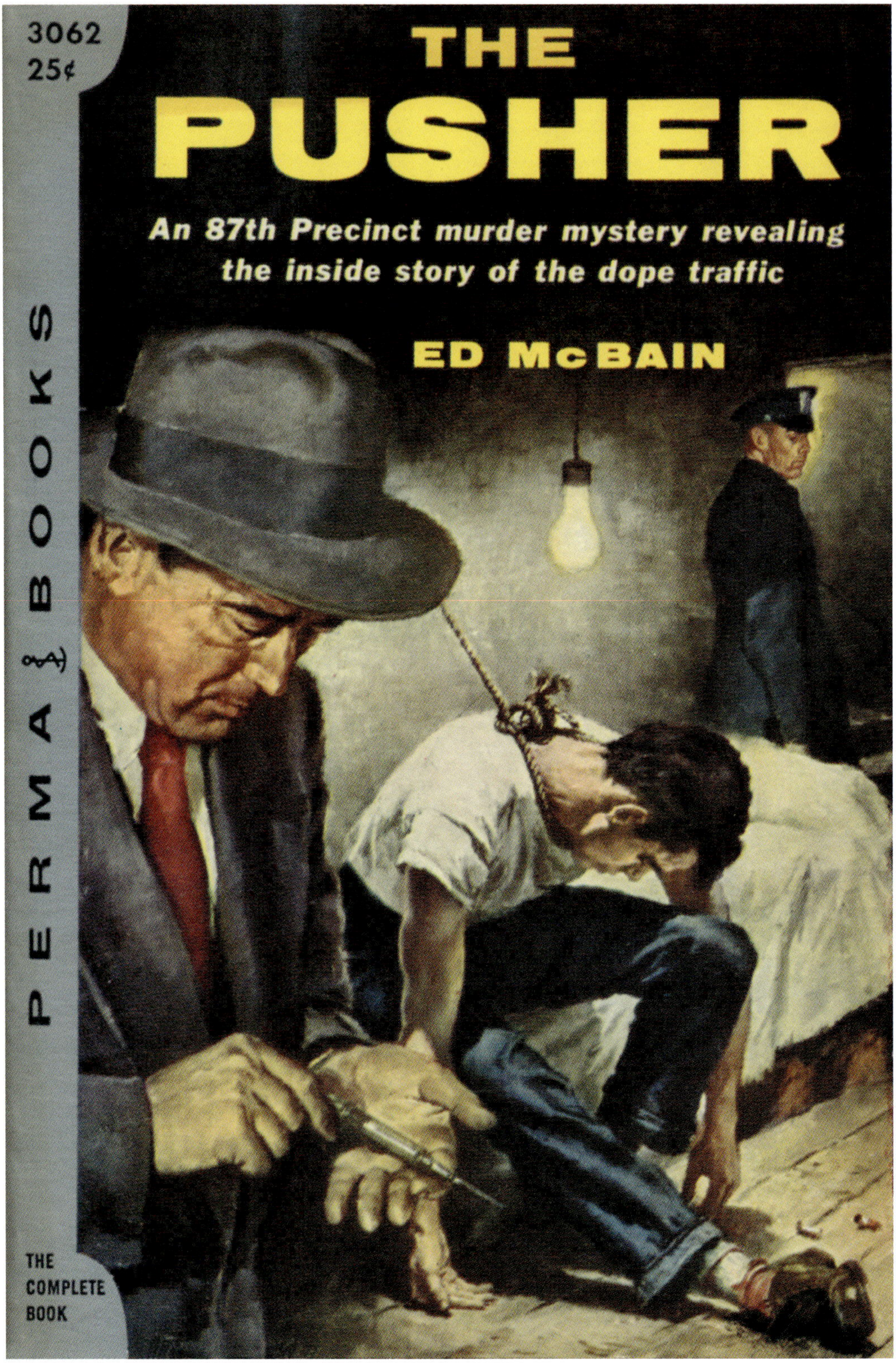

"His sister was on heroin! She sold her body to pay for it. She gave him his first shot as a joke. in a short time, he was on it steady."

Ed McBain [Evan Hunter, b. Salvadore Lombino] • ***The Pusher*** • PERMA 3062 • 1956
COVER BY CHARLES BINGER • PBO

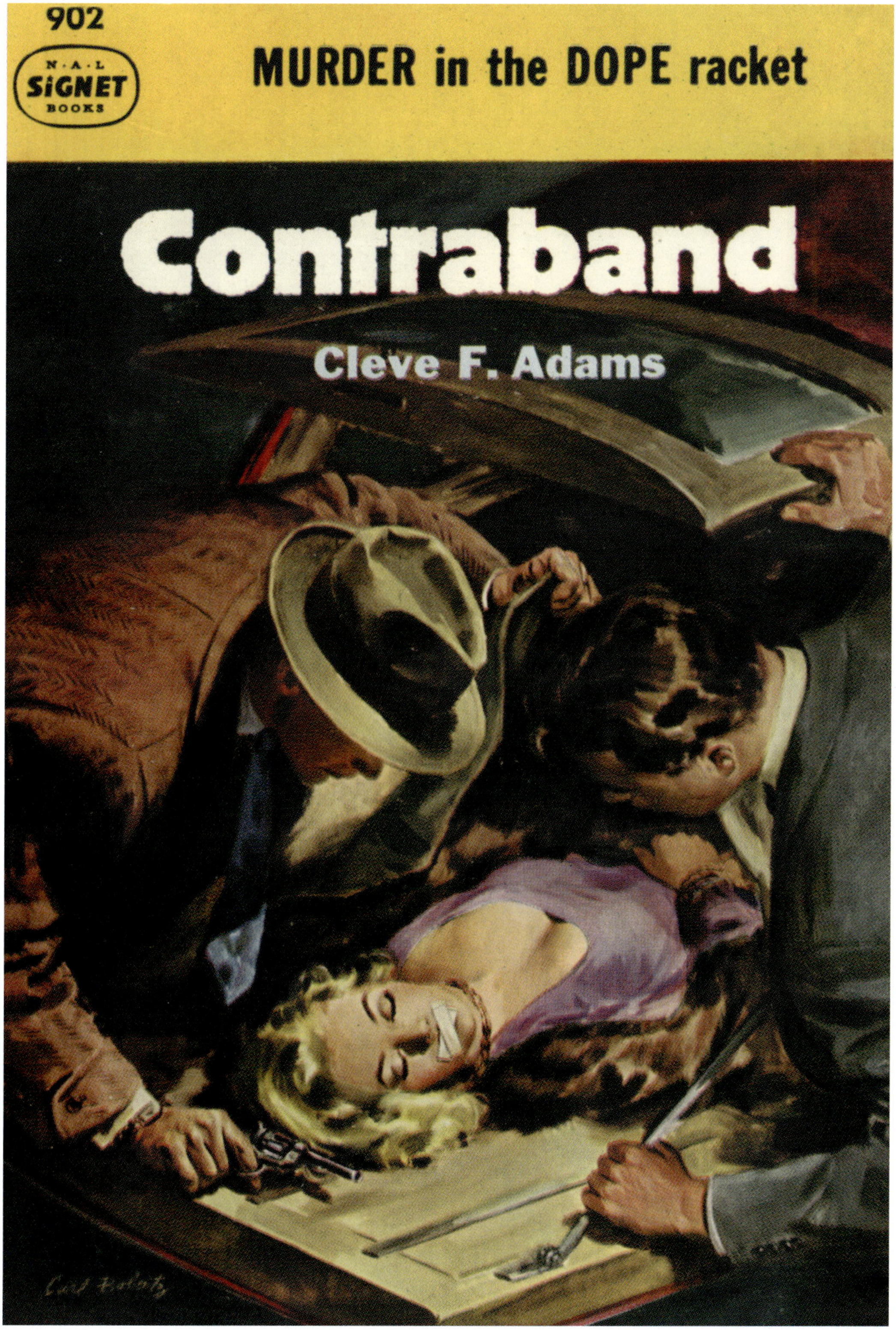

Cleve F. Adams [Vera Adams] • ***Contraband*** • SIGNET 902 • 1951 • REPRINT

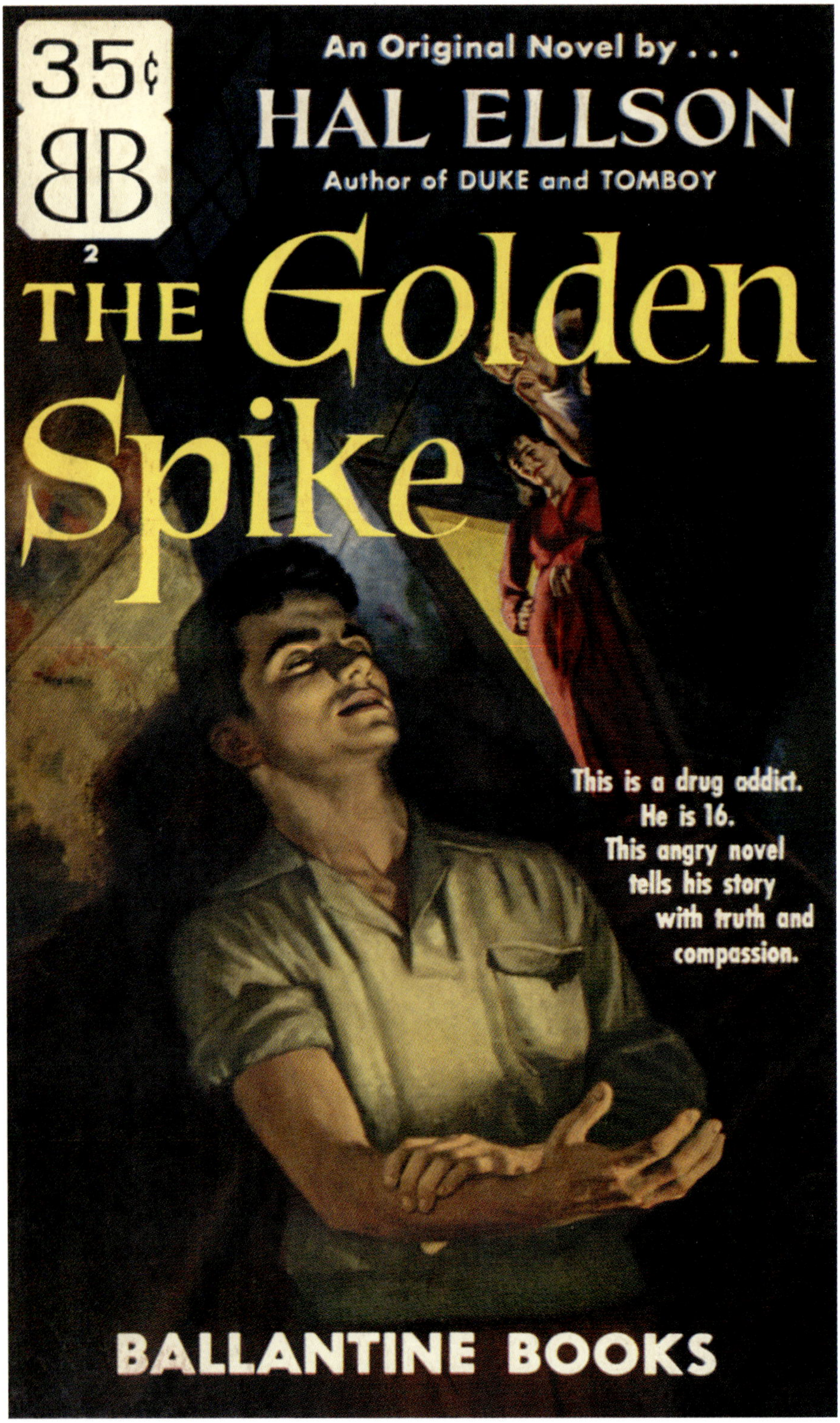

Hal Ellson • ***The Golden Spike*** • BALLANTINE 2 • 1952 • COVER BY ROBERT MAGUIRE • PBO

"Paper sacks full of death and destruction peddled wholesale... Two cigarettes, brown and far from innocent."

David Dodge • ***It Ain't Hay*** • DELL 270 • 1949 • COVER BY GERALD GREGG • REPRINT

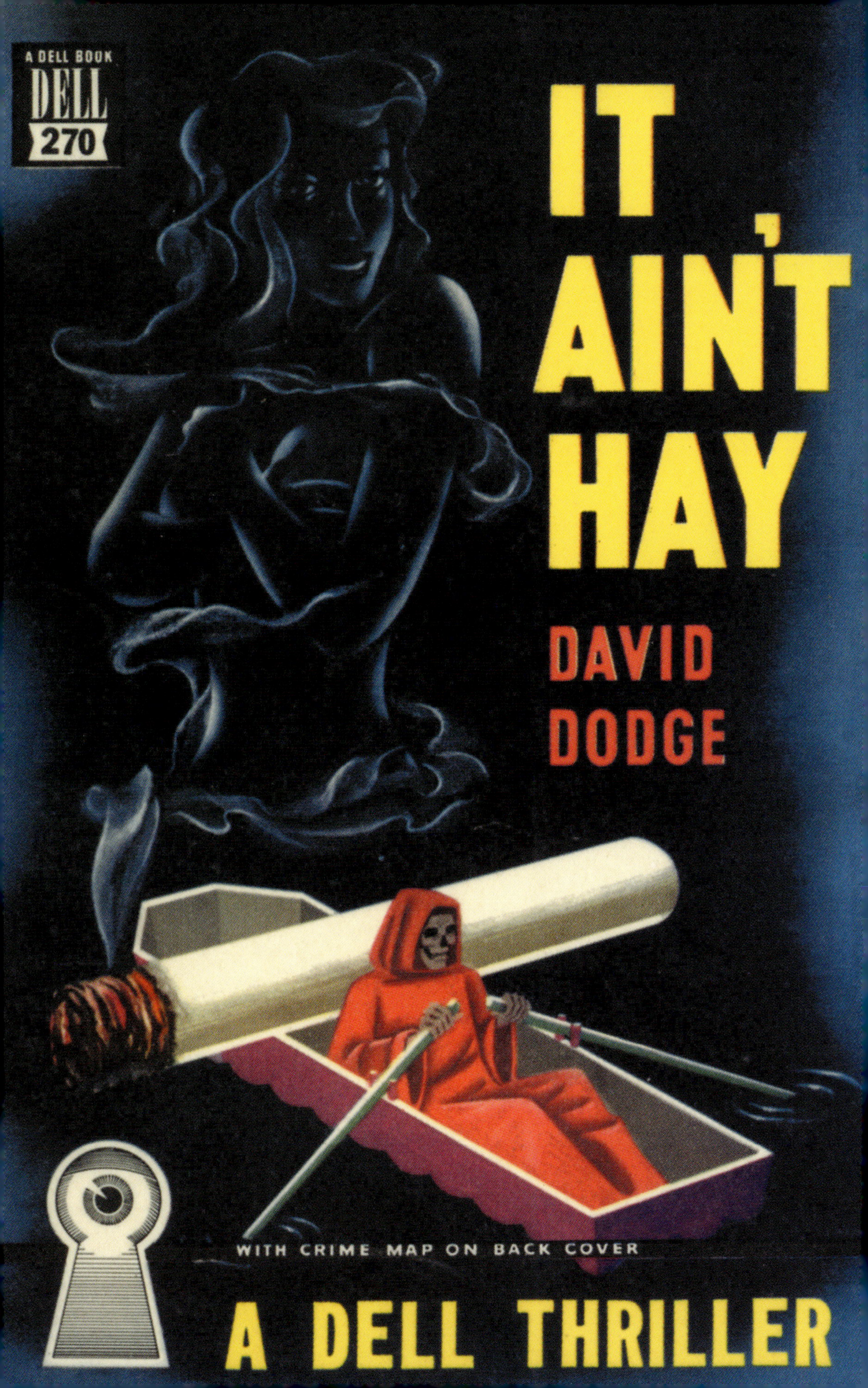
A DELL BOOK
DELL
270
IT AIN'T HAY
DAVID DODGE
WITH CRIME MAP ON BACK COVER
A DELL THRILLER

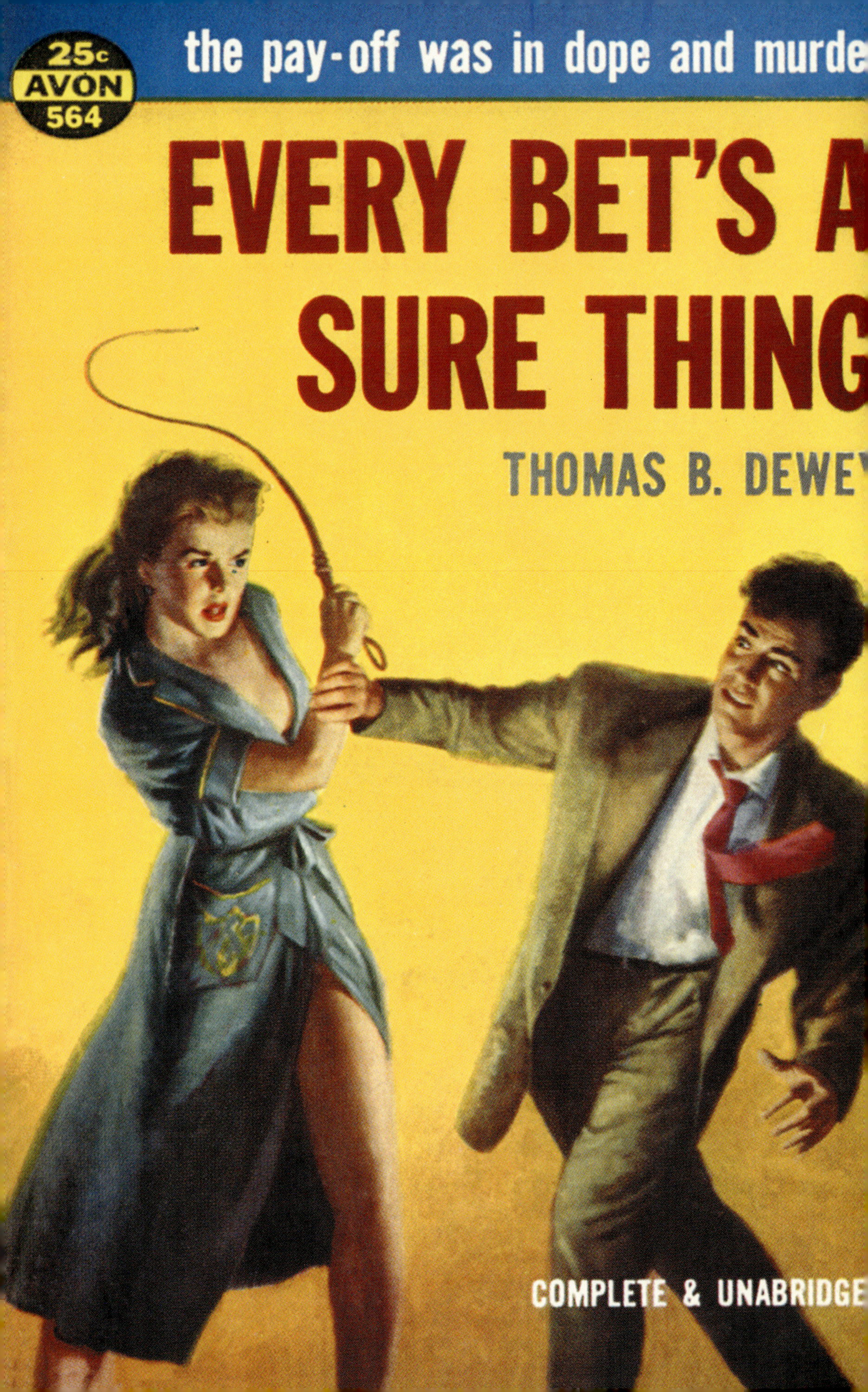
25c
AVON
564
the pay-off was in dope and murde
EVERY BET'S A
SURE THING
THOMAS B. DEWEY
COMPLETE & UNABRIDGE

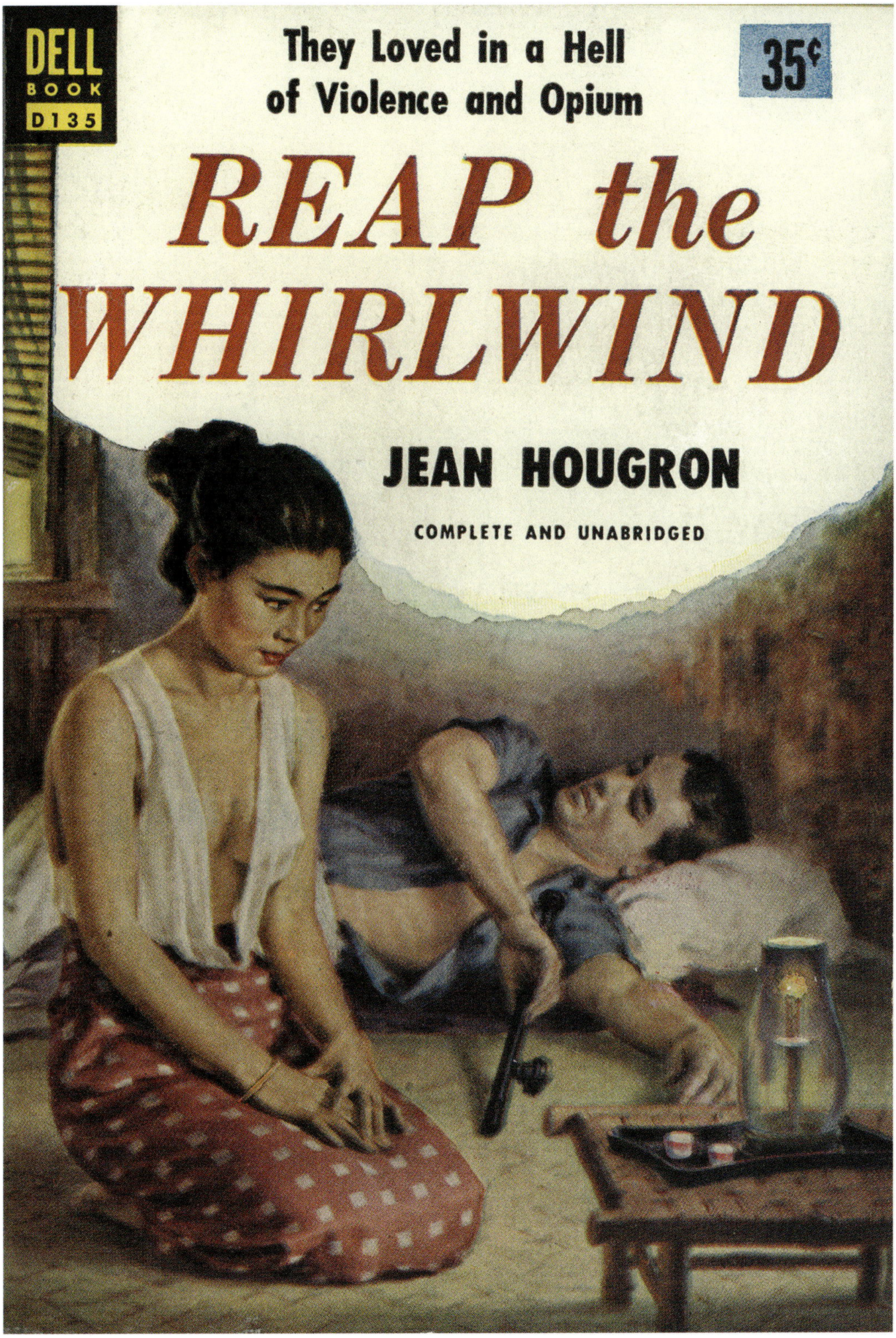

Jean Hougron • ***Reap the Whirlwind*** • DELL D135 • 1954 • COVER BY GRIFFITH FOXLEY • REPRINT

Thomas B. Dewey • ***Every Bet's a Sure Thing*** • AVON 564 • 1954

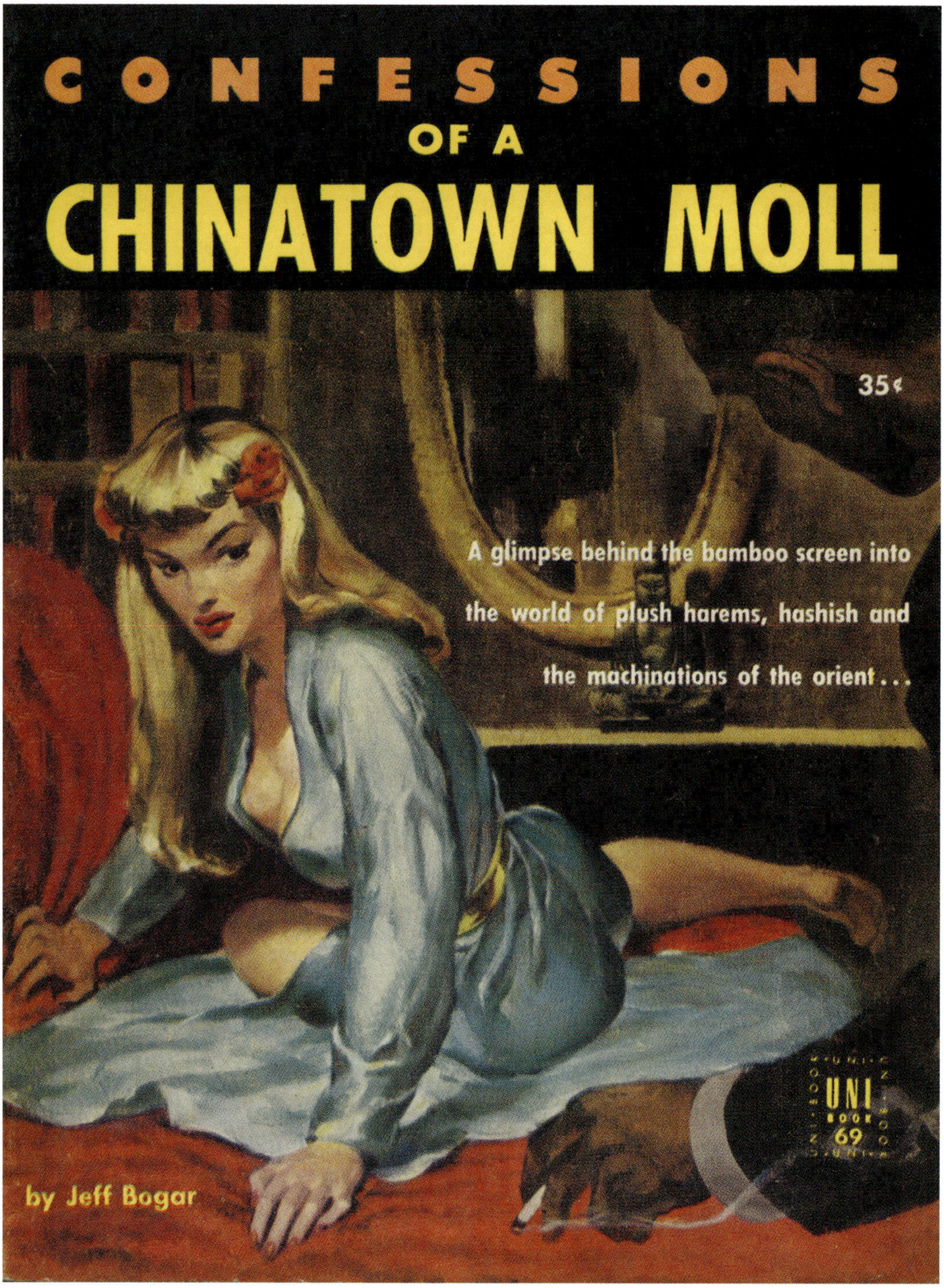

"If I were you I would not smoke, honored friend," he said, "opium is a vile poison — to the mind as well as to the body."

Jeff Bogar (pseud.) • ***Confessions of a Chinatown Moll*** • UNI-BOOK NO. 69 • 1953 • PBO

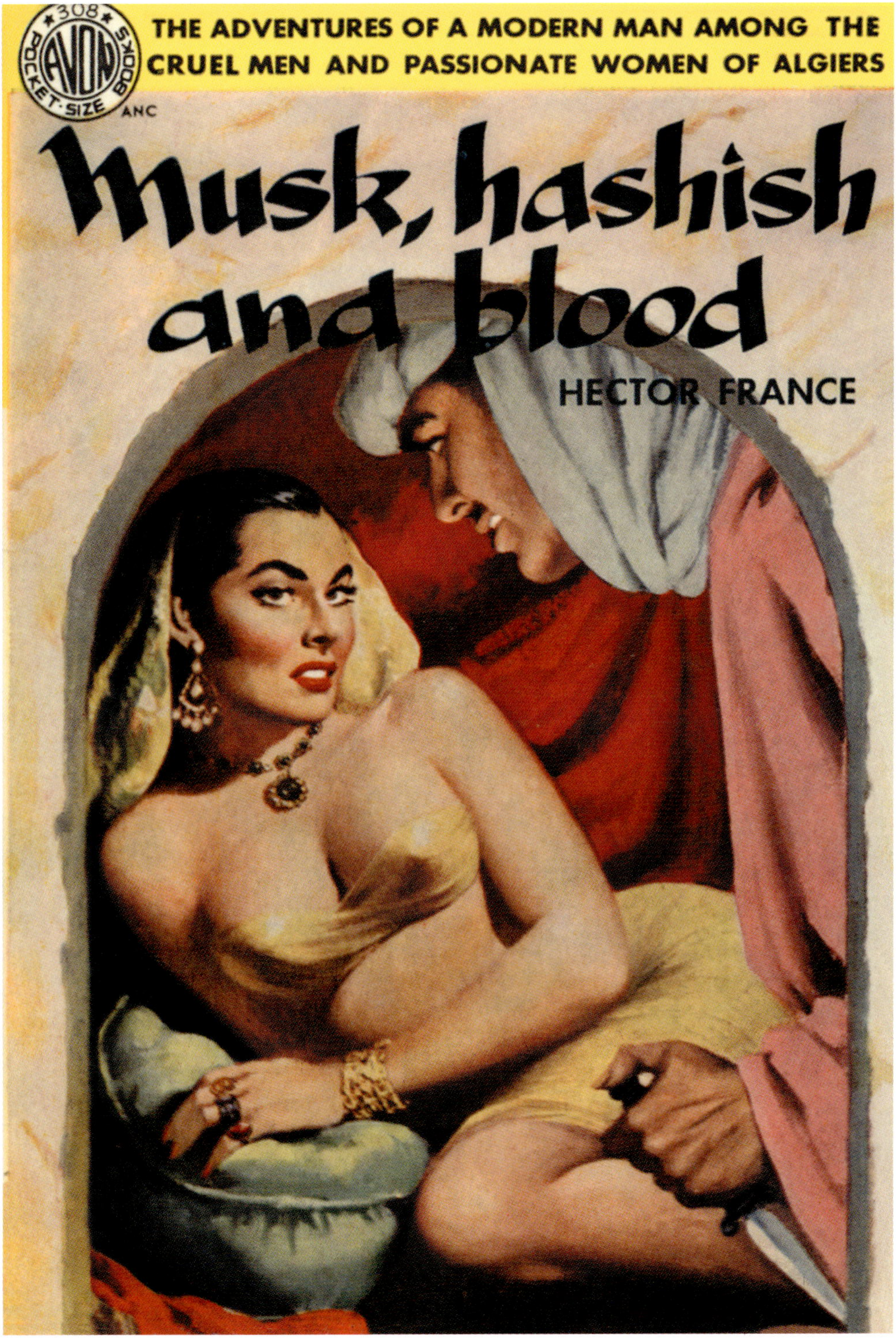

Reprint of the Charles Carrington 1899 first edition, probably but not certainly translated from an original French manuscript of France's by Maurice Boissard, who did many translations for the publisher. There is no evidence of an original edition in French.

Hector France (1837–1908) • ***Musk, Hashish and Blood*** • AVON 308 • 1951

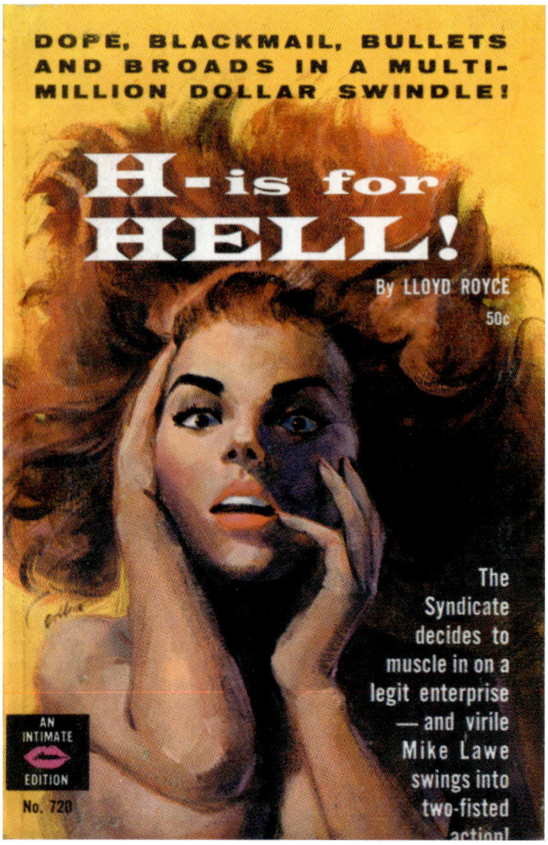

Lloyd Royce • ***"H" Is for Hell***
INTIMATE EDITION 720 • 1963 • PBO

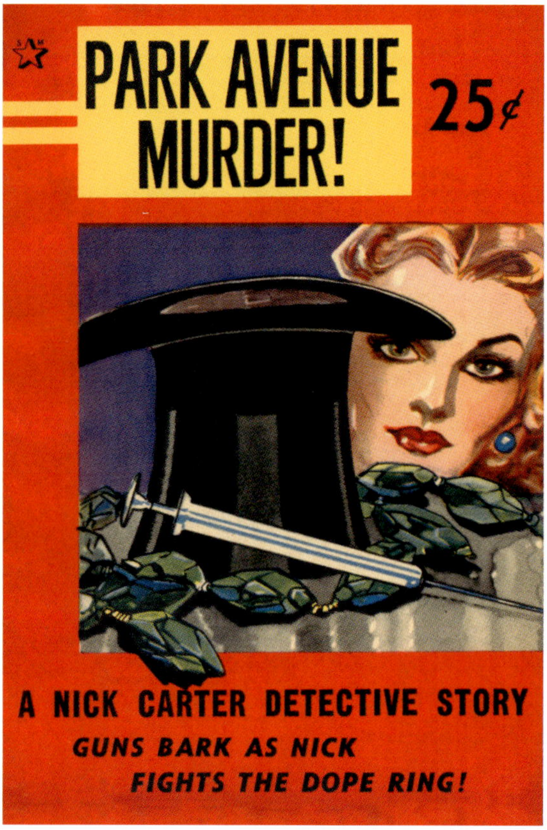

Park Avenue Murder! • VITAL #4
1946 • PBO DIGEST

Joseph Joesten • ***Dope, Inc.***
AVON 538 • 1953 • PBO

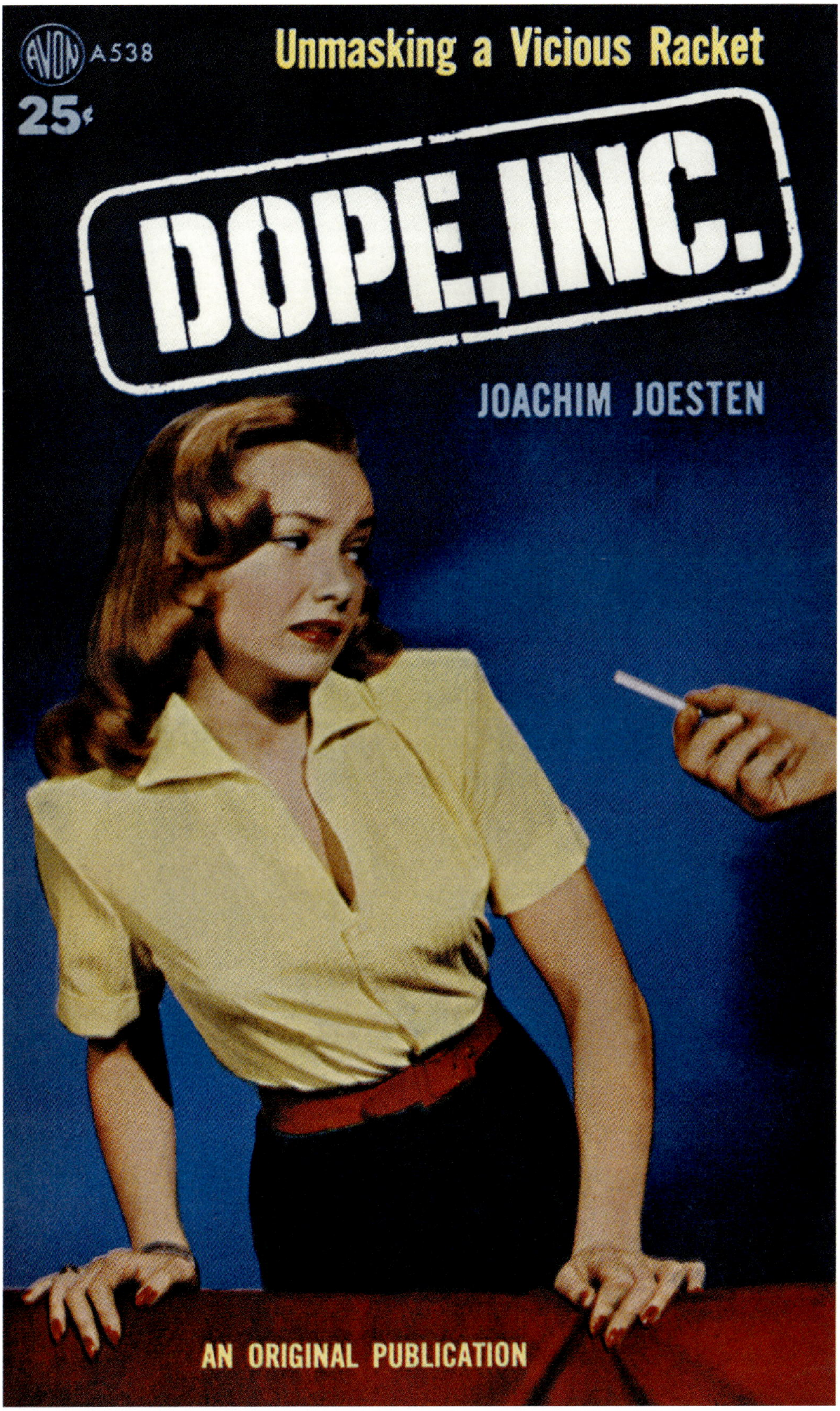
AVON
A538
25¢
Unmasking a Vicious Racket
DOPE, INC.
JOACHIM JOESTEN
AN ORIGINAL PUBLICATION

"The box contained nothing but a hypodermic syringe, a spoon, and a small alcohol lamp, the standard rig of horse rides. then I noticed the residue of fine white powder which coated the bottom of the box.

"Wynn said, 'Carter says that powder is heroin.'

"Getting a little on my finger, I touched it to my tongue. 'Uh huh. Cut with milk sugar.'

"...Grimaldi didn't even look very concerned when we found the cache. It wasn't cut horse he was riding on but full-strength op. Apparently, he treated himself better than he did his clients. He was still riding high enough not to care about much of anything at the moment. But that would change when he had been sitting cold for a while in a cell."

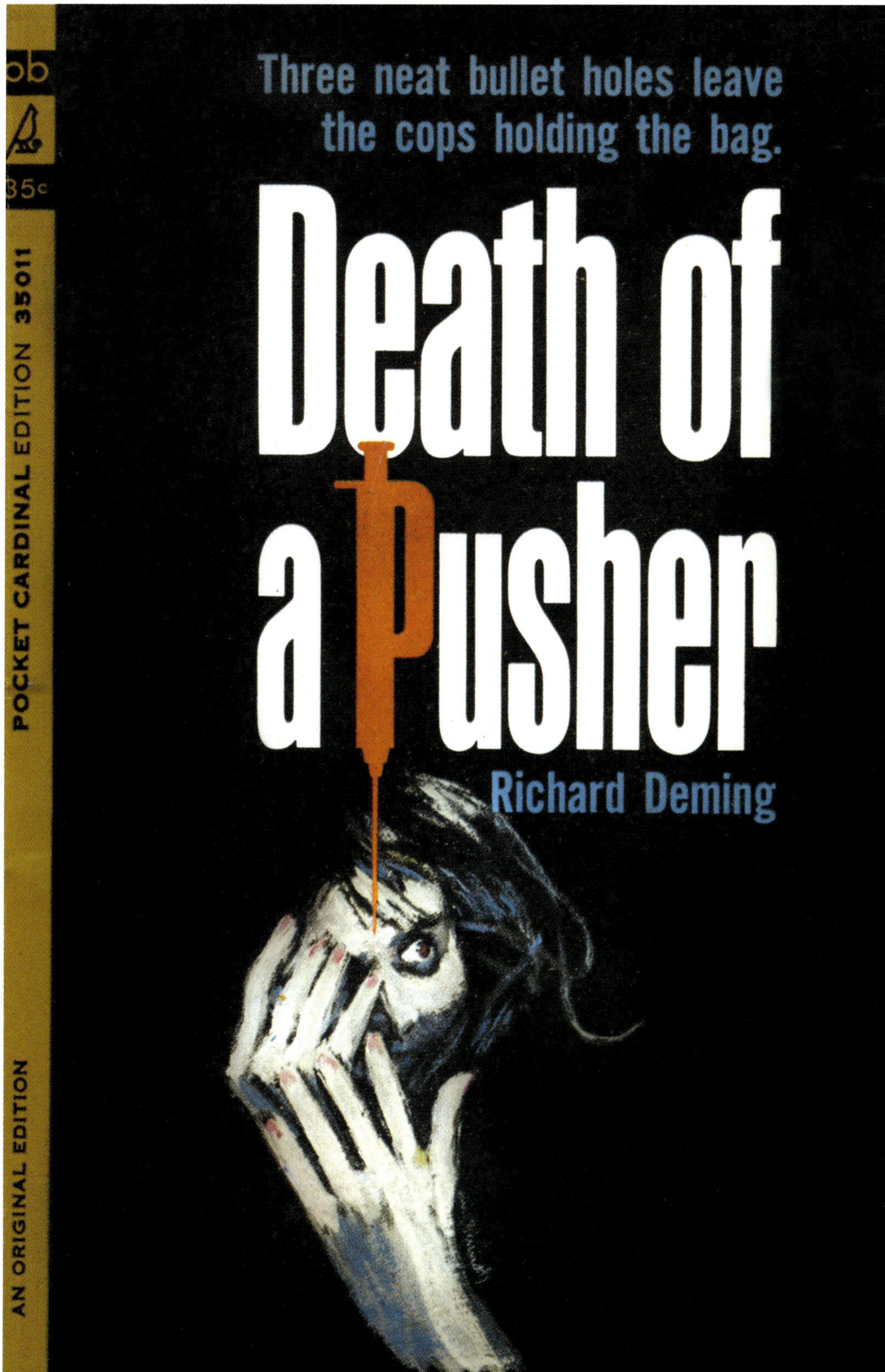

Richard Deming • ***Death of a Pusher*** • POCKET CARDINAL 35011 • 1964 • PBO

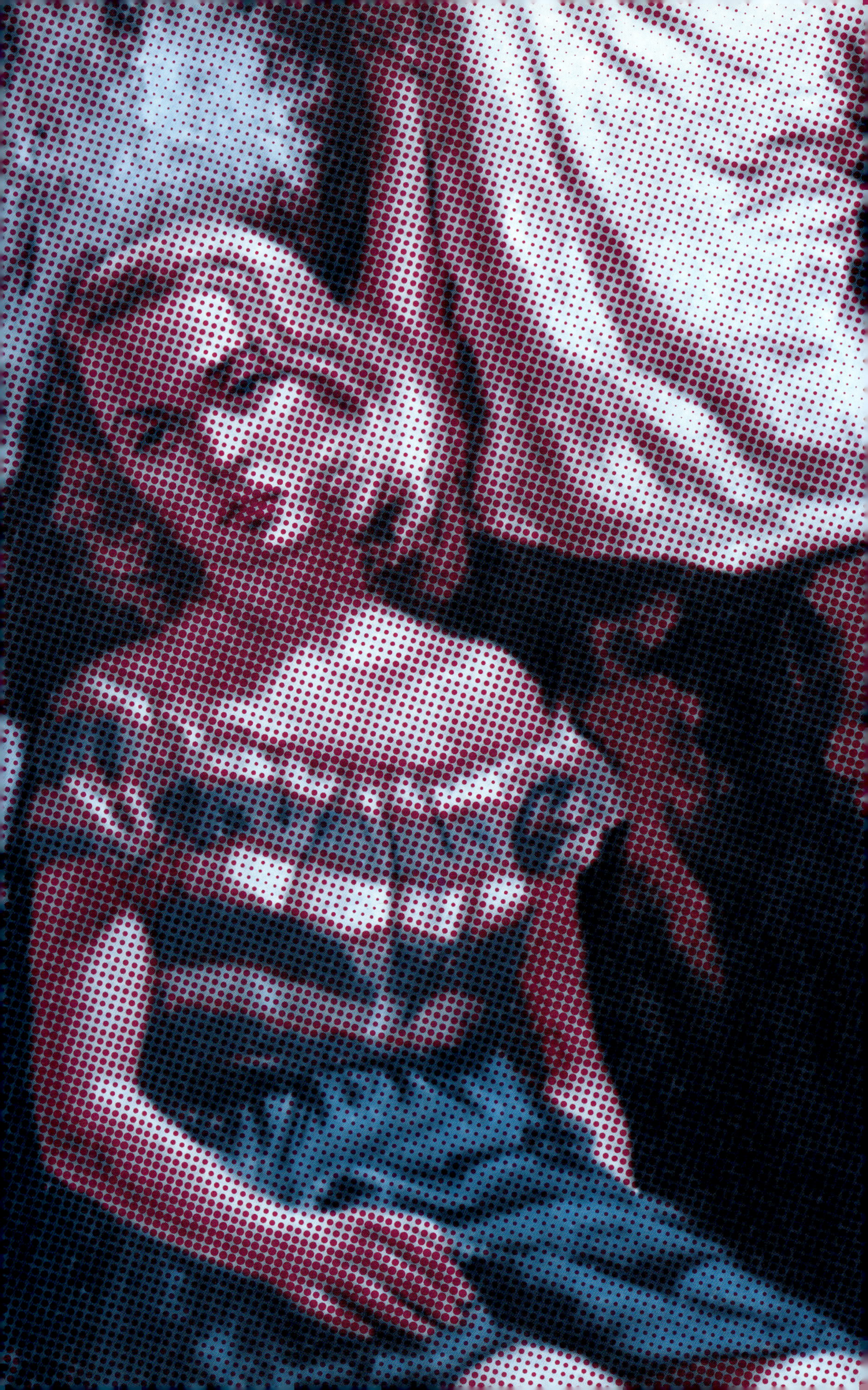

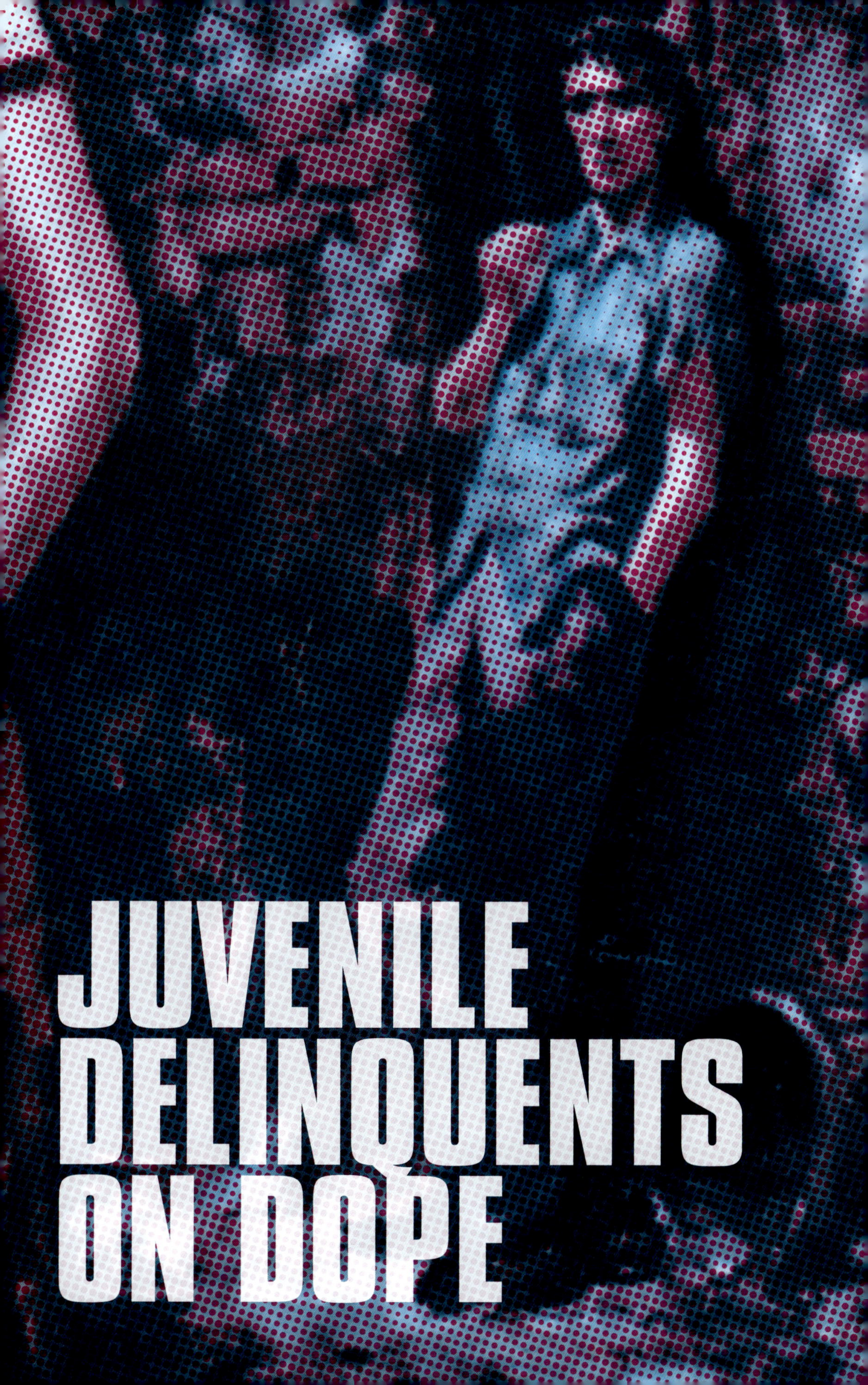
JUVENILE
DELINQUENTS
ON DOPE

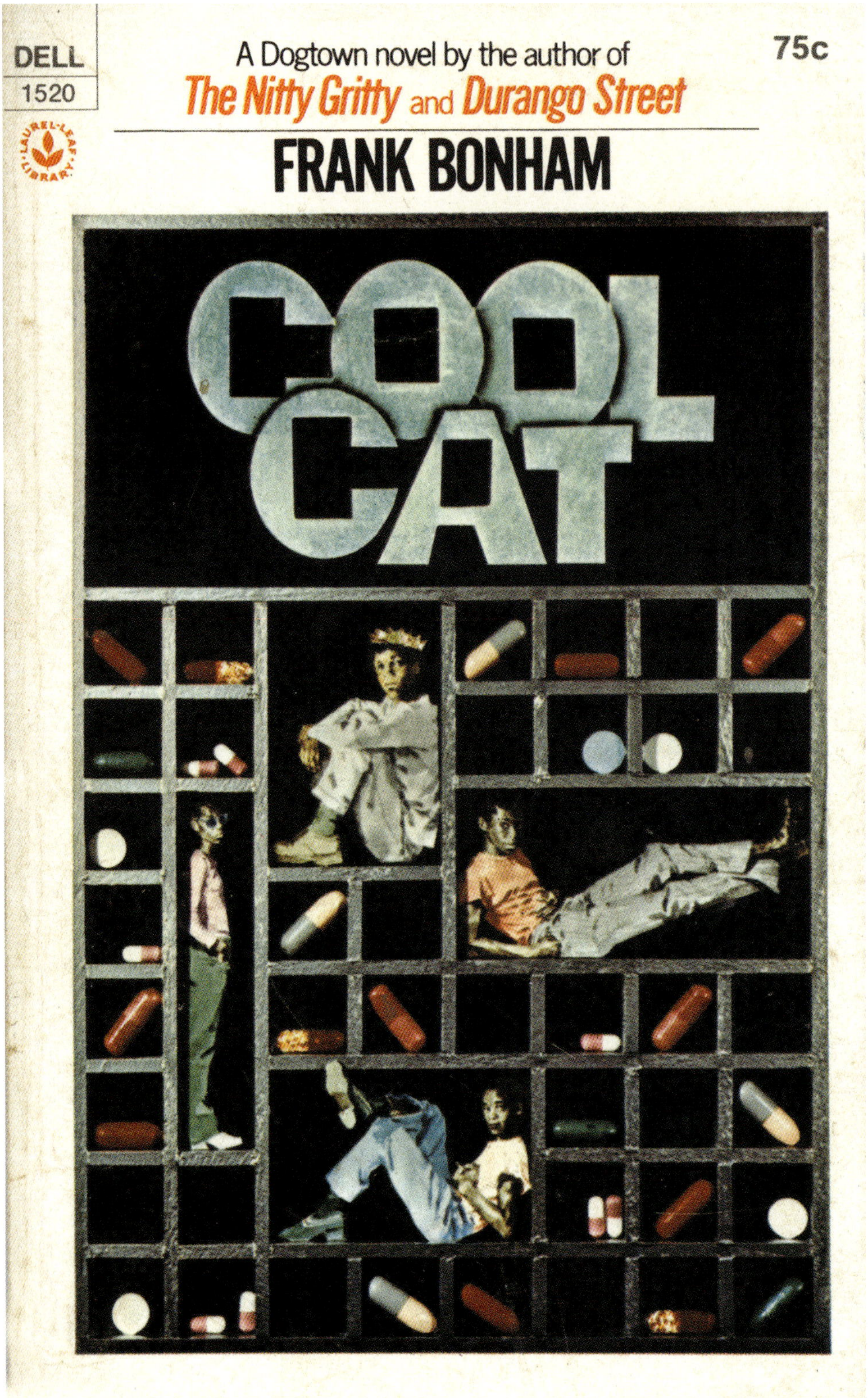

Frank Bonham • ***Cool Cat*** • DELL 1520 • 1971 • REPRINT

Floyd Miller • ***The Dream Peddlers*** • POPULAR LIBRARY 787 • 1956 • PBO

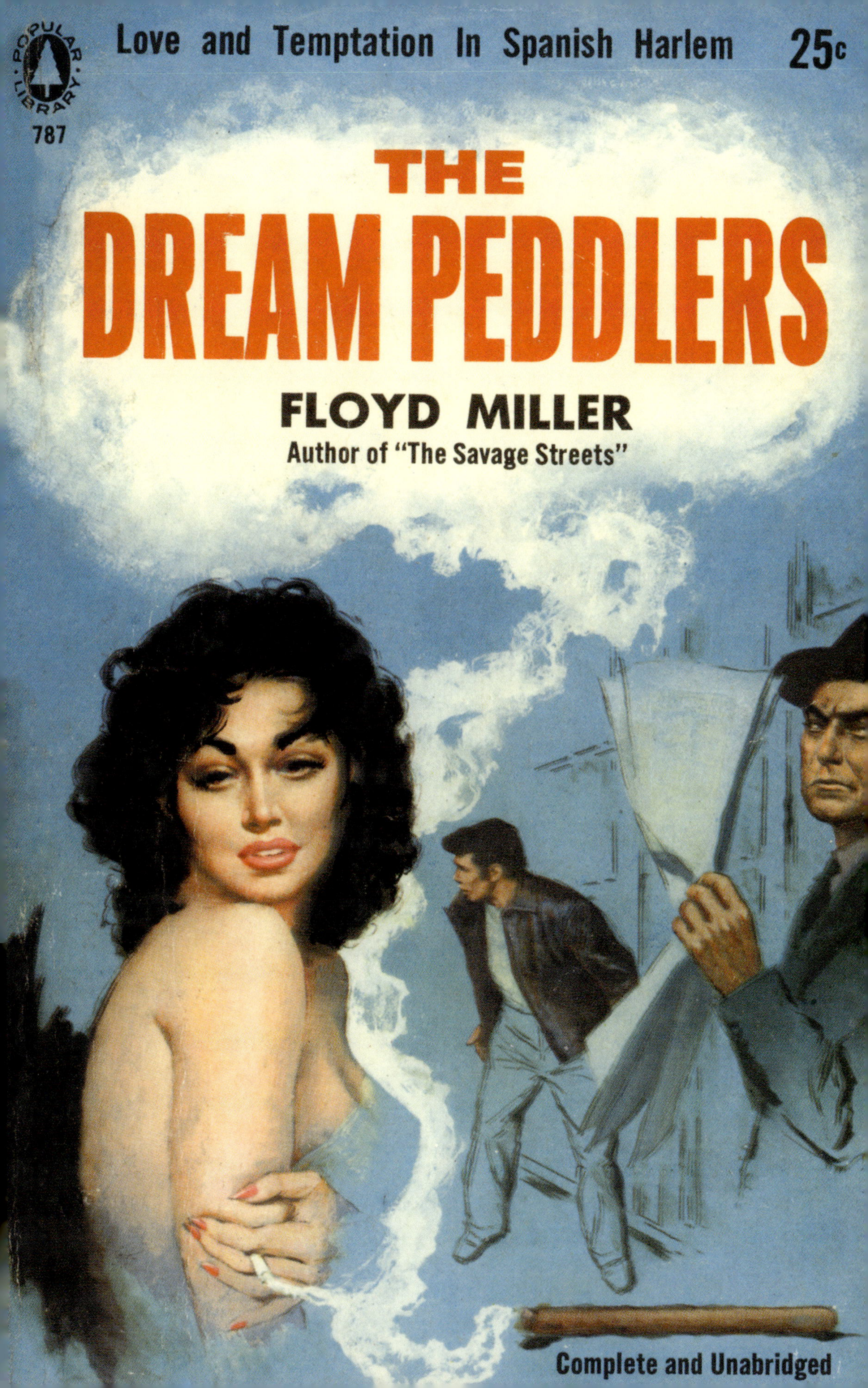
POPULAR LIBRARY
787
Love and Temptation In Spanish Harlem
25c
THE DREAM PEDDLERS
FLOYD MILLER
Author of "The Savage Streets"
Complete and Unabridged

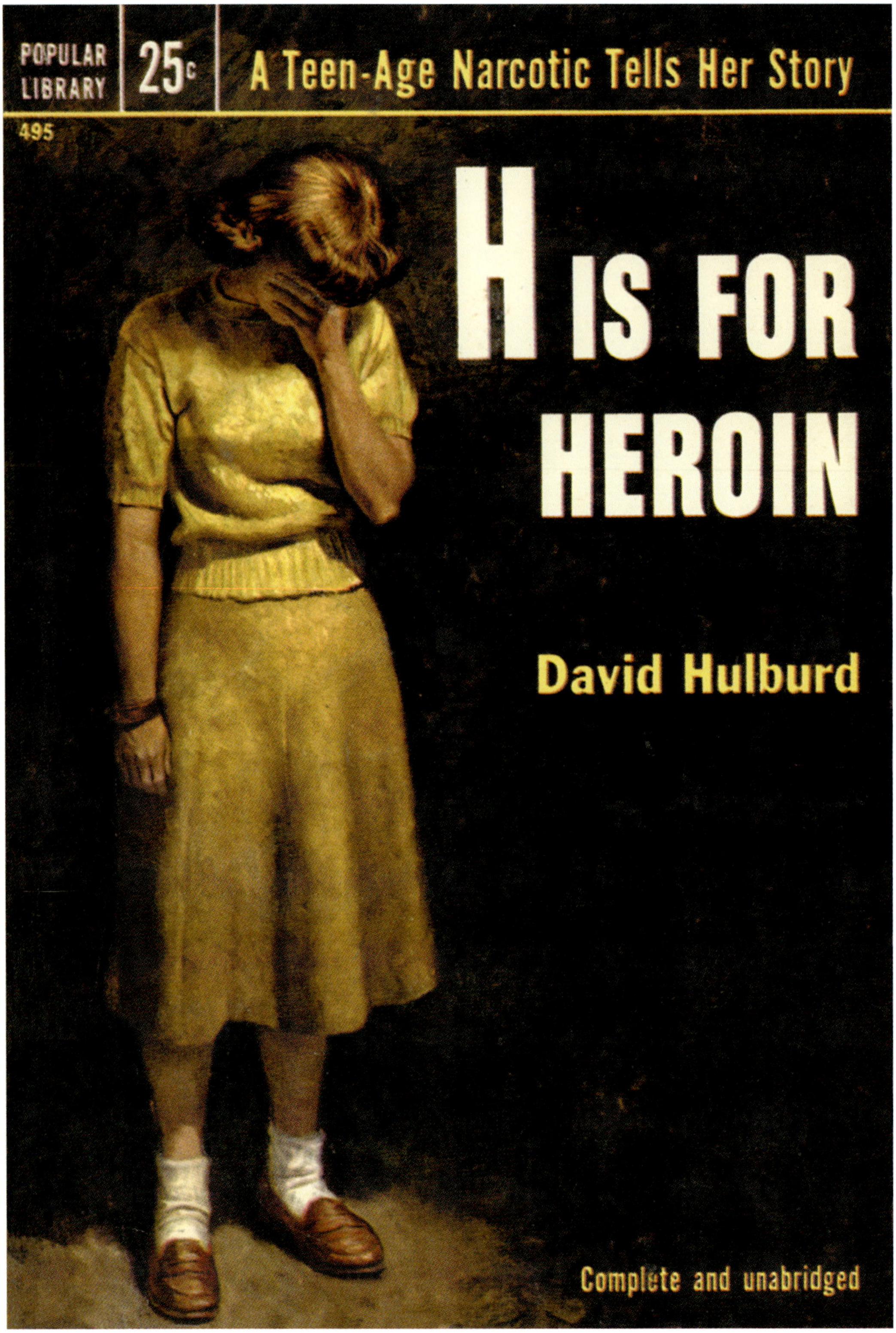

"Dope always gives you a raw deal. Take it from me. I know. I'm only seventeen but I married Eddy because he gives me heroin...This is my story — and it's not a pretty one."

David Hulburd • ***H Is for Heroin*** • POPULAR LIBRARY 495 • 1953 • COVER BY RAFAEL DESOTO • REPRINT

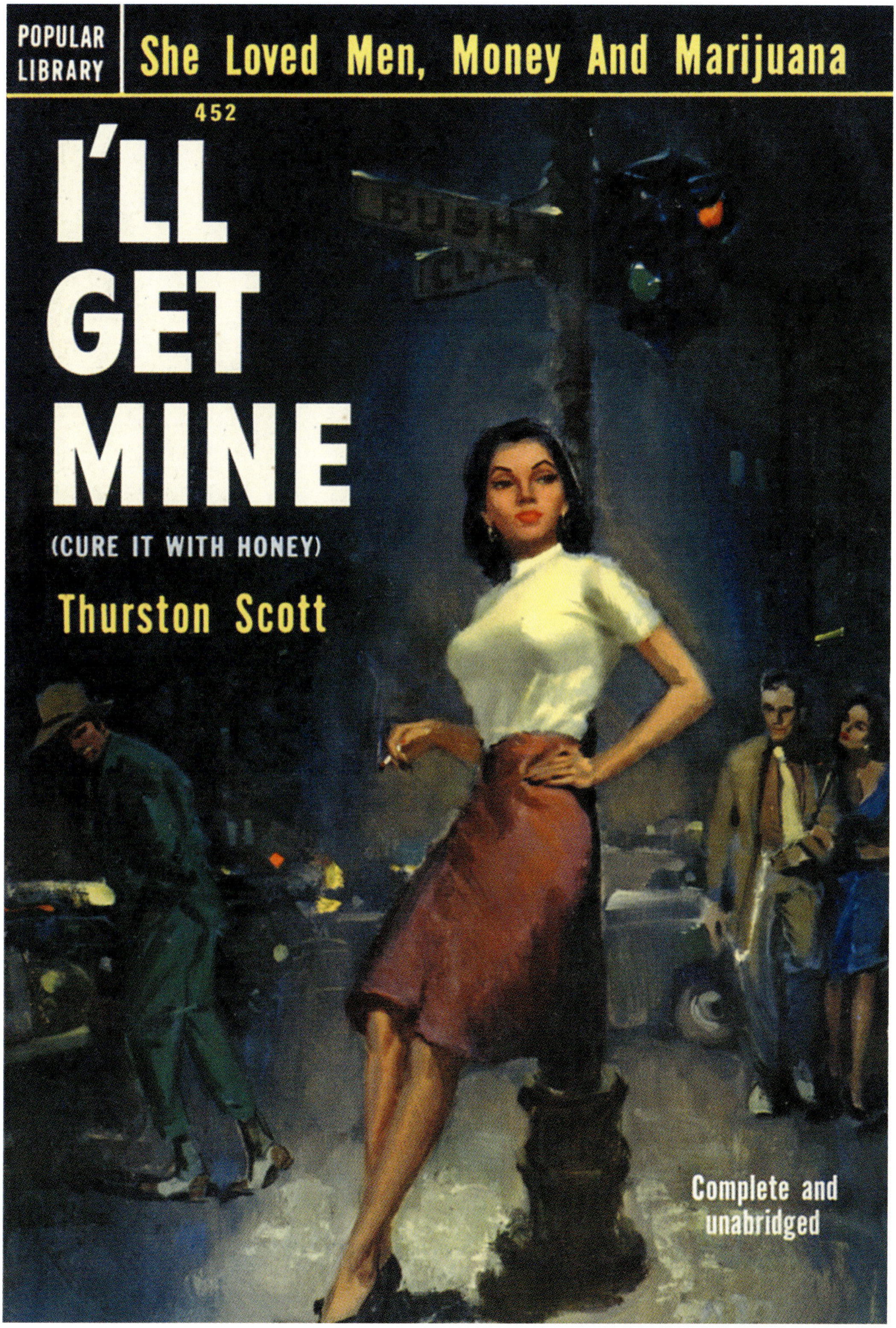

"I kissed her hand, tasting the musky odor of marijuana that clung to her lips."
—from *I'll Get Mine,* [Strange girl: lips on her hand.]

Thurston Scott • ***I'll Get Mine (Cure It With Honey)*** • POPULAR LIBRARY 452 • 1952 • COVER BY A. LESLIE ROSS • REPRINT

"'Hi, Rita. Want some charge?' Rita knew what he meant all right. Marijuana. The kids at school had a dozen names for it — gauge, pod [sic], charge, boom, muggles, weed, dynomite [sic], dream stuff, jive. The big cigarettes were bombers, the thin ones sticks or reefers. The cheapest of all were bammies, mixed with grass or catnip... 'Bammies won't hurt you, kid, but take it easy, drag in slow and not too deep then let it out fast. That way it won't reach you so soon....' Rita was staring straight ahead... Everything began to cloud over. The smoke in the room became solid, revolving in slow spirals...She felt that if she spread her arms she could float up to the top of the room, go anywhere she wanted to."

Wenzell Brown • ***Gang Girl*** • AVON 560 • 1954 • PBO

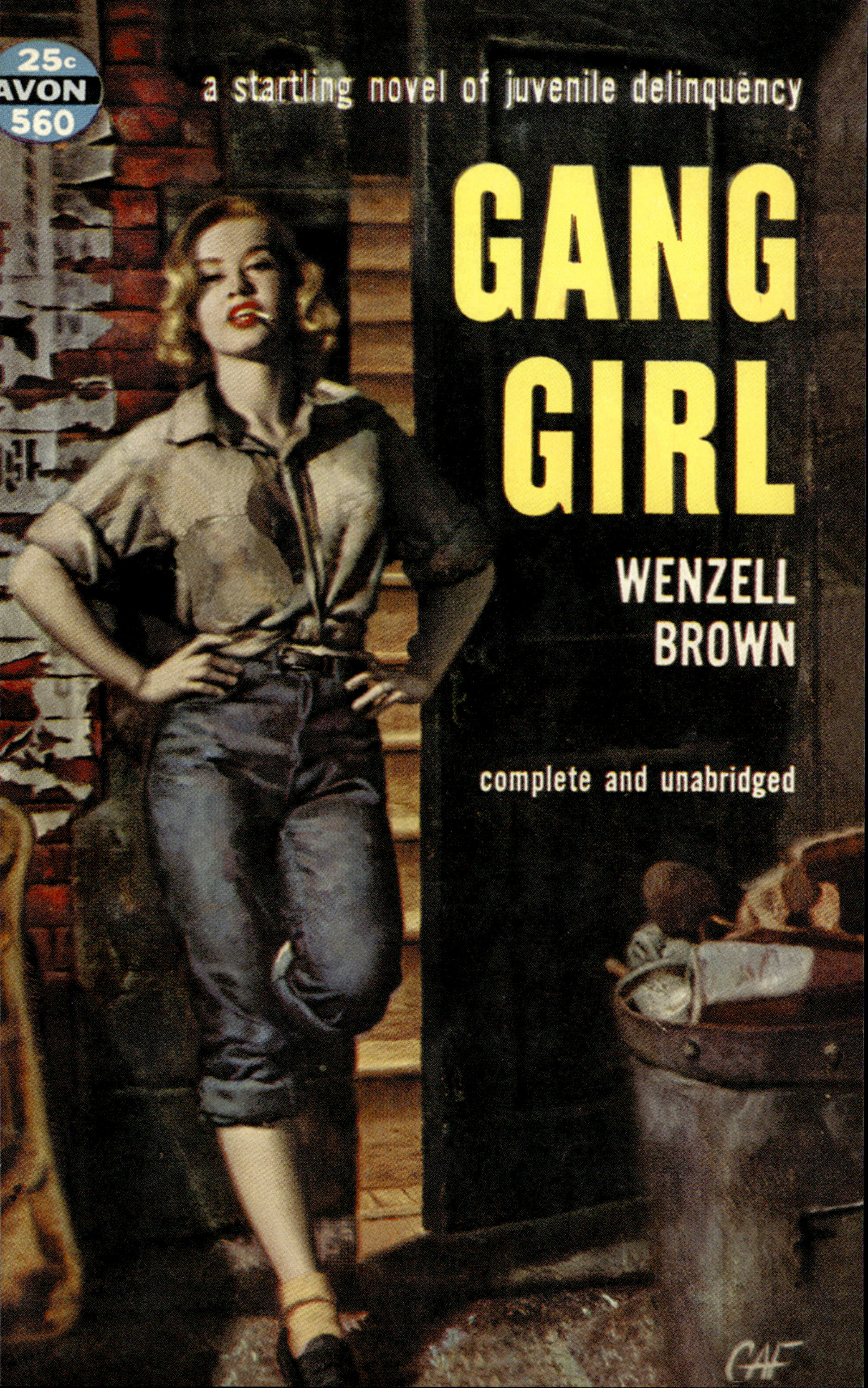
25c
AVON
560
a startling novel of juvenile delinquency
GANG
GIRL
WENZELL
BROWN
complete and unabridged

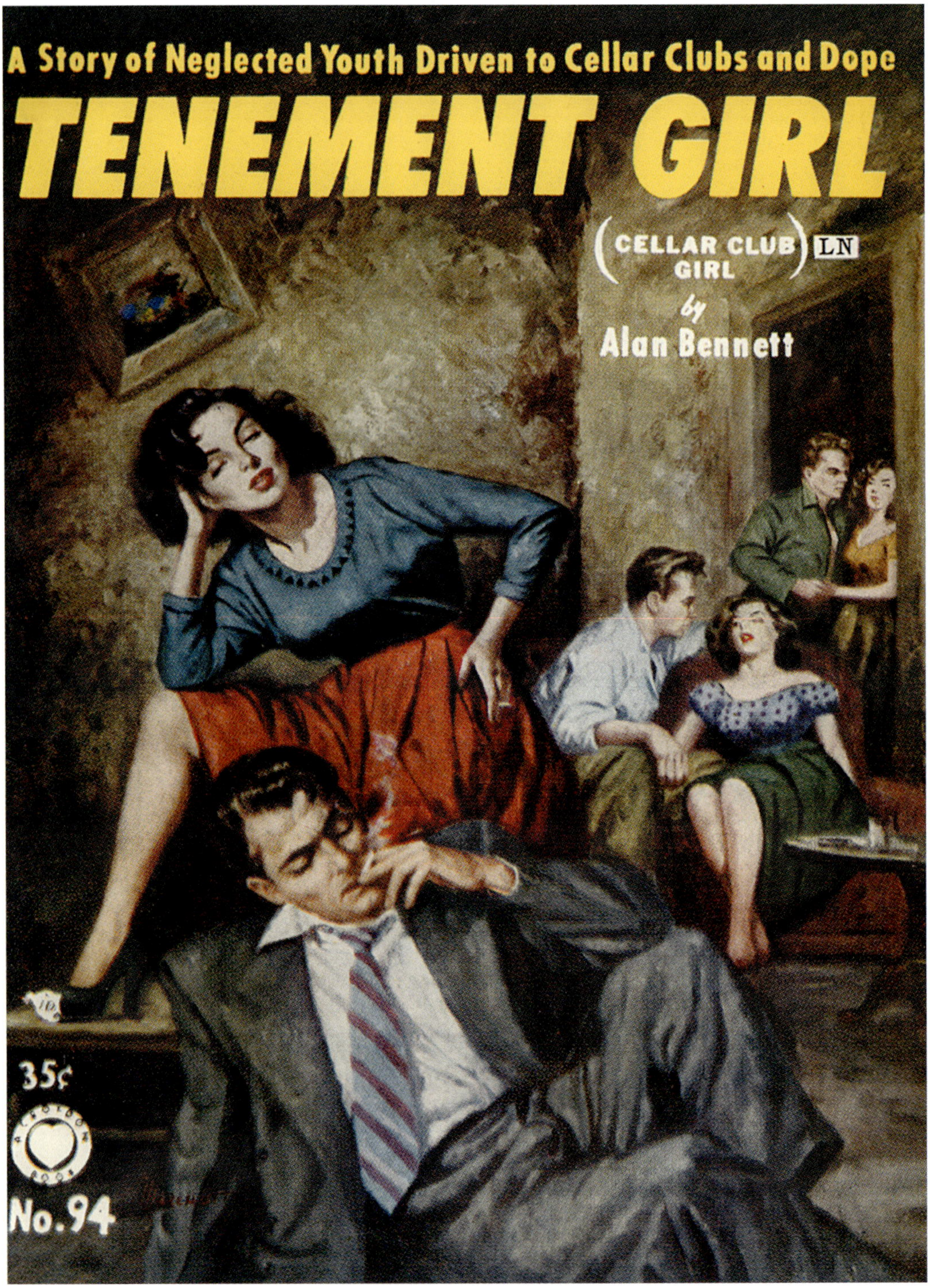

"'I'm not bad. I'm not bad,' she moaned. Why didn't her parents love her the way she wanted? Lisa wanted their love desperately. How could she make them understand that she couldn't study any more, couldn't stay home nights, couldn't explain her activities? She was a dope addict and there was no salvation for her."

Alan Bennett • ***Tenement Girl,*** a.k.a. ***Cellar Club Girl*** • CROYDEN 94 • 1955 • COVER BY LOU MARCHETTI
PBO DIGEST • 2D EDITION • ORIGINALLY PUBLISHED 1953

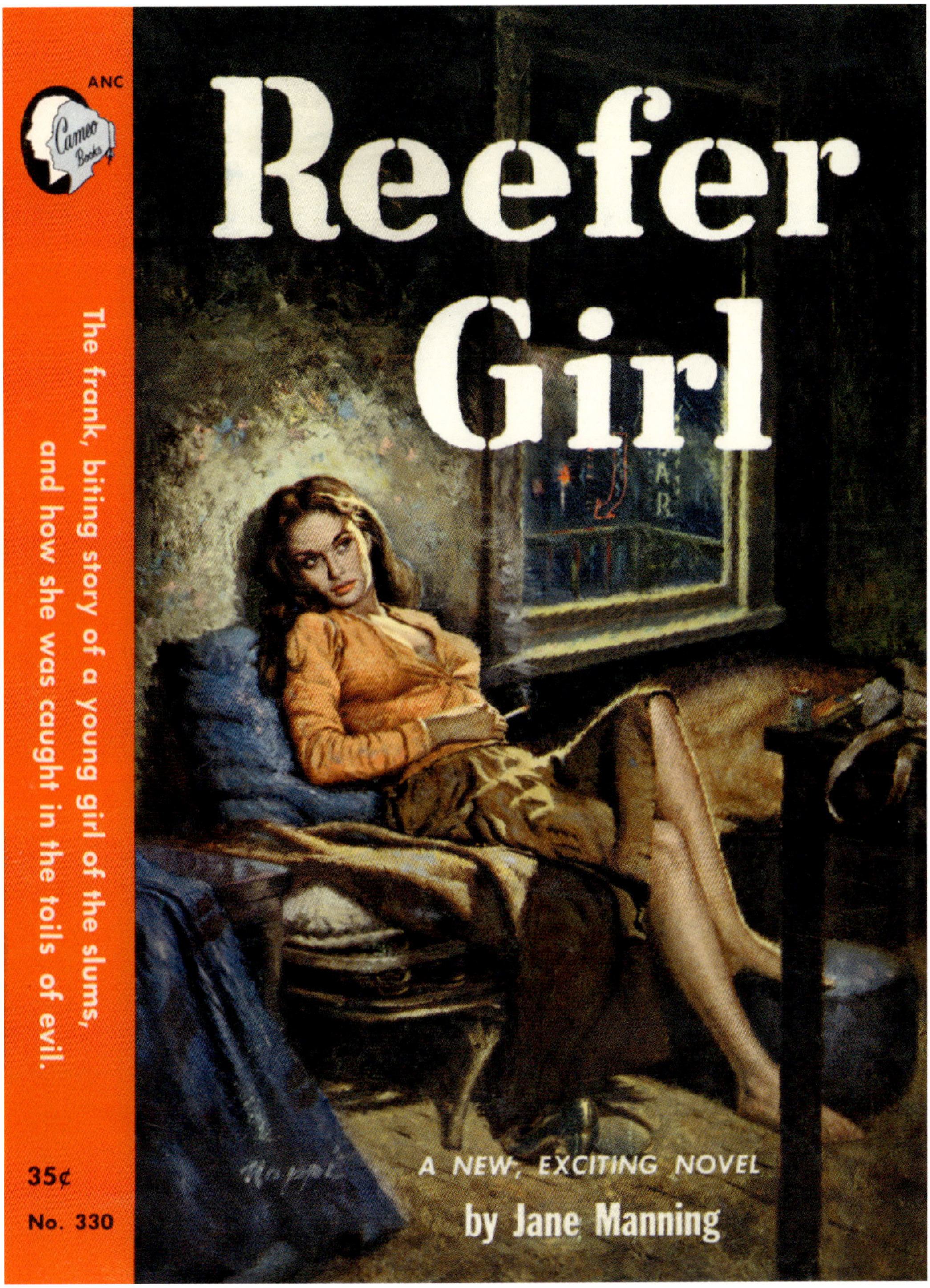

"She remembered all too well what it was like to be without dope. The need for a jolt would start like the need for a cigarette and would turn into excruciating pain. Every muscle would tighten up. It felt like the muscles in your legs were like iron chairs that someone was turning, twisting, making you scream... There was no way out of this trap, no way but death...or kicking the habit...and she could never do that."

Jane Manning [Ruth Manoff] • ***Reefer Girl*** • CAMEO 330 • 1953 • COVER BY RUDOLPH NAPPI • PBO

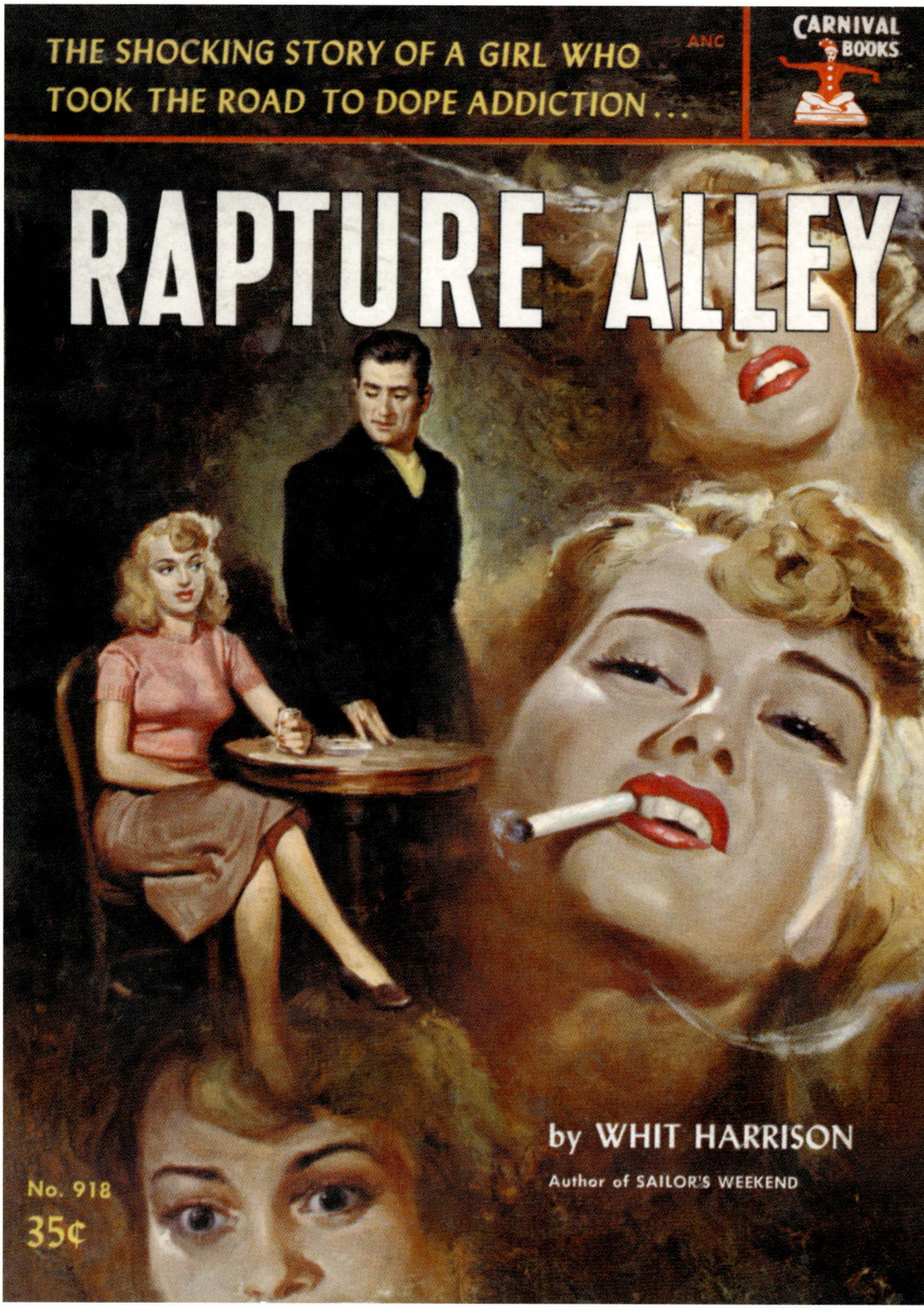

Whit Harrison [Harry Whittington] • ***Rapture Alley*** • CARNIVAL 918 • 1953 • COVER BY RUDOLPH BELARSKI • PBO

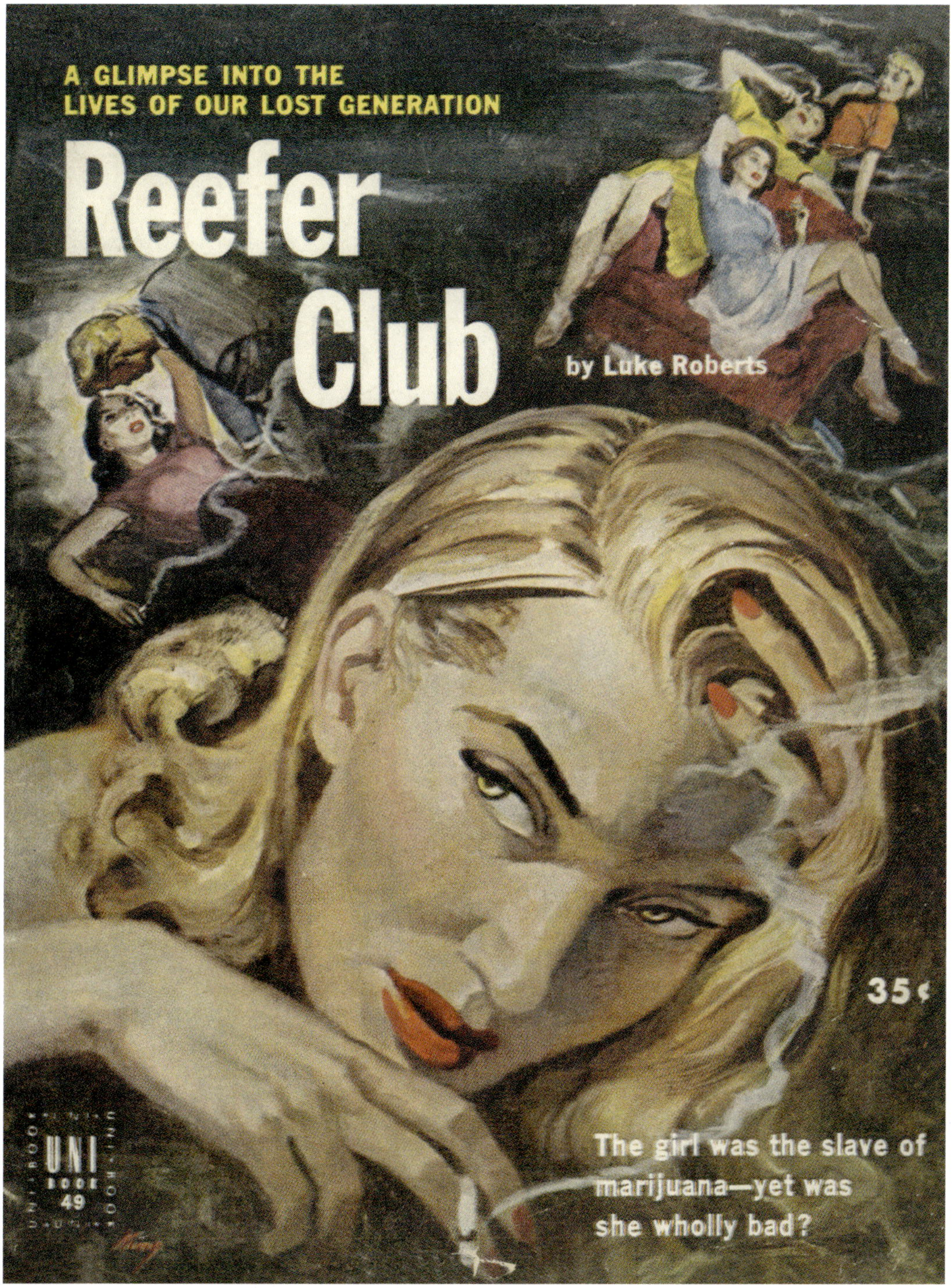

Luke Roberts [Robert Ehrenzweig] • ***Reefer Club*** • UNI BOOKS 49 • 1953 • COVER BY WARREN KING • PBO DIGEST
REPRINTED AS *REEFER GIRL* • STALLION BOOK 213 • WITH SAME COVER AS *BASEMENT GANG*

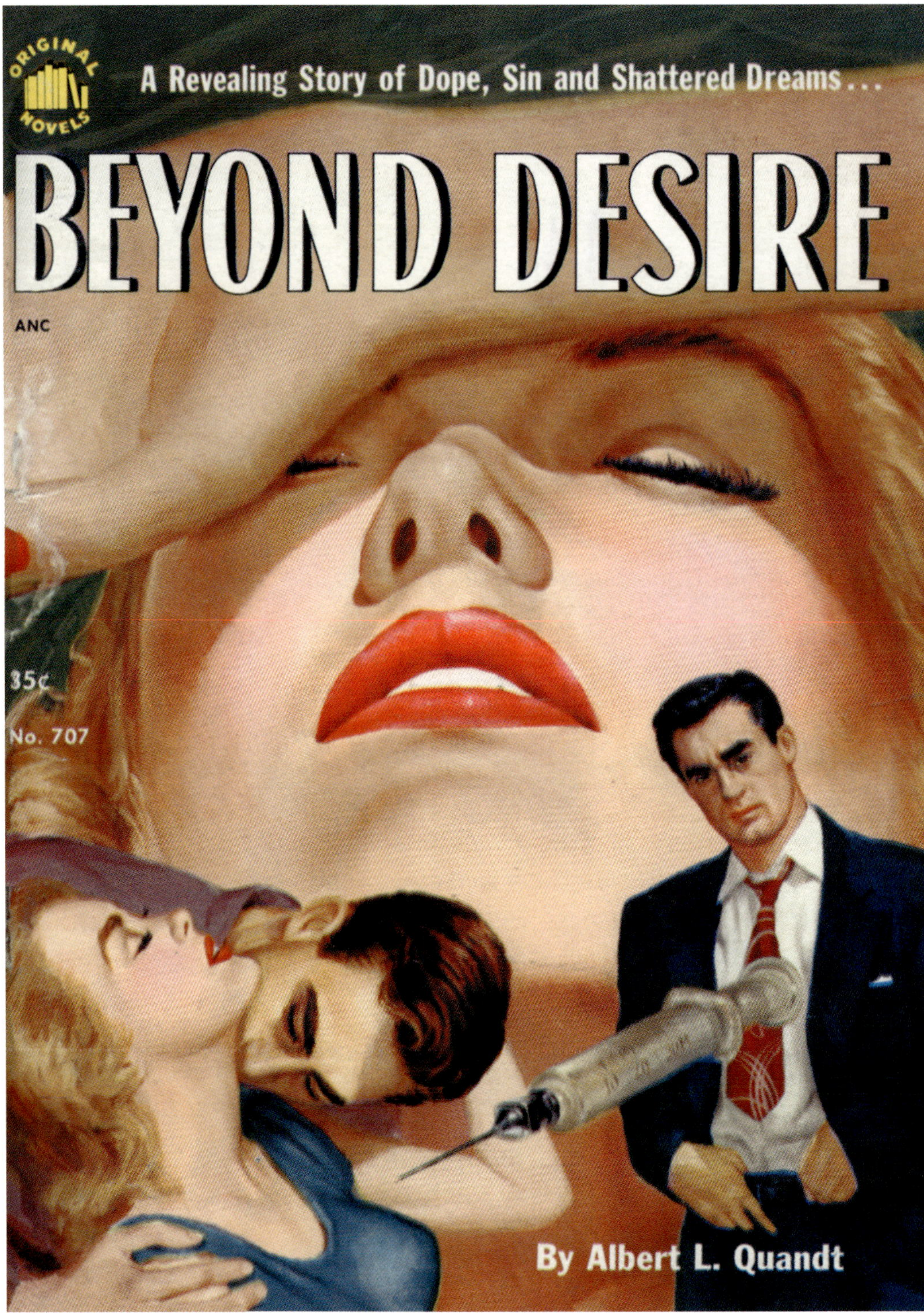

"This is the story of a girl who passed through that door, in search of something she could not name, but wanted deeply. It is also the story of how she struggled back to the light on the other side of the door..."

Albert L. Quandt • ***Beyond Desire*** • ORIGINAL NOVELS 707 • 1952 • COVER BY ROBERT SCHULTZ
PBO DIGEST • FIRST EDITION

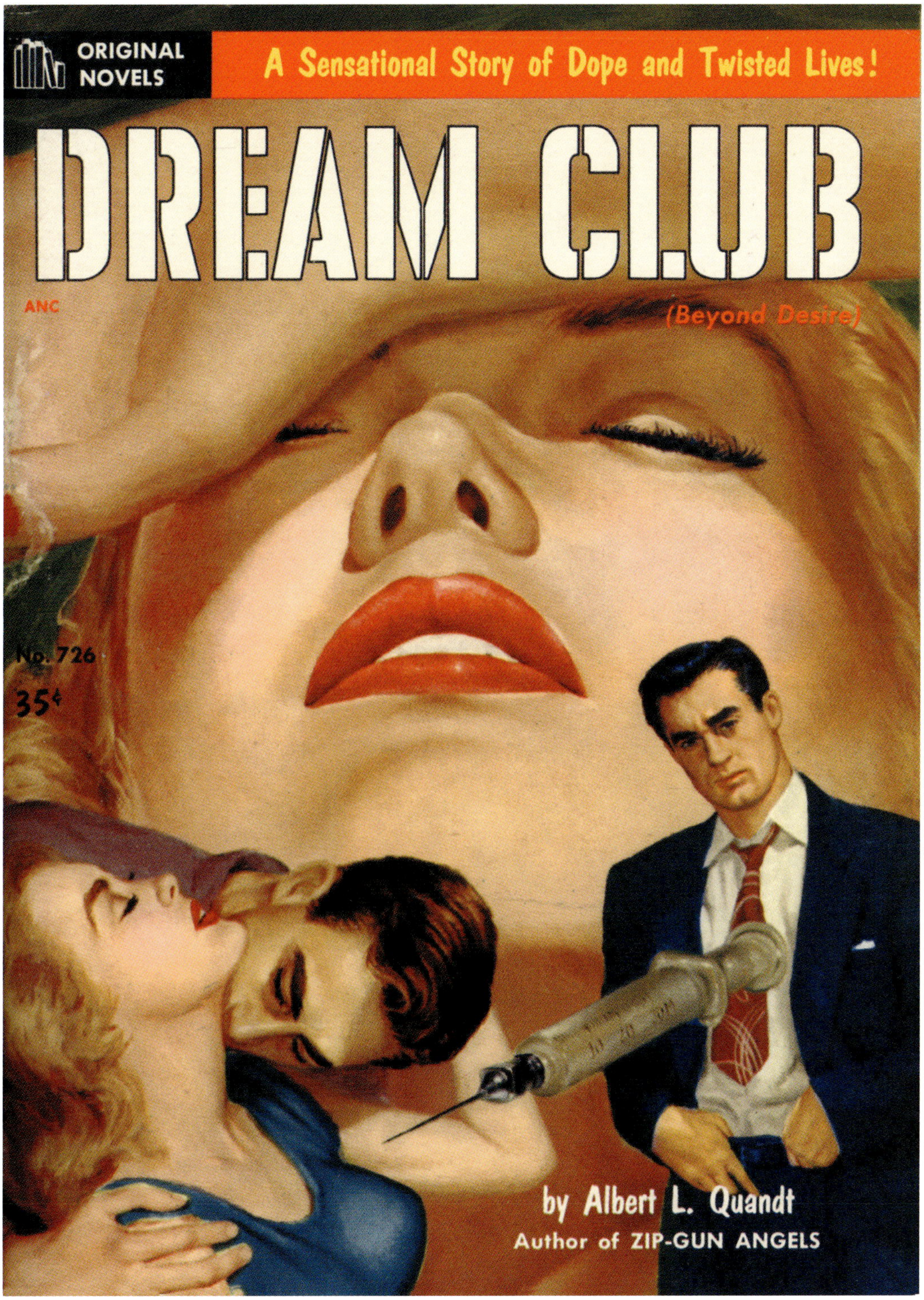

"This is the story of a publisher who passed through that door of deception, in search of something he could not name but was sort of like extra profits, and wanted deeply, like money."

Albert L. Quandt • ***Dream Club*** • ORIGINAL NOVELS 726 • 1953 • COVER BY ROBERT SCHULTZ
PBO DIGEST • SAME BOOK, SAME COVER, DIFFERENT TITLE

"Today habit-forming drugs are easily accessible to teenagers. They can be bought in school yards, playgrounds, candy shops, or on street corners. They are distributed at high school dances, in pool rooms, at parties. Their use has spread out from the big cities to invade the small towns and even rural communities. And while such conditions exist, it is inevitable that many youngsters will experiment with these drugs and that some of them will land 'on the hook.'"

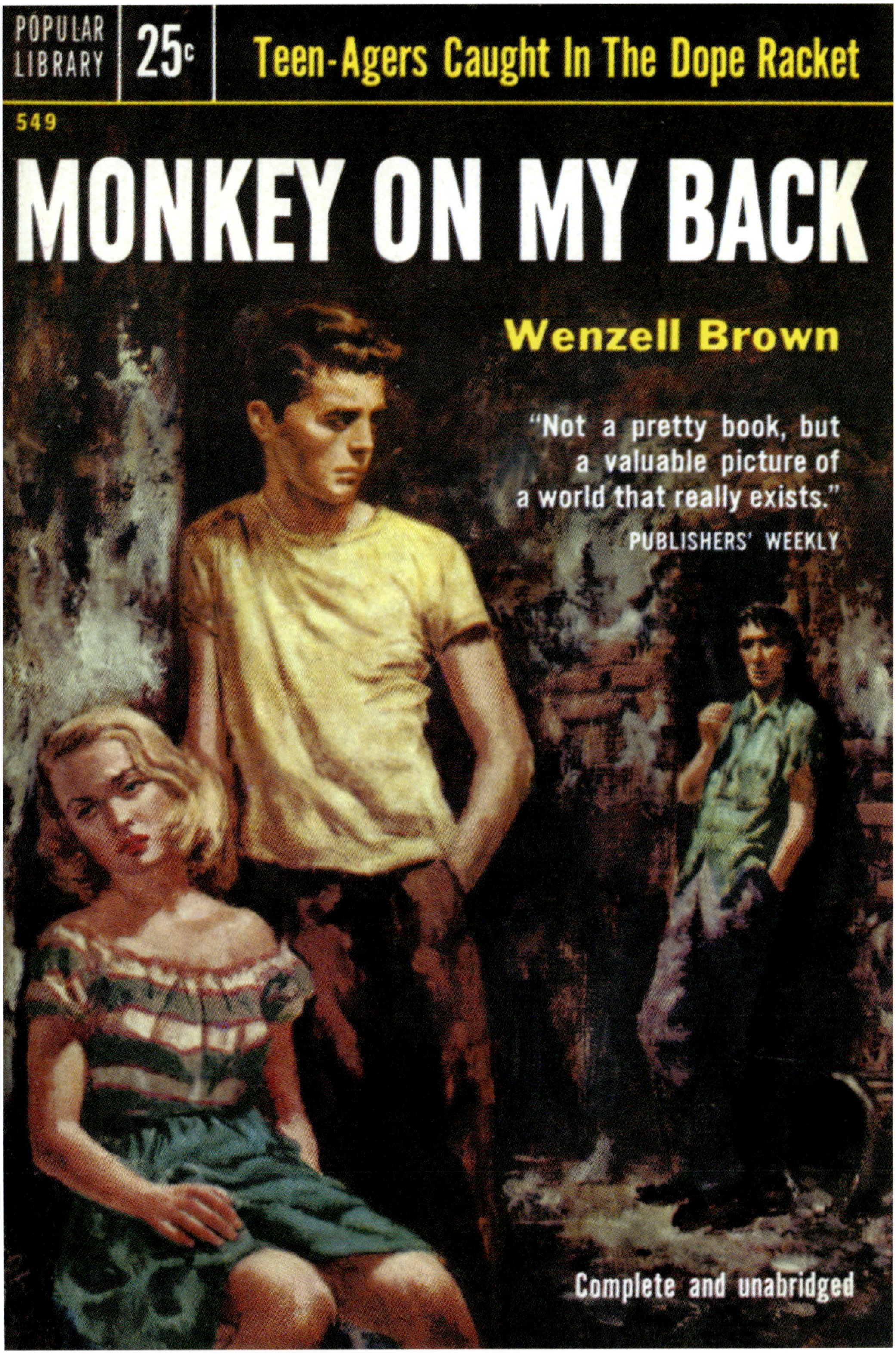

Wenzell Brown • ***Monkey on My Back*** • POPULAR LIBRARY 549 • 1954 • COVER BY OWEN KAMPEN • PBO

25c COMPLETE • UNABRIDGED POPU LIBR

MEET THE TEEN-AGE ADDICT

On this strange journey into the fantastic world of juvenile "junkies," you will meet:

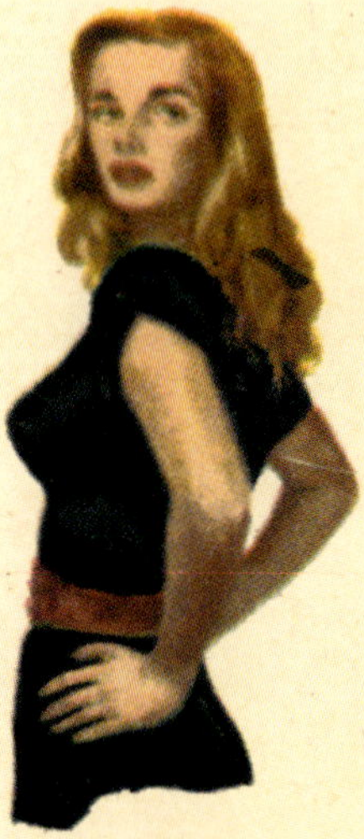

ROSA—the trailer camp girl who got her first "fix" from her addict husband on their wedding night.

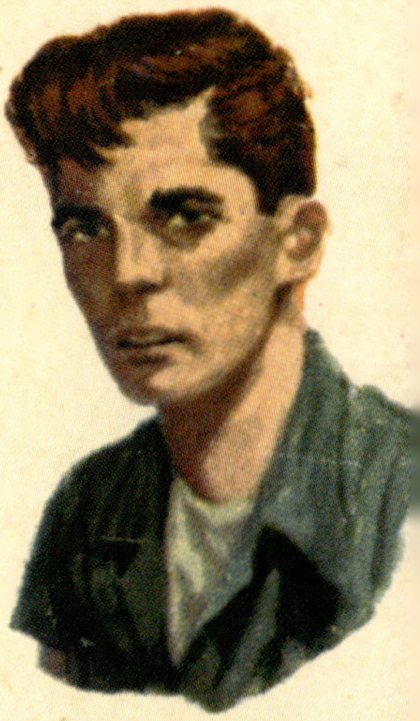

DAVE—the rich boy who started "blasting just for kicks" and got caught in the narcotics trap.

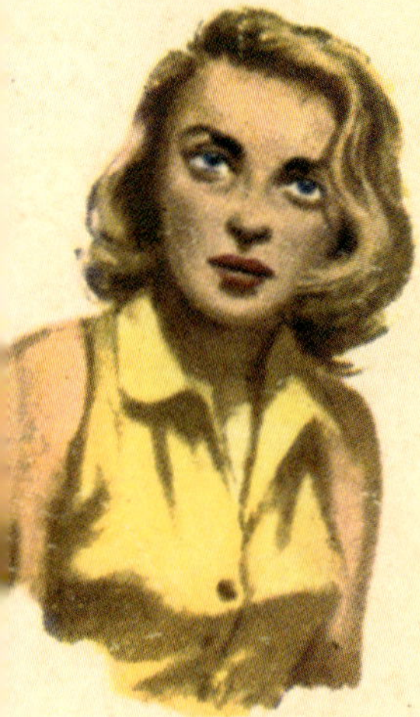

JOANNE—the Times Square girl who took a "hot shot" and was taken for a ride.

And other teen-age addicts driven to every degradation to keep "the monkey off their backs."

"If you're the parent of a teen-ager, or if you have a child about to enter that phase of life, you should read this book."

Arkansas GAZETTE

PRINTED IN THE UNITED STATES

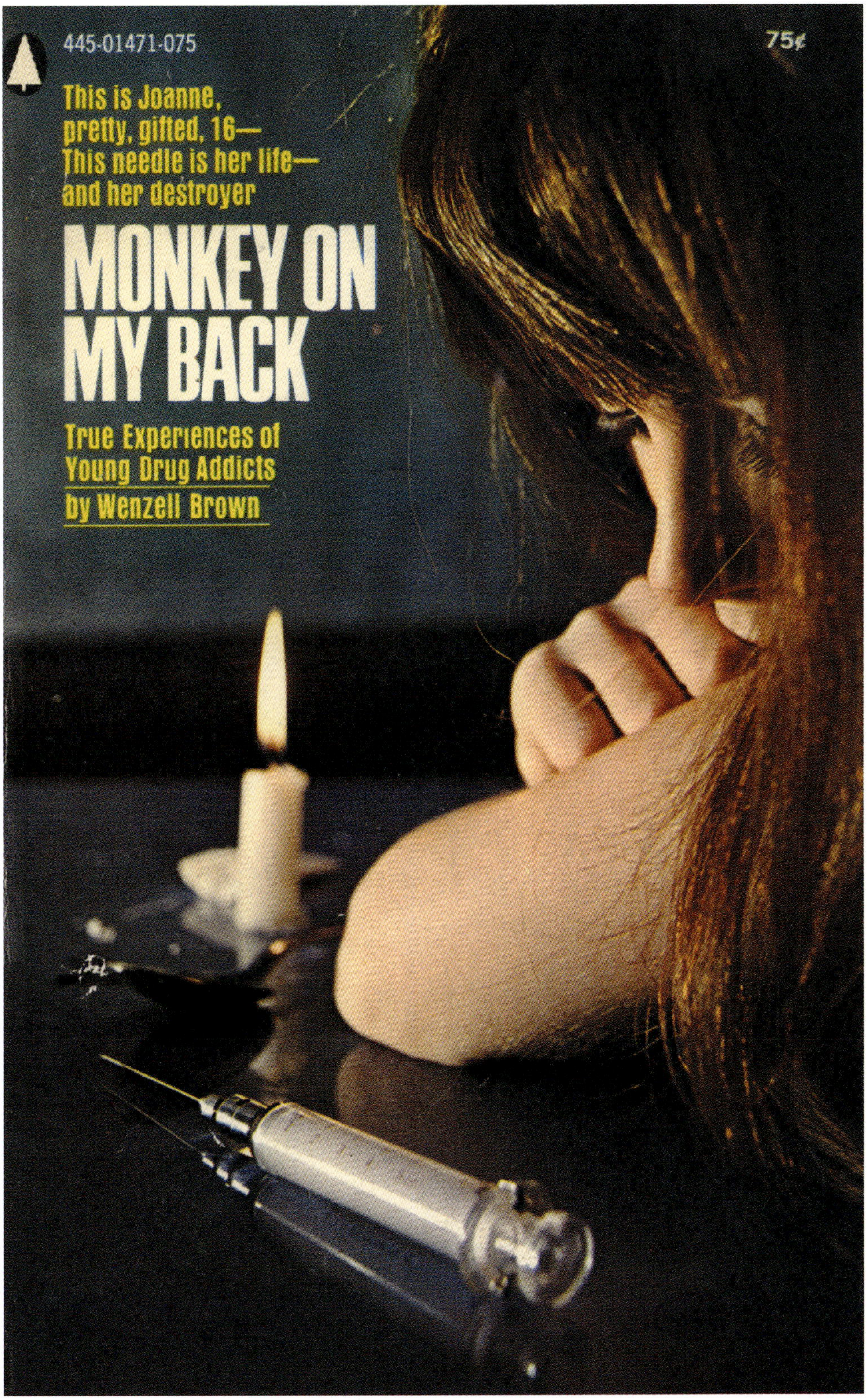

Wenzell Brown • ***Monkey on My Back*** • NEW YORK: POPULAR LIBRARY 4455-01471-075
N.D. (C. 1966) • REPRINT OF 1954 EDITION

Opposite page: Back cover of *Monkey on My Back* • 1954

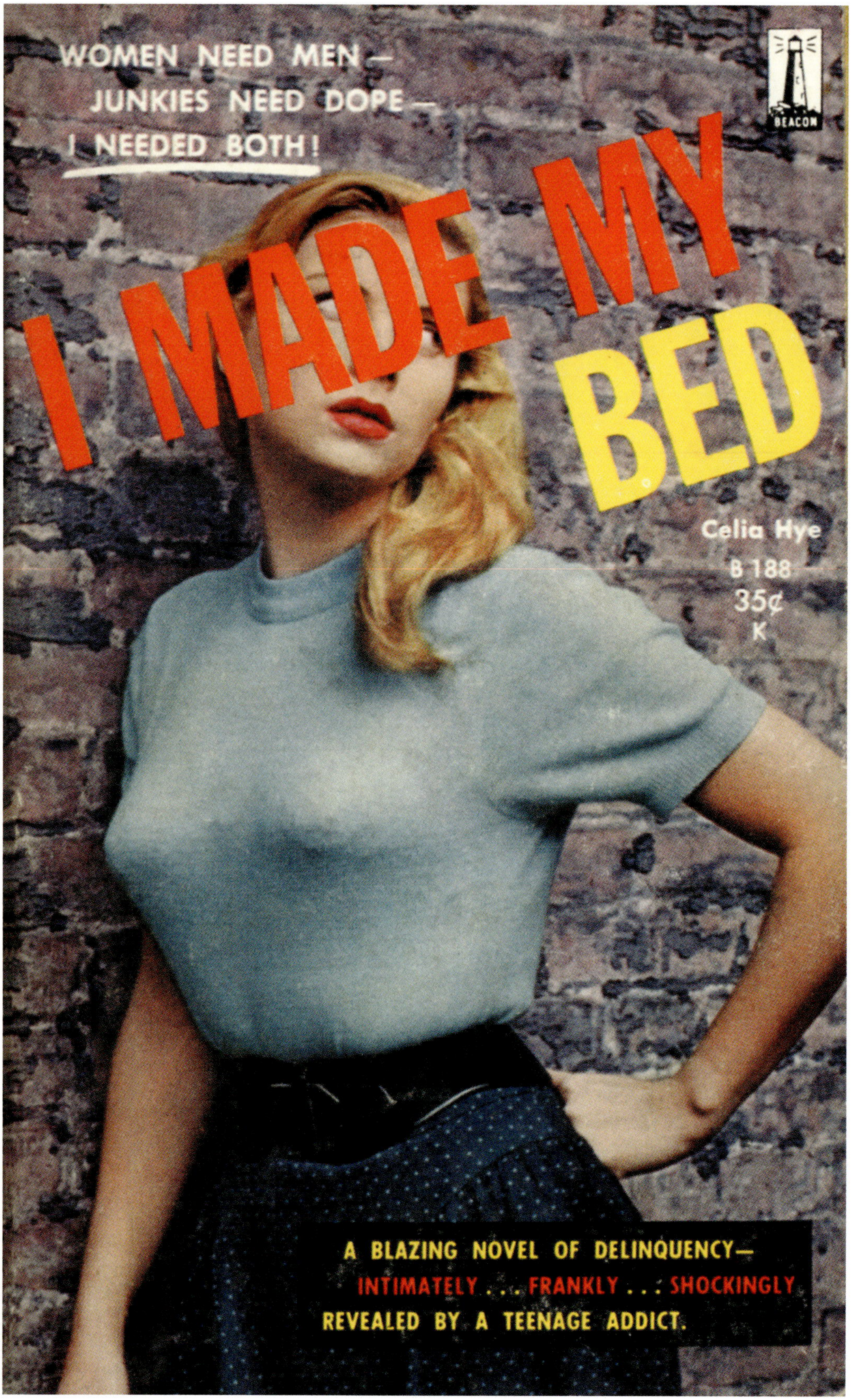
WOMEN NEED MEN—
JUNKIES NEED DOPE—
I NEEDED BOTH!
BEACON
I MADE MY BED
Celia Hye
B 188
35¢
K
A BLAZING NOVEL OF DELINQUENCY—
INTIMATELY . . . FRANKLY . . . SHOCKINGLY
REVEALED BY A TEENAGE ADDICT.

"Here is the tragic story of a degraded girl, every word of it shocking — every word of it is true! Fresh out of high-school, Celia Hye fell in love with Bernie, the baby-faced leader of a pillaging street gang. He taught her how to steal, and worse, how to take narcotics. For awhile, she was happy, getting her kicks where she could find them, living in her private world of drug-mad dreams."

Celia Hye • ***I Made My Bed***
BEACON 188 • 1958 • PBO

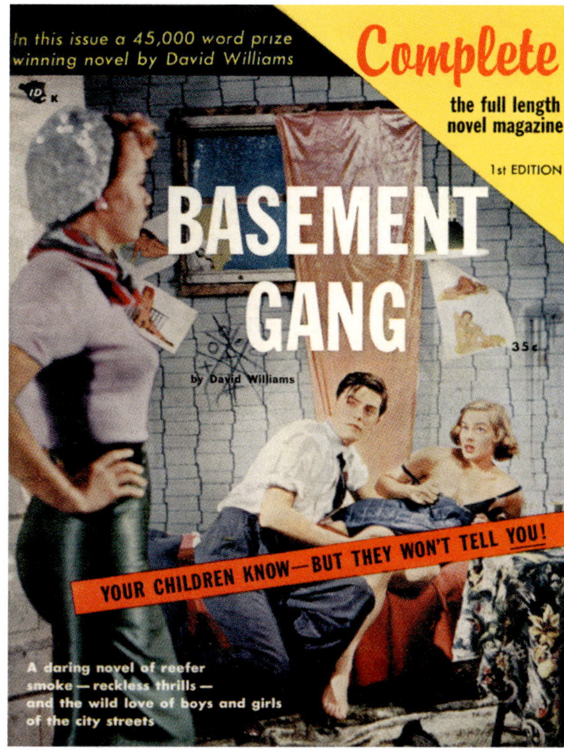

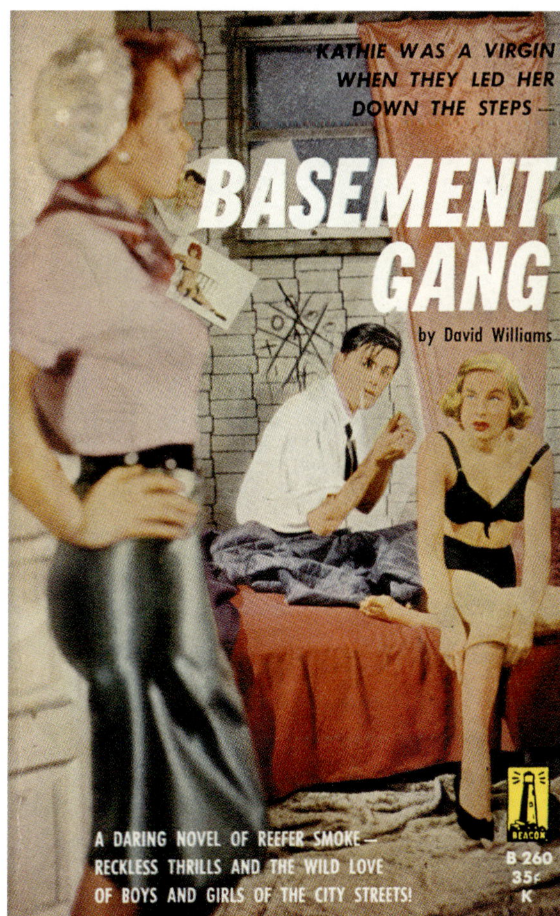

Katie "had heard about reefers and she had heard that many youths in the neighborhood smoked them and she was filled with horror of what she heard."

David Williams [Arnold Stroog]
Basement Gang • INTIMATE #32 • 1953
PBO DIGEST

David Williams [Arnold Stroog]
Basement Gang • BEACON 260 • 1959
REPRINT OF INTIMATE #32

"You're Valerie Jordan and you've just had your first puff of a reefer. You're not scared. Why should you be? Nobody can kid you because you know marijuana is not habit-forming. So what's the big deal if a girl wants a kick?

"But there comes a day when a kick is not enough. You're feeling down, like you were underground, and you know you've got to have a jolt, a blast — heroin!

"The next step? A bigger jolt, a louder blast — to the tune of thirty dollars a day — and that's a lot of bread.

"It means picking up men — half a dozen a day — what does it matter? You're in paradise. Until the blast wears off and you've got to face reality again: you're hooked, chained, a teen-age dope addict."

Valerie Jordan (pseud.) • ***I Am A Teen-Age Dope Addict*** • MONARCH MB-526 • 1962 • PBO.

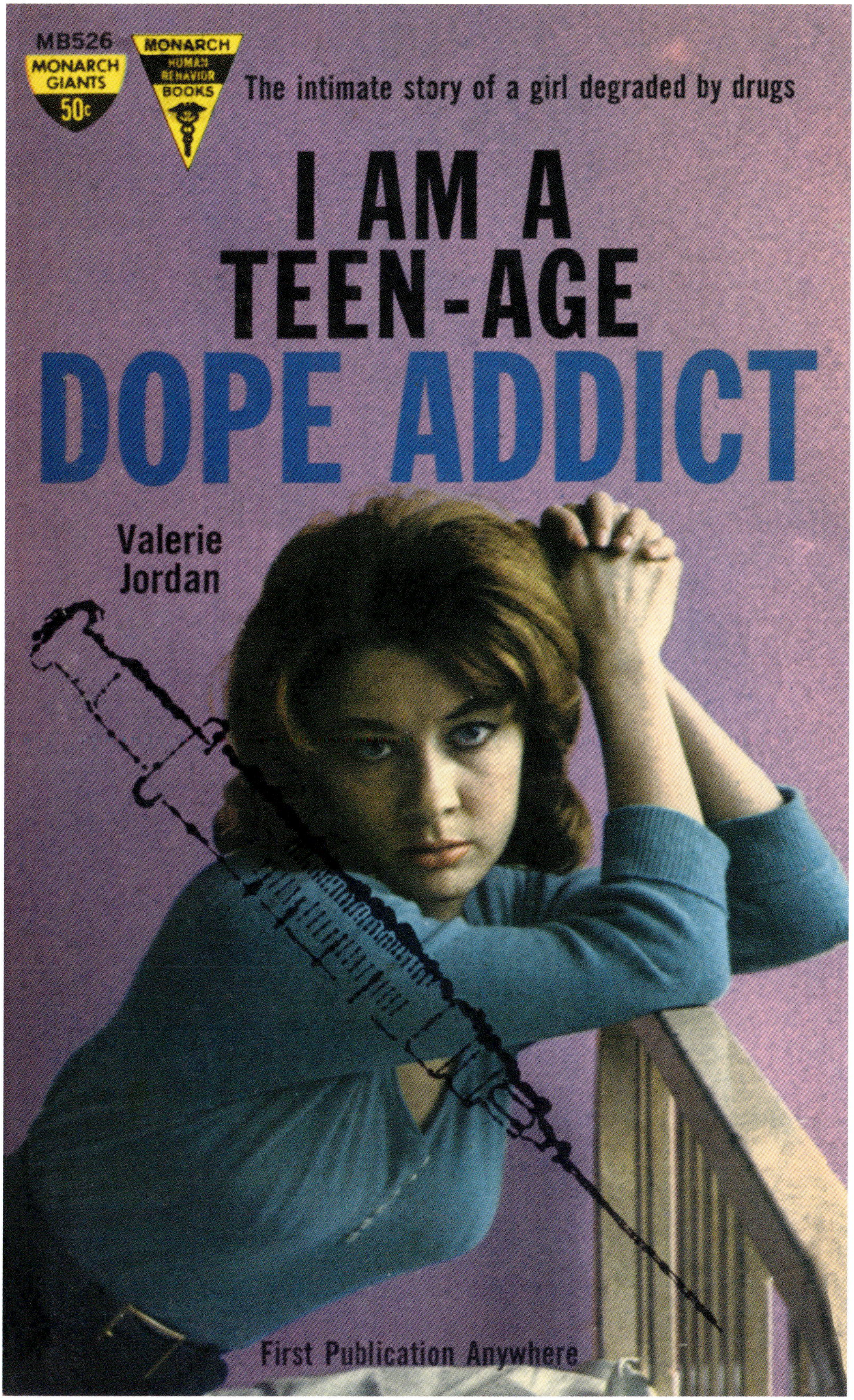
MB526
MONARCH GIANTS
50c
MONARCH HUMAN BEHAVIOR BOOKS
The intimate story of a girl degraded by drugs
I AM A
TEEN-AGE
DOPE ADDICT
Valerie
Jordan
First Publication Anywhere

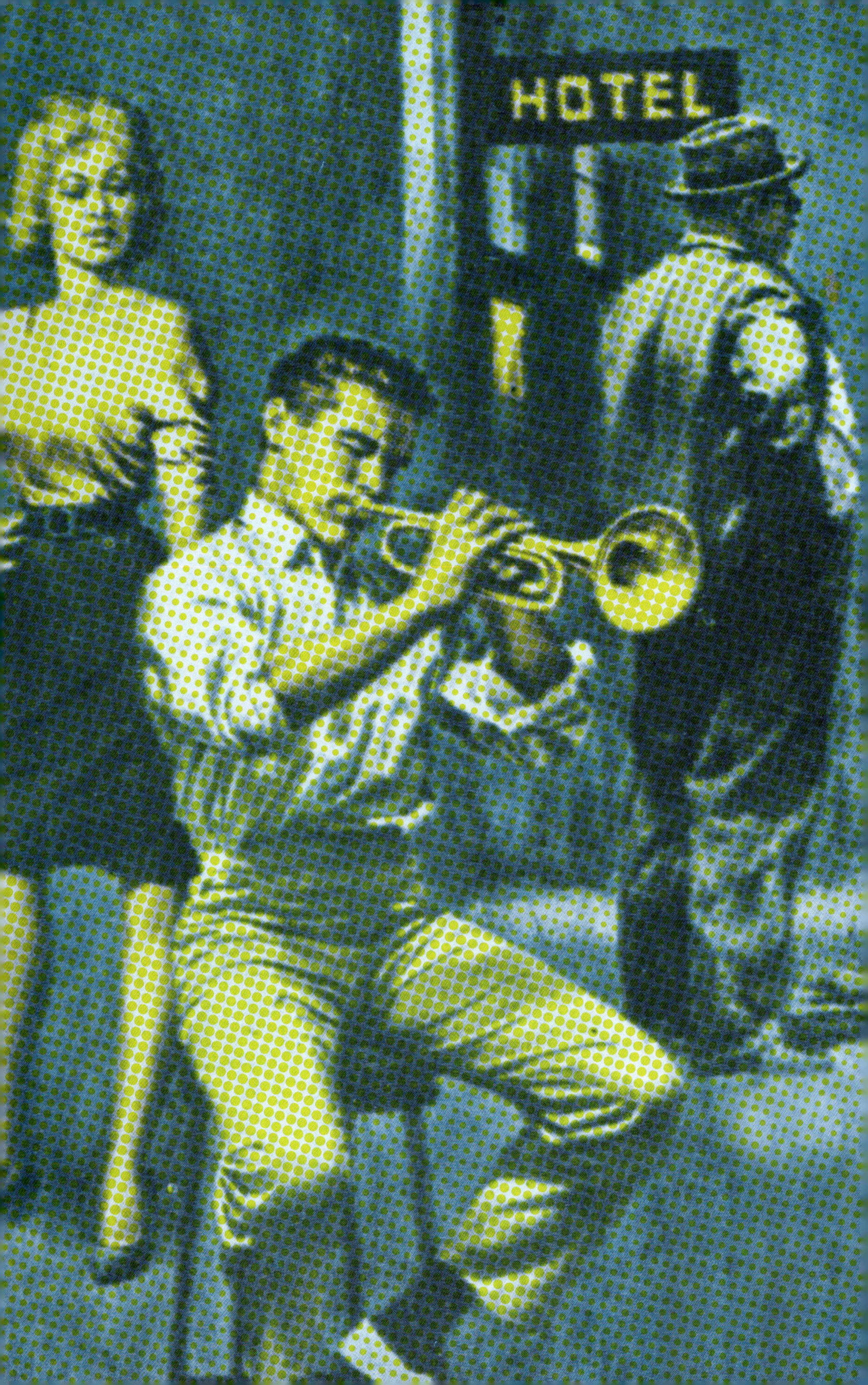
HOTEL

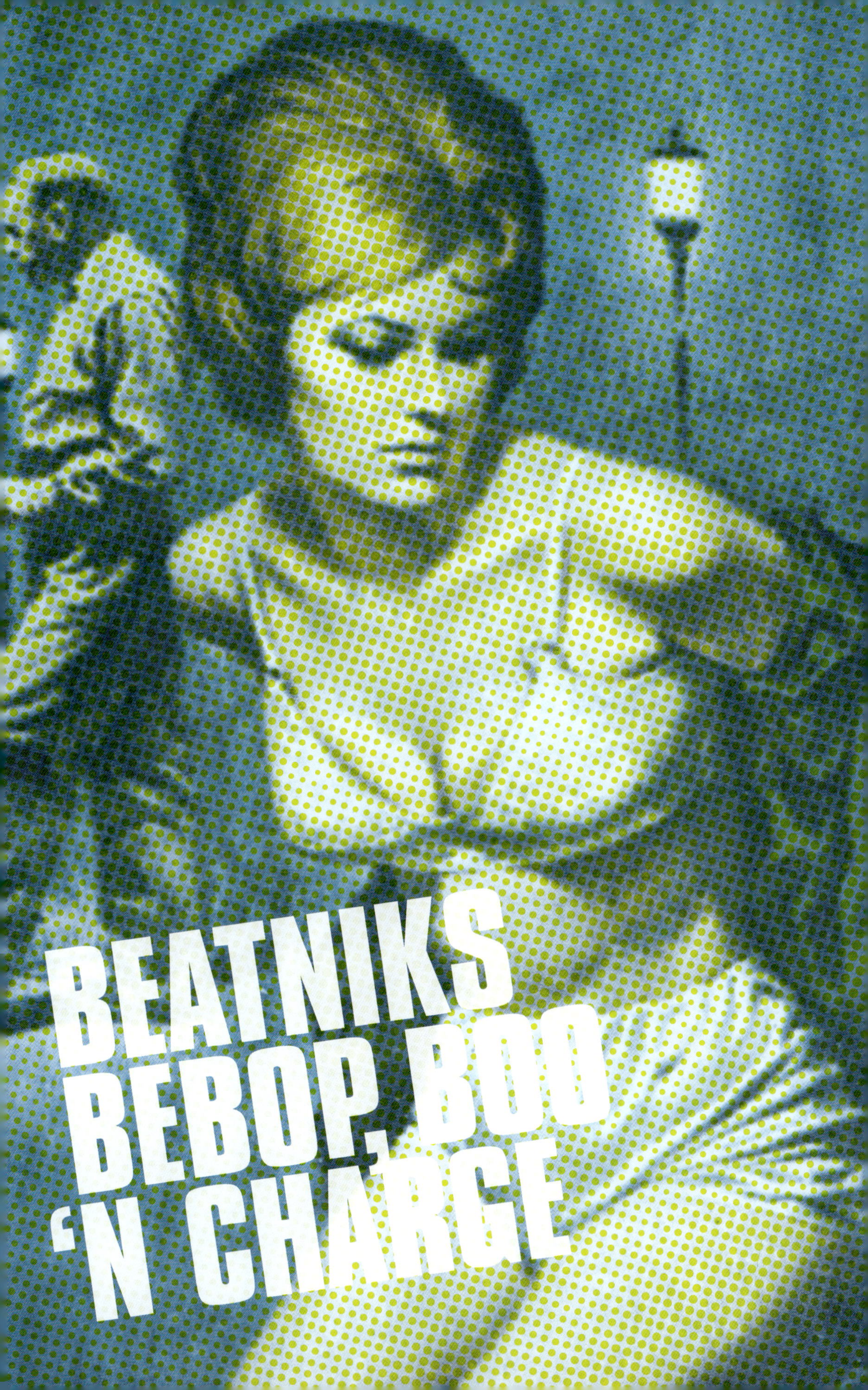
BEATNIKS
BEBOP, BOO
'N CHARGE

Co-founder of the Beats, who, with Kerouac, gave the movement its name, Holmes is now largely forgotten but was, aside from Burroughs, arguably the best writer of them all. His book *GO!* (1952) was the first novel from the group to be published; alas, not in paperback until 1980. His short story "Tea For Two," published in the proto-Beat journal *Neurotica* (Vol. I No. 2, 1948), is an early Beat gem about a young couple meeting in a jazz club and their getting-to-know-you conversation in ultracool hipster argot while sharing joints. *The Horn* is one of the best jazz-'n-drugs books written.

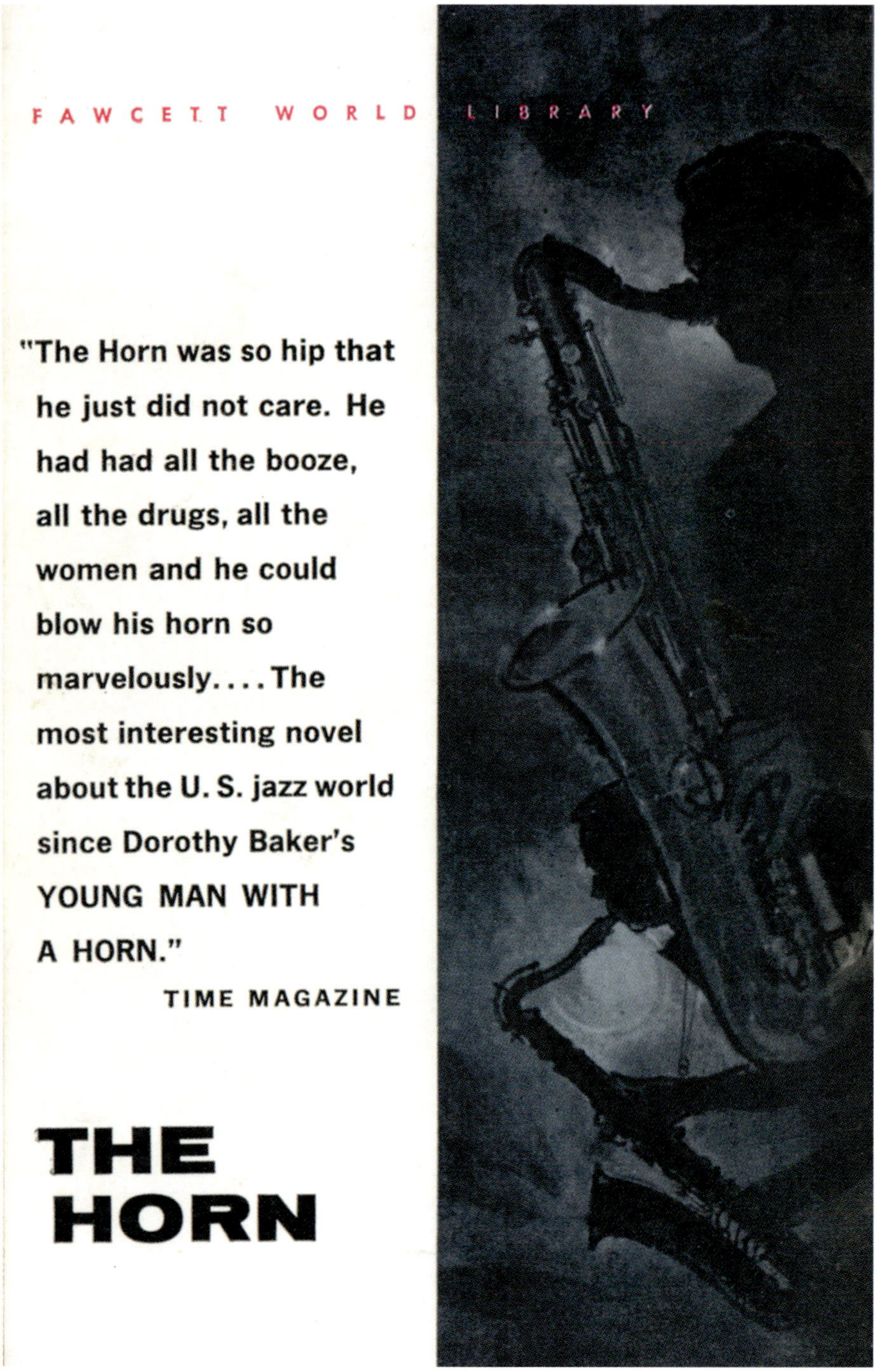

John Clennon Holmes (1926-1988) • ***The Horn*** • CREST S-307 • 1959 • COVER BY MITCHELL HOOKS • REPRINT

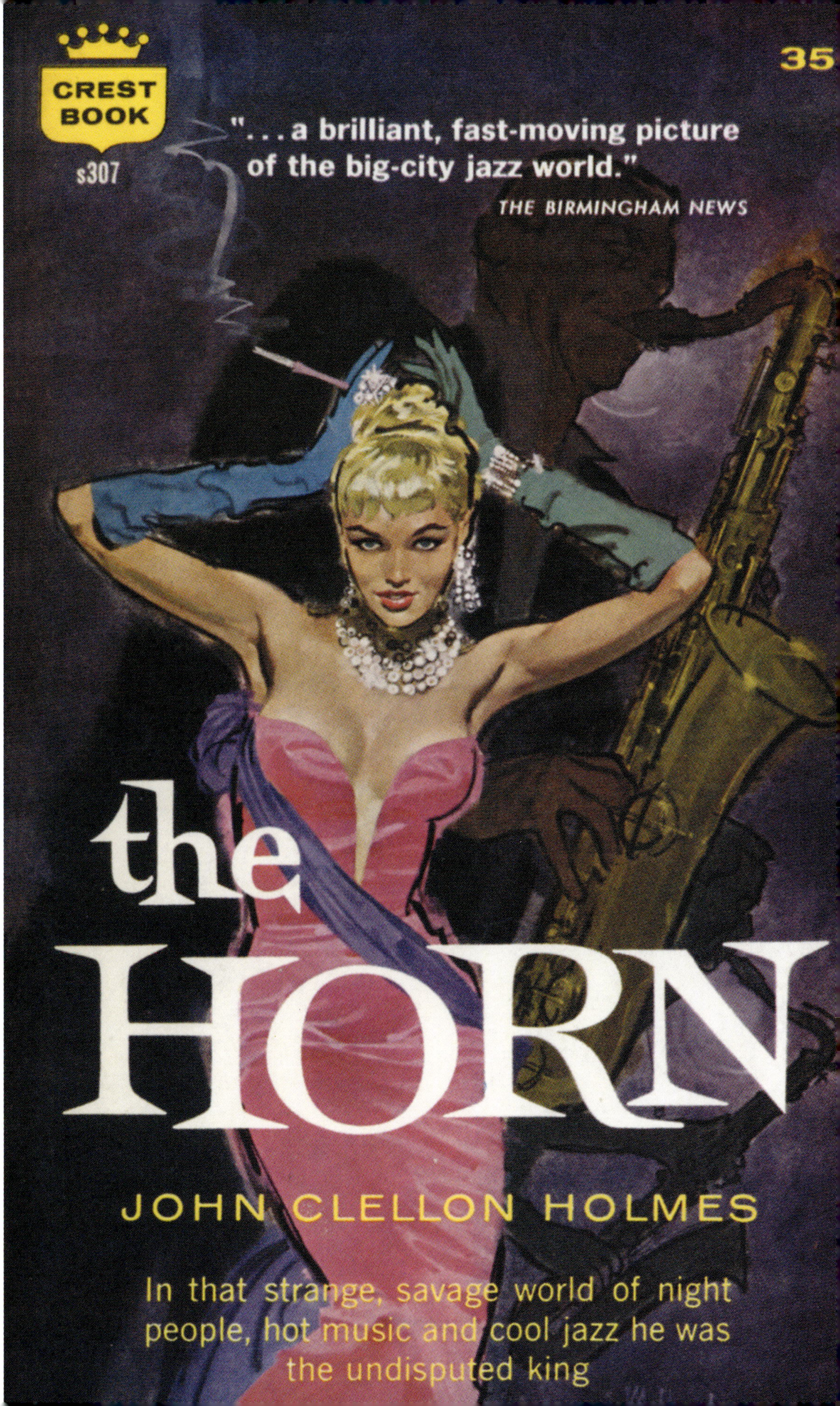
CREST BOOK
s307
35
". . . a brilliant, fast-moving picture of the big-city jazz world."
THE BIRMINGHAM NEWS
the HORN
JOHN CLELLON HOLMES
In that strange, savage world of night people, hot music and cool jazz he was the undisputed king

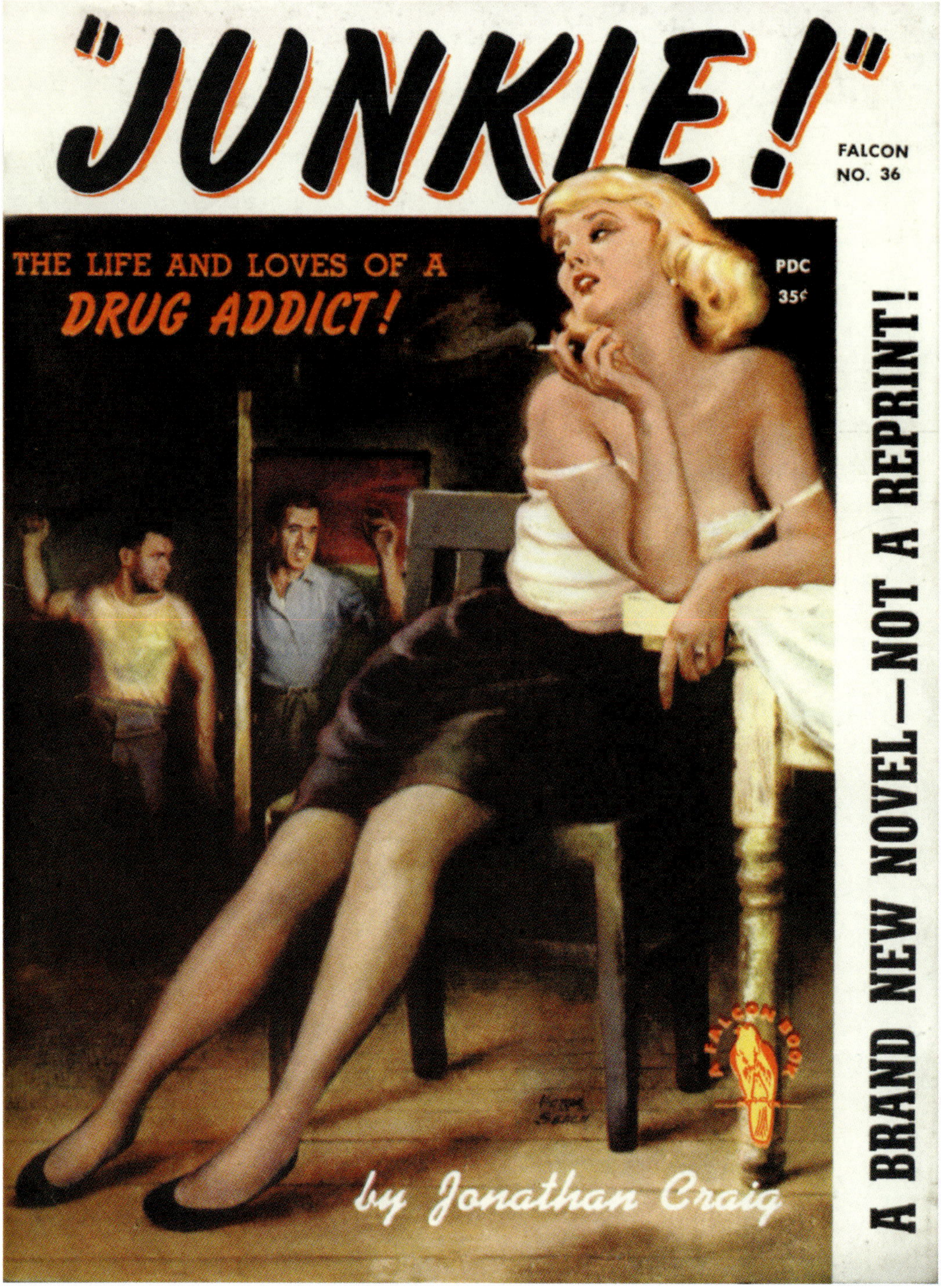

Jonathan Craig (Frank E. Smith) • ***Junkie*** • FALCON BOOKS 36 • 1952 • PBO

Jonathan Craig (Frank E. Smith) • ***Frenzy*** • NEW YORK: LANCER 70-013 • 1962
REPRINT OF *JUNKIE* • FALCON BOOKS • 1952

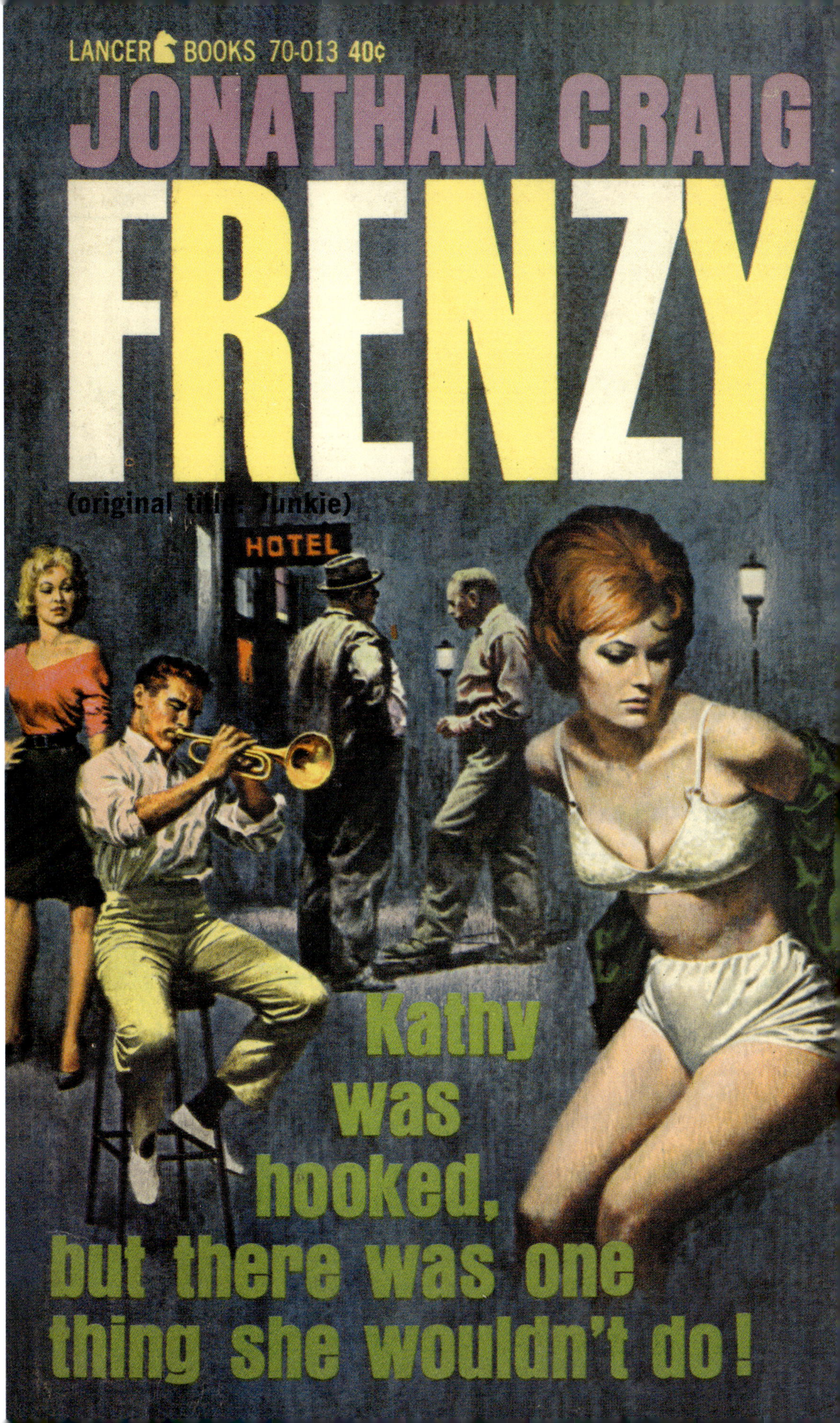
LANCER BOOKS 70-013 40¢
JONATHAN CRAIG
FRENZY
(original title: Junkie)
HOTEL
Kathy was hooked, but there was one thing she wouldn't do!

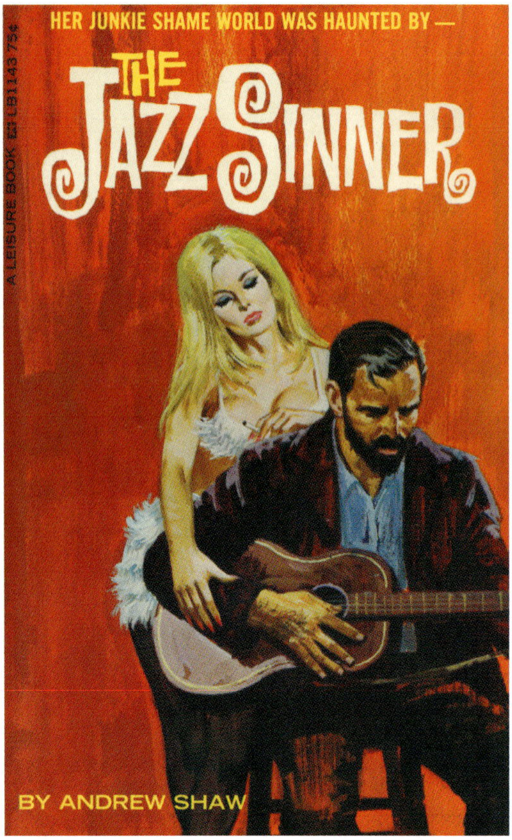

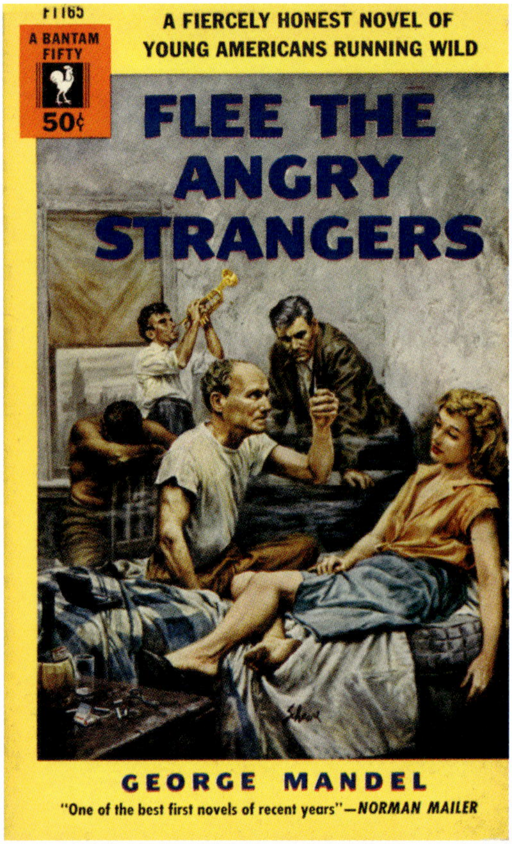

Andrew Shaw (pseud.) • ***The Jazz Sinner***
LEISURE BOOKS LB1143 • 1966 • COVER BY ROBERT BONFILS • PBO

George Mandel • ***Flee the Angry Strangers***
BANTAM 1165 • 1953 • COVER BY HARRY SCHAARE REPRINT

Evan Hunter [b. Salvador Lombino]
Quartet in "H" • CARDINAL C236 • 1956
COVER BY TOM DUNN • REPRINT OF SECOND ENDING

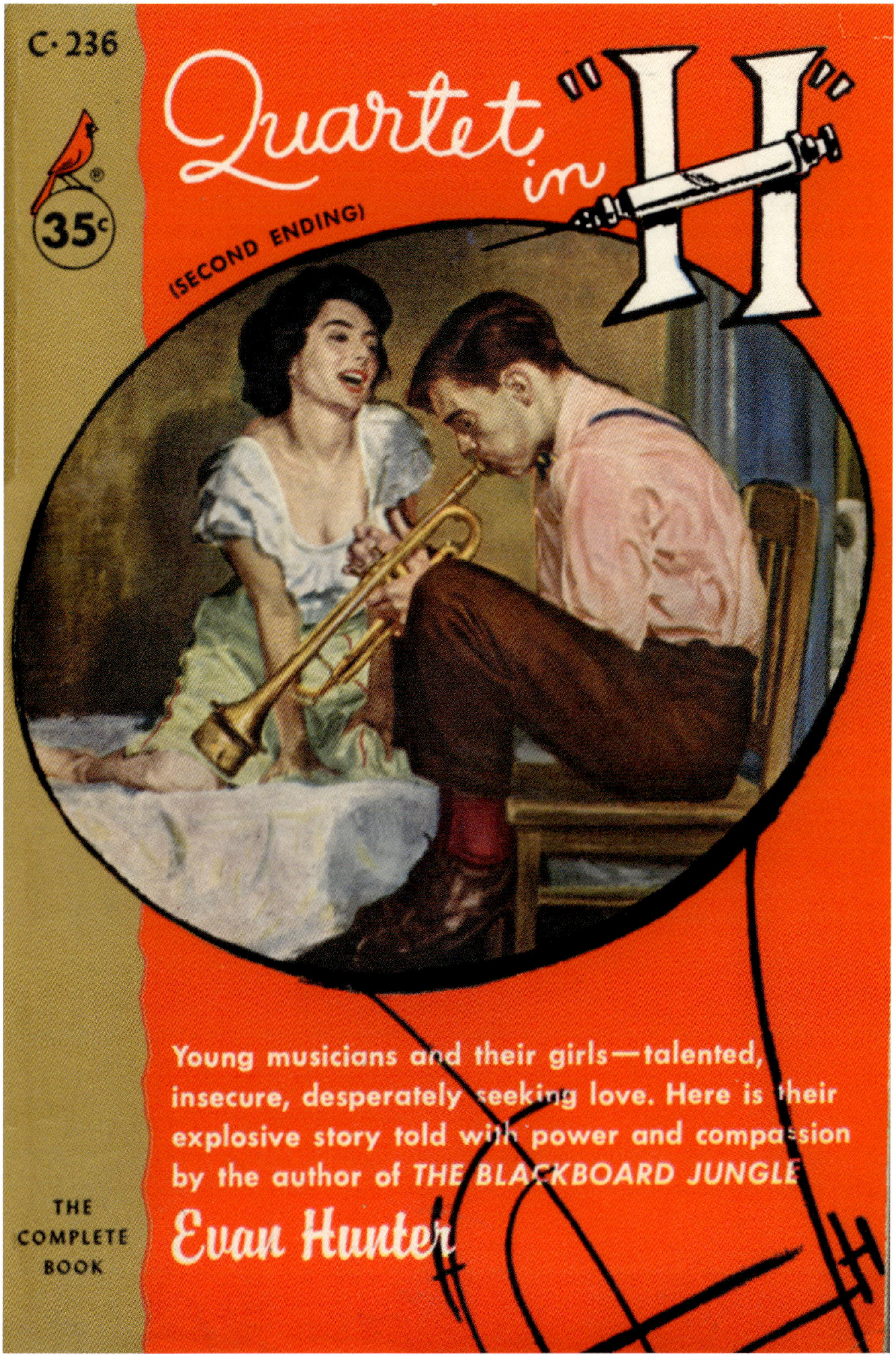

"Andy Silvers played trumpet in a small band. He was more than good — he was a genius...But Andy started looking for kicks. It was small time stuff at first — just benzadrine...but soon Andy went on to marijuana, and then to the killer drug — HEROIN!"

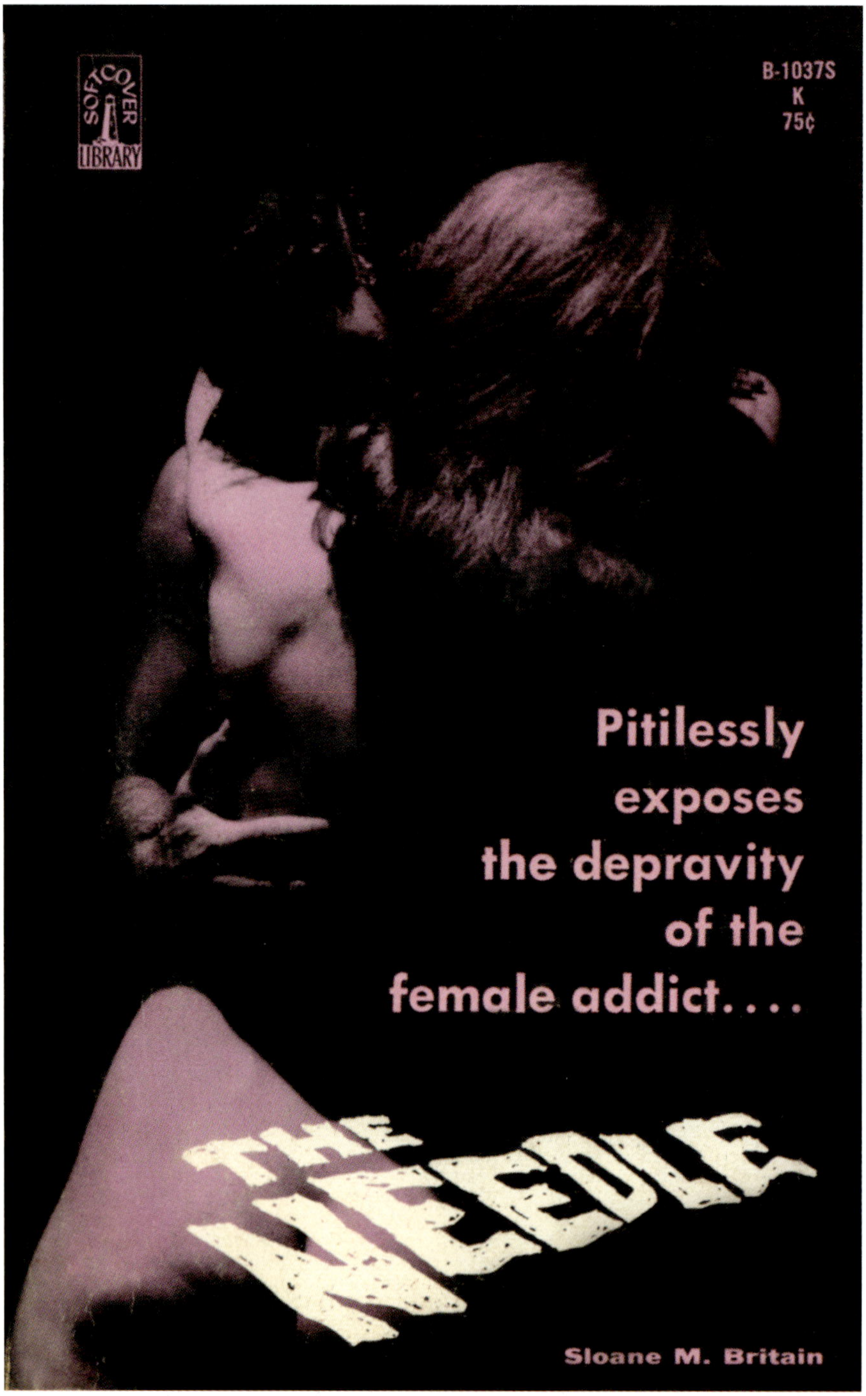

"One look at Gina and you knew she was a nice girl — nice on top, nice on bottom, even nicer in between. Furthermore, she had nice ideas, nice morals, and a nice head on her beautiful shoulders. But a beatnik named Bob slipped her a charge of heroin one night. After that, Gina was not so nice... First came the orgies of dope and dizzying lust. Then the long transports of shameless ecstasy in the grip of the drug. And finally, selling that nice body of hers to anybody for any purpose."

Sloane M. Britain • ***The Needle*** • BEACON 237 • 1959 • PBO
REPRINT OF UNI BOOK 19 • ALSO REPRINTED IN 1954 AS STALLION BOOKS #204

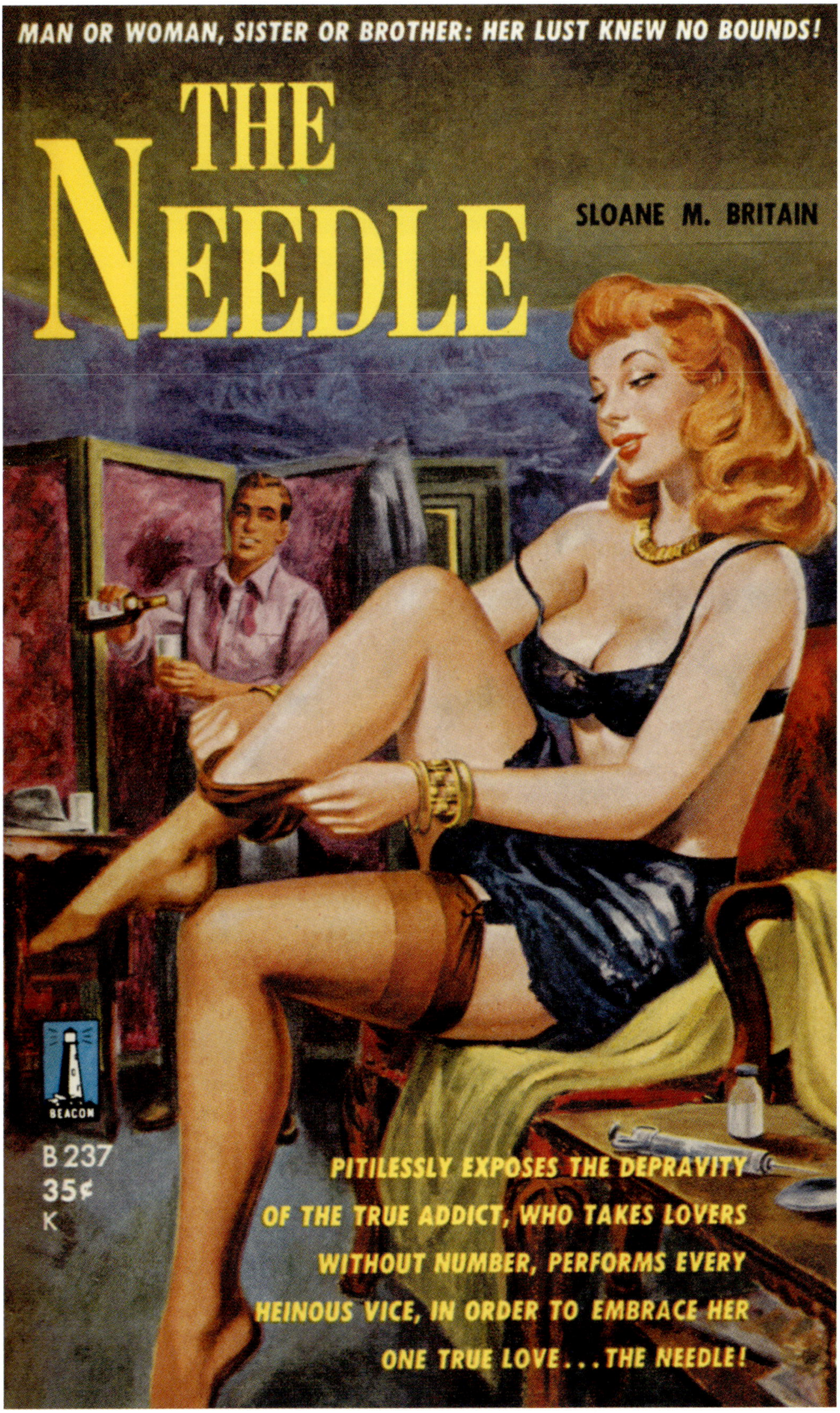
MAN OR WOMAN, SISTER OR BROTHER: HER LUST KNEW NO BOUNDS!
THE NEEDLE
SLOANE M. BRITAIN
BEACON
B 237
35¢
K
PITILESSLY EXPOSES THE DEPRAVITY OF THE TRUE ADDICT, WHO TAKES LOVERS WITHOUT NUMBER, PERFORMS EVERY HEINOUS VICE, IN ORDER TO EMBRACE HER ONE TRUE LOVE... THE NEEDLE!

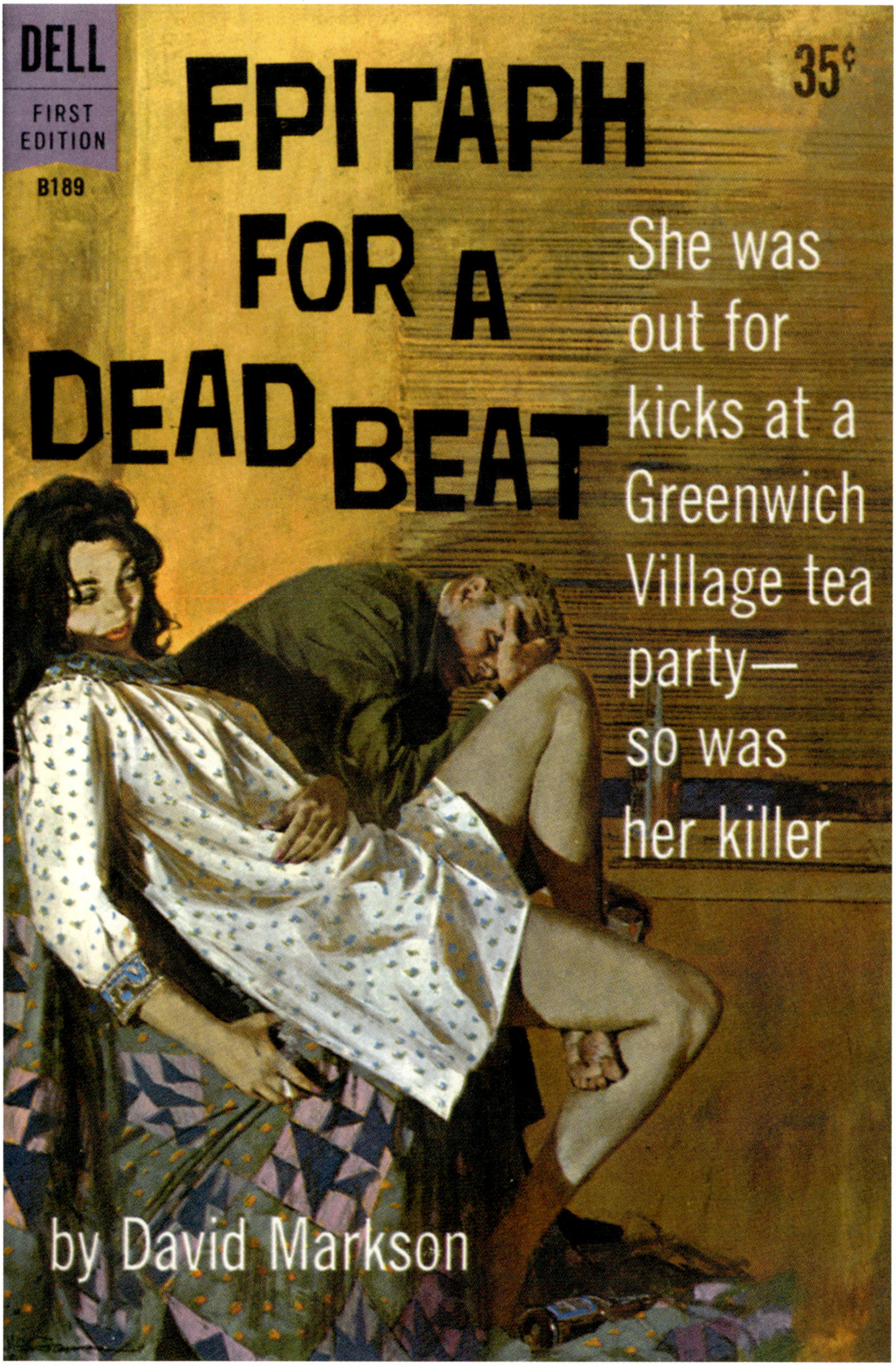

David Markson • ***Epitaph for a Deadbeat*** • DELL FIRST EDITIONS B189 • 1961 • COVER BY ROBERT MAGUIRE • PBO

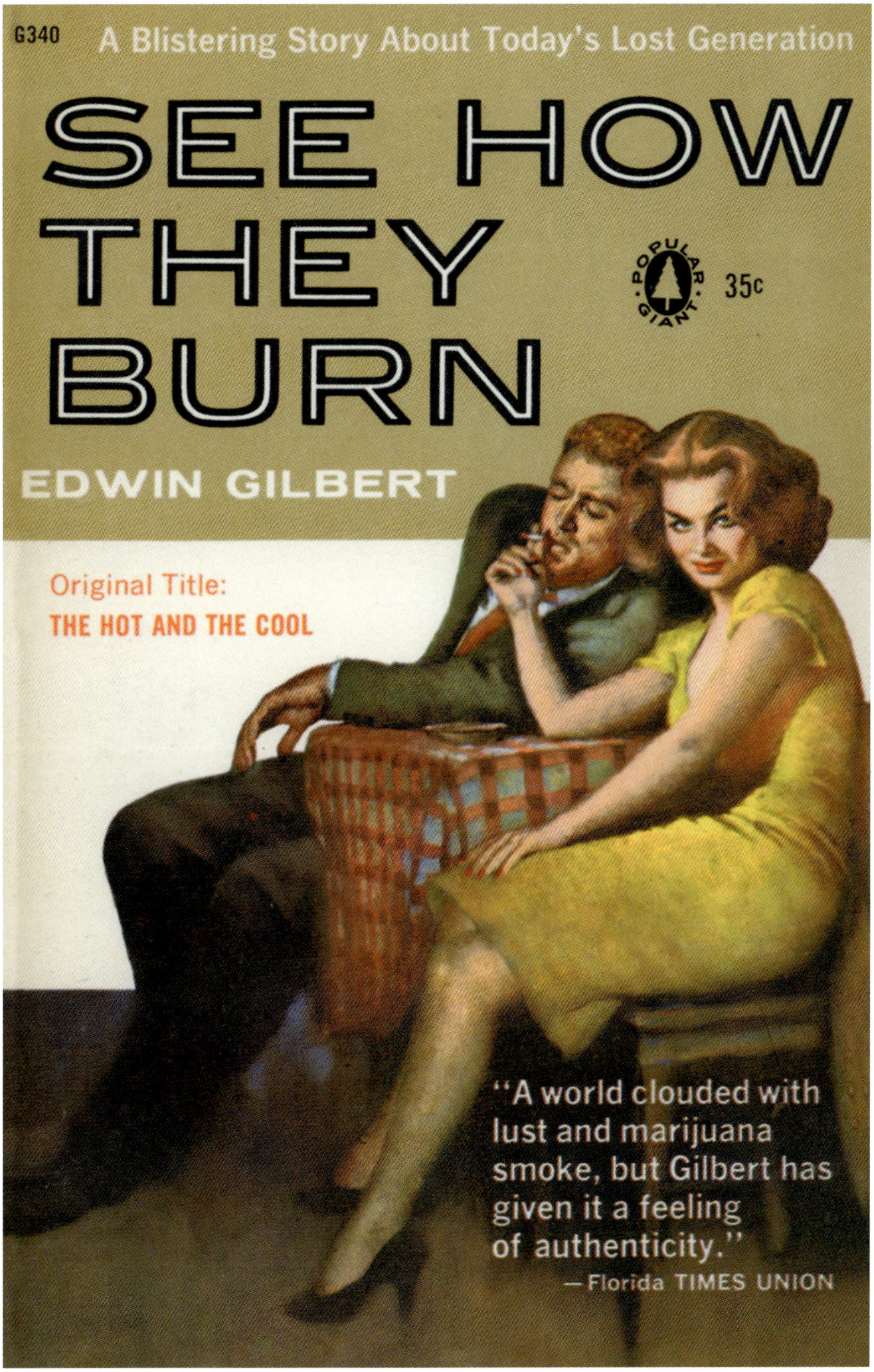

Edwin Gilbert • ***See How They Burn*** • POPULAR LIBRARY G340 • 1959 • REPRINT

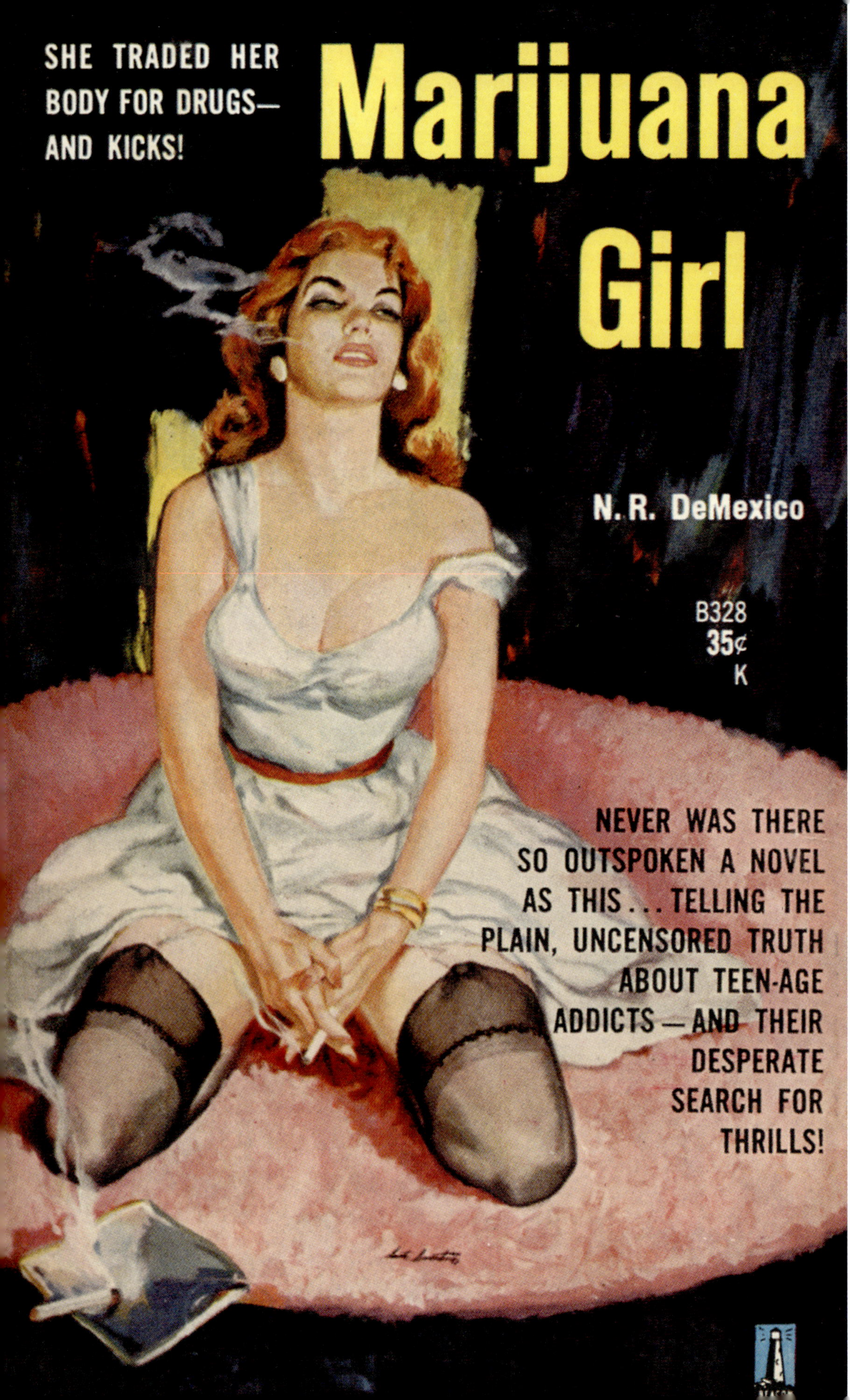
SHE TRADED HER BODY FOR DRUGS— AND KICKS!
Marijuana Girl
N.R. DeMexico
B328
35¢
K
NEVER WAS THERE SO OUTSPOKEN A NOVEL AS THIS . . . TELLING THE PLAIN, UNCENSORED TRUTH ABOUT TEEN-AGE ADDICTS — AND THEIR DESPERATE SEARCH FOR THRILLS!

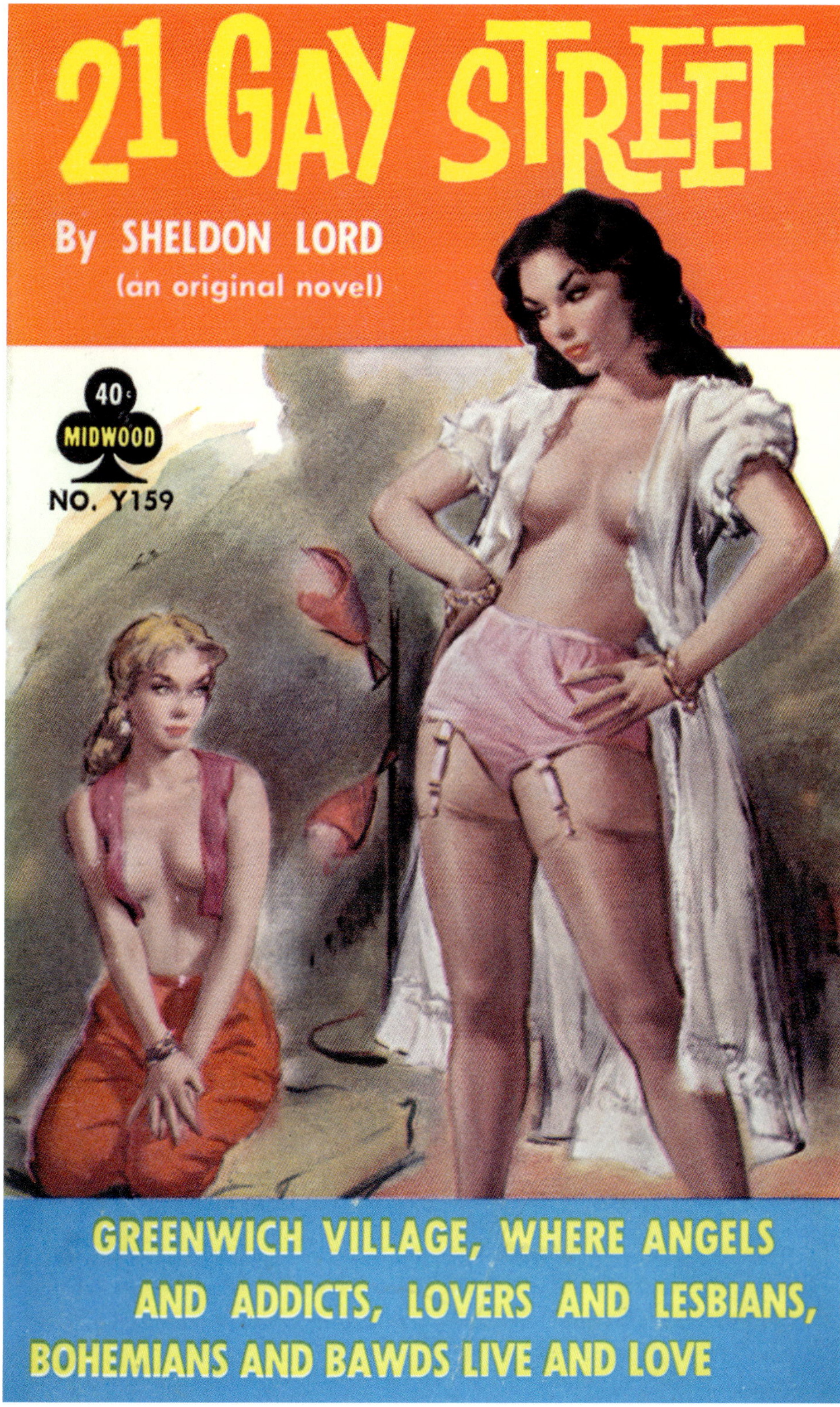

Sheldon Lord [Lawrence Bloch] • ***21 Gay Street*** • MIDWOOD Y-159 • 1962 • COVER BY PAUL RADER • PBO

N.R. DeMexico • ***Marijuana Girl*** • BEACON 328 • 1960 • COVER BY AL ROSSI • REPRINT OF UNI BOOK 19
ALSO REPRINTED IN 1954 AS STALLION BOOKS #204

Soon after being introduced to drugs by a jazz-scene boyfriend, 21-year-old Sheila's "health was not what it ought to be, and her money was running low, too. Cocaine cost heavily. She was into debt to a dozen people. Nothing seemed to matter, though, as long as she got her kicks. She finally took the cocaine in her arm. She could stay high on it for hours. When she switched over to heroin, she hardly noticed the transition.

"...The jolt was really just what she was looking for. Sheila began to feel sorry for people who didn't know the way every worry, every fear, every anxiety disappeared."

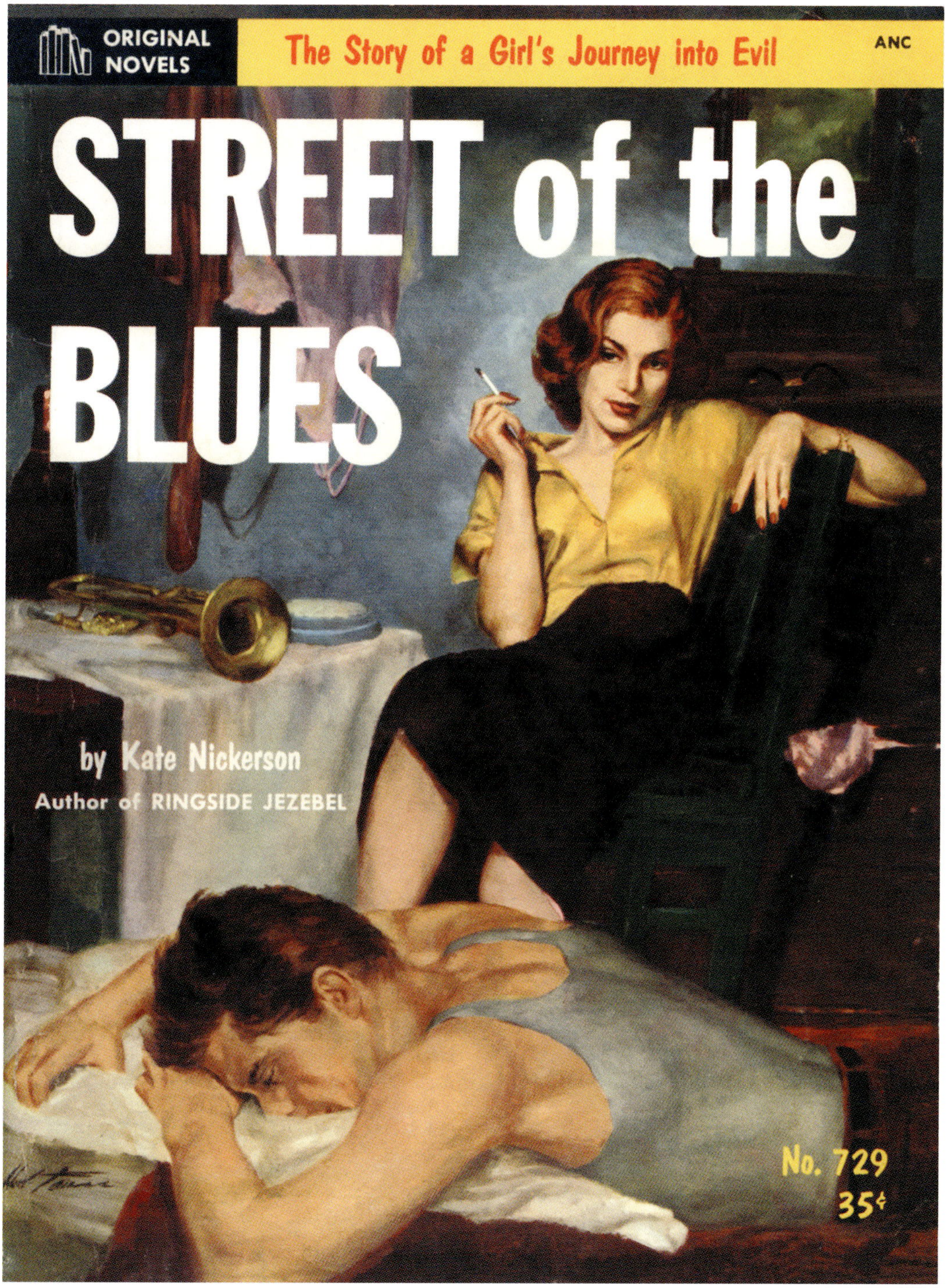

Kate Nickerson • ***Street of the Blues*** • ORIGINAL NOVEL 729 • 1952 • COVER BY HERB TAUSS • PBO DIGEST
REPRINTED BY MCFADDEN IN 1967

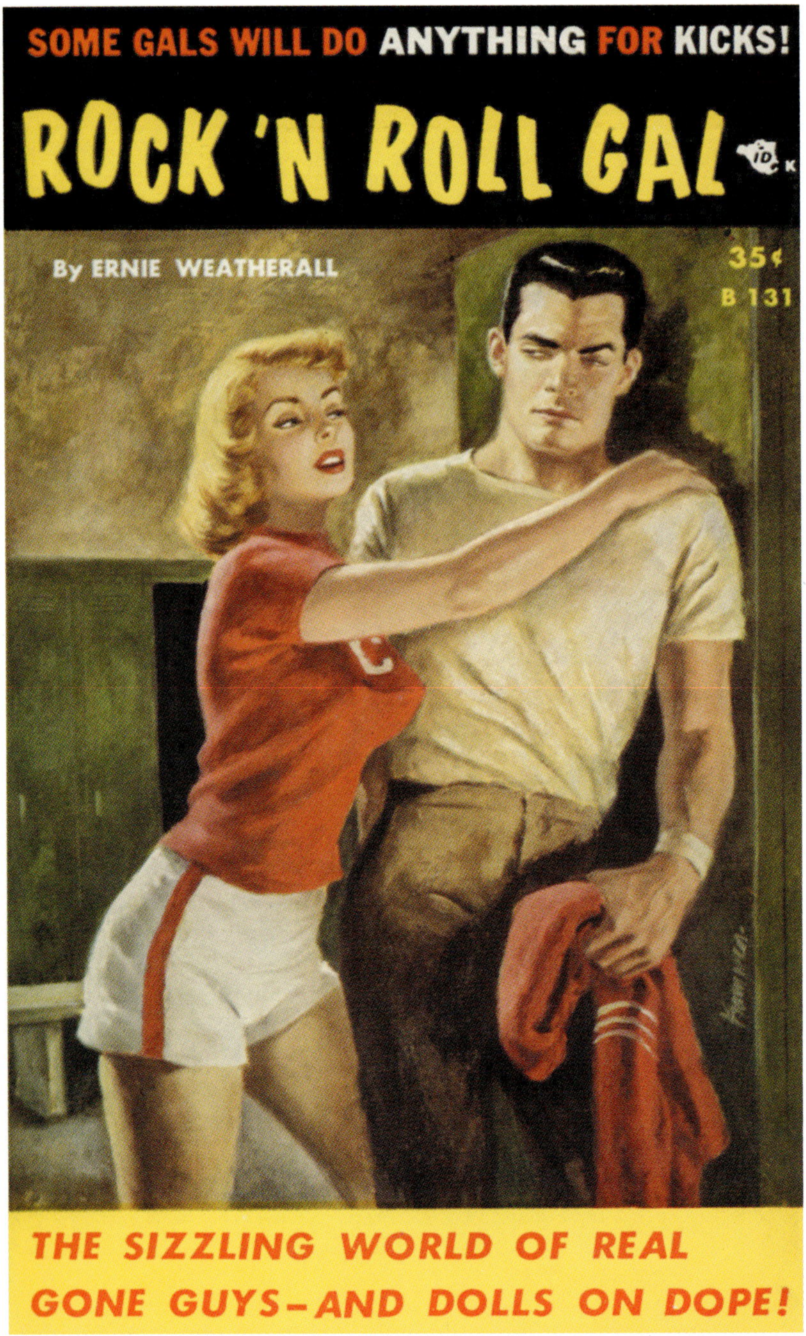

Alas, not an early sex, drugs and rock 'n roll novel but rather the story of a top bebop trumpet player, the drug scene, doped-up babes, and a jazz songstress who sells out to rock 'n roll and connives to get our hero to sell out, too. But he's a man of principle and high musical standards.

So he murders her. Then, consumed with remorse...

"I want a charge, Shorty. The white stuff.'

"He looked at me funny-like. 'Just take a skin-pop. You won't get hooked that way.'

"'On the main-line, Shorty."

"He looked at me again. 'Okay, baby. If you want to ride on horse, I'm your man..'"

Ernie Weatherall • ***Rock 'n Roll Gal*** • BEACON 131 • 1957 • COVER BY OWEN KAMPEN • PBO

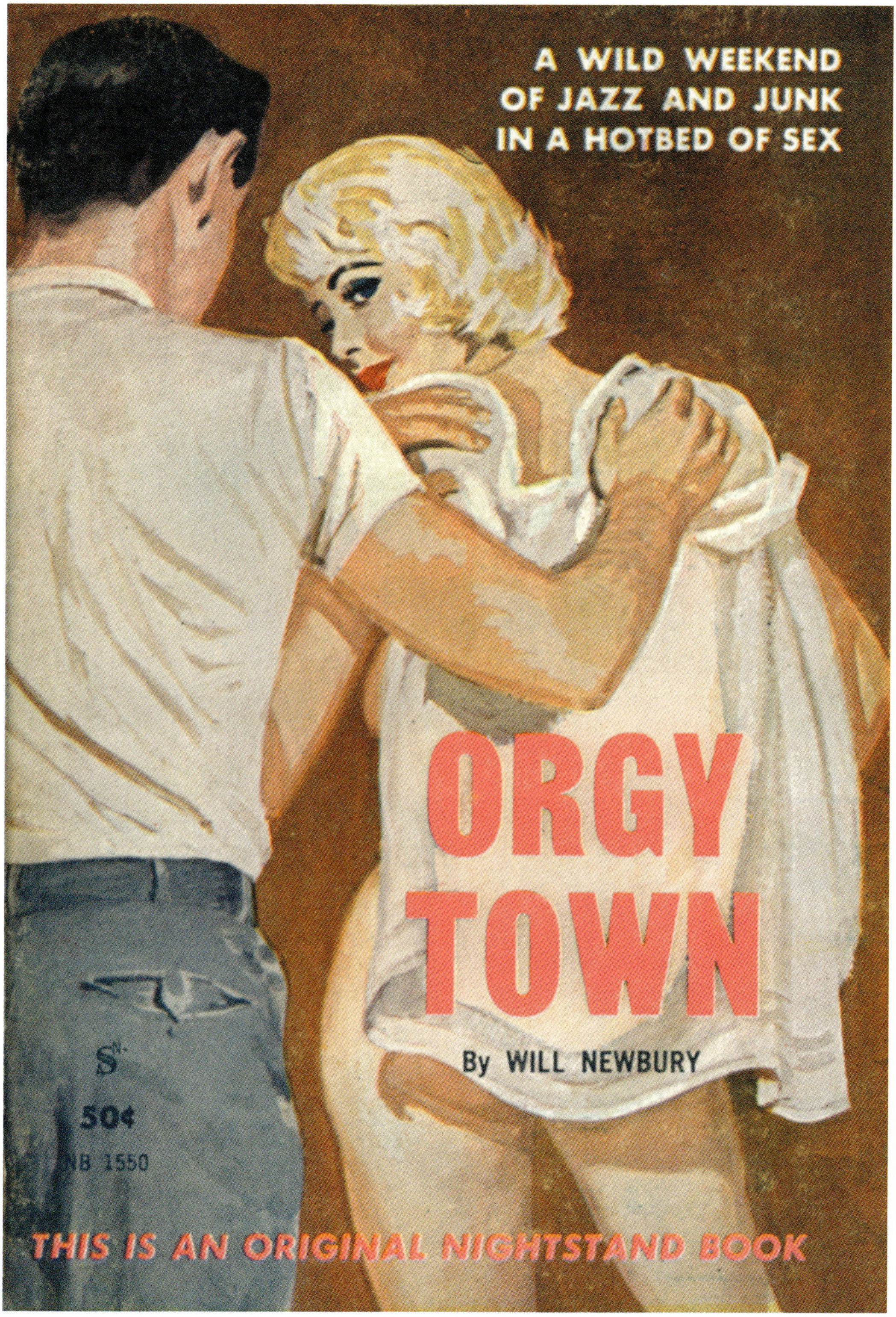

Will Newbury • ***Orgy Town*** • NIGHTSTAND NB1550 • 1961 • COVER BY HAROLD W. MCCAULEY • PBO

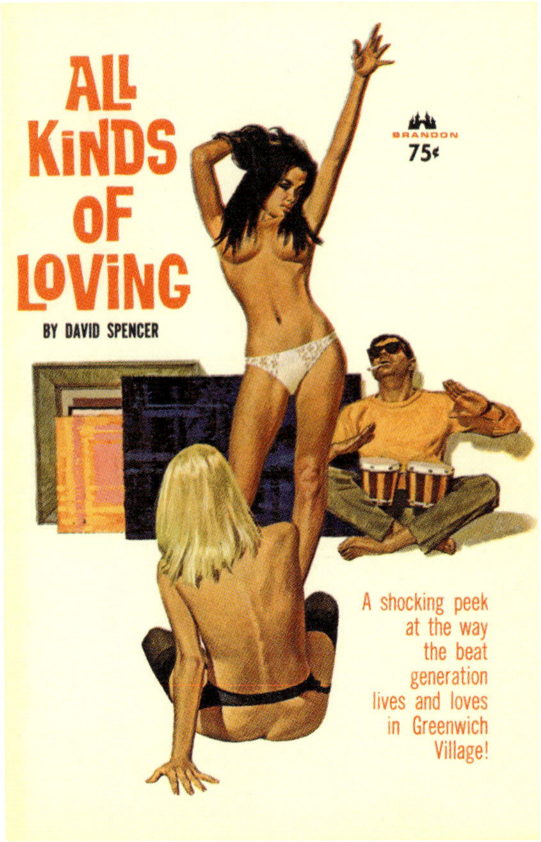

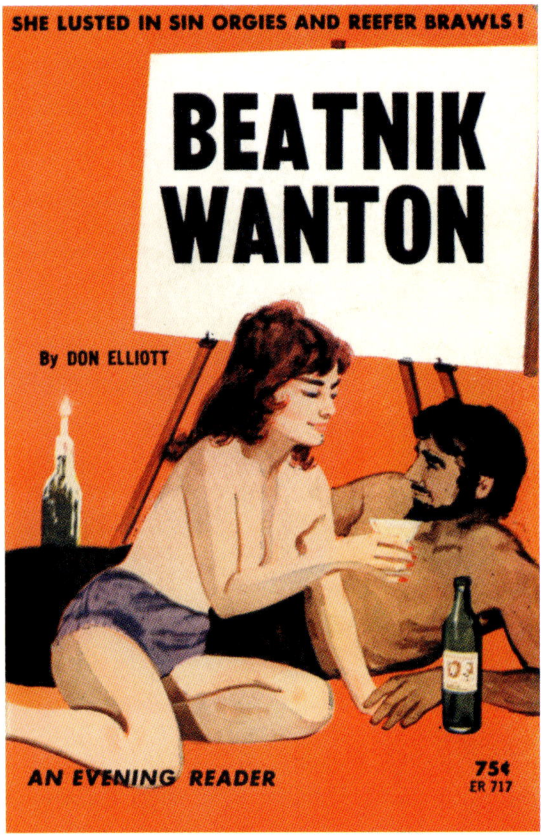

"When untamed young Beatniks get high, they're eager to try all kinds of loving!" (wrapper blurb).

David Spencer • ***All Kinds of Loving***
BRANDON HOUSE 722 • 1965 • PBO

Don Elliott [Robert Silverberg] • ***Beatnik Wanton***
EVENING READER ER 717 • 1964 • PBO

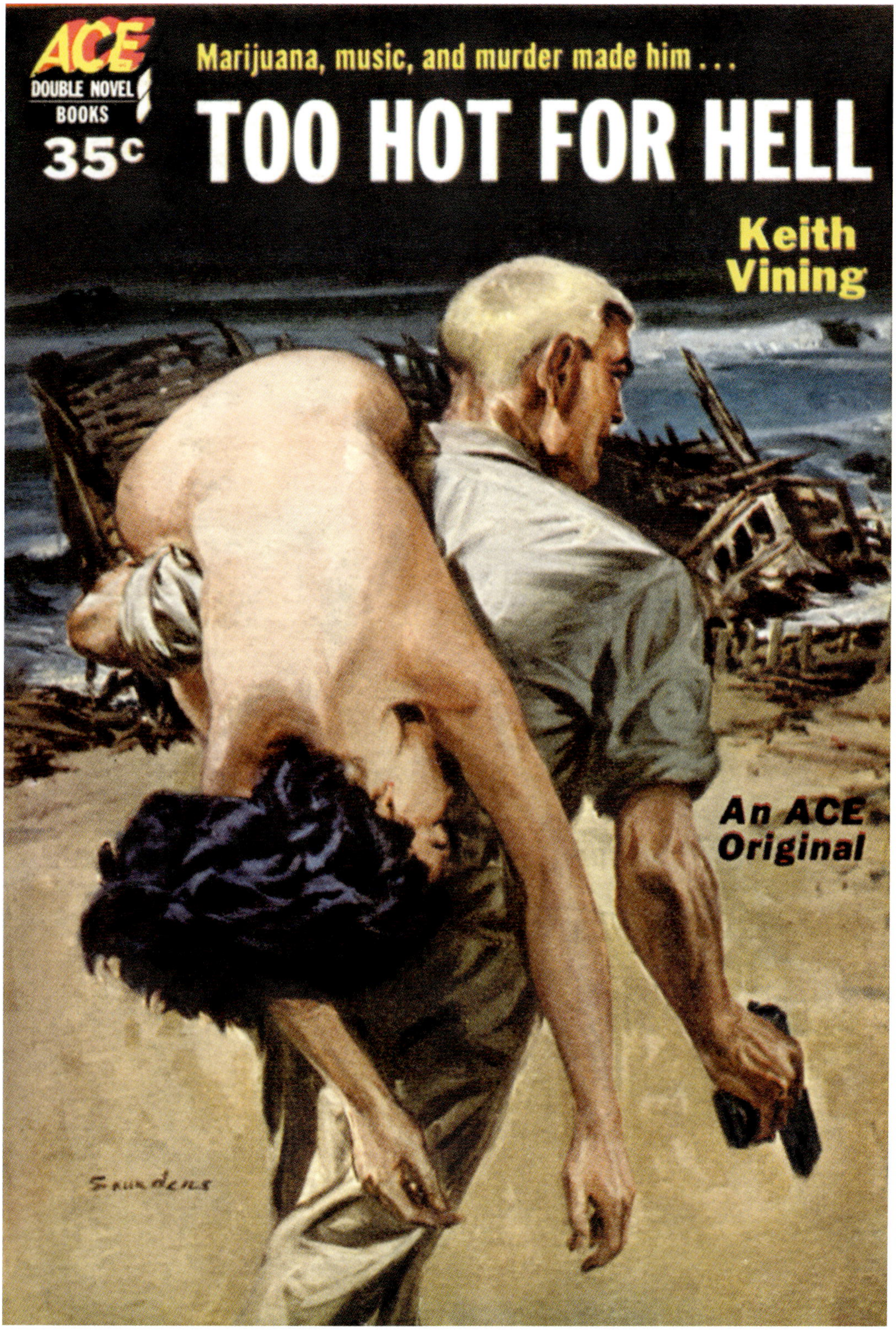

"High on a drugged cloud of lust, Jack Norman came down to earth with a hard shock when his marijuana-guided fingers closed with murderous fury around Gerry De Lange's deceiving throat."

Keith Vining • ***Too Hot for Hell*** • ACE D-1 • 1952 • COVER BY NORMAN SAUNDERS • PBO

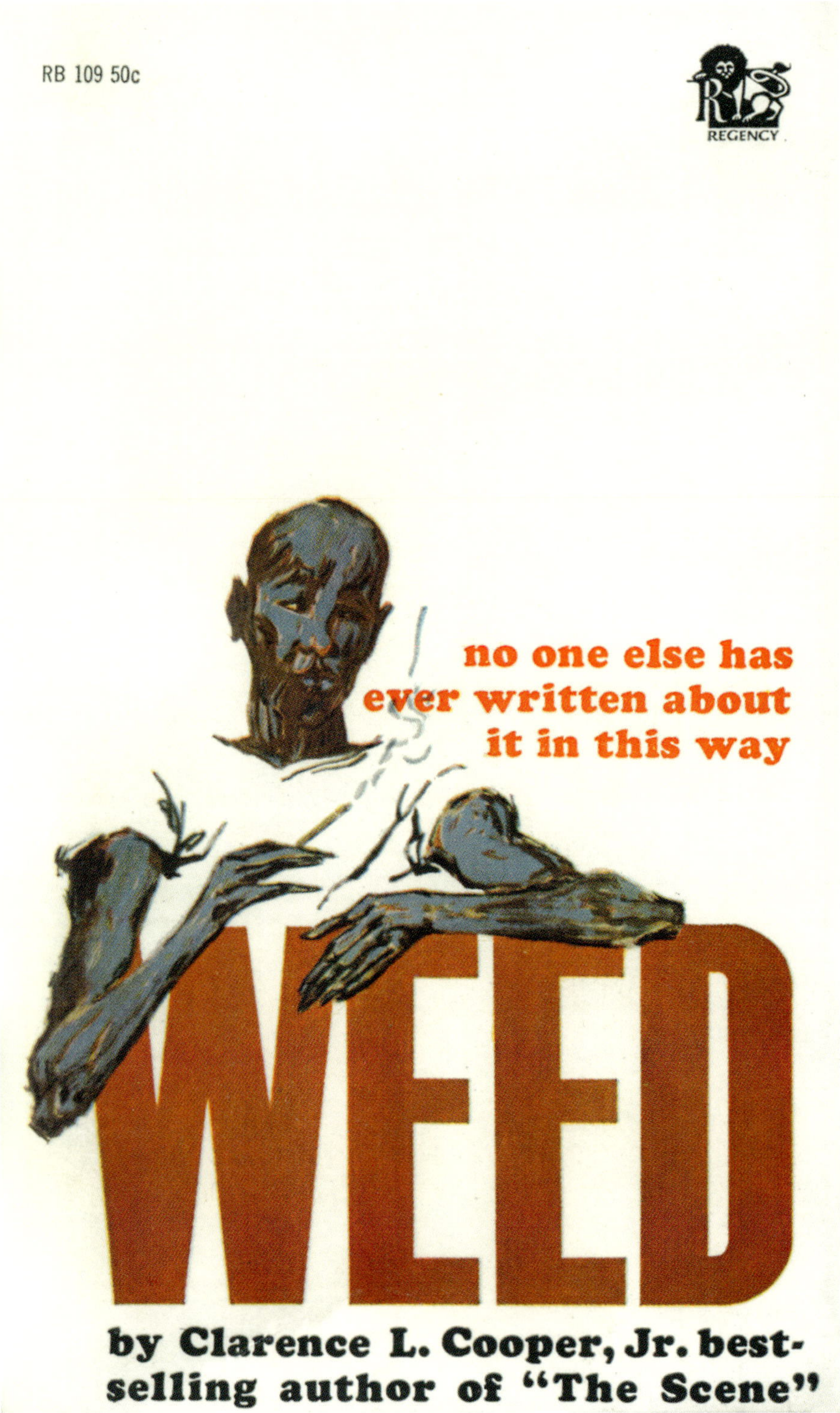

"Boo, pot, gangster, weed...they have many names for the green weed of pleasure."

Clarence L. Cooper • ***Weed*** • REGENCY RB109 • 1961 • COVER BY W.A. SMITH • PBO

Ellison was editor at pornographer Wm. Hamling's Regency Books, a straight imprint.

Harlan Ellison • ***Gentleman Junkie*** • REGENCY 102 • 1961 • COVER BY LEO AND DIANE DILLON • PBO

RB 102
50¢

REGENCY

ANTI-SEMITISM
JUVENILE DELINQUENCY
NEGRO PREJUDICE • JAZZ MUSICIANS
BEATNIKS • NARCOTICS ADDICTION

Raw, vital, uncompromising—here are portraits of the lost, the damned, the helpless, trying to get a handle on life. A startling collection of "hip" stories by an impressive young writer, torn from the shadows of a twilight world.

GENTLEMAN JUNKIE

and other stories of the hung-up generation

BY HARLAN ELLISON

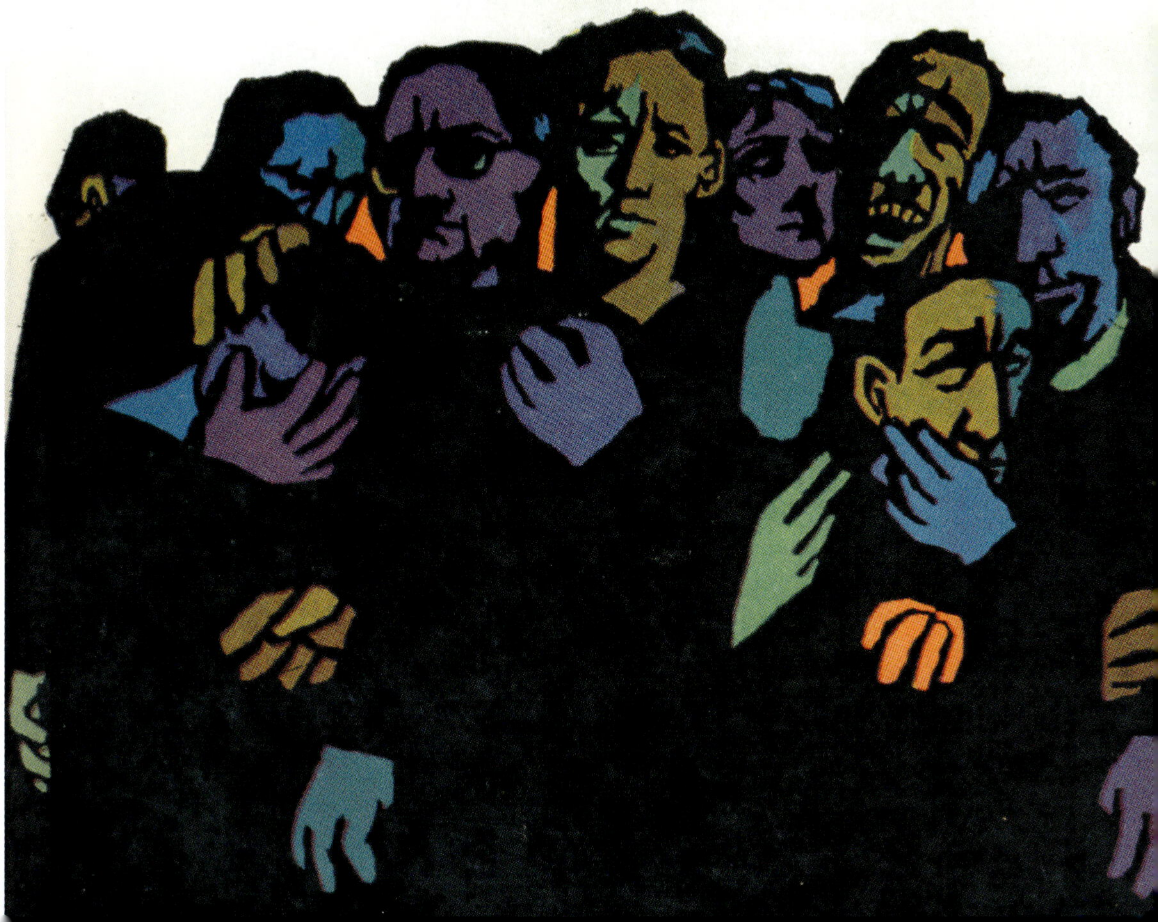

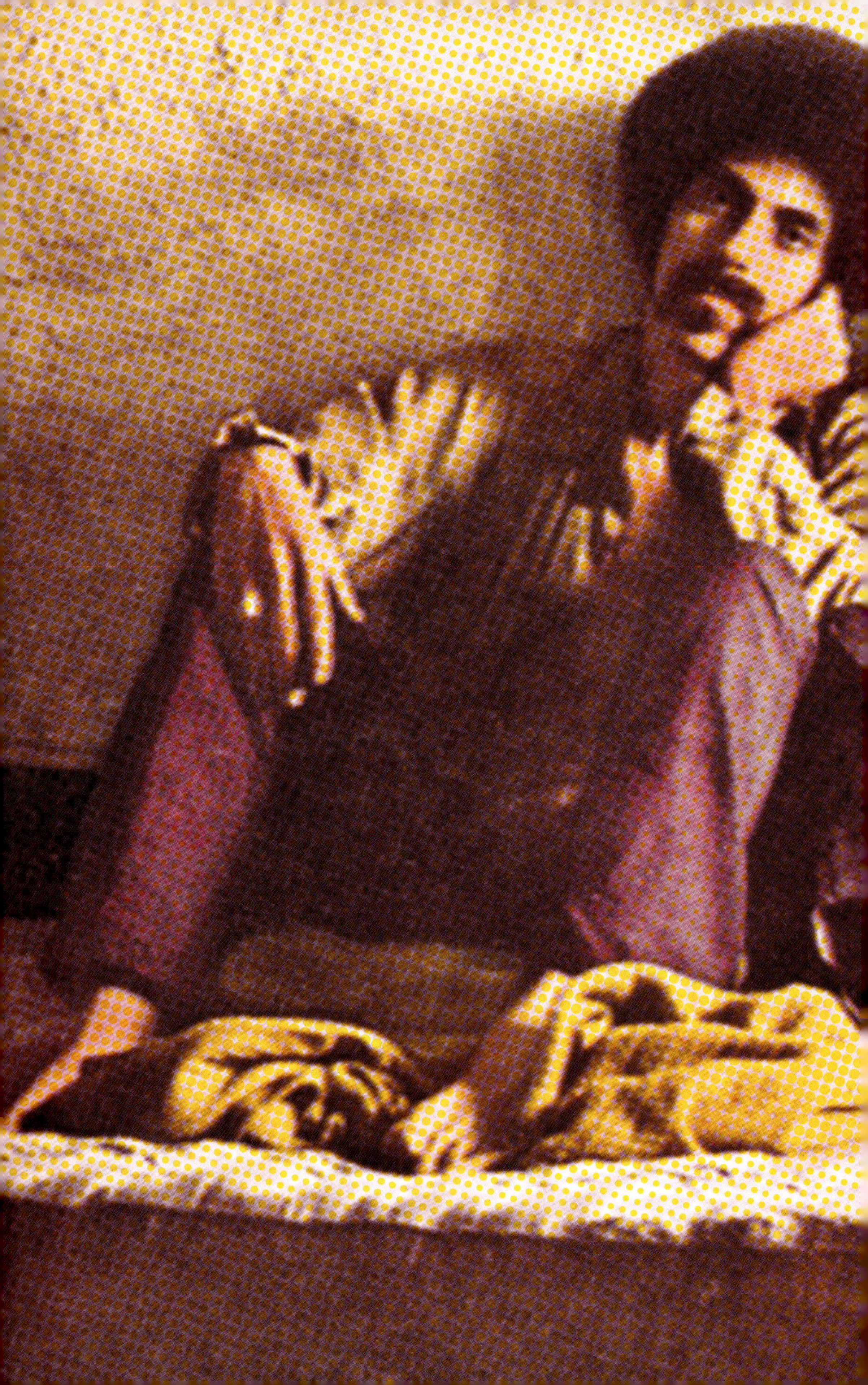

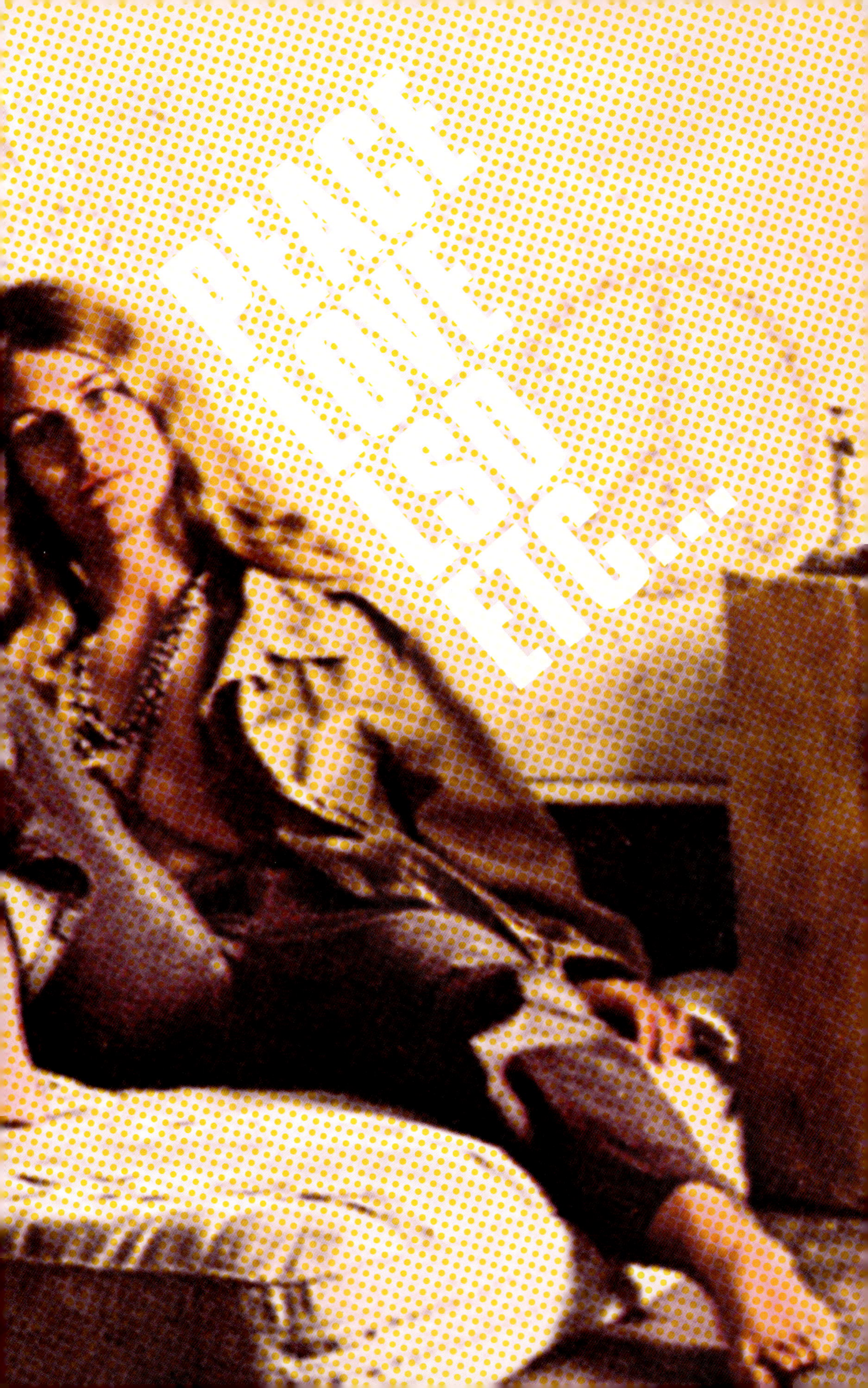
ETC...

THE PYSCHEDELIC SET HAPPENING WITH KNEE DEEP GRASS, DISCORDS, HASH BROWNIES, AND ROCKING-HORSE BUSES WITH LIGHTS

"You're stoned, baby! And it's a totally groovy experience. Whole new realms of sight and sound — of beauty — seem to be born all about you...Someone passes around a pizza...you eat a piece — slowly savoring each morsel to be tossed around your taste buds...the food of the Gods — in a commonplace pizza!...You have tripped out."

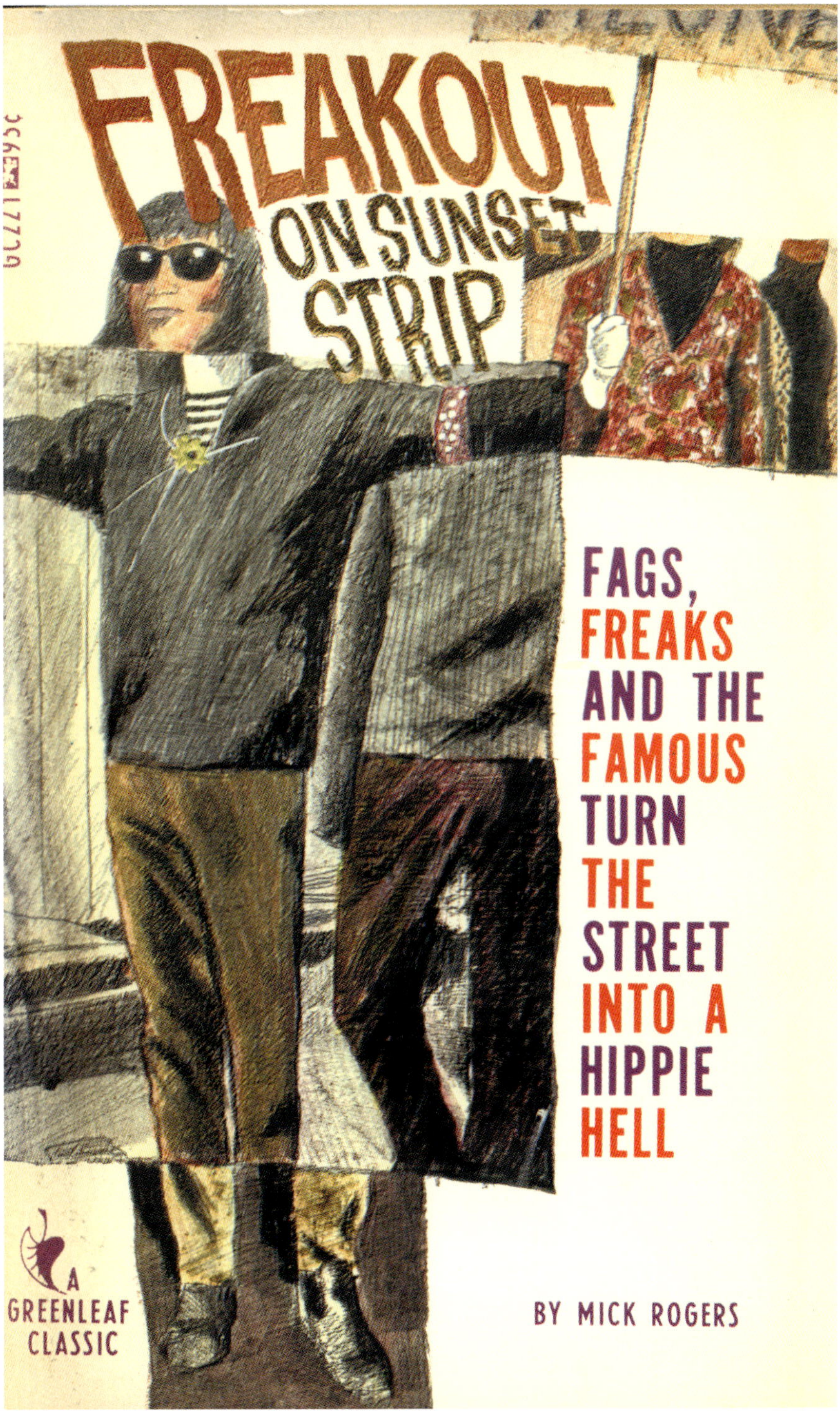

Mick Rogers [Donald F. Glut] • ***Freakout on Sunset Strip*** • GREENLEAF GC221 • 1967
COVER BY HARRY BREMNER • PBO

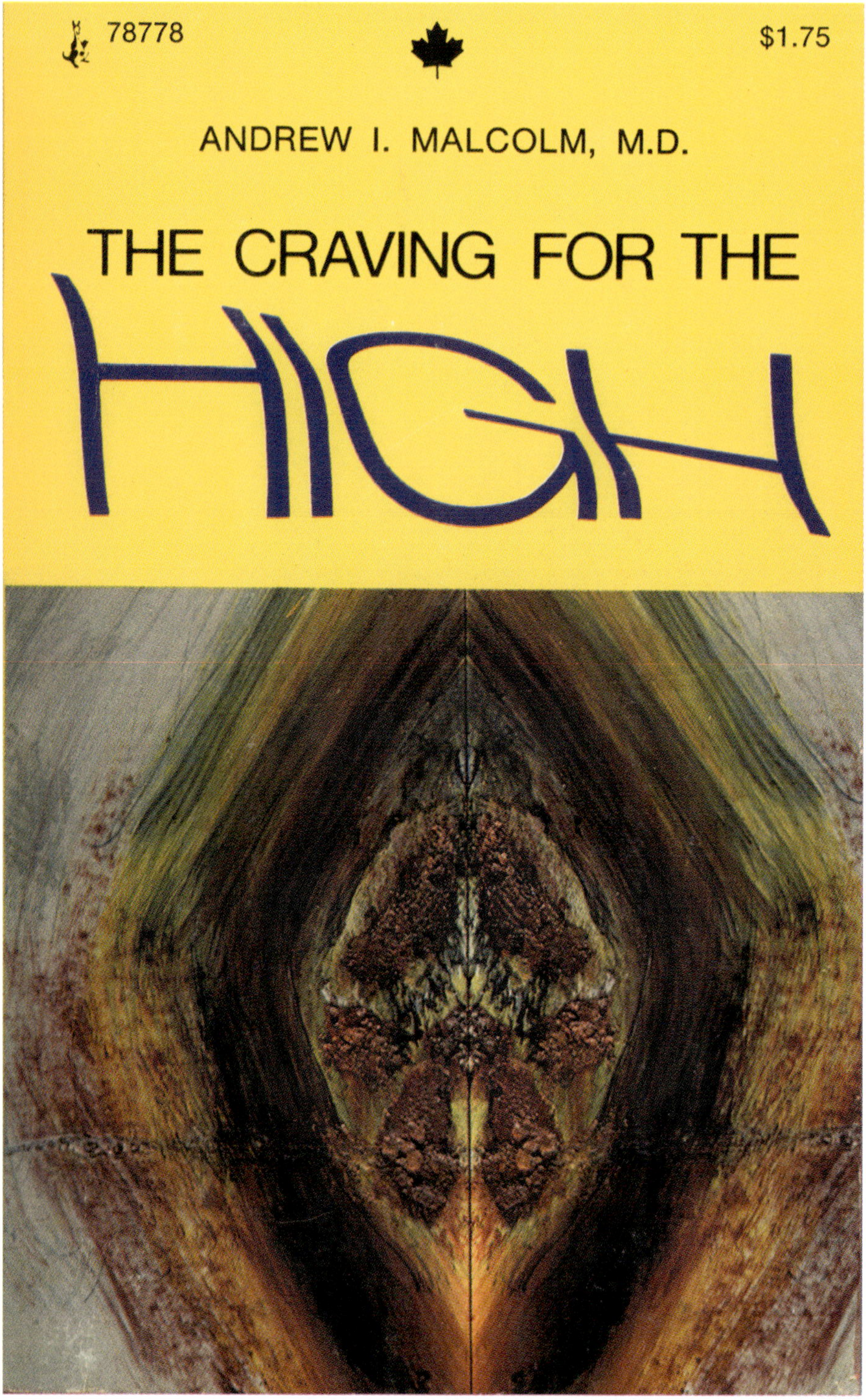

Andrew I. Malcolm • ***The Craving for the High*** • POCKET BOOKS 78778 • 1975 • PBO

Contains the complete text of Crowley's *The Herb Dangerous*, including Crowley's translation of Baudelaire's "The Poem of Hashish," and extracts from H.G. [Fitz Hugh] Ludlow's *The Hasheesh Eater*. With introductory essay by occultist Regardie.

Israel Regardie • ***Roll Away the Stone: An Introduction to Aleister Crowley's Essays on the Psychology of Hashish*** • Llewellyn • 1968 • Cover by Carlola Williams • First Edition

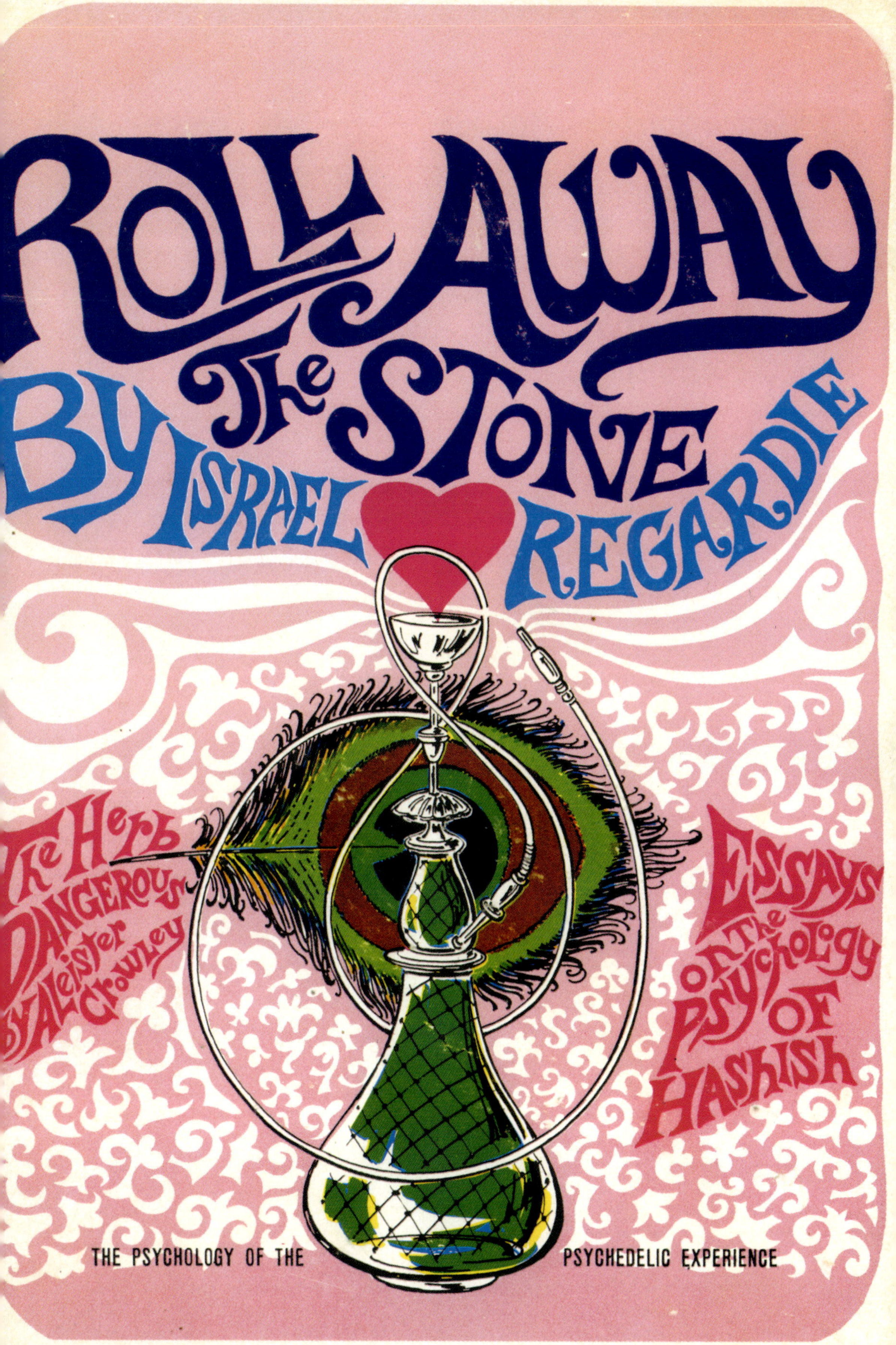
ROLL AWAY
The STONE
BY ISRAEL REGARDIE
The Herb DANGEROUS by Aleister Crowley
ESSAYS ON The PSYCHOLOGY OF HASHISH
THE PSYCHOLOGY OF THE
PSYCHEDELIC EXPERIENCE

“Malcolm Wren was stoned. Pot was the only way he could forget the heavy days inflicted upon him by the sick, mechanized society he was trapped in. Walking the smog-drenched streets of Los Angeles, he tried to find the one pleasure that might free him...finally, desperately, he turned to LSD and pitched headlong over the brink into a desperate, brutal crusade for his lost confidence. It was his last chance.”

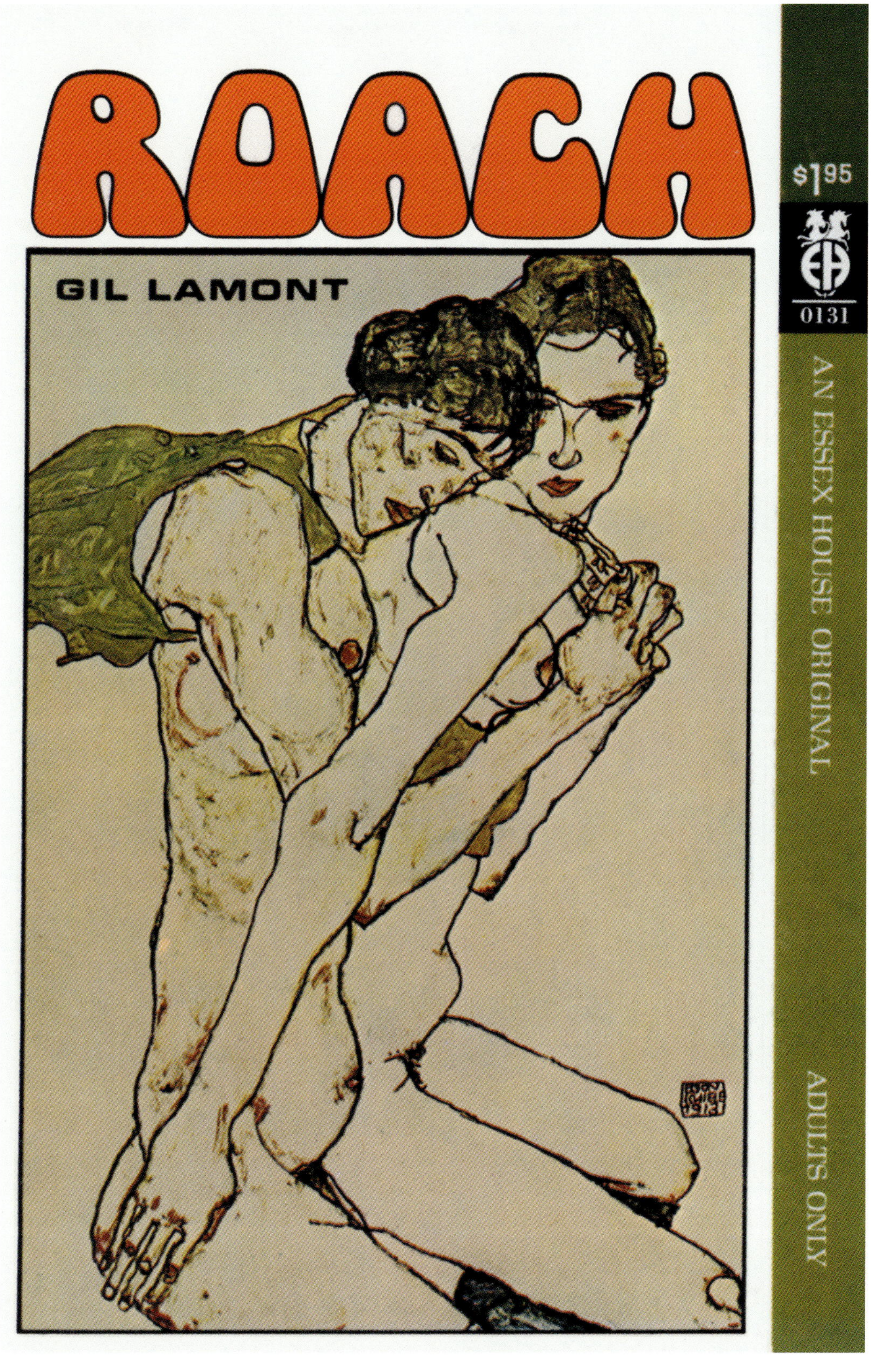

Gil Lamont • ***Roach*** • ESSEX HOUSE 131 • 1969 • COVER BY EGON SCHIELE • PBO

A Paperback Original | The Olympia Press Inc.

THE AMPHETAMINE MANIFESTO

BY HARVEY COHEN

Handling prose with the delicate skill of a poet, Harvey Cohen has succeeded in doing what so many writers have tried and failed, to literally synthesize a "trip" in words. And what a trip it is, as he leads you on this Odyssey to the alien, misty lands of the "Counter-Culture". You look at conventional America through his eyes, an experience strangely akin to being transported into the mind of a fish viewing the angler. Often disturbing, always fascinating, THE AMPHETAMINE MANIFESTO is unquestionably one of the more important statements to emerge from a world that is to most Americans totally incomprehensible. When you've read this book, you will comprehend, but you may wish you had preserved your innocence, for you can never see yourself in quite the same way again.

Printed in U.S.A.

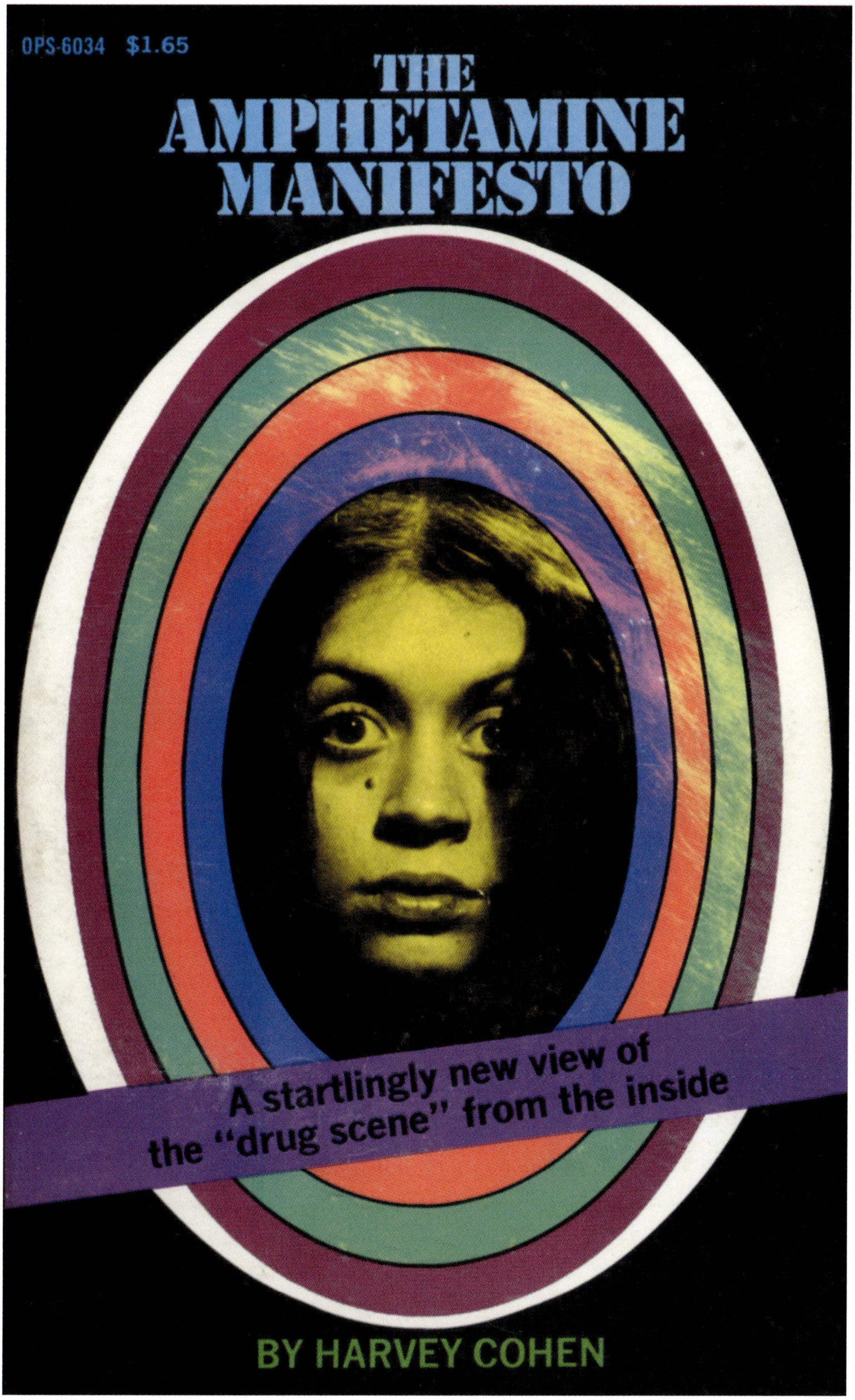

Harvey Cohen • ***The Amphetimine Manifesto*** • OLYMPIA PRESS-NY OPS-6034 • 1972
COVER BY HARVEY & IRA COHEN, AND DON SNYDER • PBO

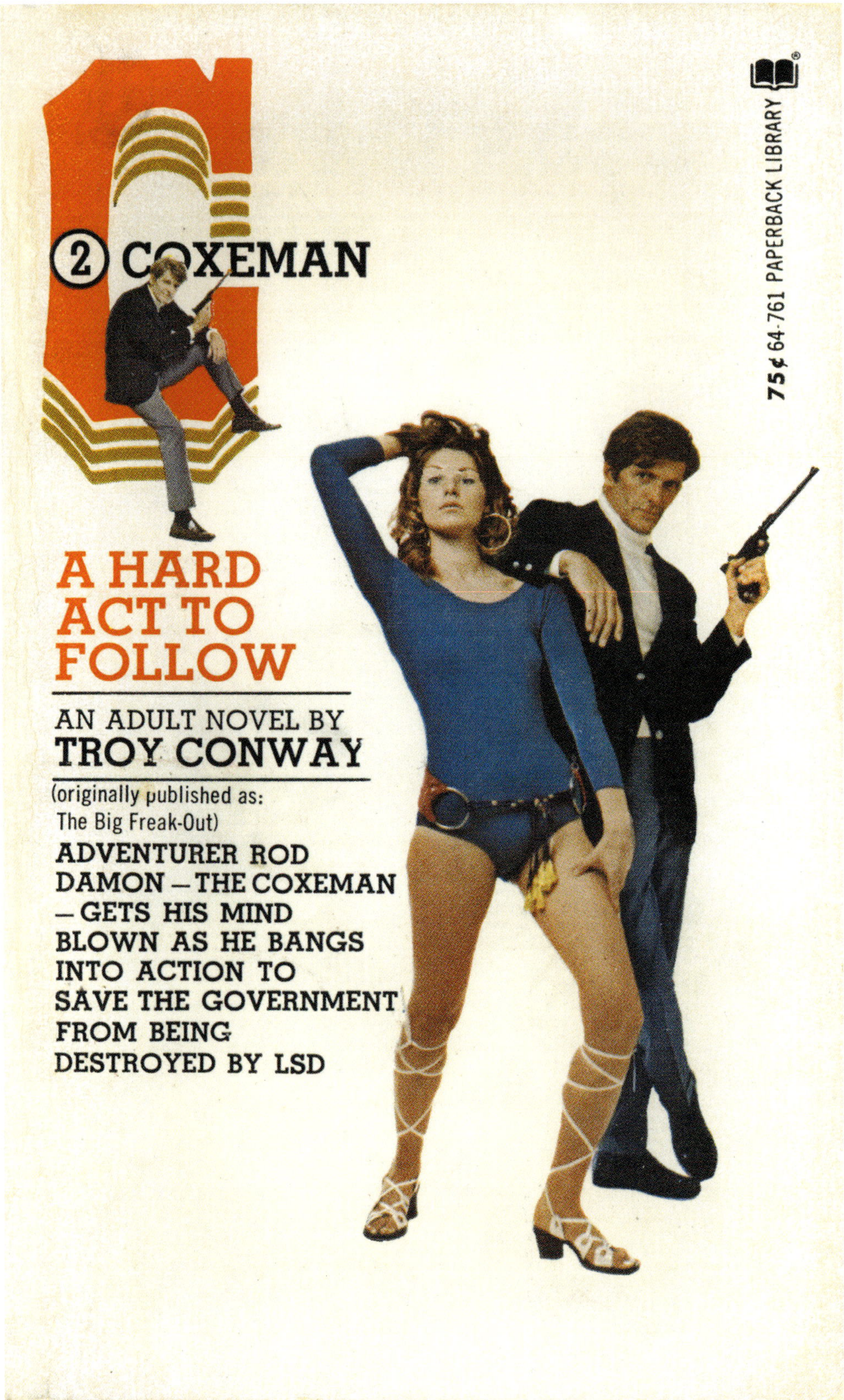

Troy Conway • ***A Hard Act to Follow*** • PAPERBACK LIBRARY 64-761 • 1972 • REPRINT

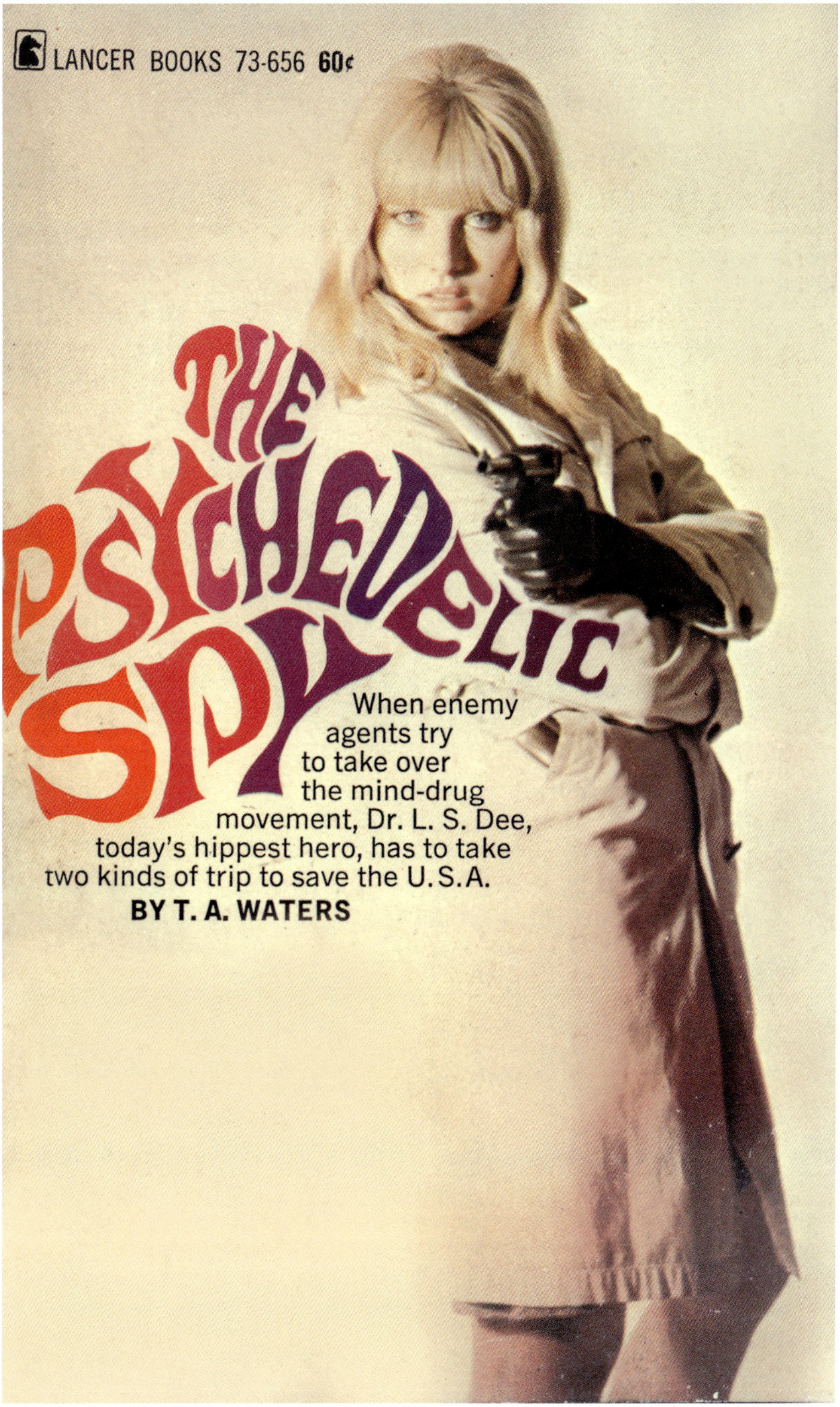

T.A. Waters (pseud.) • ***The Psychedelic Spy*** • LANCER 73-656 • 1967 • PBO

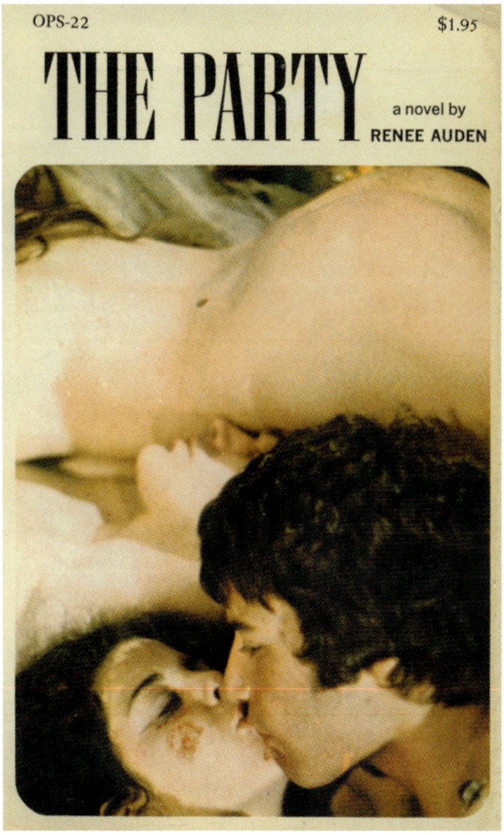

"'...I really don't dig ammies [amyl nitrate, a.k.a. "poppers"] that much anymore...they give me vertigo. I mean, you just outgrow some things.'

"'...Yeah, I guess ammies are kind of kid stuff,' Clara admitted. 'I still like them, though.'

"Clara put the white plastic tube in her nostril and took a deep sniff. 'Different strokes for different folks, eh?' she giggled cheerfully.

"Felicity nodded. 'Wish I could get a hold of some good coke,' she said wistfully. 'It's so hard to come by. Now that Lee's been busted, I don't know anybody who handles it.'

"'Yeah, coke's nice,' Clara agreed. 'Nobody wants to deal it though — too expensive for most people, not enough profit in it, I guess.'"

Renee Auden [Uta West] • ***The Party*** • OLYMPIA PRESS NY OPS-22 • 1971 • TRUE FIRST EDITION

The White Rabbit is the White Hophead in this sly, witty parody of Alice in Wonderland incorporating sex, drugs (LSD, etc.), rock 'n roll, and student protest.

Jackson Short [Peter Hochstein] • ***Blue Alice***
DELL 0733 • 1972 • PBO

Lambert Macy • ***Lovemaster***
SOFTCOVER LIBRARY 1033 • 1967 • PBO

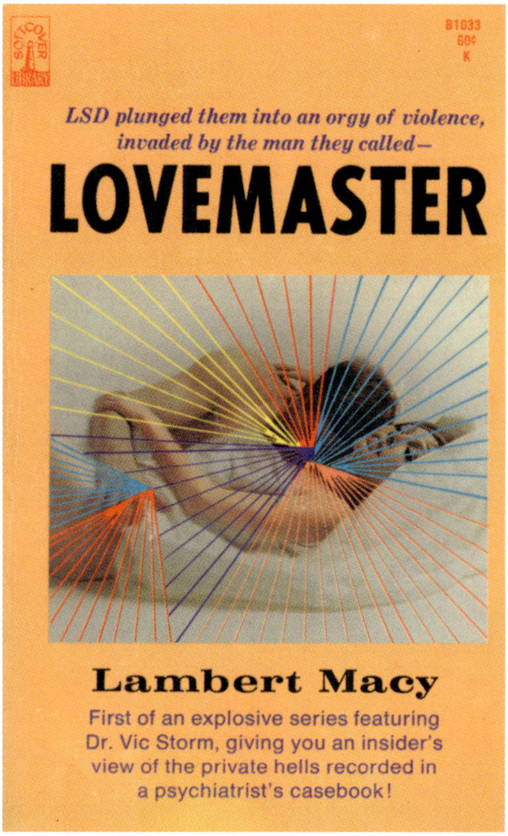

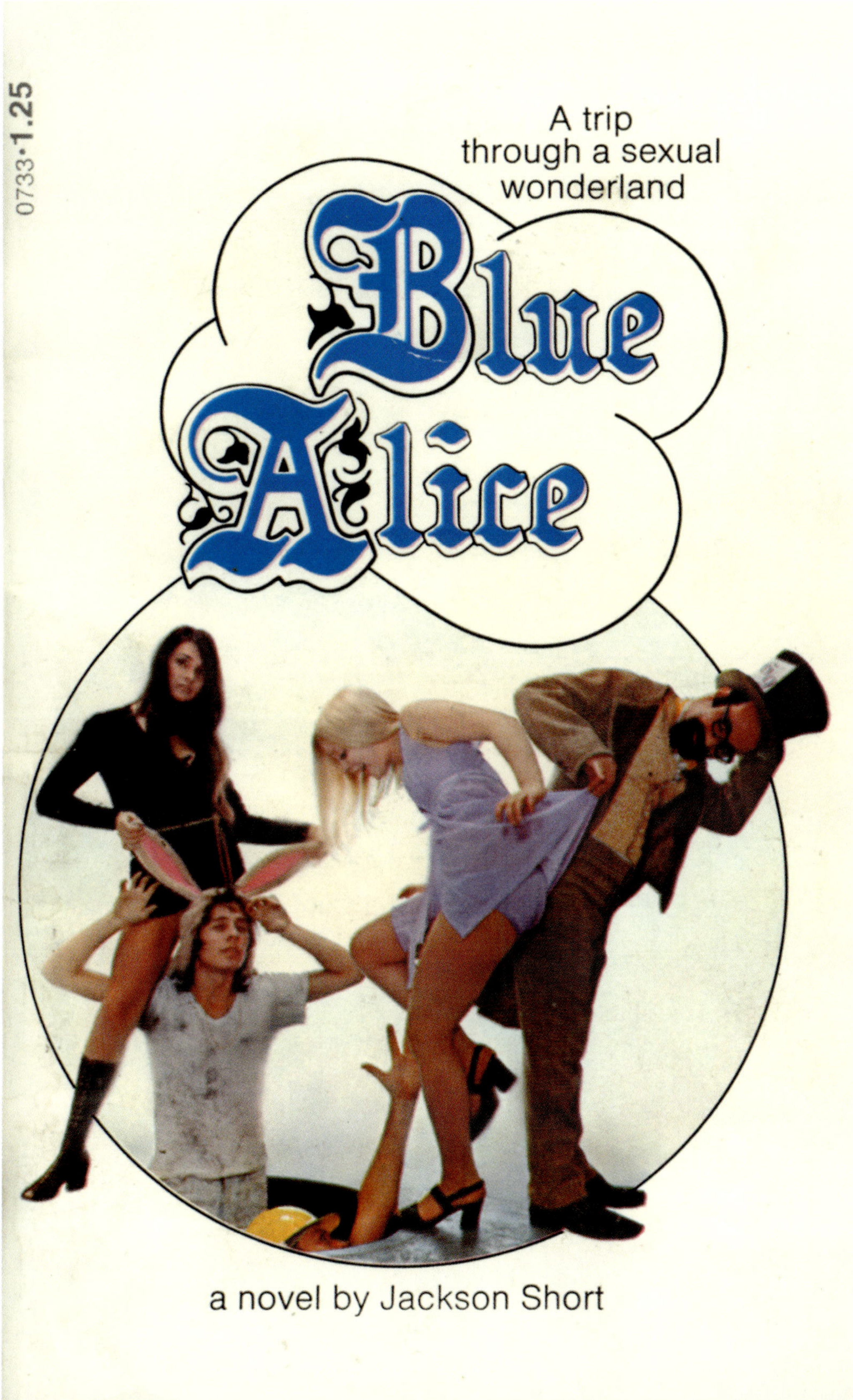
0733·1.25
A trip
through a sexual
wonderland
Blue
Alice
a novel by Jackson Short

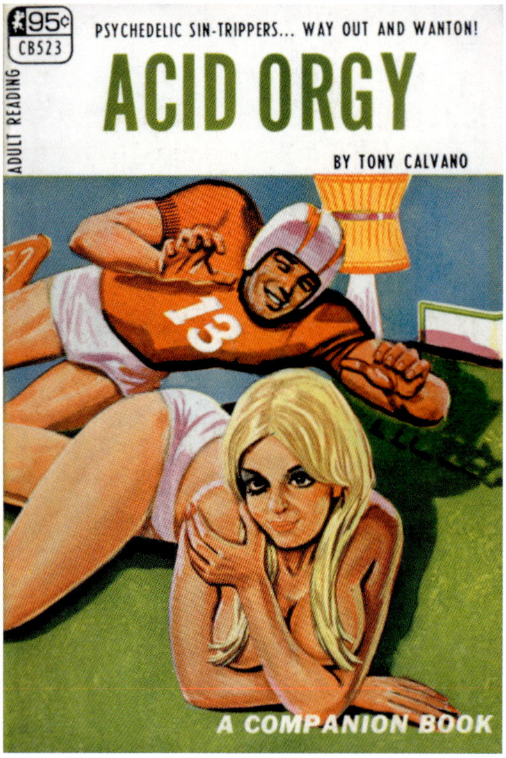

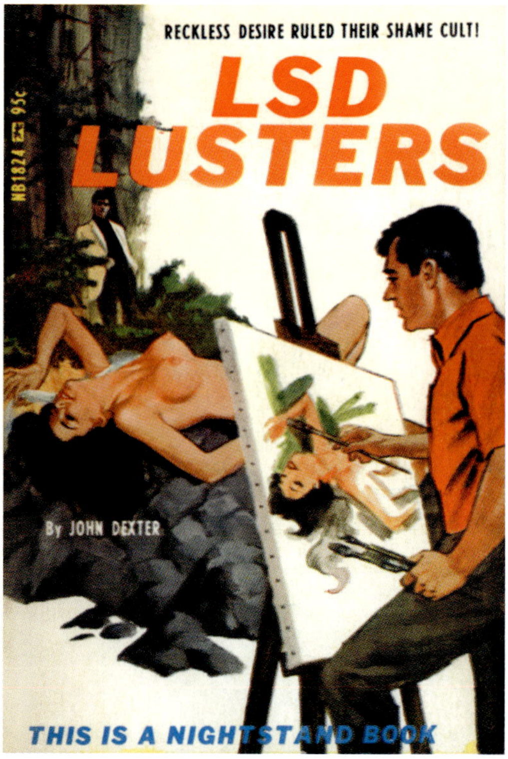

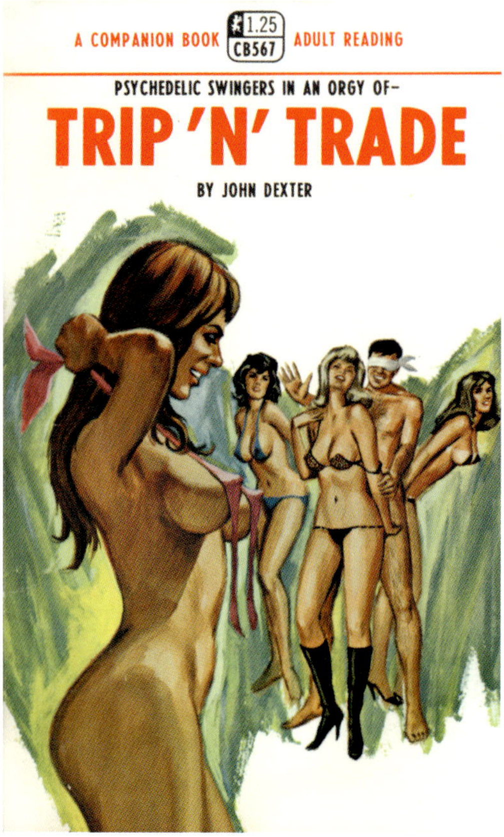

Tony Calvano [Thomas P. Ramirez] • ***Acid Orgy***
COMPANION BOOKS CB523 • 1967
COVER BY CANNIZZARO • PBO

John Dexter (pseud.) • ***LSD Lusters***
NIGHTSTAND NB 1824 • 1967 • PBO

John Dexter (pseud.) • ***Trip 'n' Trade***
COMPANION BOOKS CB567 • 1968
COVER BY ED SMITH • PBO

Marcus Miller [Milo Perichitch or Samuel Dodson]
LSD Orgy • COMPANION BOOK CB 519 • 1967
COVER BY ED SMITH • PBO

ADULT READING

LSD ORGY

HEIR PSYCHEDELIC SIN-TRIP PASSED THE POINT OF NO RETURN!

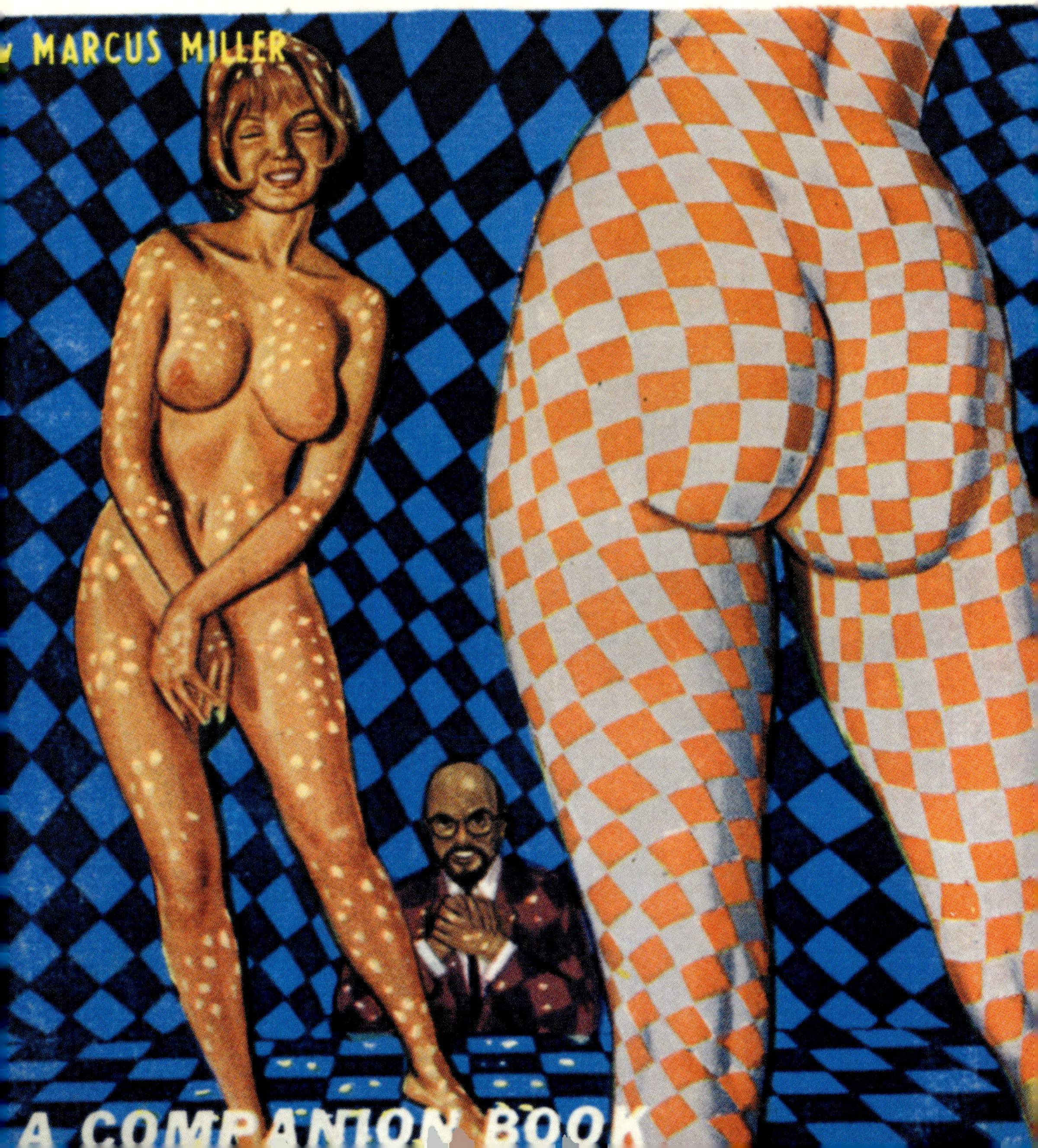

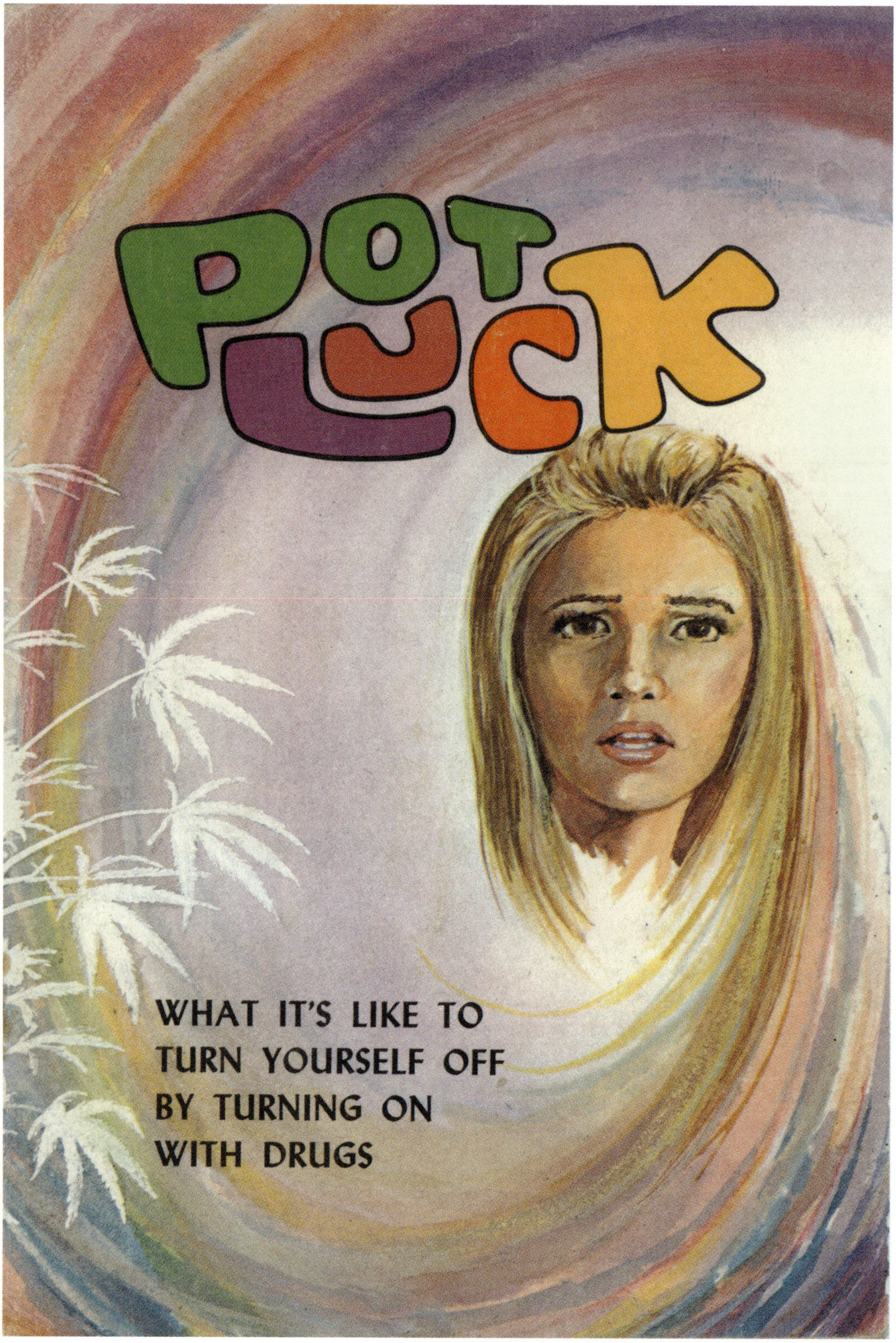

Barbara Herrera • ***Pot Luck*** • PACIFIC PRESS PUBLISHING ASSOCIATION • 1970 • PBO

John S. Simon • ***The Sign of the Fool: Memoirs From The Haight-Ashbury 1965–68*** • ACE 76350 • 1969 • PBO

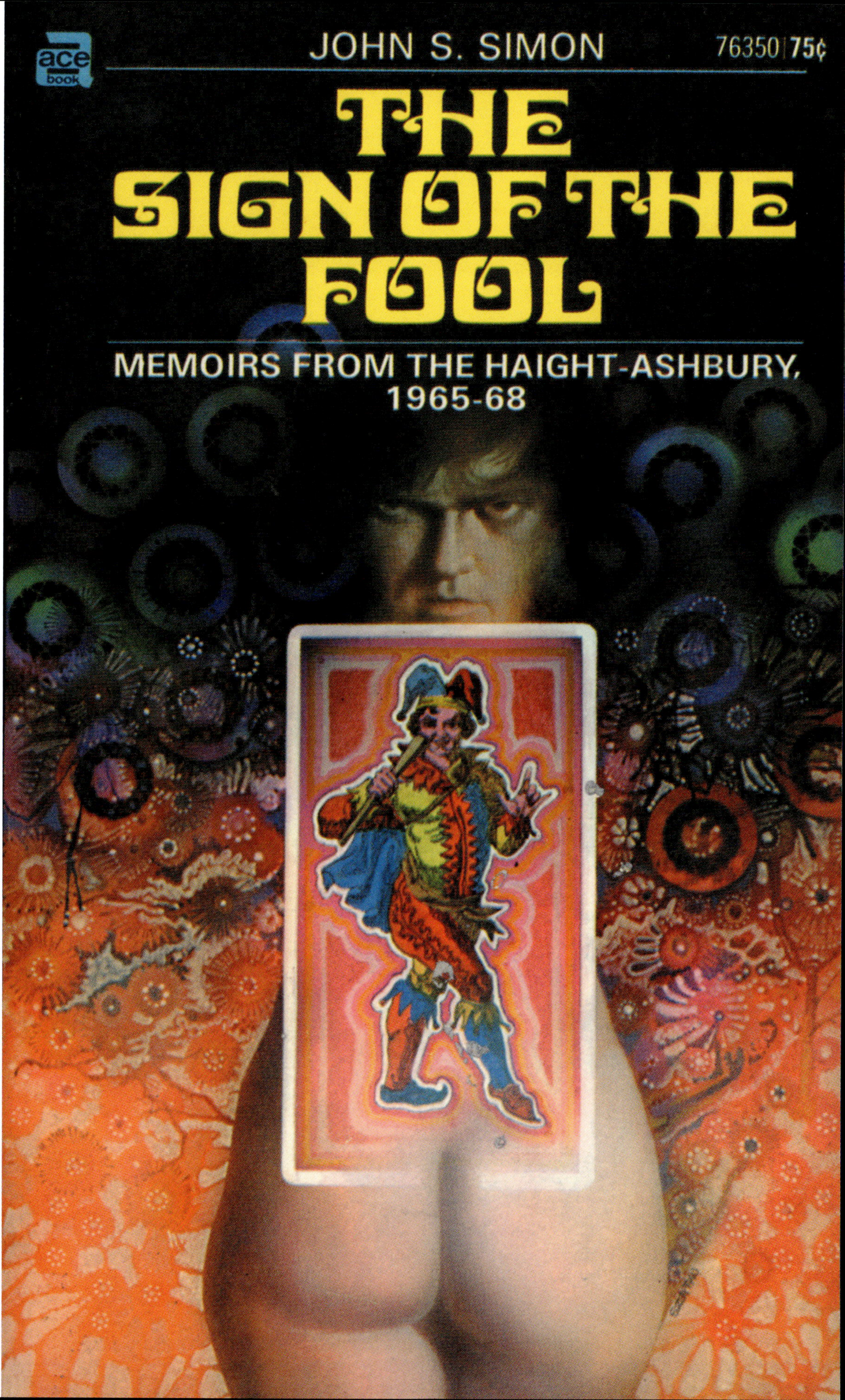
ace book
JOHN S. SIMON
76350 75¢
THE SIGN OF THE FOOL
MEMOIRS FROM THE HAIGHT-ASHBURY, 1965-68

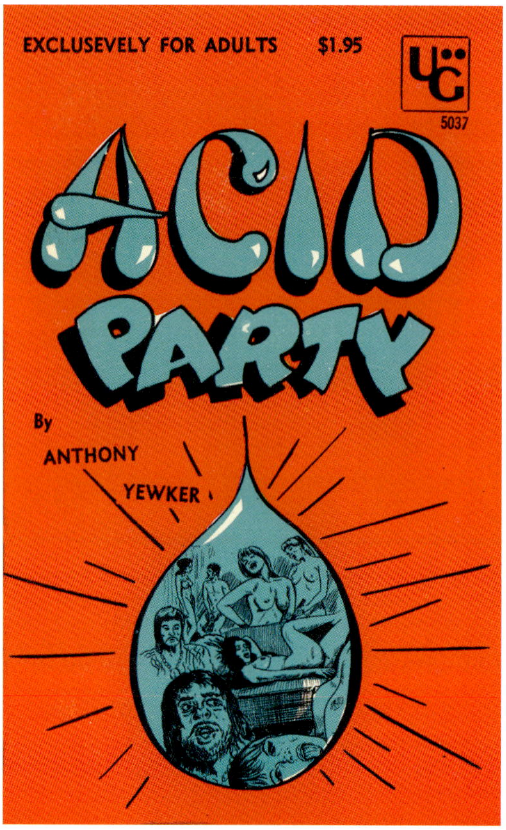

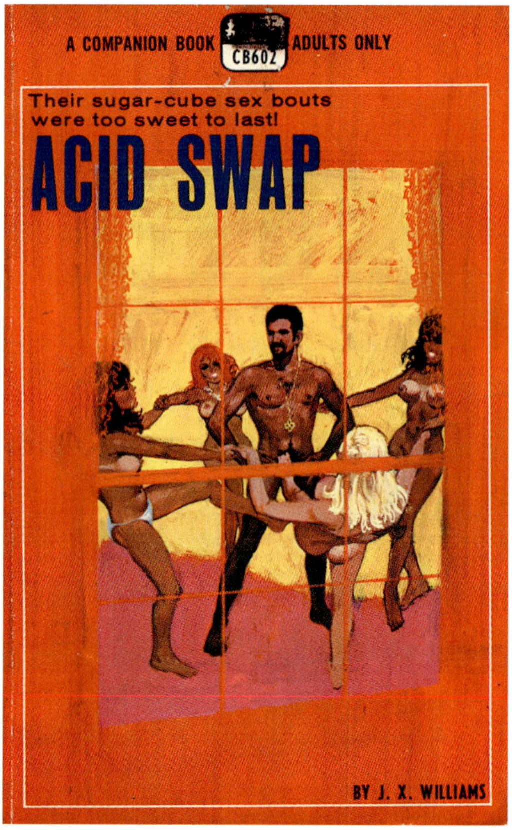

Anthony Yewker (pseud.) • ***Acid Party*** • BELL HOUSE (UNITED GRAPHICS) UG-5037 • 1969 • PBO

"Maybe we'll never know who killed her. Maybe the murderer will never be sure. Because you don't need a motive to kill someone under LSD. They have to be there when your mind explodes and you've got a knife or a gun in your hand."

J.X. Williams (pseud) • ***Acid Swap*** • COMPANION BOOKS CB602 • 1969 • COVER BY ROBERT BONFILS • PBO

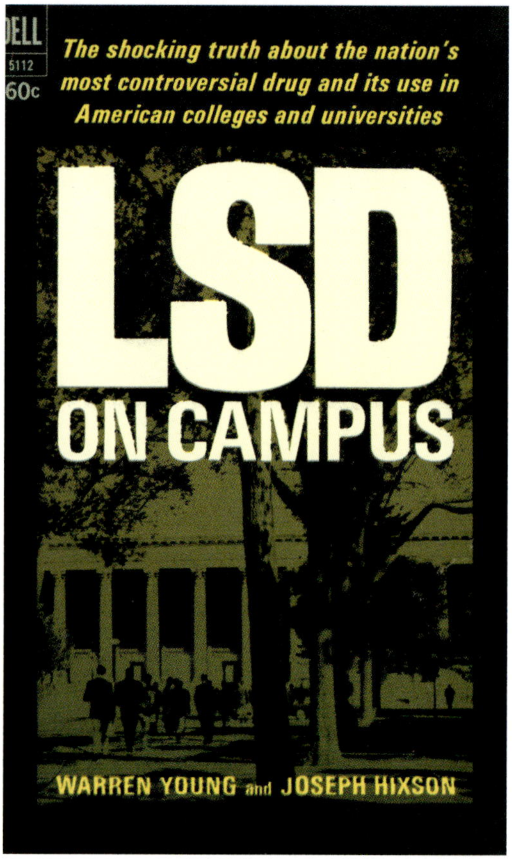

Warren Young and Joseph Hixson • ***LSD on Campus*** DELL 5112 • 1966 • PBO

The authors acknowledge Timothy Leary for his help with the book.

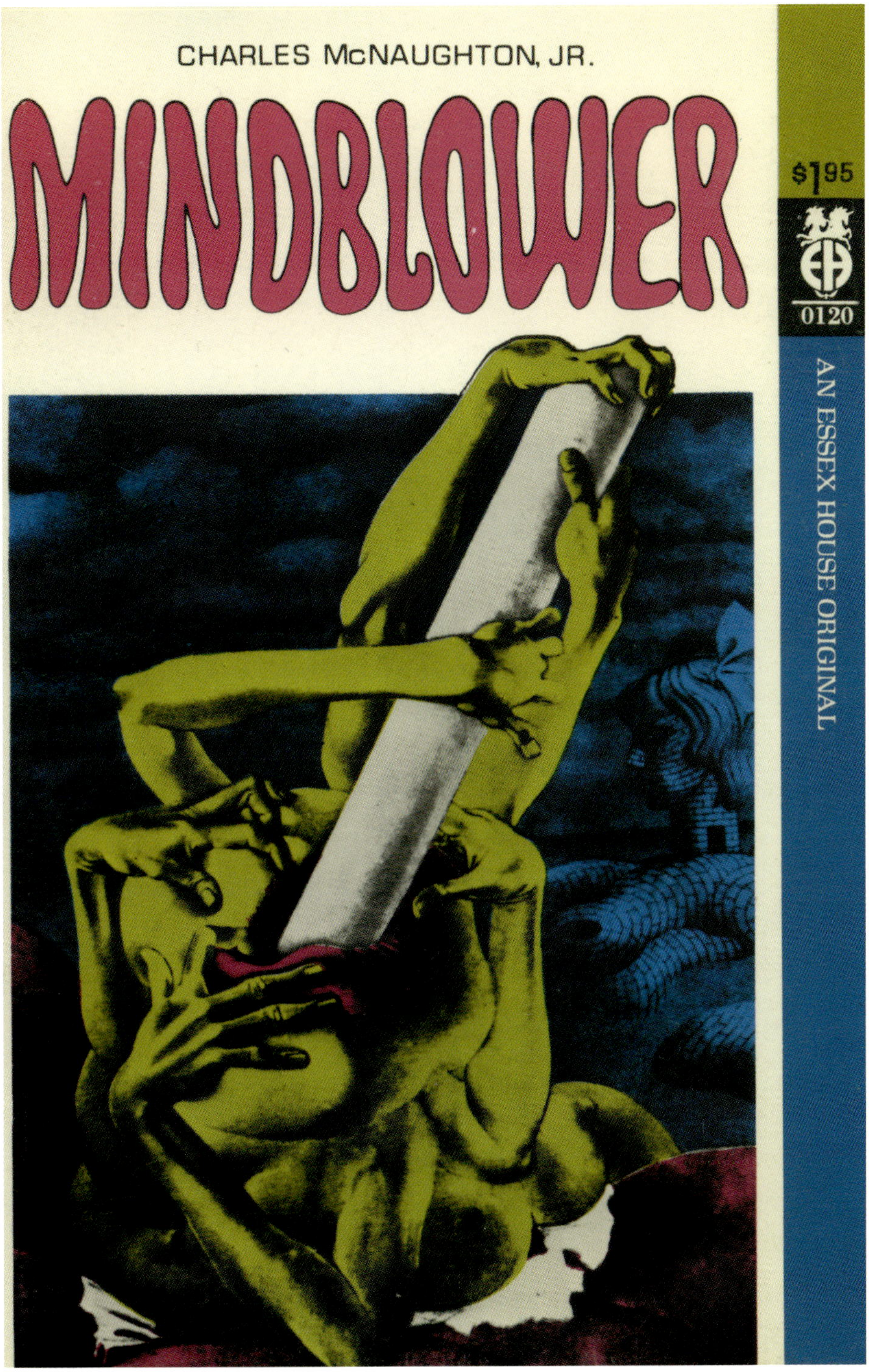

"Jack Flasher deeply felt all the poetic romance of a mystical adventurer. He halted a moment to gaze at the much fabled and long sung Haight-Ashbury.

"In his peak then, 600 micrograms of LSD magnifying, accelerating his thinking-associating processes about a thousand times or so. Idea after idea, association after association sped past the grain of sand that was now his consciousness in such a torrential deluge that his mind couldn't possibly walk a straight path if his life depended on it."

Charles McNaughton Jr. • ***Mindblower*** • ESSEX HOUSE 0120 • 1969 • COVER ART BY HANS BELLMER • PBO

"A lot of people who say they ought to know, say that LSD will never do permanent harm, but never's a big word in reference to mind and I think there's always the chance that some poor fool might crack a one-way dimension...I did some quick bartering and came up with two more doses to take along because I never know when to quit. I've always wanted to continue beyond X point. That is, I've always been kind of dumb.

"After three weeks high on methadrine [crystal meth] the comedown isn't necessarily bad, but the participant's frame of mind can steer it anywhere from mere exhaustion to suicidal desperation, with hundreds of nefarious variations in between. So I knew it was going to hit me terrible...I wished I could stop time right then and stay between places forever, never to arrive, never to arrive anywhere... if I'd had a gun I'd gladly have blown my brains out all over the place."

William Burroughs Jr. • ***Speed*** • OLYMPIA PRESS-NY • OPS/2 • 1970 • COVER BY IRA COHEN & BILL DEVORE • PBO

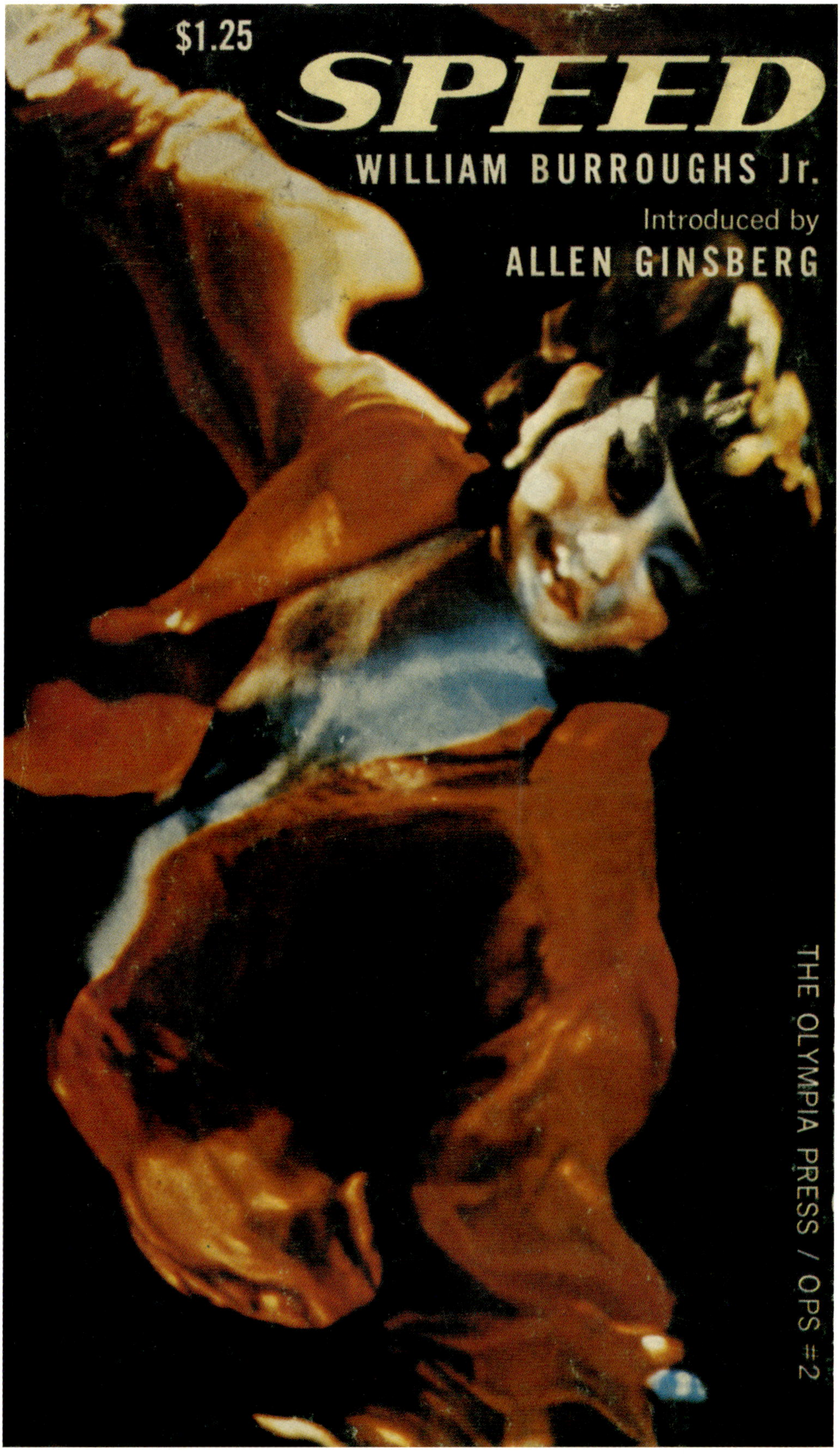
$1.25
SPEED
WILLIAM BURROUGHS Jr.
Introduced by
ALLEN GINSBERG
THE OLYMPIA PRESS / OPS #2

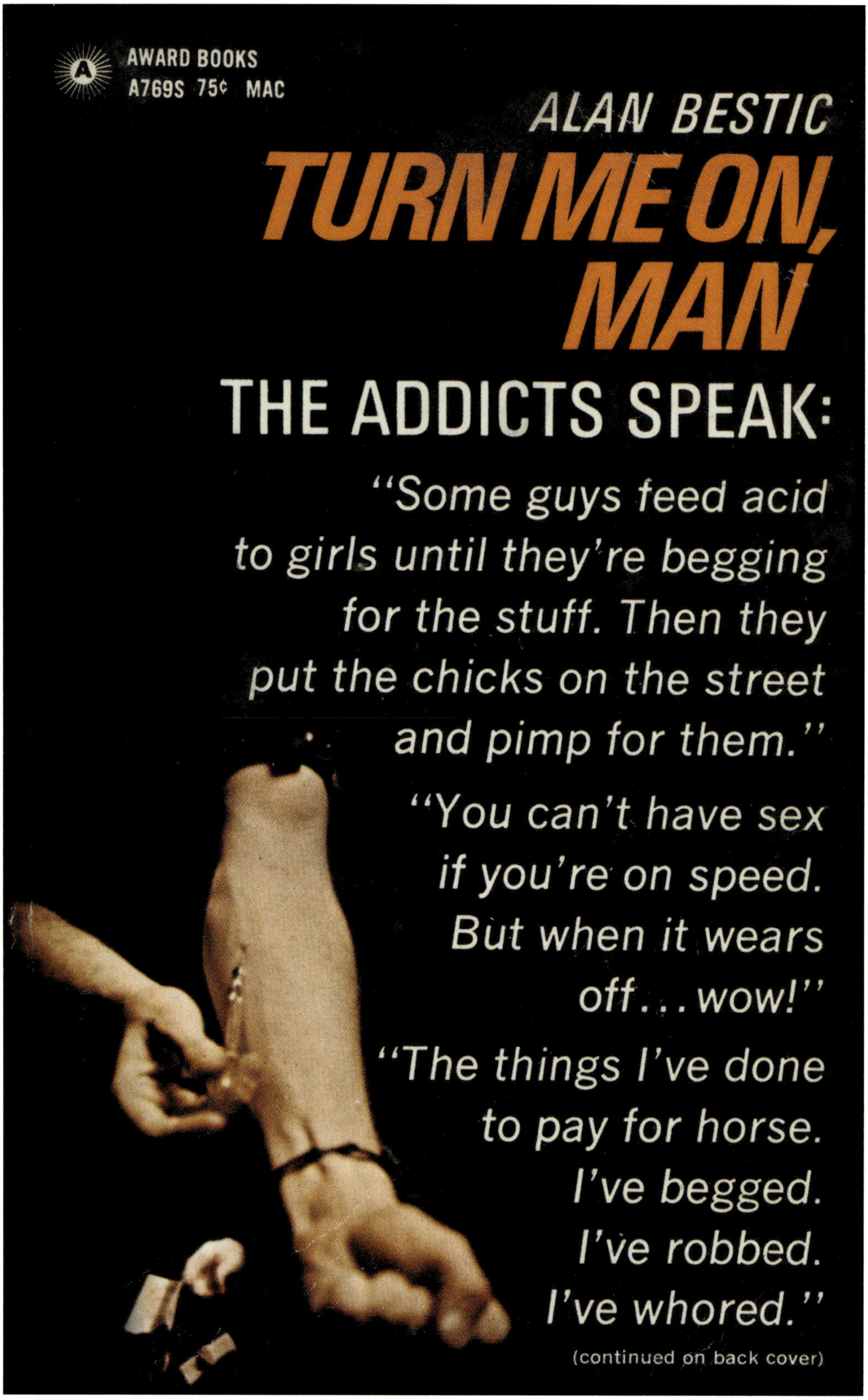

Alan Bestic • ***Turn Me On, Man*** • AWARD A769S • 1970 • REPRINT OF U.K. FIRST EDITION

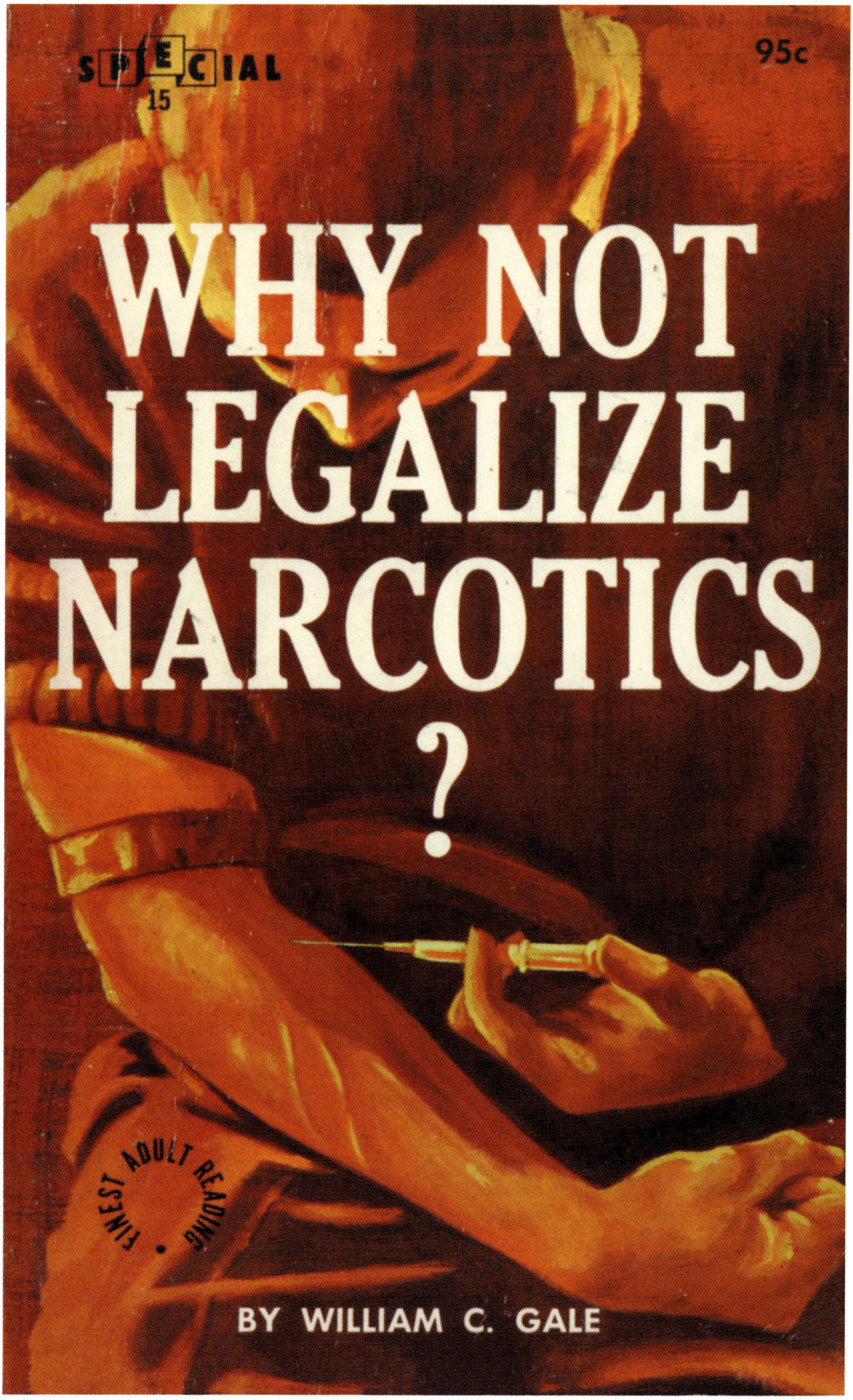

William C. Gale • ***Why Not Legalize Narcotics?*** • PUBLISHER'S EXPORT CO. SP15 • 1967 • PBO

"Where it's at — pushing, scoring, tripping, group sex, grass, acid, speed, and smack. It is a psychedelic nightmare with Mardi Gras characters — White Rabbit, Chocolate George, The Beast, Black Preacher, Teddybear — against a landscape of madness" (*Chicago Daily News*)

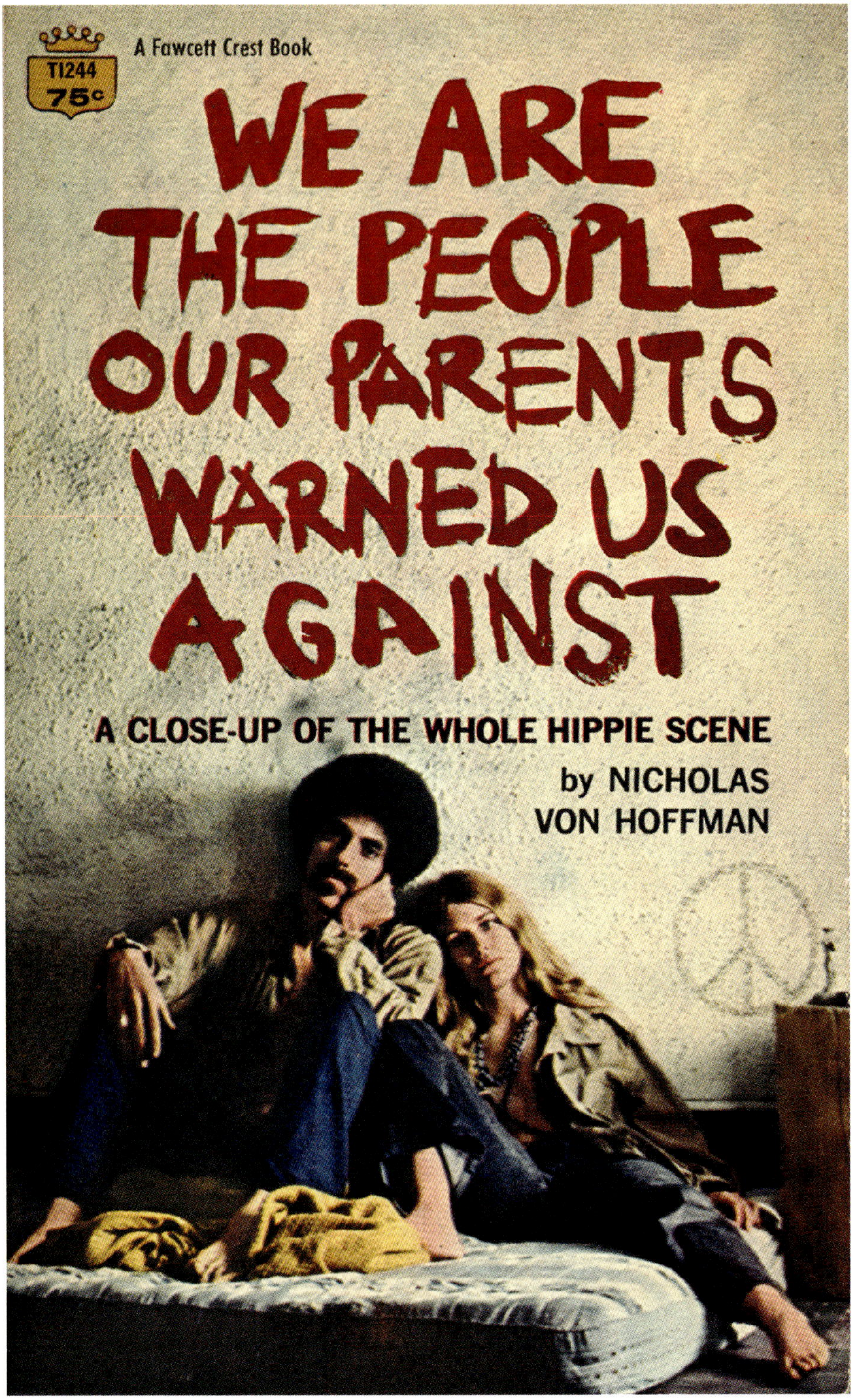

Nicholas Von Hoffman • ***We Are the People Our Parents Warned Us Against*** • CREST T-1244 • 1969 • REPRINT

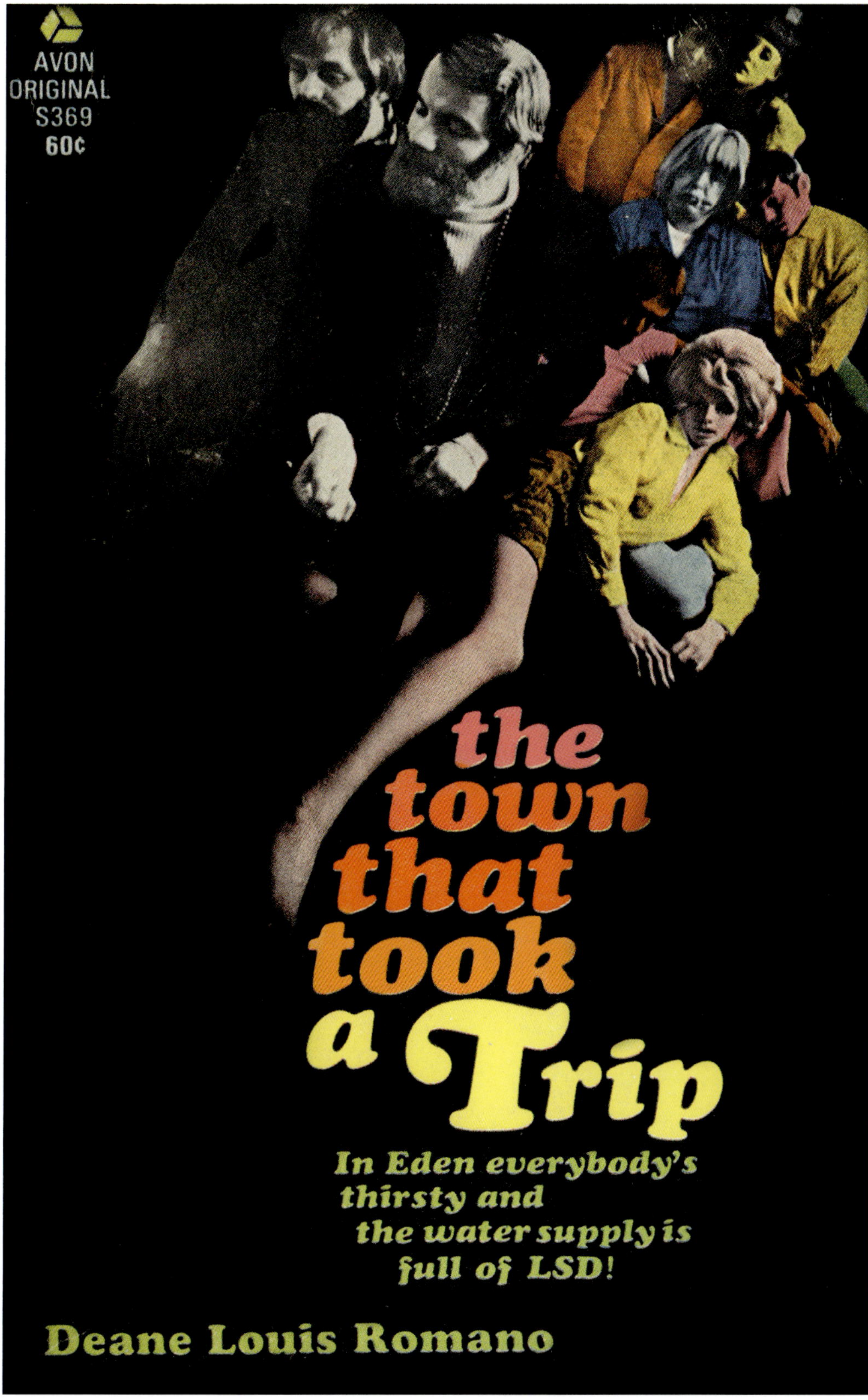

Deane Louis Romano • ***The Town That Took a Trip*** • AVON S369 • 1968 • PBO

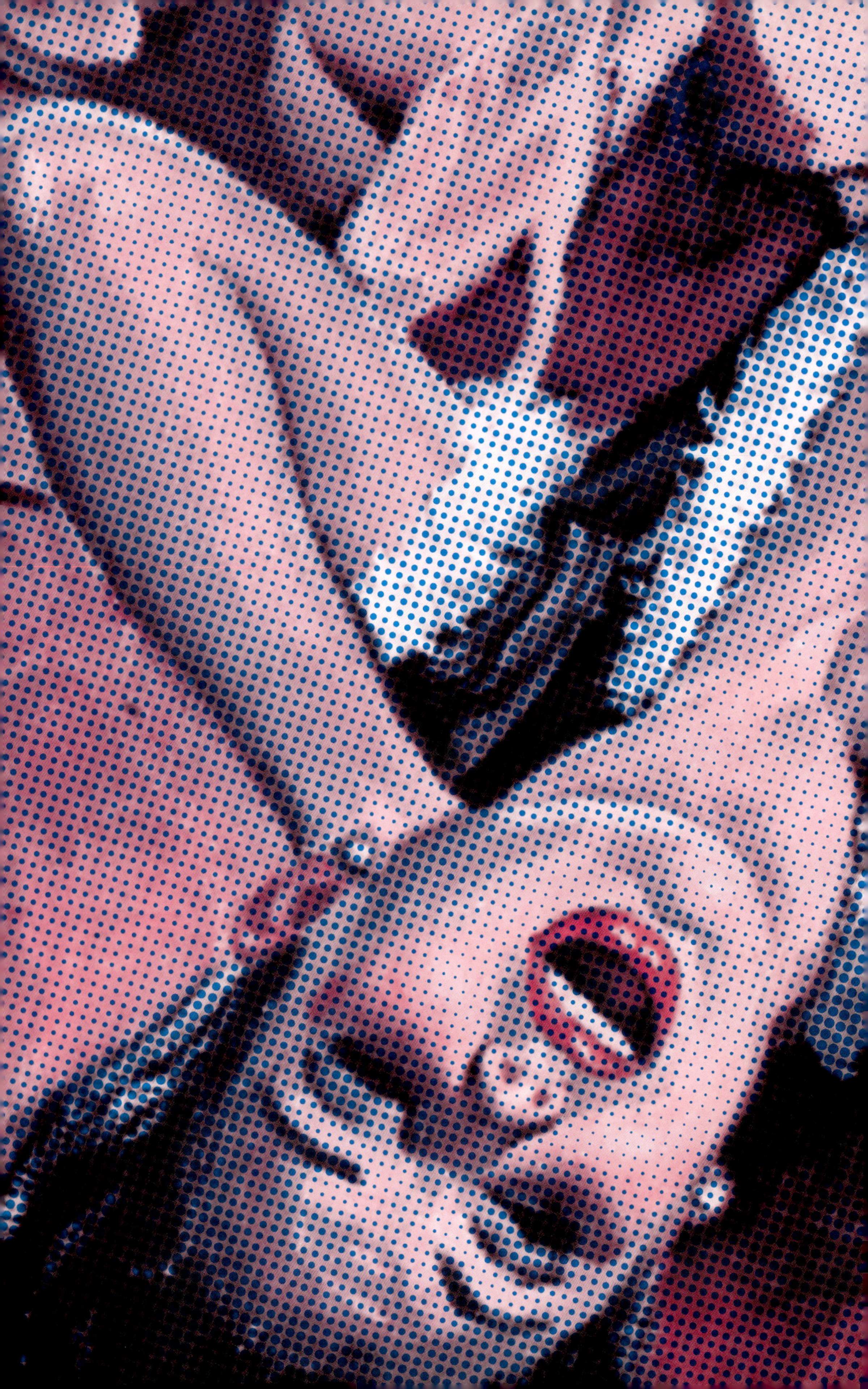

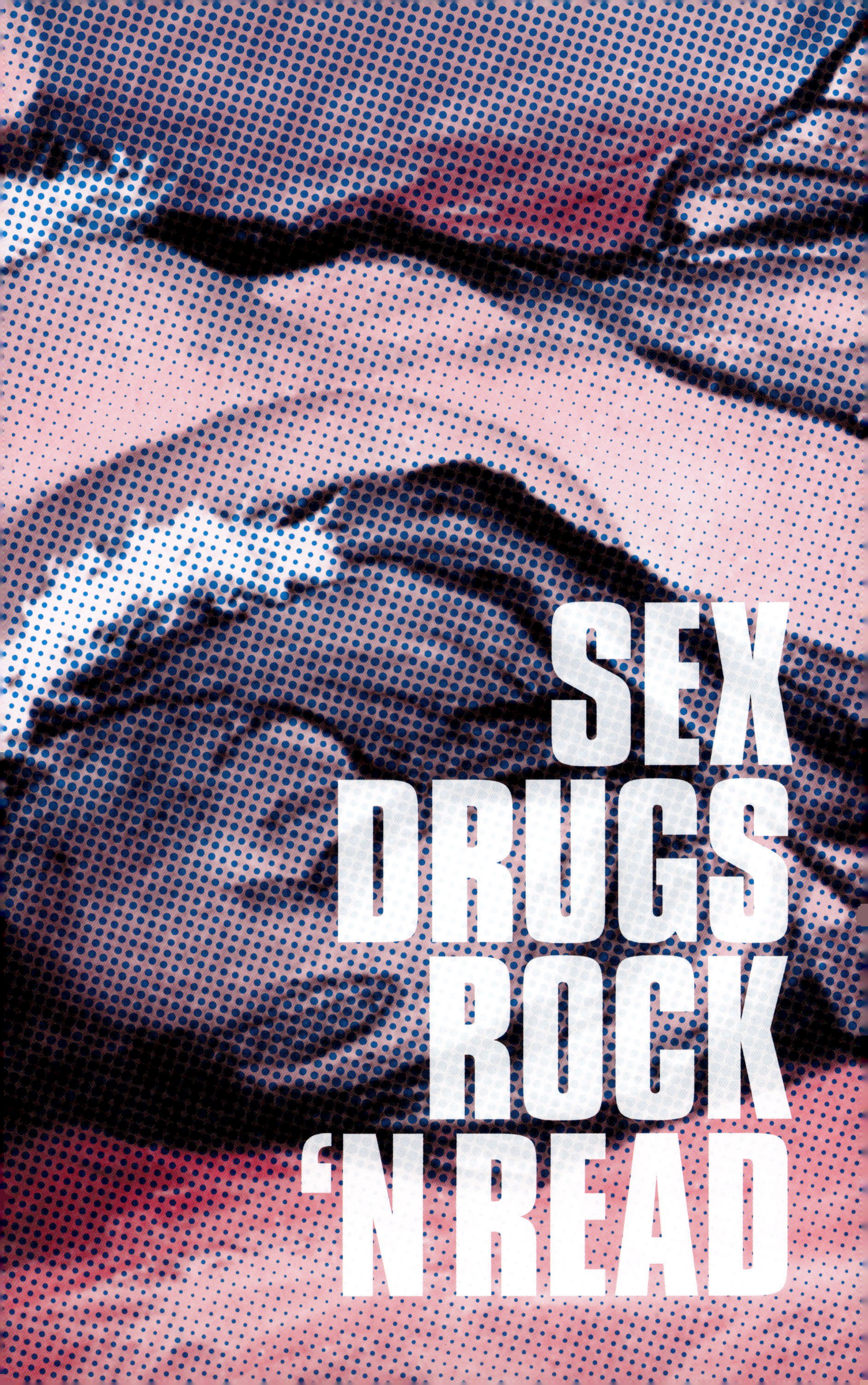
SEX
DRUGS
ROCK
'N READ

"Their kicks came from a needle...the brutal, explosive story of hopheads on the loose and the victims they ravage to vent their hyped emotions..."

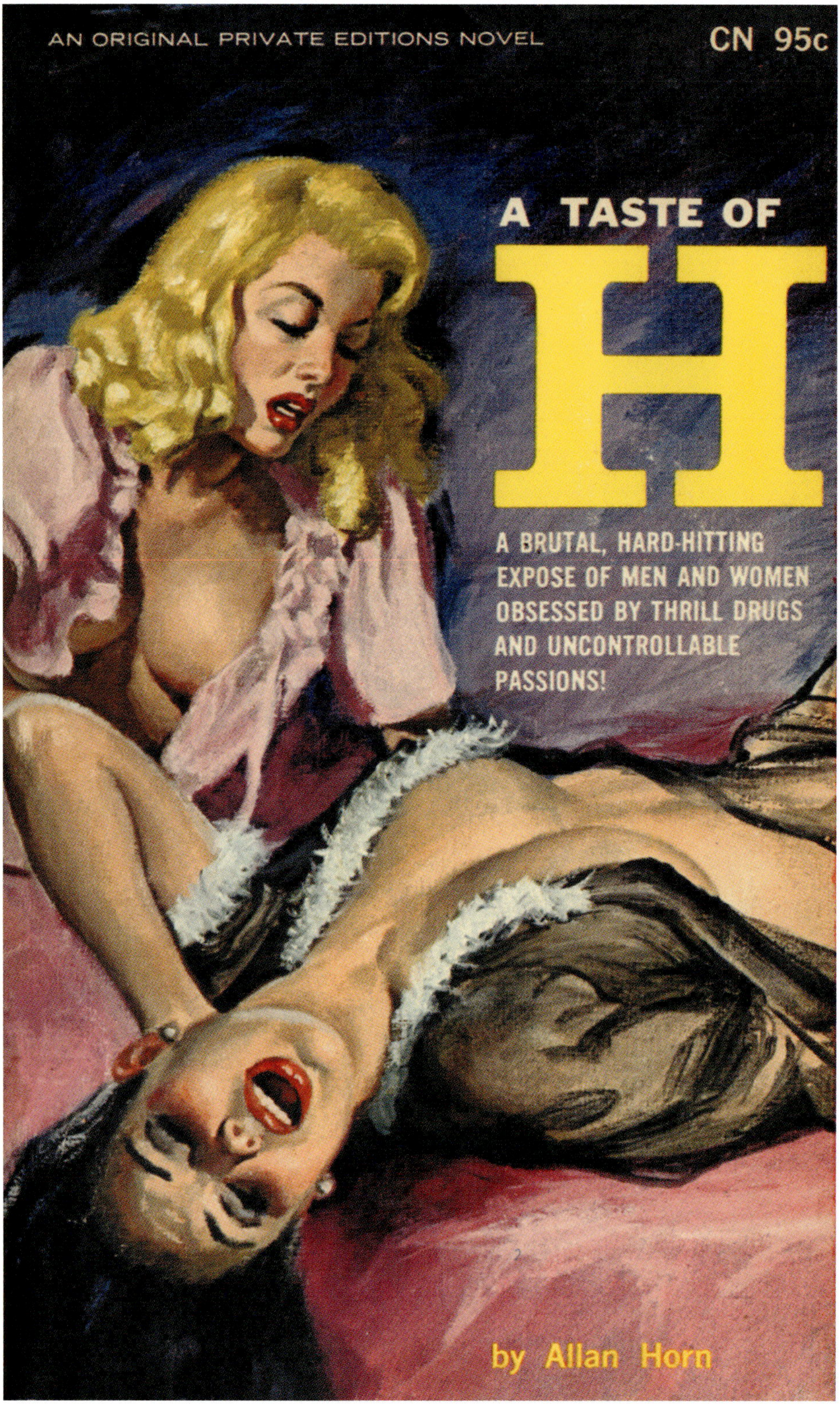

Allan Horn • ***A Taste of H*** • PRIVATE EDITIONS PE384 • 1969 • PBO

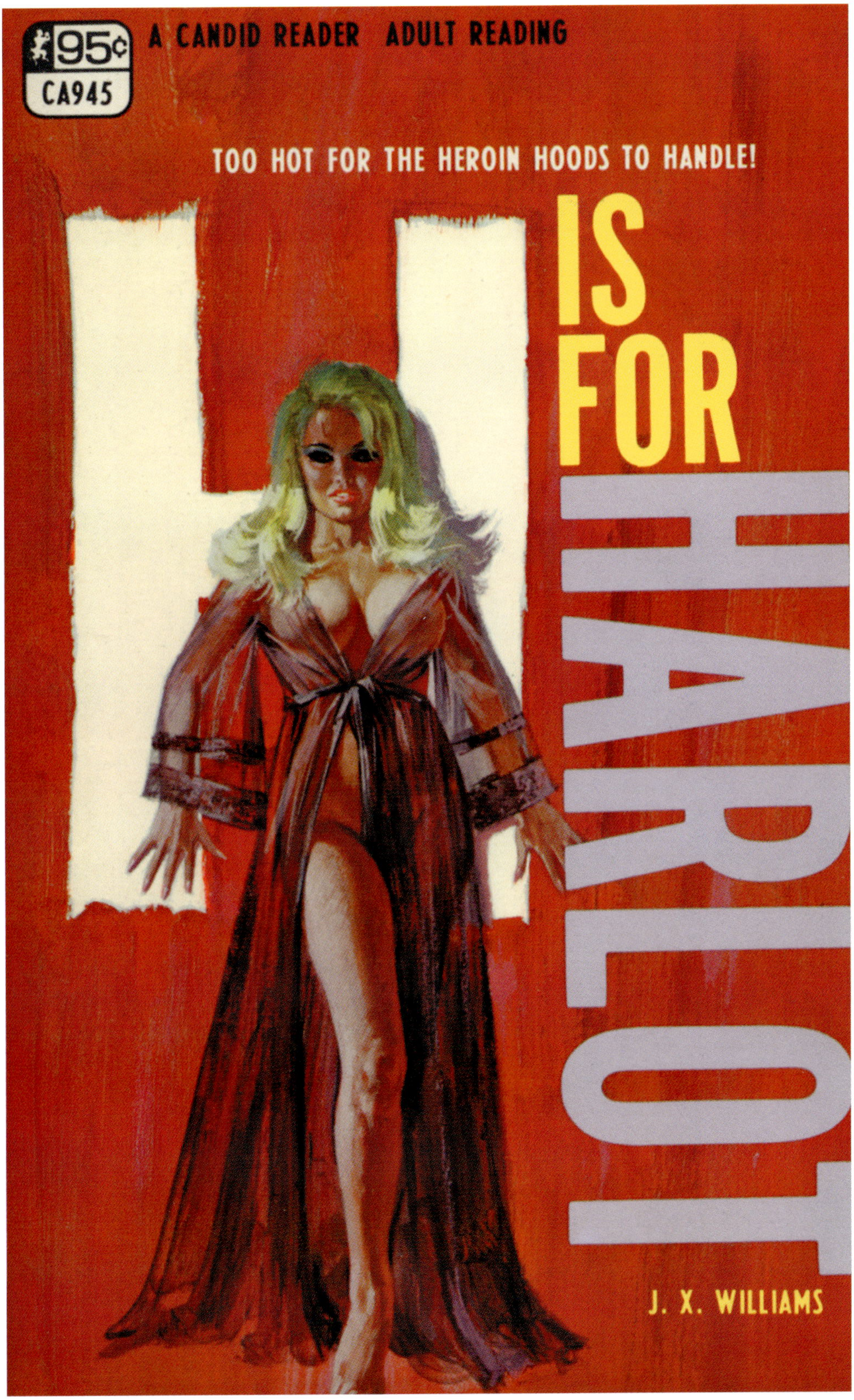

J.X. Williams (pseud.) • ***H Is For Harlot*** • CANDID READER 945, N.D., CA • 1967 • COVER BY ROBERT BONFILS • PBO

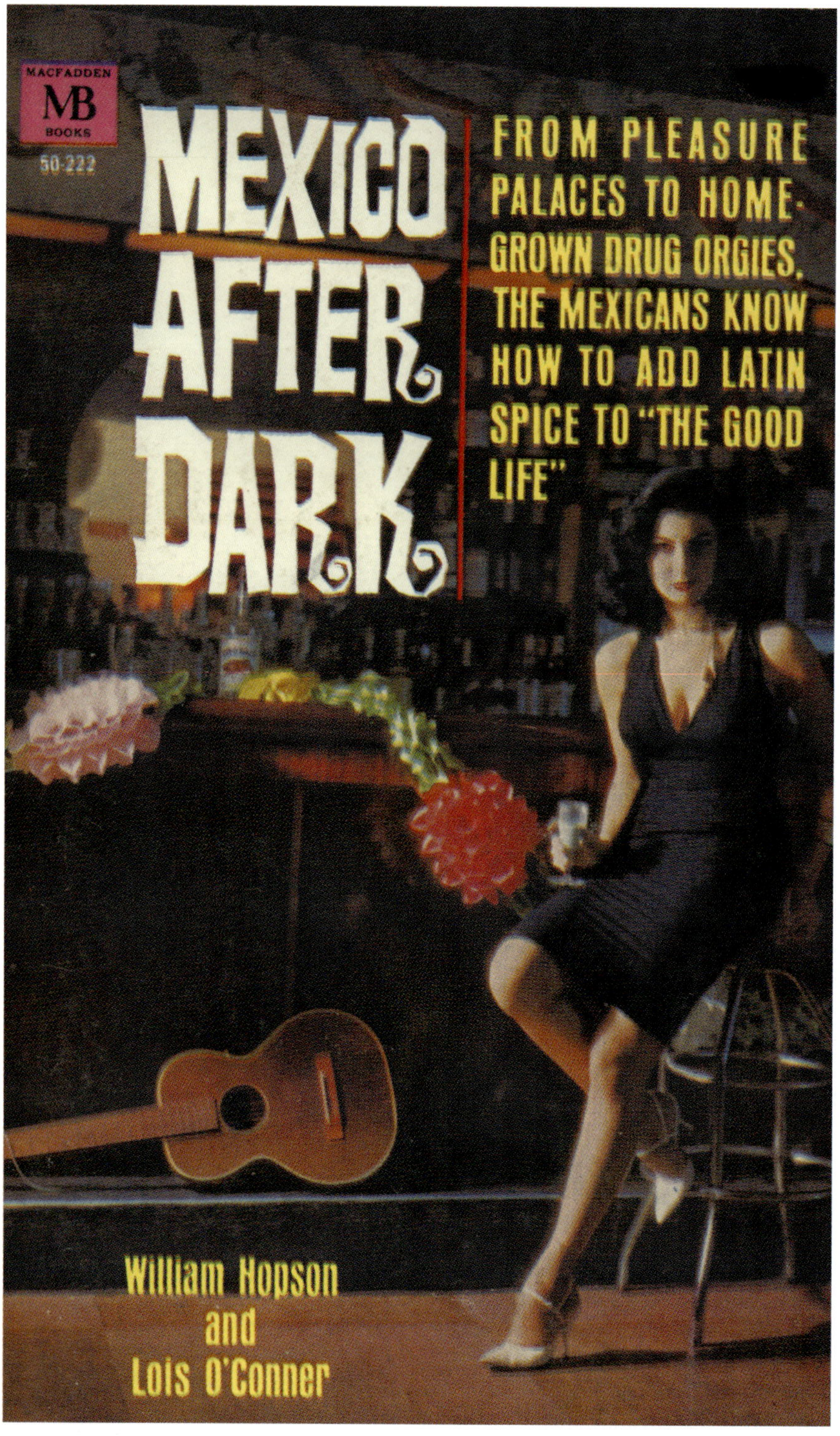

"The heat is on in Tijuana, partly because of the hue and cry over narcotics. Now you buy your happiness pills only on prescription at the Tijuana drugstores. Formerly you just stepped up and bought what you wanted, at about two cents a pill. Narcotic traffic has now been chased underground, and a pill now costs about a dollar. Such is the high cost of government intervention."

William Hopson and Lois O'Conner • ***Mexico After Dark*** • MCFADDEN MB 50-222 • 1964
PBO • COURTESY TONY JACOBS

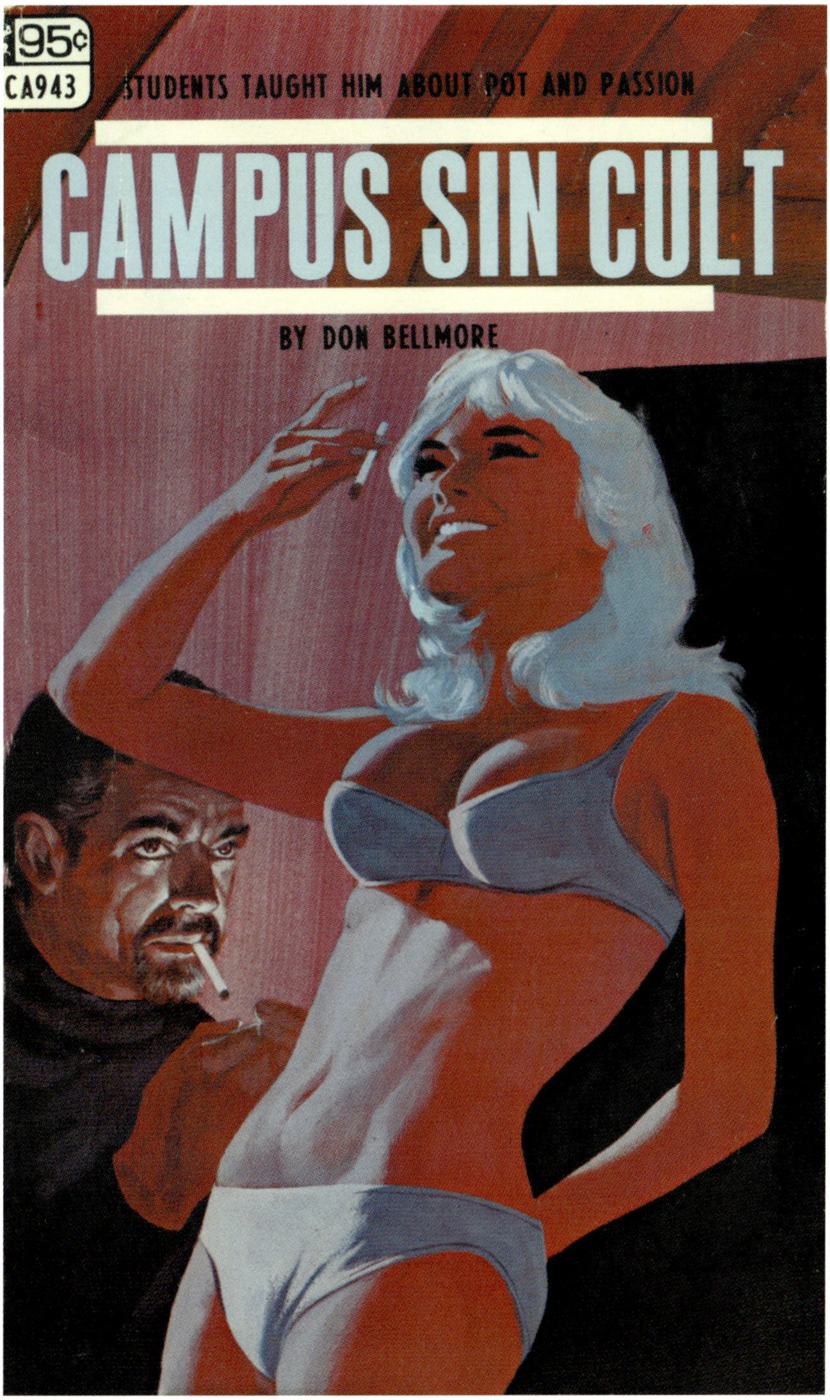

"'Remember, it's the marijuana problem we're interested in this time.'

"Russ blanched. 'This time?'

"'Drugs today — protesters tomorrow,' Dean Huggans said firmly. 'We've decided to start on the smaller problems first...'"

"'...Huggans means it,' Russ said...'too much adverse publicity lately about drugs and sex on college campuses...Euphemia?'"
"'Shhhh...Puff, baby,' she said, 'it's dream time.'"

Don Bellmore [George H. Smith] • ***Campus Sin Cult*** • CANDID READER CA943 • 1968
COVER BY ROBERT BONFILS • PBO

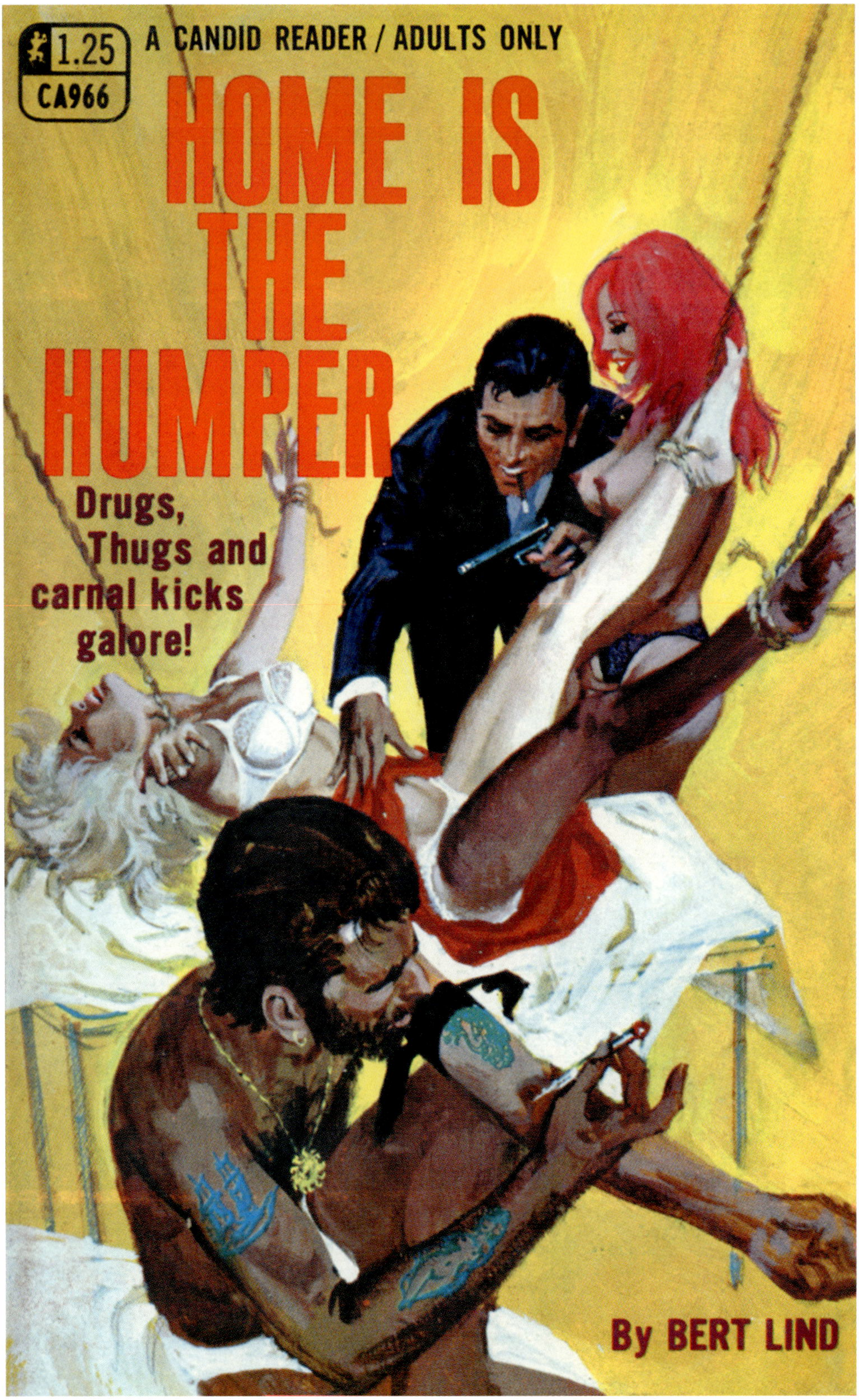

Bert Lind (pseud.) • ***Home Is for the Humper*** • CANDID READER 966 • 1968 • COVER BY ROBERT BONFILS • PBO

John Dexter (pseud.) • ***Narco Nympho*** • LEISURE BOOKS LB1197 • 1967 • COVER BY ROBERT BONFILS • PBO

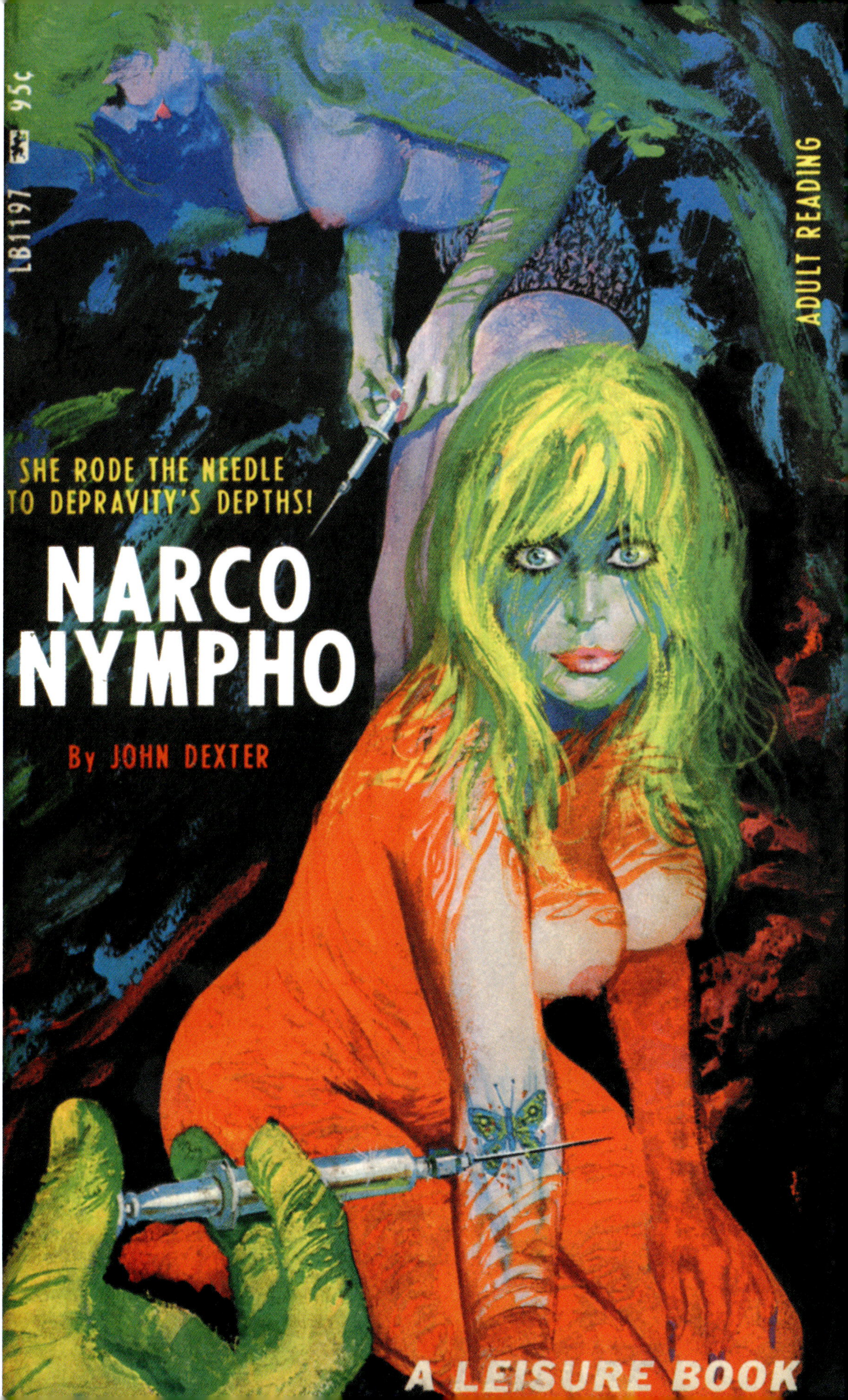
LB1197
95¢
ADULT READING
SHE RODE THE NEEDLE
TO DEPRAVITY'S DEPTHS!
NARCO
NYMPHO
By JOHN DEXTER
A LEISURE BOOK

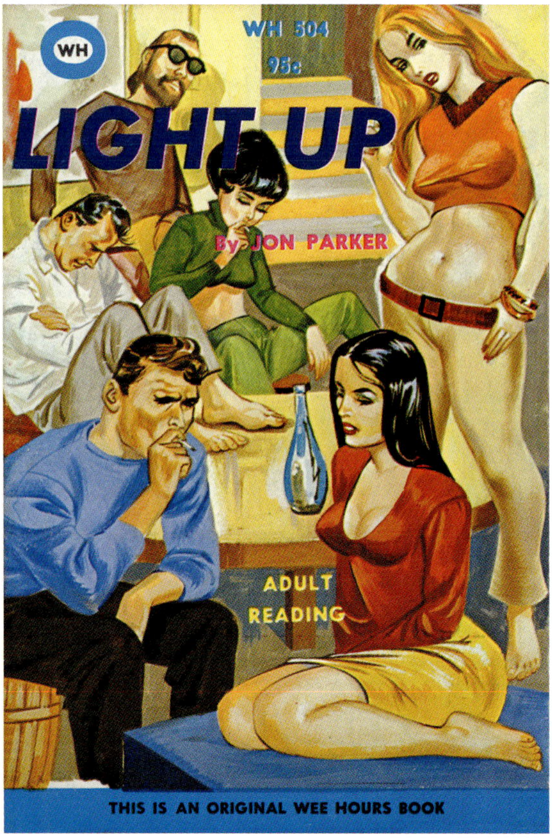

"Saturday night in Greenwich Village meant a real wild bash. It meant going to those attic parties where LSD and reefers held sway.

"...a hopped up Beatnik poet dared Lila, the Pop artist: 'Bet you can't do what a girl wants to do.'

"'Bet you I can!' Lila had taken more than her customary dose of LSD, dropping just a speck of the liquid on a sugar cube, sticking it under her tongue and then draining it until there was nothing left — but a real wild kick that made her tear off her clothes, stand nude before the circle of Bohemians, then proceed to stroke and fondle herself, losing contact with reality. LSD was like that. So was Lila."

Jon Parker (pseud.) • ***Light Up*** • WEE HOURS 504
1966 • COVER BY BILL ALEXANDER • PBO

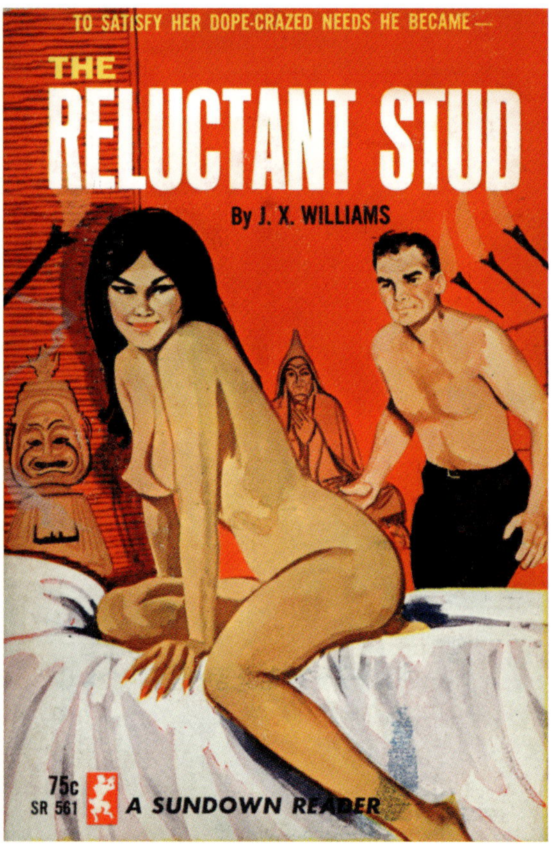

J.X. Williams [house pseudonym, here of Arthur Plotnick] • ***The Reluctant Stud***
SUNDOWN READER SR561 • 1965 • PBO

Gregg Stevens • ***The Auto-Mated Swap***
COMPANION BOOKS CB654 • 1969
COVER BY ROBERT BONFILS • PBO

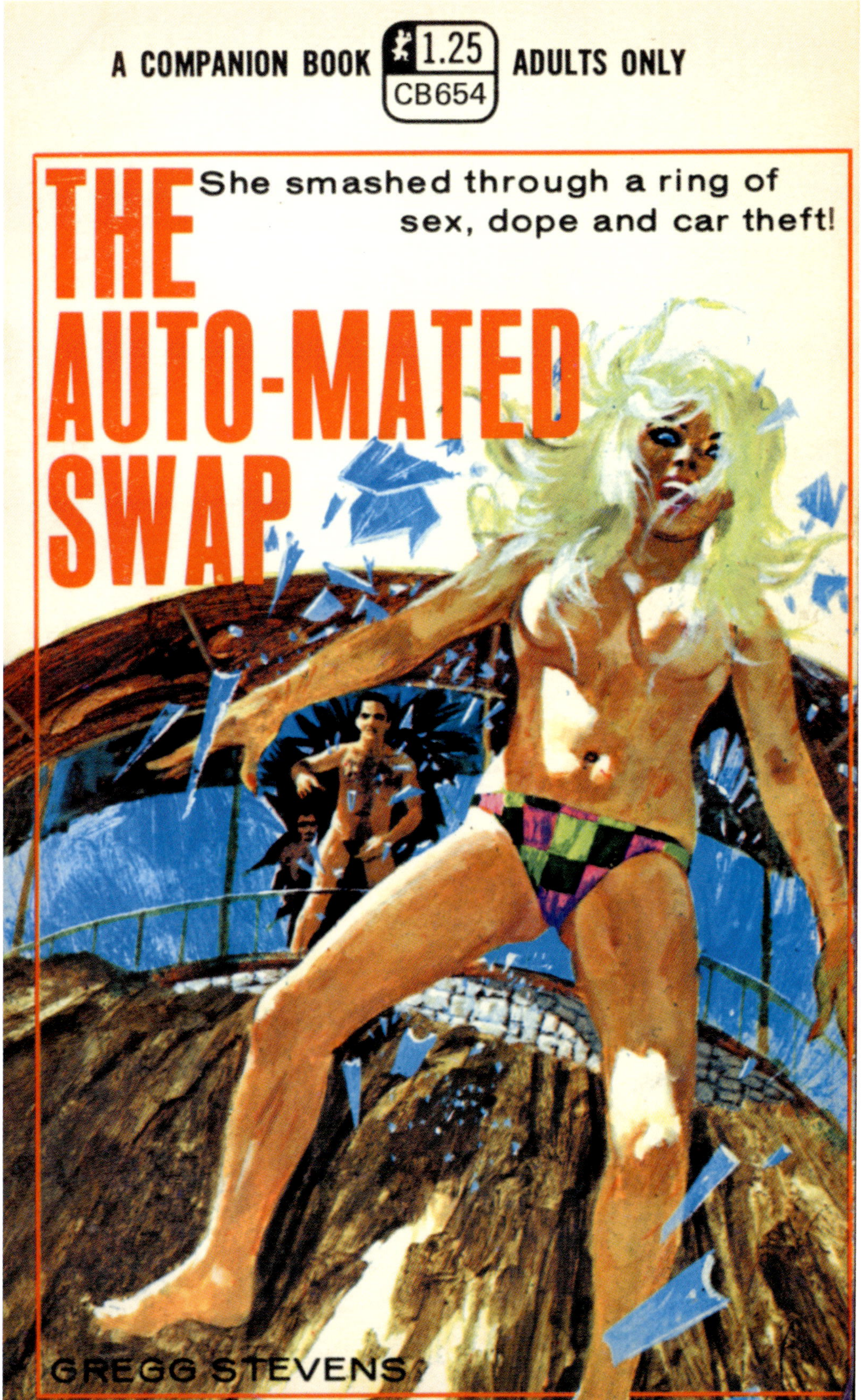
A COMPANION BOOK
1.25
CB654
ADULTS ONLY
THE AUTO-MATED SWAP
She smashed through a ring of sex, dope and car theft!
GREGG STEVENS

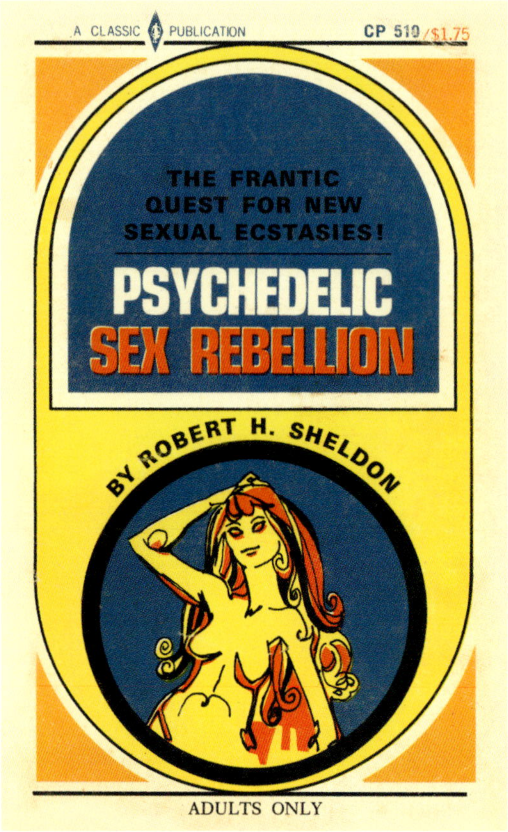

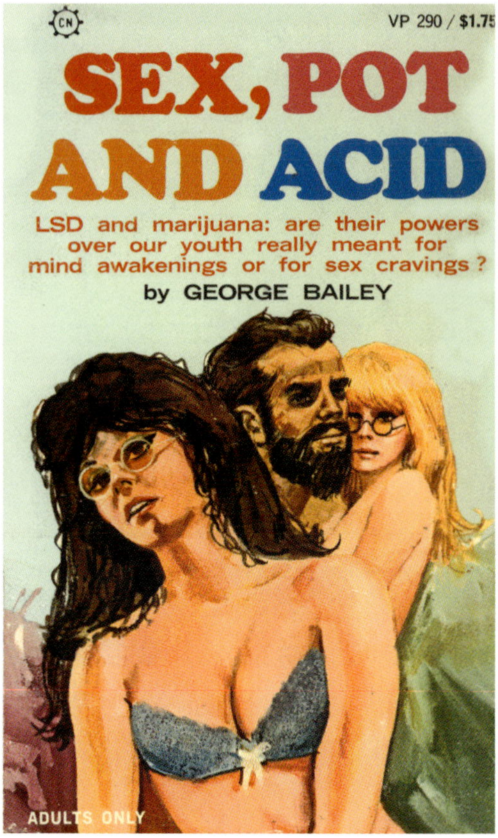

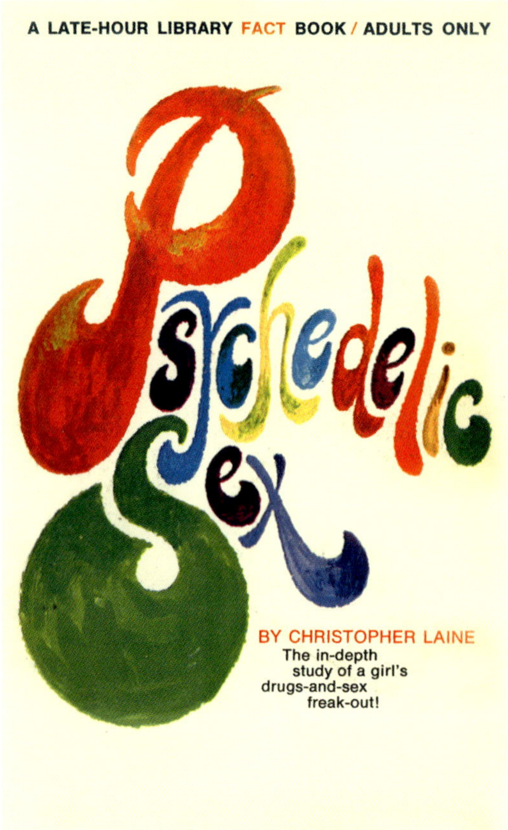

Robert H. Sheldon • ***Psychedelic Sex Rebellion***
CLASSIC PUBLICATIONS [EDWARD S. SULLIVAN, A.K.A. JULES GRIFFON] CP-510 • 1968 • PBO

George Bailey (pseud.) • ***Sex, Pot and Acid***
VICEROY VP290 • 1968 • PBO

Christopher Laine (pseud.) • ***Psychedelic Sex***
LATE HOUR LIBRARY • 811 • 1967 • PBO

Opposite page: Ralph Benton (pseud.)
Psychedelic Sex • VICEROY VP283 • 1968 • PBO

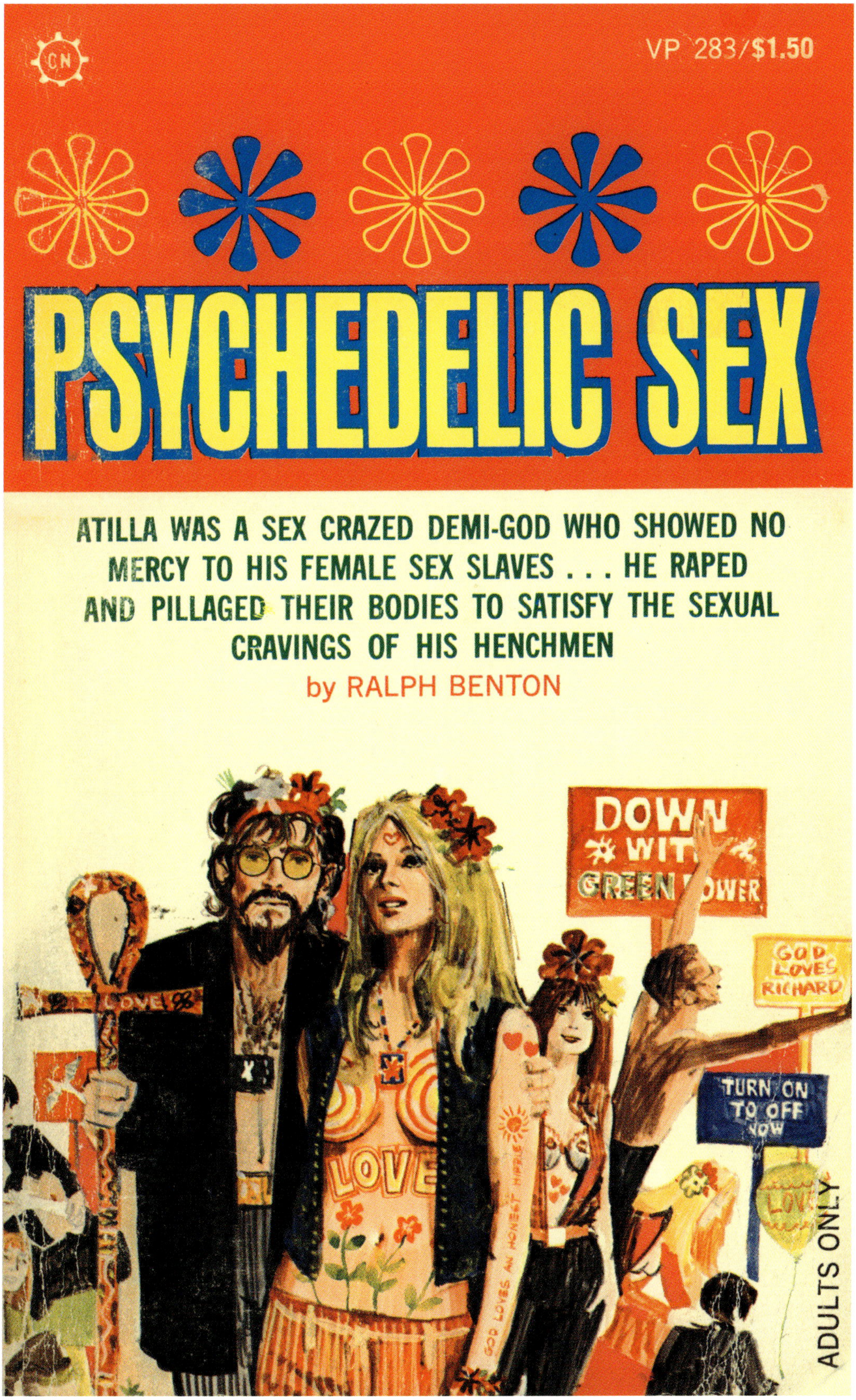
VP 283/$1.50
PSYCHEDELIC SEX
ATILLA WAS A SEX CRAZED DEMI-GOD WHO SHOWED NO MERCY TO HIS FEMALE SEX SLAVES . . . HE RAPED AND PILLAGED THEIR BODIES TO SATISFY THE SEXUAL CRAVINGS OF HIS HENCHMEN
by RALPH BENTON
DOWN
GREEN
GOD LOVES RICHARD
TURN ON TO OFF
LOVE
ADULTS ONLY

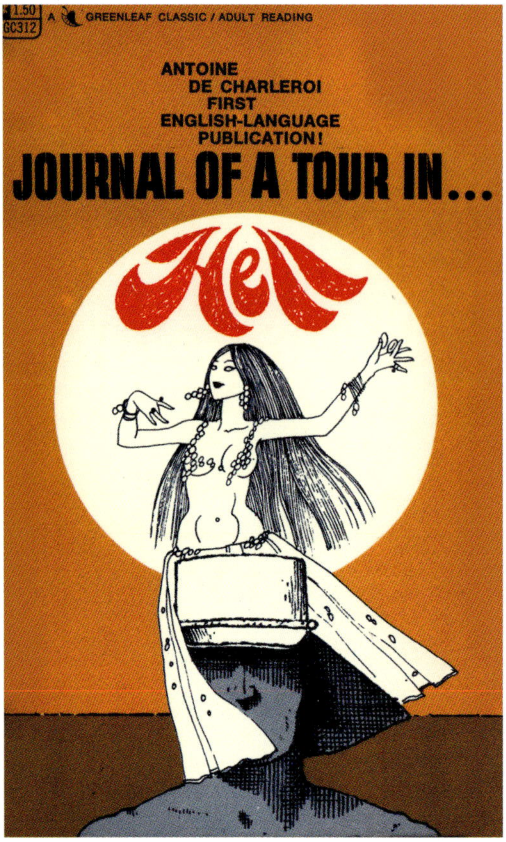

"I had never tried kif. I had heard that with some it brought elation and with others nausea. When I am bent on love-making, I do not take chances…Bramont smoked contentedly. When the weed was nearly gone I consented to have two draws of it. Perhaps it would intensify the thrill of passion, but it had no effect on me whatever. I suppose I expected to see garish phantoms in the air. I did not."

First American Edition, a reprint of an unknown French-in-English original source edition circa 1955–1960. Sex and kif (hashish) smoking in North Africa amongst French Foreign Legionnaires and the native populace.

Antoine de Charleroi (pseud.) • ***Journal of a Tour in Hell*** • GREENLEAF CLASSICS GC312 • 1968
COVER BY HARRY BREMNER • FROM THE AUTHOR'S COLLECTION

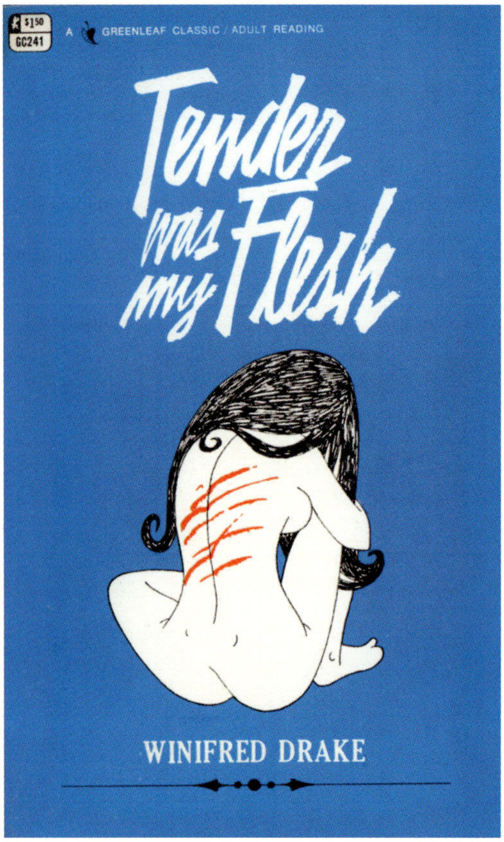

"'When you going to try the real thing? How about now?'

"'Try what?'

"'H. Come on.' Mary took her by the arm. 'Come on in the kitchen and I'll fix you up. It's the greatest.'

"'Well, maybe,' Susan hesitated. 'Which way?'

"'A shot's the best, but you can sniff it, if you want. Come on.'

"…Susan took it. 'I've heard this usually makes you sick the first time.'

"'Yeah, sometimes. But there's a first time for everything, kid, and after that you're ridin' high.'"

Winifred Drake [Deny Bryant] • ***Tender Was My Flesh*** • GREENLEAF CLASSICS GC241 • 1967
COVER BY HARRY BREMNER • REPRINT OF OLYMPIA PRESS TC-6 (1955) • FROM THE AUTHOR'S COLLECTION

Eric Jay (pseudo) • ***Pussies and Pot*** • CANDID READER 978 • 1969 • COVER BY HARRY BREMNER • PBO

Peter Jenkins (pseud.) • ***Drugged Into Sin***
LIVERPOOL LIBRARY PRESS 111 • 1968 • PBO

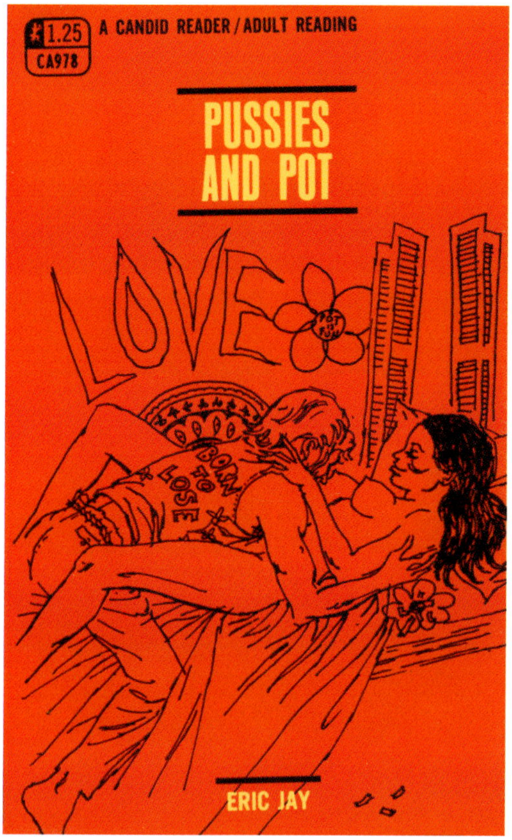

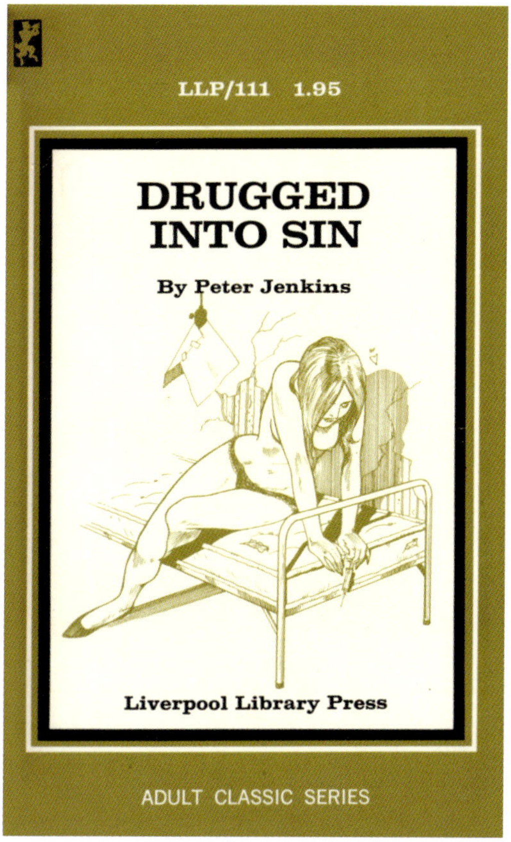

"'What are they smoking,' she finally asked, as she watched them pass around the pipe a few more times.

"'Hashish and opium,' he told her. 'You should try it, it's very relaxing.'

"'No, I don't think so,' she said but he had already motioned for the pipe and was holding it for her.

"'Try it,' he told her and his tone of voice made it more an order than an offer...'It will make the evening more pleasant if you do,' he laughed, 'and you're going to be here for the evening, so you may as well enjoy yourself.'

"...The smoke filled her lungs and she coughed. The taste was acrid and she thought that she might get sick but she didn't...her head began to feel numb in a feathery-light sort of way and the music seemed to be resounding in her brain, almost as if the notes were coming from within her...her head nodded up and down in time to the music...She could feel the effects of the dope and she felt lethargic, listless and completely uncaring, time seemed to have stopped..."

Ann Garner (pseud.) • ***Opium Den*** • LIVERPOOL LIBRARY PRESS LLP134 • 1968 • PBO

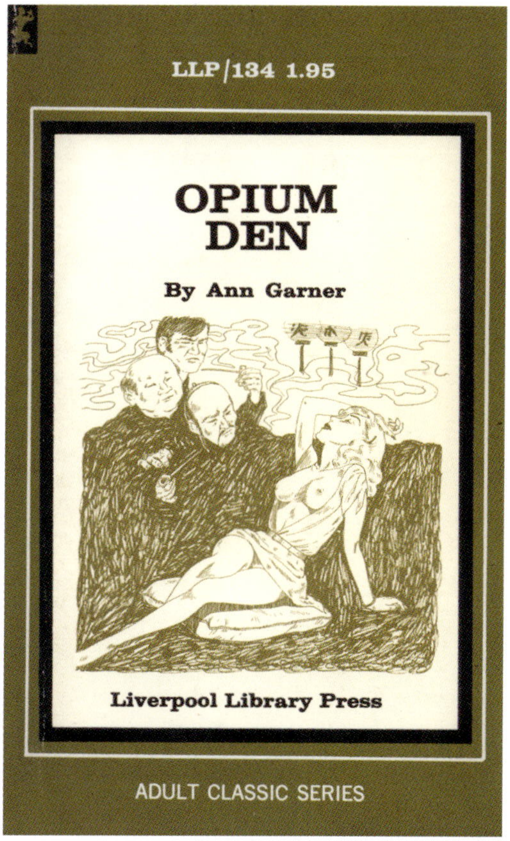

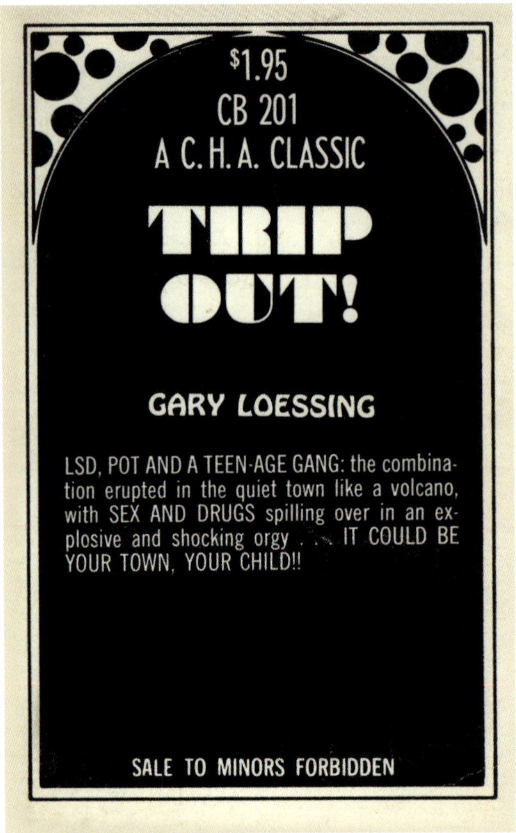

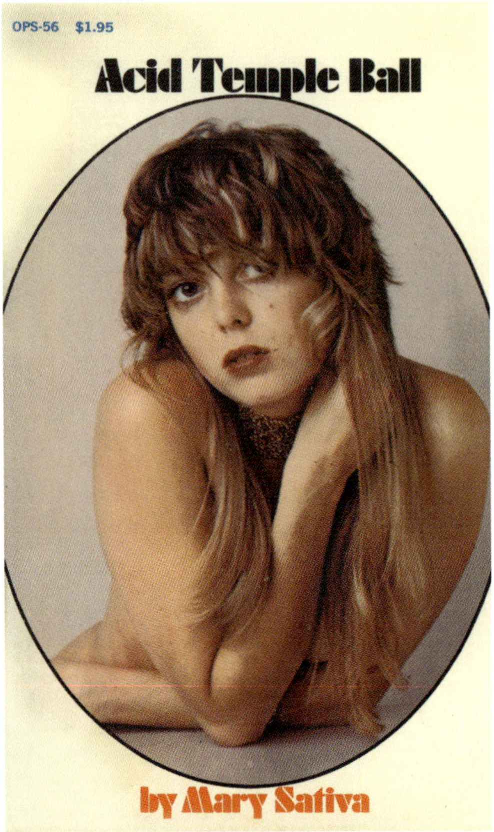

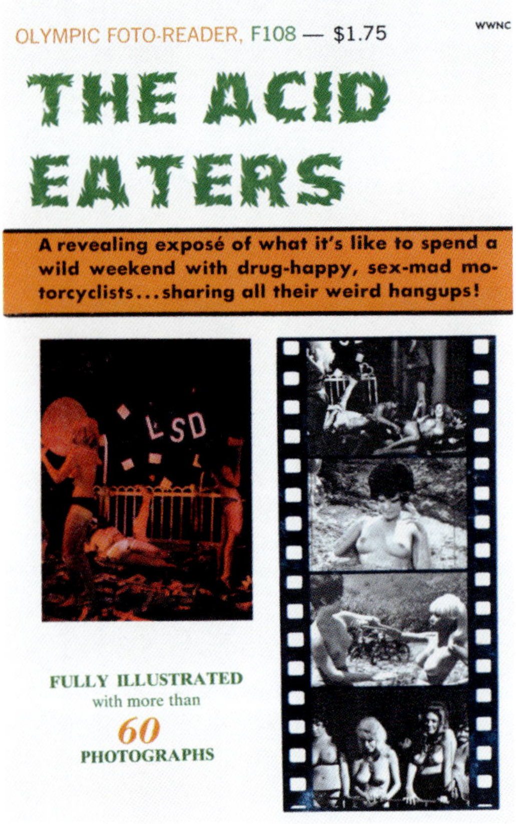

"...Jesse's flesh is melting and merging like colored lights. I peer through the patterns at him, he smiles. The smile opens, shooting darts of light in spreading whirlpools in the room. Moves his hands before my eyes and leaves a rail of golden, dripping images, like a harpsichord arpeggio."

Mary Sativa [Sharon Rudahl] • ***Acid Temple Ball***
OLYMPIA PRESS-NY OPS-56 • 1972
REPRINT OF OLYMPIA PRESS-NY TRAVELLER'S COMPANION TC2228 • 1969

Gary Loessing • ***Trip Out!*** • C.H.A. CLASSICS CB201
1969 • PBO

The Acid Eaters • OLYMPIC FOTO-READER F108
1967 • PBO

Peter Kevin • ***The Pimp's Needle***
BARCLAY HOUSE 7423 • 1974 • PBO

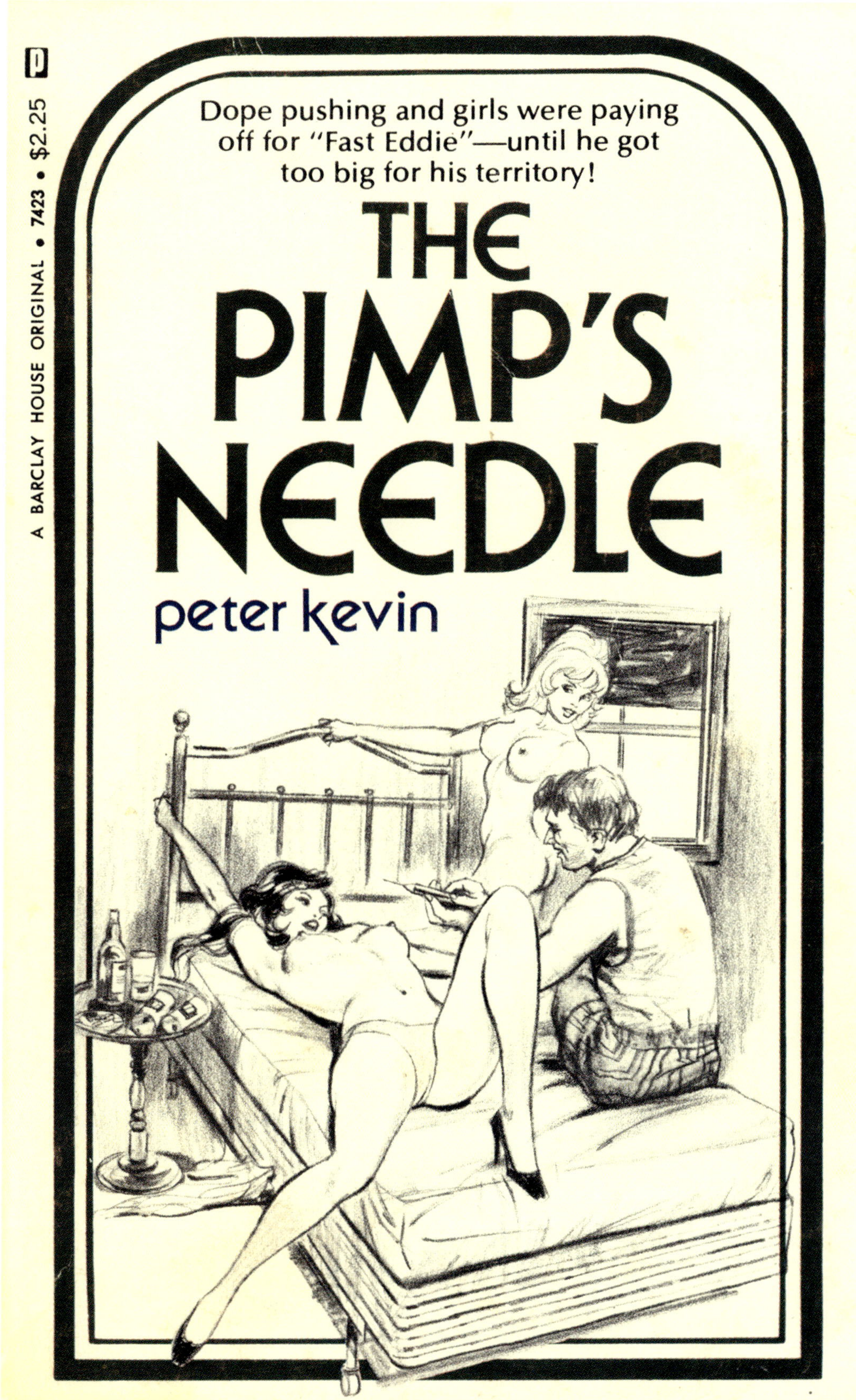
A BARCLAY HOUSE ORIGINAL • 7423 • $2.25
Dope pushing and girls were paying off for "Fast Eddie"—until he got too big for his territory!
THE PIMP'S NEEDLE
peter kevin

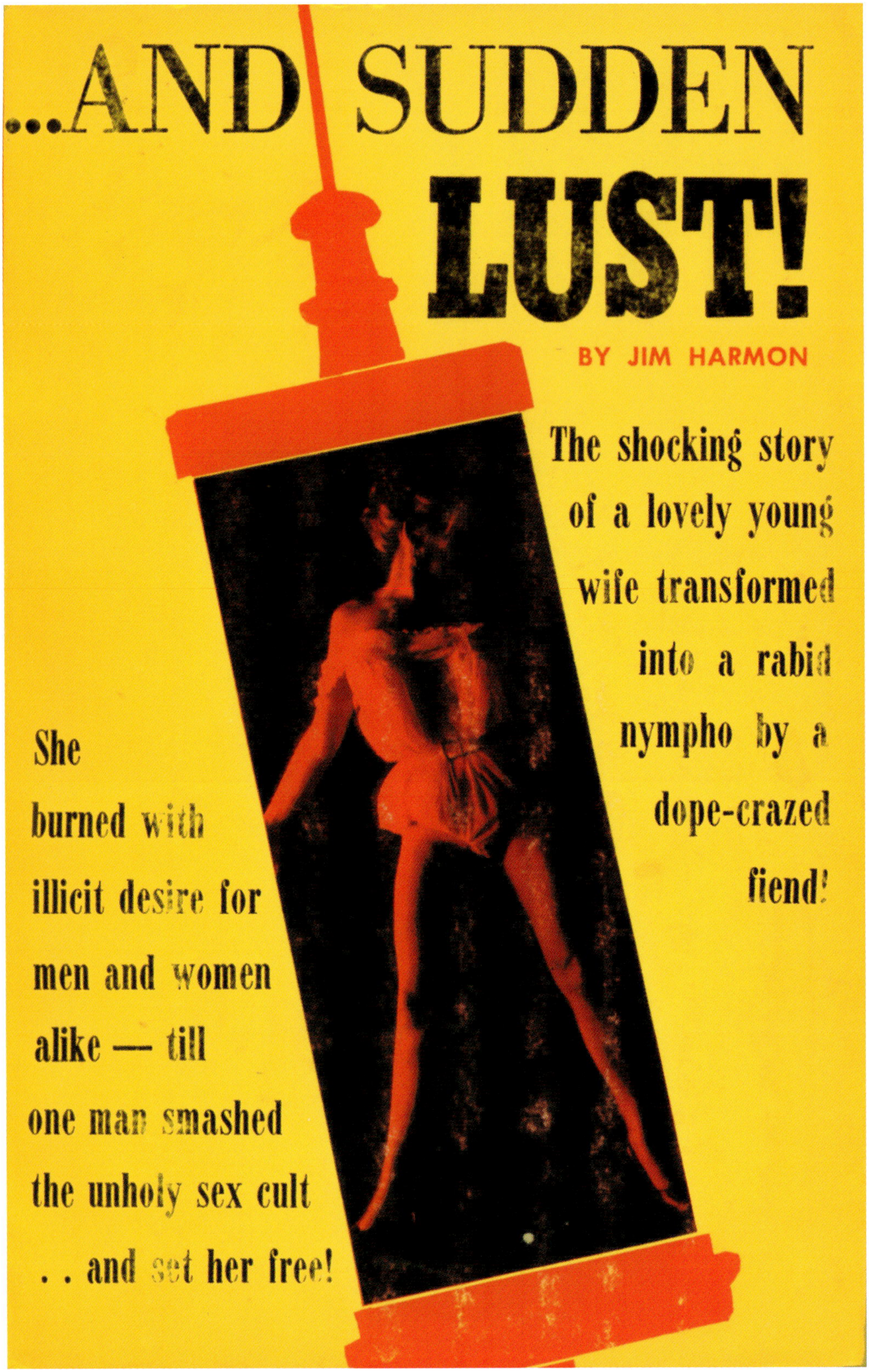

Jim Harmon • ***...And Sudden Lust!*** • PAGAN 102 • 1962 • PBO • COURTESY TONY JACOBS

Andrew Shaw (pseud.) • ***Fraternity of Shame*** • LEISURE BOOKS 1134 • 1966 • COVER BY ROBERT BONFILS • PBO

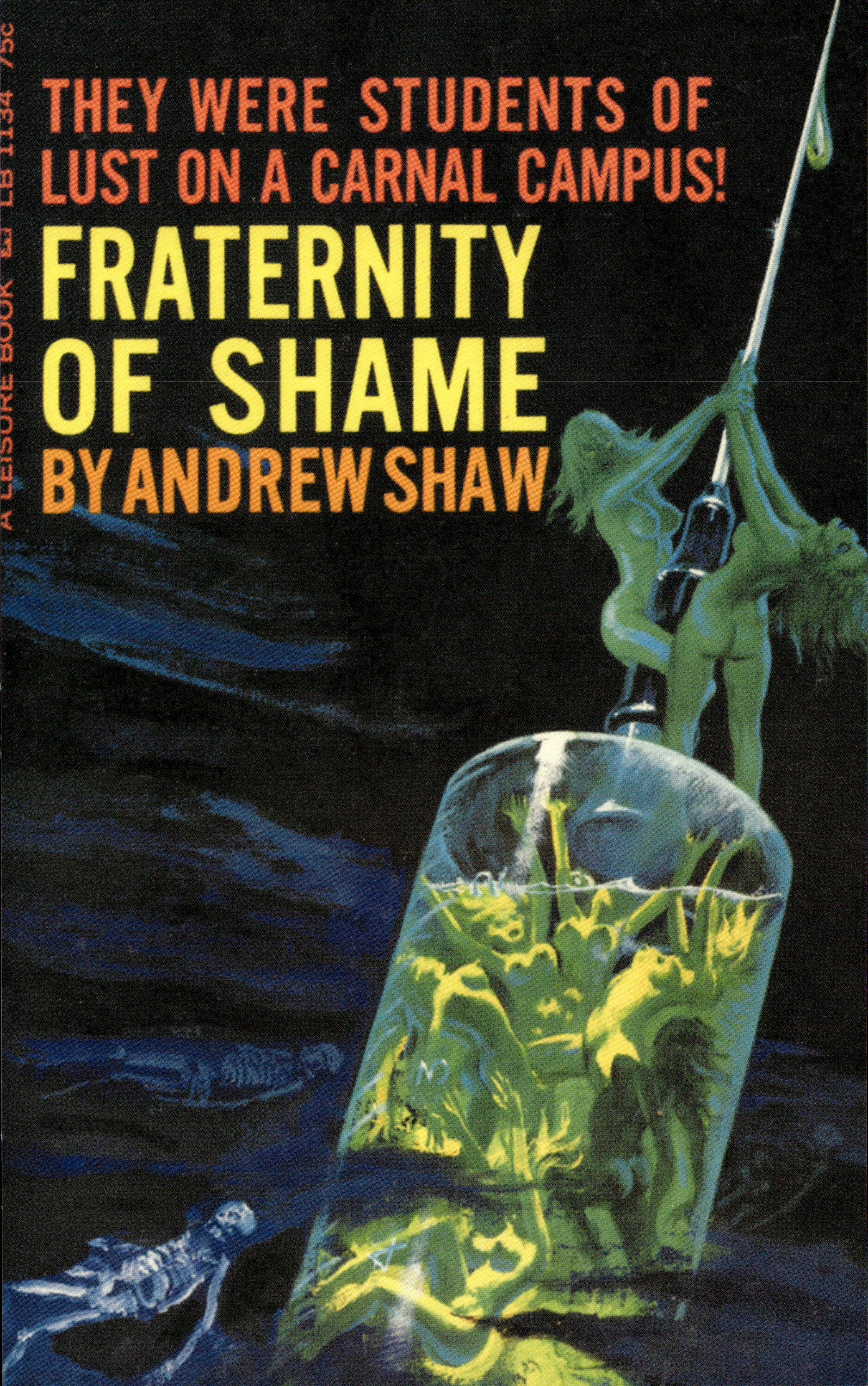
A LEISURE BOOK LB 1134 75c
THEY WERE STUDENTS OF LUST ON A CARNAL CAMPUS!
FRATERNITY OF SHAME
BY ANDREW SHAW

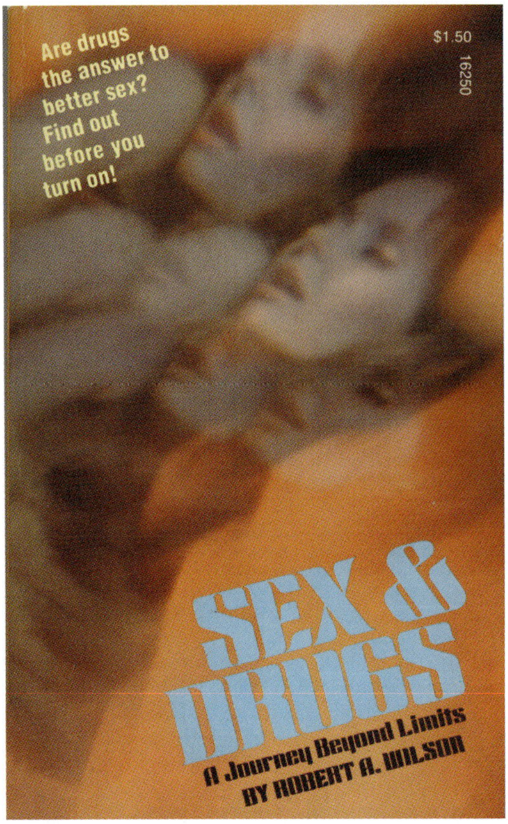

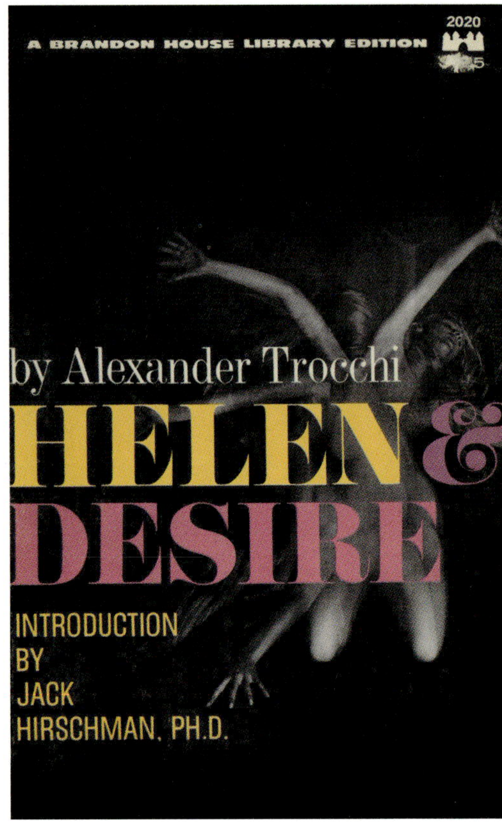

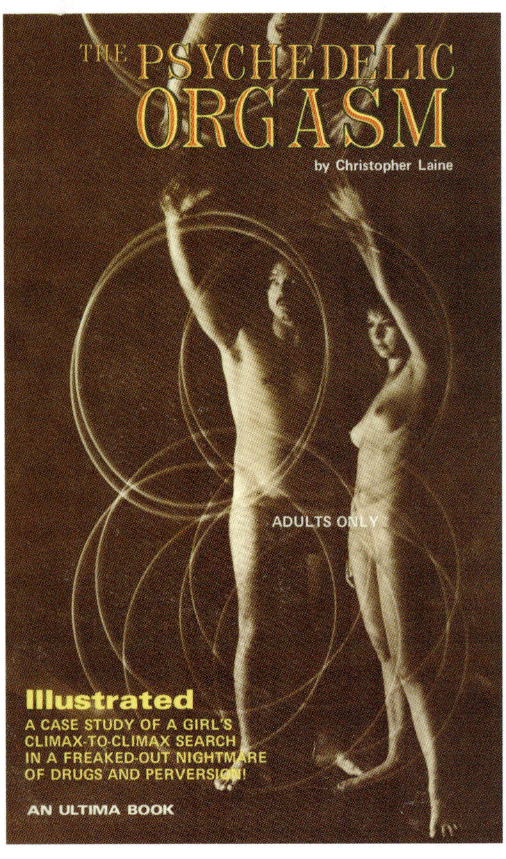

Arguably the best contemporary non-fiction treatment of the subject, written by the author of many respected speculative fiction and metaphysical volumes.

Robert A[nton]. Wilson • ***Sex & Drugs***
PLAYBOY PRESS 16250 • 1975 • REPRINT

"I have lusted as it were to melt out of myself, to become the anonymous and vibrant spasm which the regular application of drugs — hashish, I believe — has made me...

"Oh God, what an ecstasy!

"Food? Its taste is very pleasant, but it is rather an effort to eat it. All I eat willingly and without reservation is the exotic mouth-ringing mixture of honey and almonds and hashish"

Alexander Trocchi (a.k.a. Frances Lengel)
Helen & Desire • BRANDON HOUSE LIBRARY EDITIONS 2020 • 1967 • REPRINT OF THE PARIS: OLYMPIA PRESS 1954 1ST EDITION • FROM THE AUTHOR'S COLLECTION

Christopher Laine (pseud.) • ***The Psychedelic Orgasm***
ULTIMA • 1969 • POB

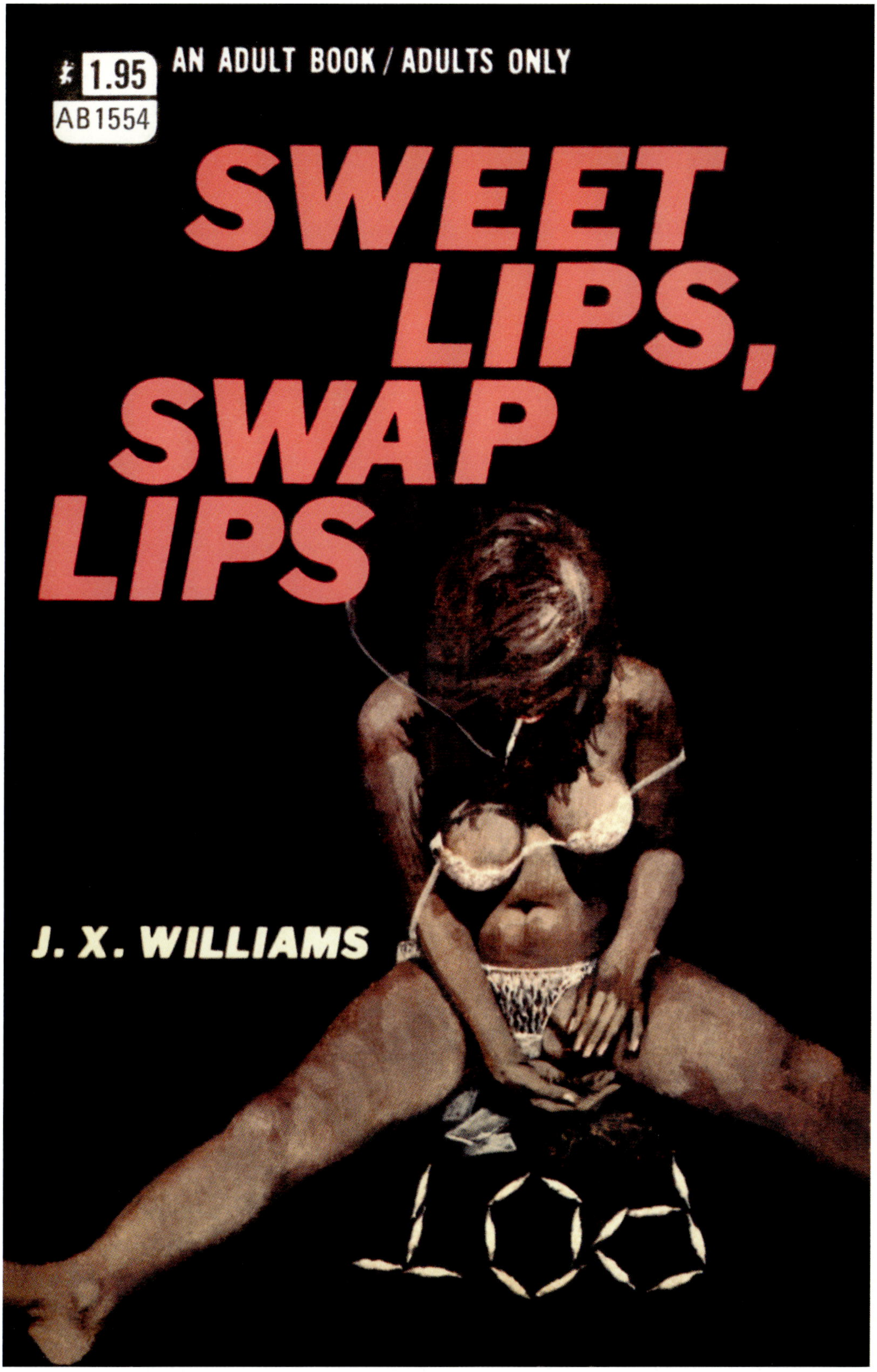

J.X. Williams • ***Sweet Lips, Swap Lips*** • ADULT BOOKS AB1554, N.D. [CA.1969–70] • COVER BY ROBERT BONFILS • PBO

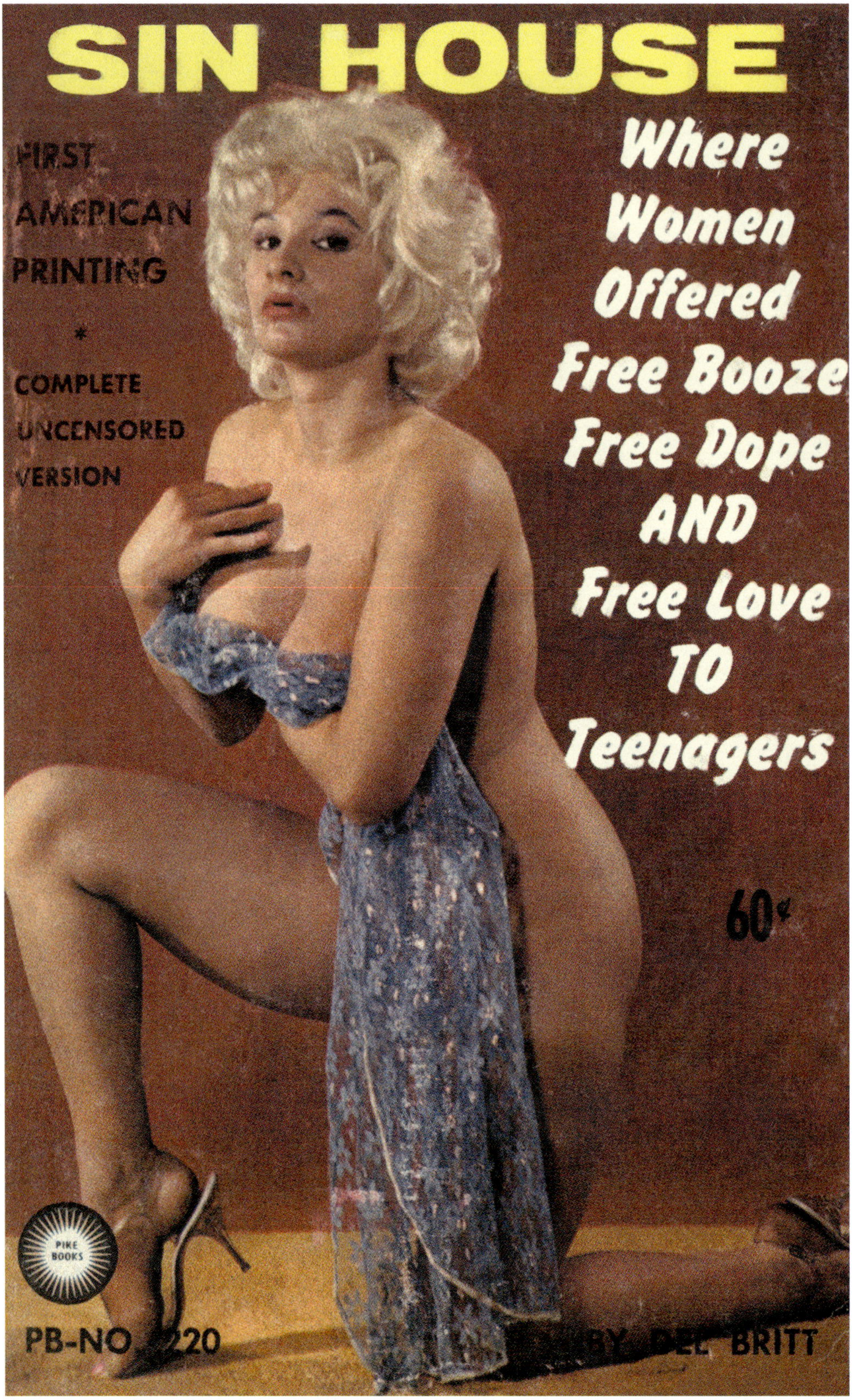

Del Britt [Dale Koby] • ***Sin House*** • PIKE 220 • 1962 • PBO

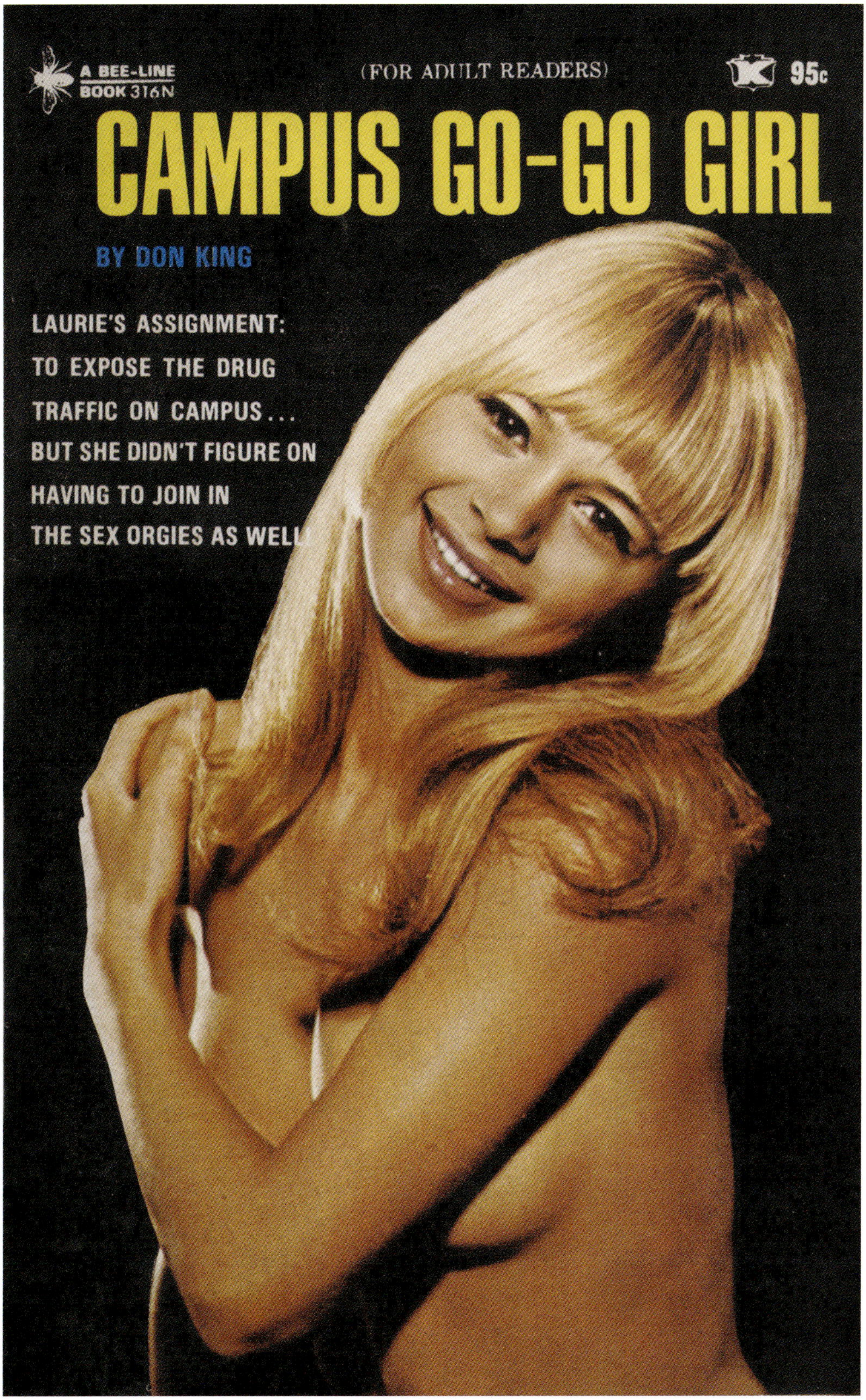

Don King • ***Campus Go-Go Girl*** • BEE-LINE 316N • 1968 • PBO

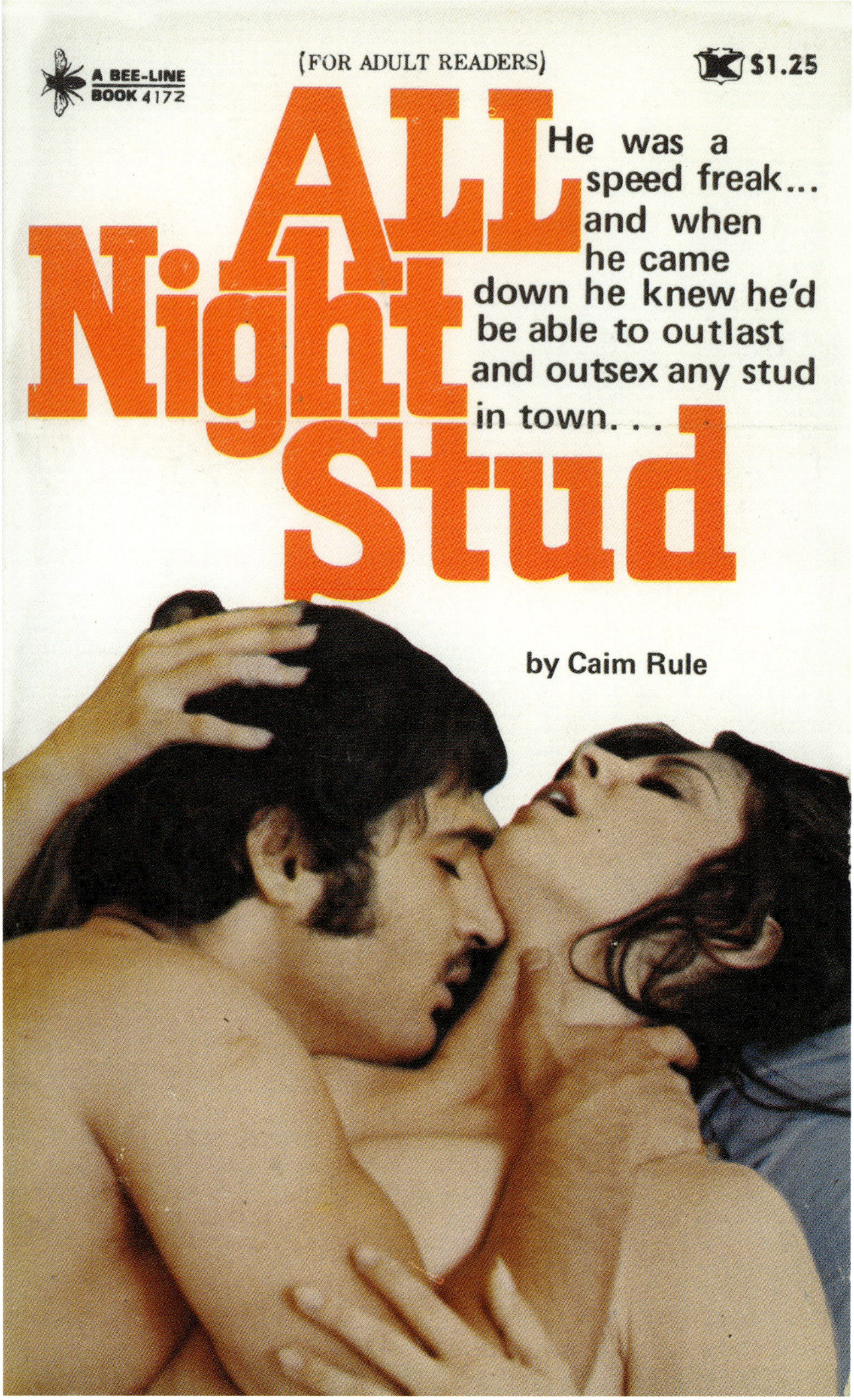

Caim Rule (pseud.) • ***All Night Stud*** • BEE-LINE 4172 • 1969 • PBO

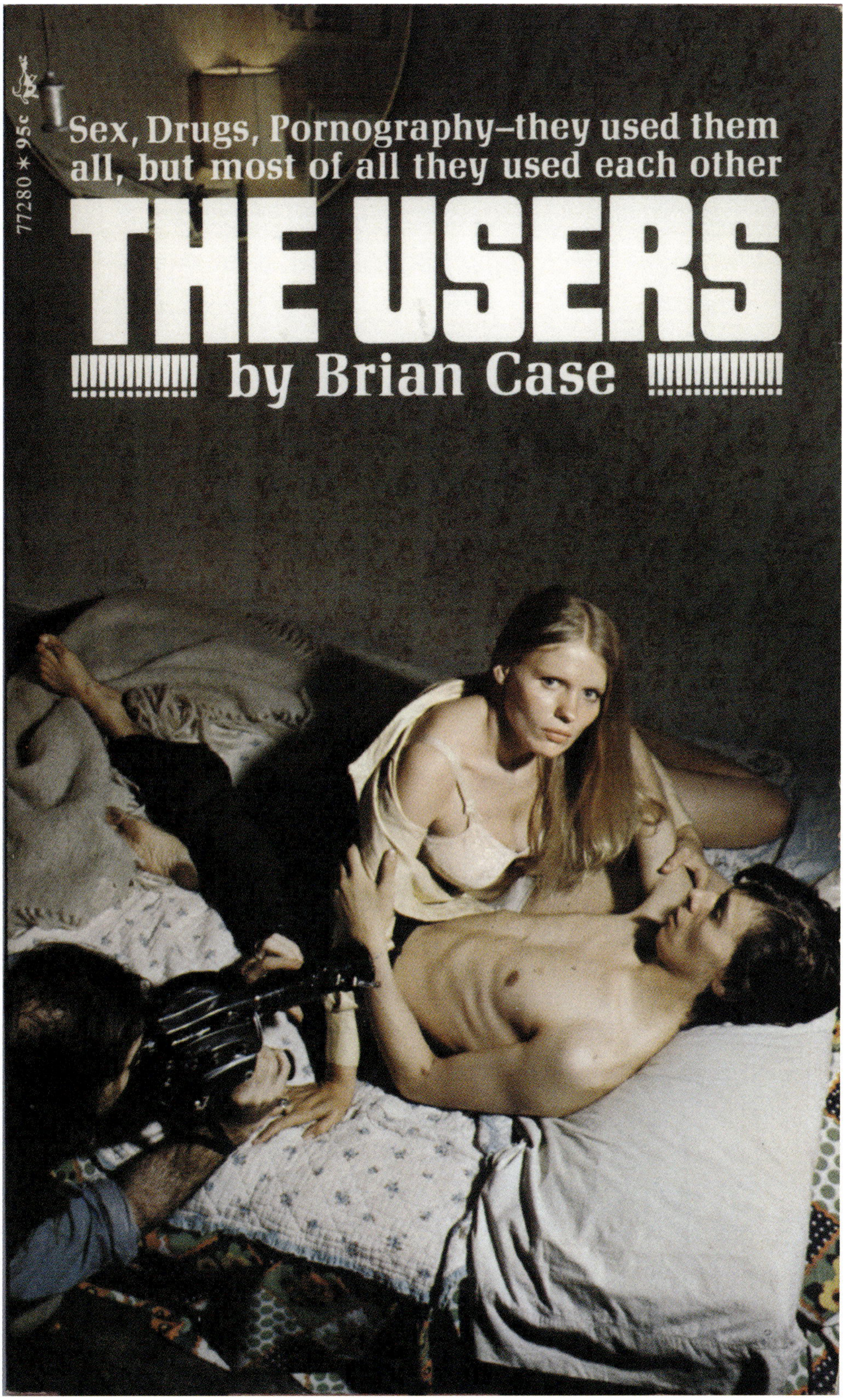

Brian Case • ***The Users*** • POCKET BOOKS 77280 • 1974 • PBO

THE INTERNATIONAL TRADE

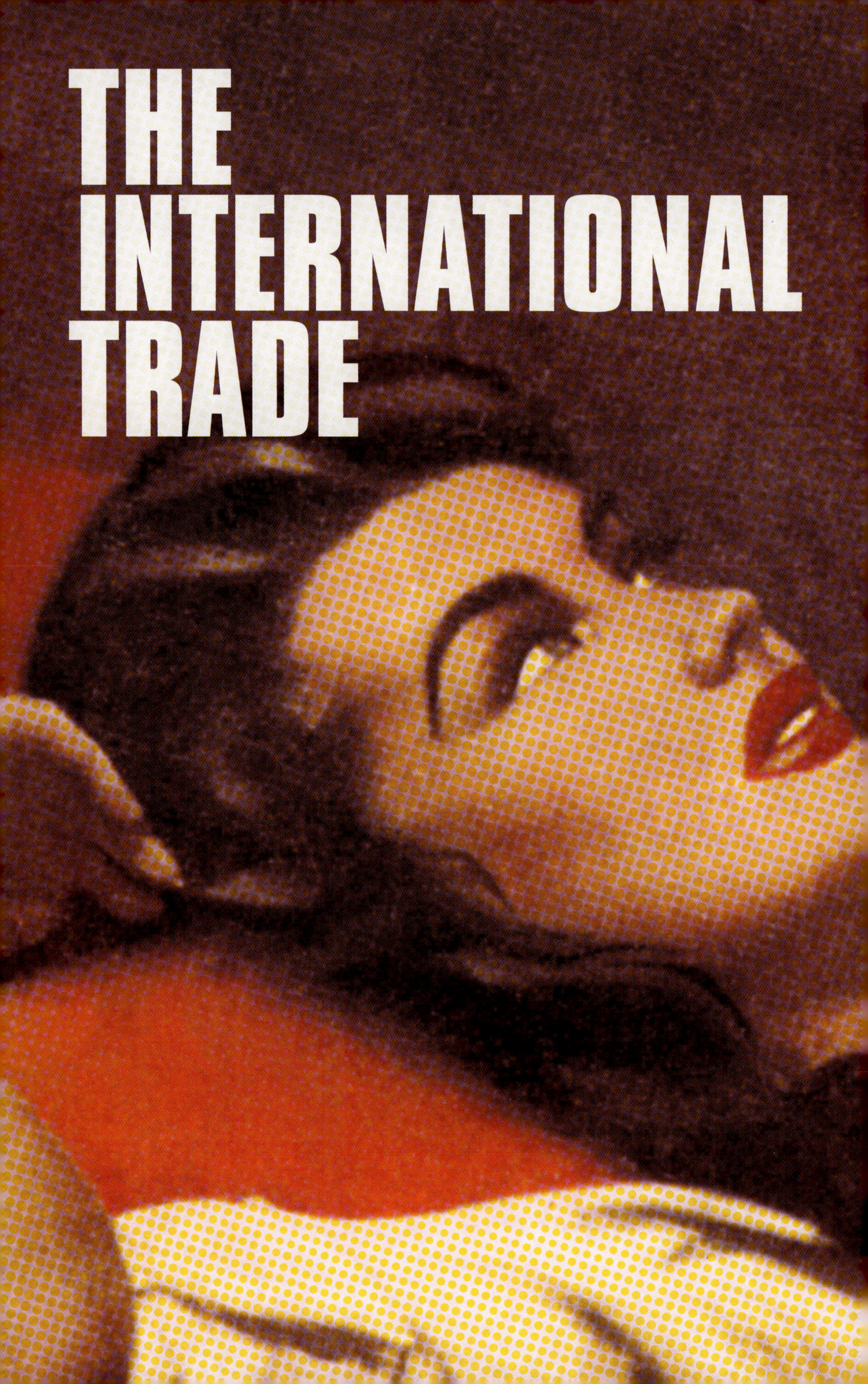

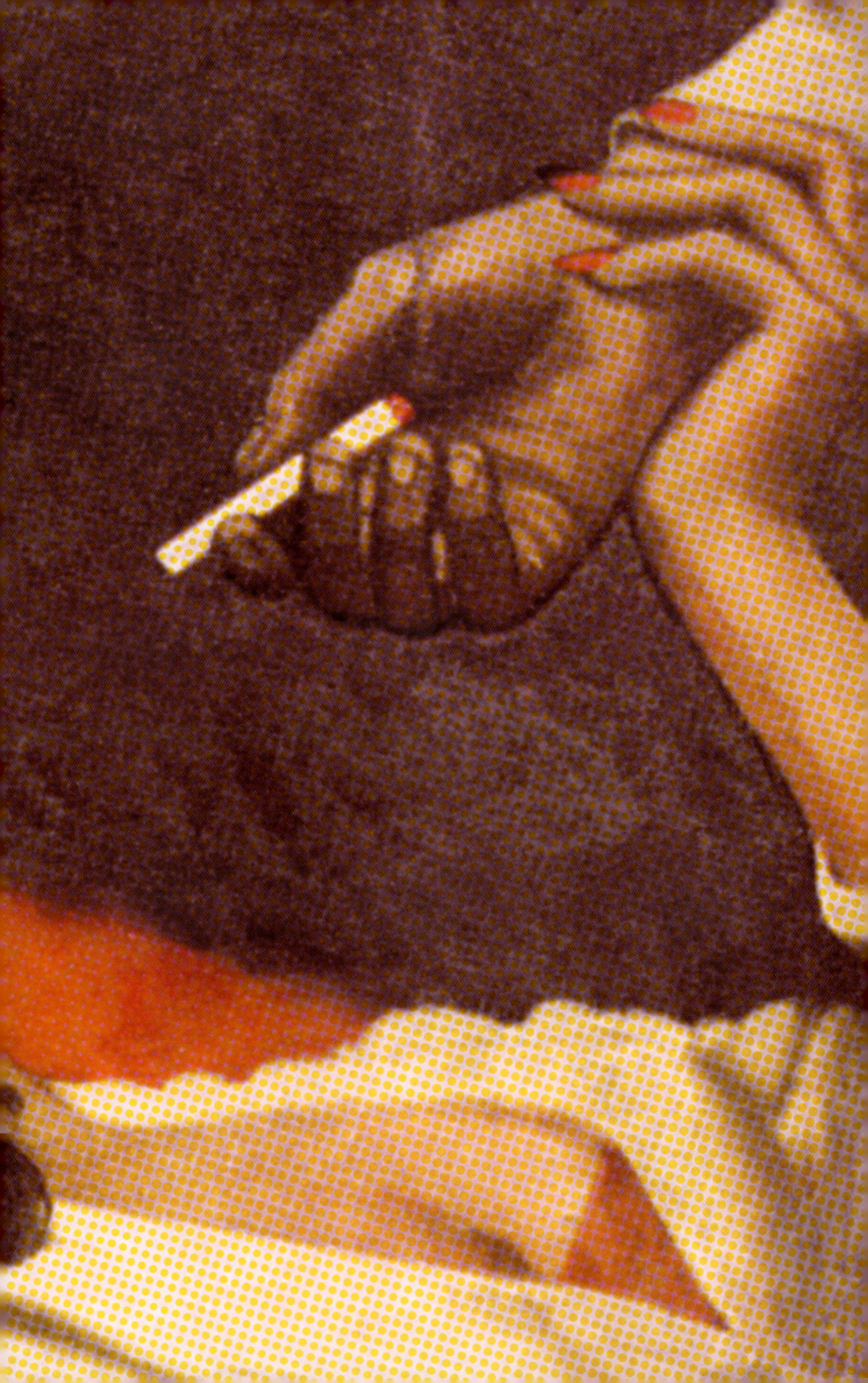

The paperback has a long tradition in Europe. From printing's origins, books were published without bindings at all; you bought them in unbound state from a bookseller and walked down the street to a binder to have them bound up, usually in leather or vellum: Books were strictly for those who could afford such extravagance.

Until the mid-20th century, books in France were routinely issued in softcover (wrappers); if they sold well, they might then be reissued in hardcover. In Great Britain, the mass-market paperback took a while longer to catch on than in the U.S., and, until the late 1960s, censorship in the U.K. was much stricter. In Europe, the volume of drug paperbacks issued were nowhere near that of the United States. And Europe has never experienced drug problems of the scope and nature as we in the U.S. have. In general, the "drug problem" is peculiar to our culture; it was viewed as The American Disease as early as the first decade of the 20th century.

No doubt due to their colonization of Southeast Asia and the mania for all things Oriental that swept Europe in the last quarter of the 19th century, the French appear to have had a particular fondness for smoking opium. But then, opium smoking has always been considered a civilized, if no less addictive, activity as opposed to shooting morphine or heroin which have traditionally been viewed with horror.

Yet the attraction to the sensational and lurid have no international boundaries, and the ambivalent attraction-repulsion to decadent sin is timeless.

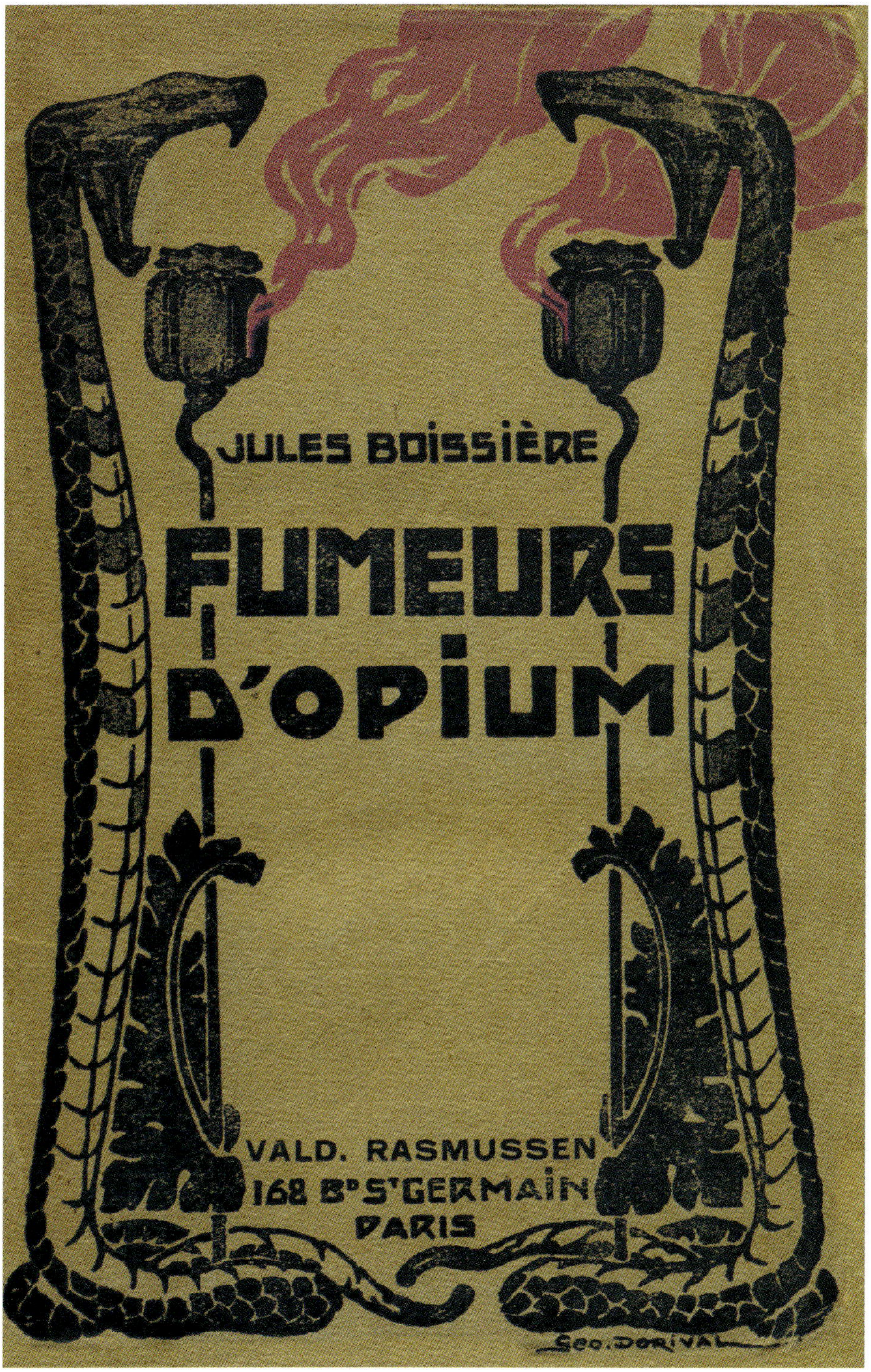

Jules Boissière • ***Fumeurs D'Opium*** • PARIS: VALD. RASMUSSEN • 1925 • COVER BY GEO. DORIVAL
LATER EDITION, ORIGINALLY PUBLISHED 1896 • COURTESY OF WILLIAM DAILEY

Jules Boissière (1863–1897), poet, traveler, Chinese scholar and opium addict, was a disciple of Mallarmé and the Symbolists. He wrote only seven books in his short life, the two on opium usage, *Fumeurs D'Opium* and *Propos d'un Intoxiqué,* his finest.

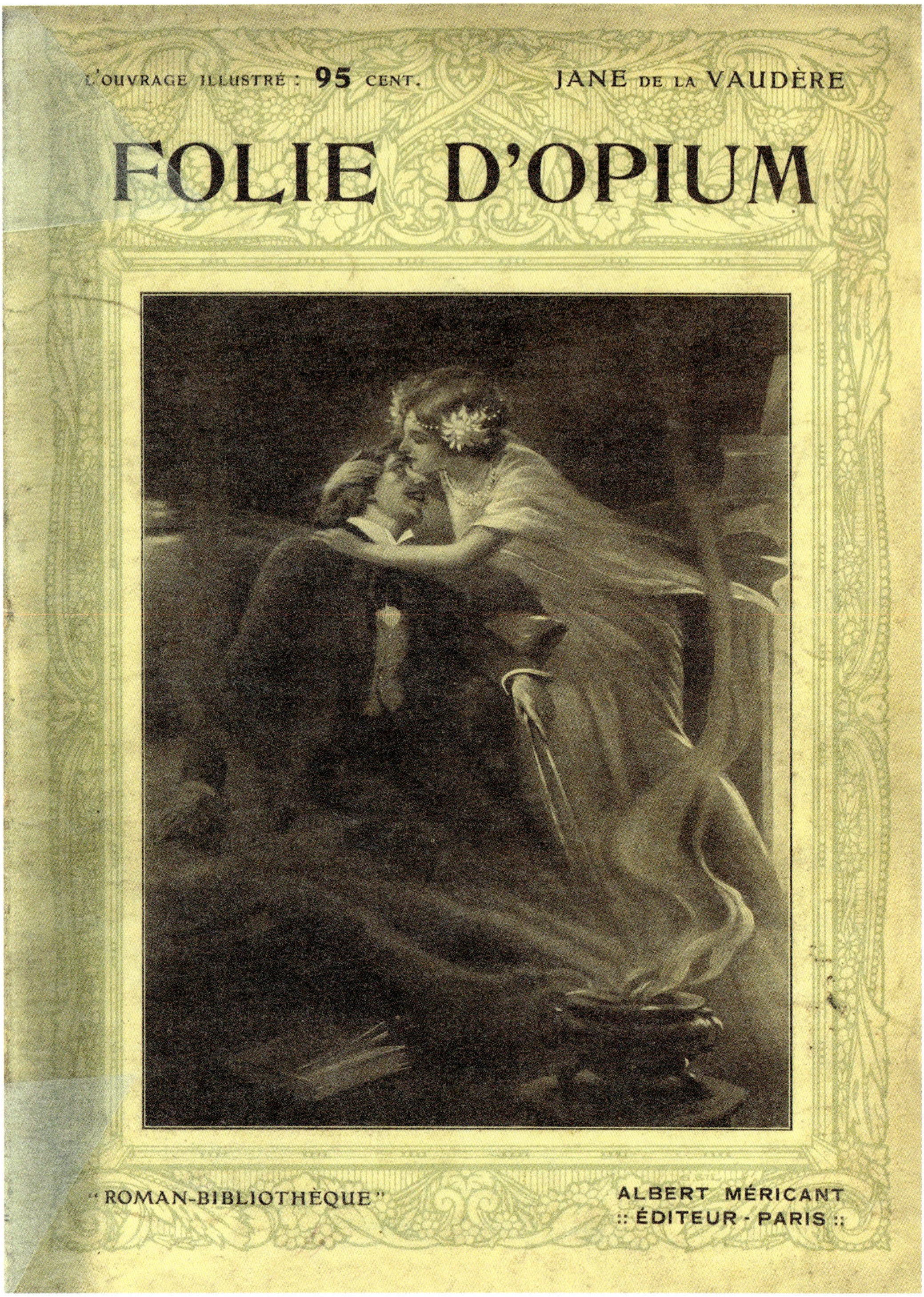

Jane de la Vaudère • ***Folie D'Opium*** • PARIS: ALBERT MÉRICANT, N.D. • CA. 1910
UNRECORDED; NO WORLDWIDE INSTITUTIONAL RECORDS • COURTESY OF THE LUDLOW-SANTO DOMINGO (LSD) LIBRARY

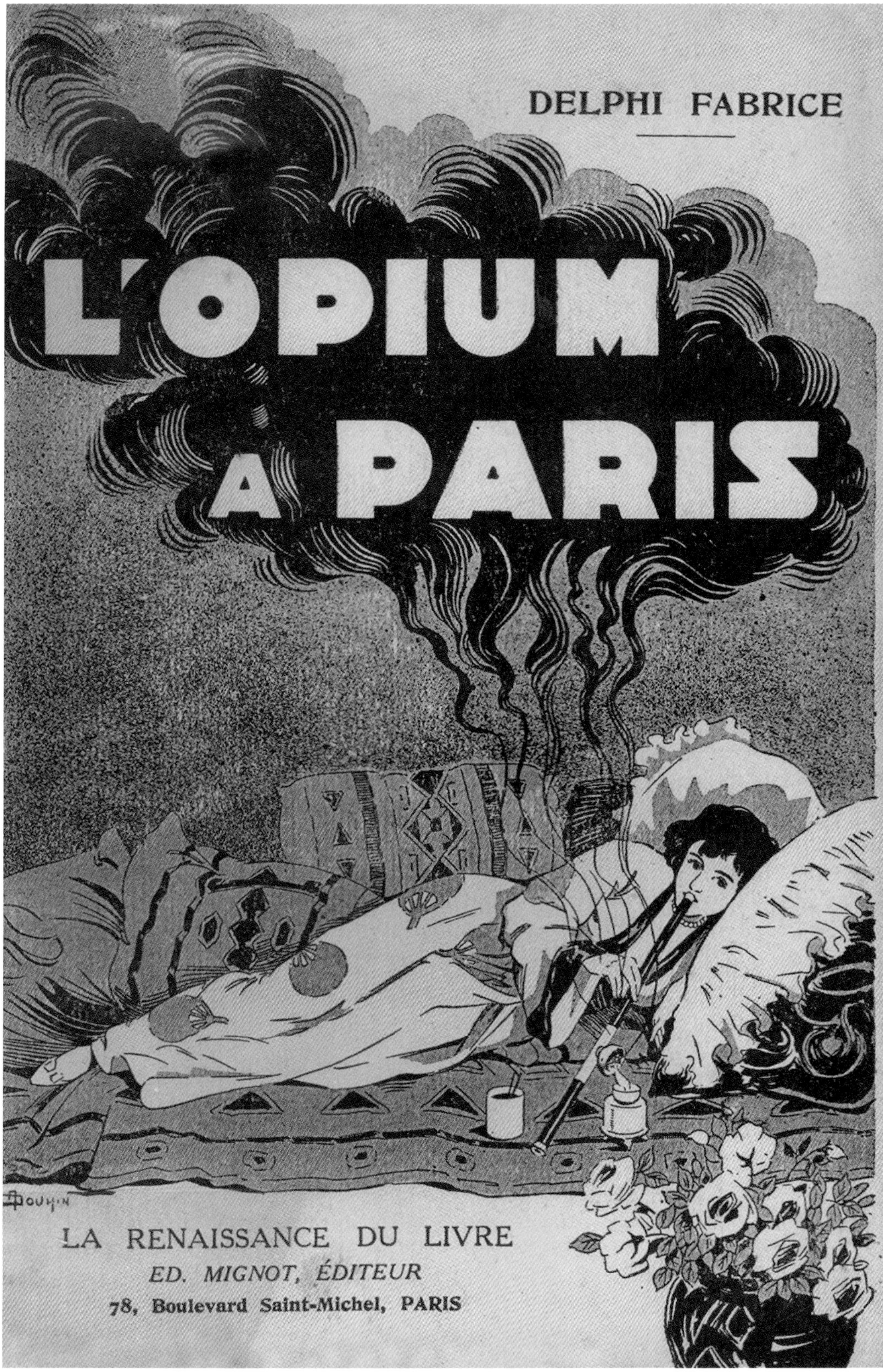

Delphi Fabrice • ***L'Opium A Paris*** • PARIS: LA RENAISSANCE DU LIVRE • 1907
COURTESY OF THE LUDLOW-SANTO DOMINGO (LSD) LIBRARY

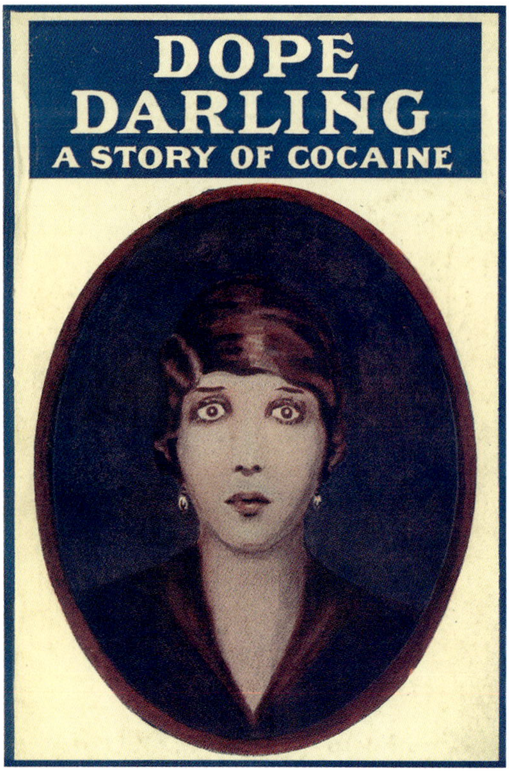

Leda Burke [David Garnett] • ***Dope Darling***
LONDON: WERNER LAURIE, N.D. • 1919
COVER ARTIST UNKNOWN • FIRST (ONLY) EDITION
COURTESY OF RALPH SIPPER

David "Bunny" Garnett (1892–1981) was a bookseller in London (Birrell & Garnett) and co-founder of Nonesuch Press, a small publisher famed for the outstanding quality and taste of its productions. He was a member of the Bloomsbury circle, marrying Vanessa Bell's daughter, scandalously 26 years his junior: Present at her birth, he, according to Carolyn G. Heilbrun's biography of the literary Garnett family, swore to marry "it" when she came of age 20 years later.

Dope Darling was his first novel, the story of a man torn between two women, one of whom is a cocaine addict. Heilbrun notes that in this book Garnett "aped the style of the women's magazine serials, used every cliché he could remember, and wrote the book as badly as he could." He succeeded. Unsurprisingly, his father, English critic, biographer, and essayist Edward Garnett, urged him to publish it under a pseudonym to protect the family name: In addition to his father's highly regarded literary reputation, his mother, Constance, was the foremost translator of the Russian novelists, and certainly his grandfather Richard Garnett (1835–1906) — literary historian, poet, critic, biographer and chief keeper of printed books at the British Museum — would have turned in his grave.

This cheaply produced, cheesy paperbound book is of the utmost scarcity with only four copies in its original state located in institutional collections worldwide; the British Library has an additional copy but it has been rebound in hardcover. Only one copy has come into the marketplace in the last 35 years. It is dearly priced into five figures, based not so much upon the book's status as the black tulip of drug literature (though, in reality, the book has little drug-related content, its desirability strictly due to its sensationalistic title and cover art) but as a scarce British modern first edition associated with the Bloomsbury group and an author who would thereafter write many critically acclaimed novels, one of which, *Aspects of Love* (1955), was adapted for the musical stage by Andrew Lloyd Webber.

Federico Trujillo • ***Amor Y Opio*** [*Love and Opium*] • MADRID: LOS CONTEMPORANIOS • 1915
COVER BY MANCHÓN • COURTESY OF THE LUDLOW-SANTO DOMINGO (LSD) LIBRARY

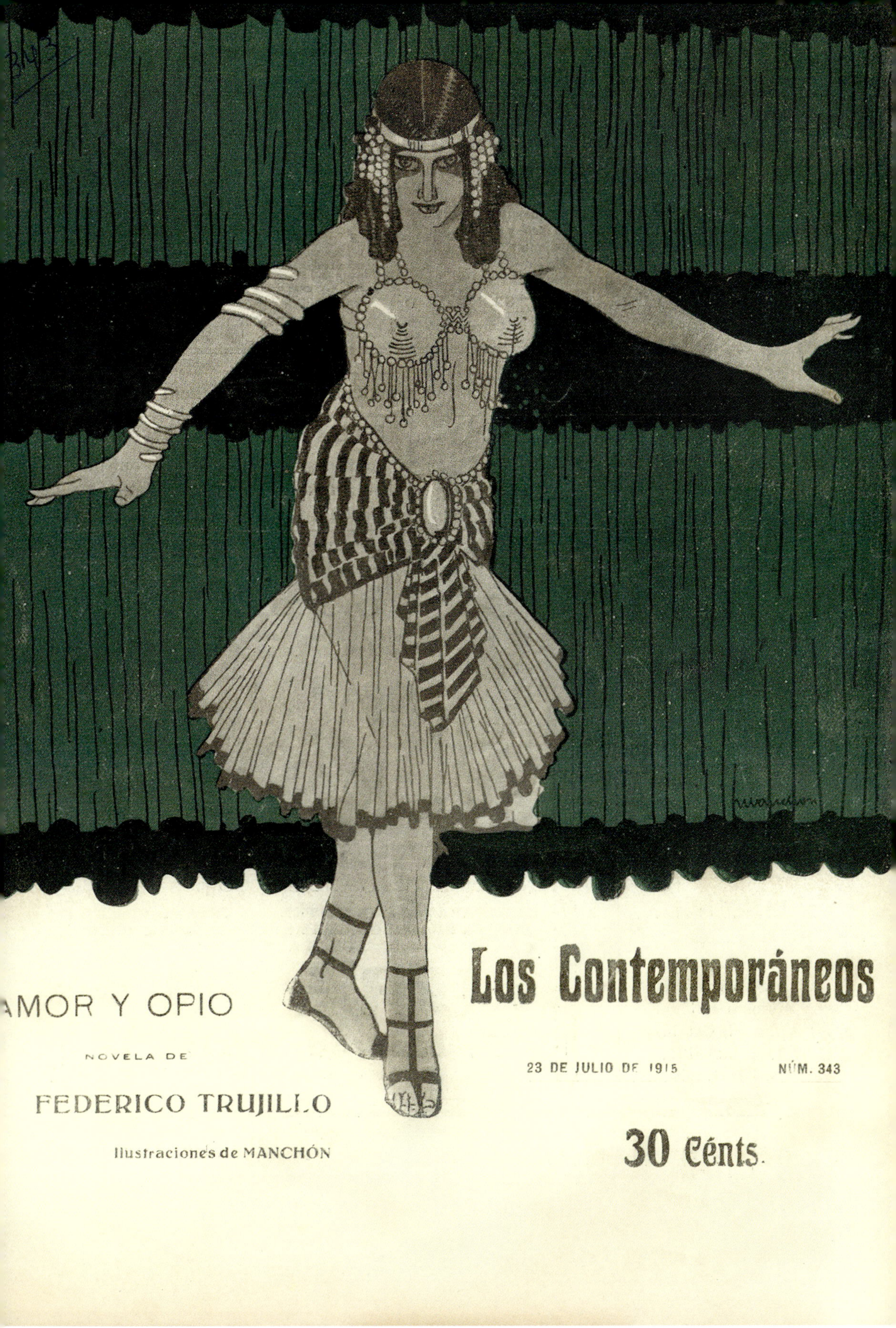
Los Contemporáneos
AMOR Y OPIO
NOVELA DE
FEDERICO TRUJILLO
Ilustraciones de MANCHÓN
23 DE JULIO DE 1915
NÚM. 343
30 Cénts.

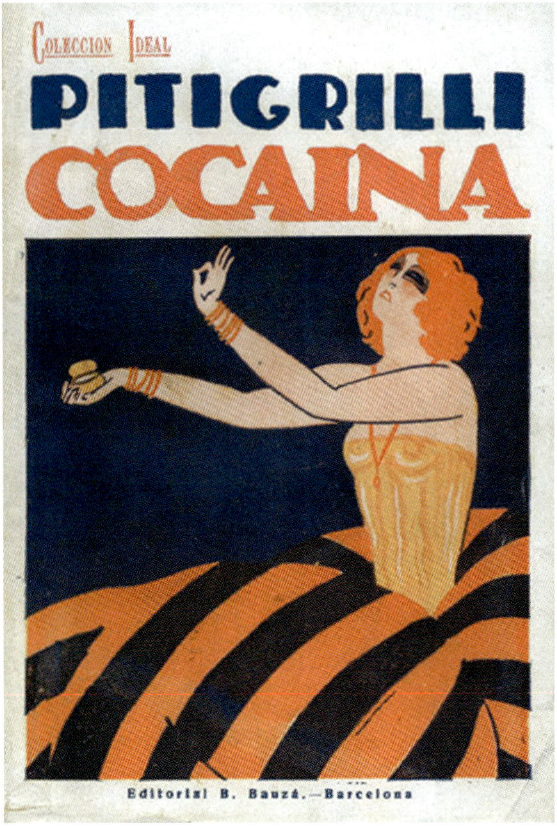

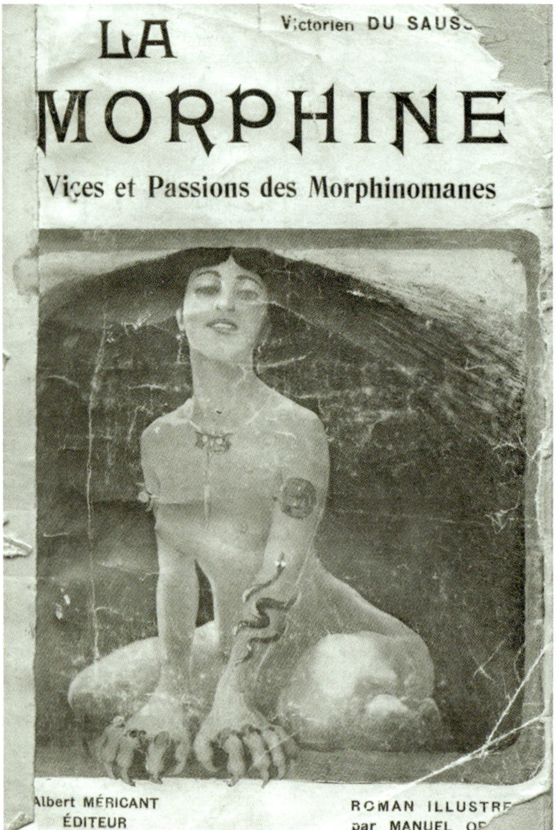

Pitagrilli [Dino Segré] • ***Cocaina*** • BARCELONA: B. BAUZA • 1923 • FIRST EDITION IN SPANISH • COURTESY OF MIRIAM LINNA

Victorien du Saussay • ***La Morfina: Novela de Horror y de Pasíon*** • MADRID: EDITORIAL CASTILLA 1921 • COVER BY RIBAS • FIRST SPANISH EDITION COURTESY OF RONALD K. SIEGEL, PH.D.

Victorien du Saussay • ***La Morphine: Vices et Passions des Morphinomanes*** • PARIS: ALBERT MÉRICANT • 1906 • COVER BY MANUEL ORAZI • COURTESY OF RONALD K. SIEGEL, PH.D.

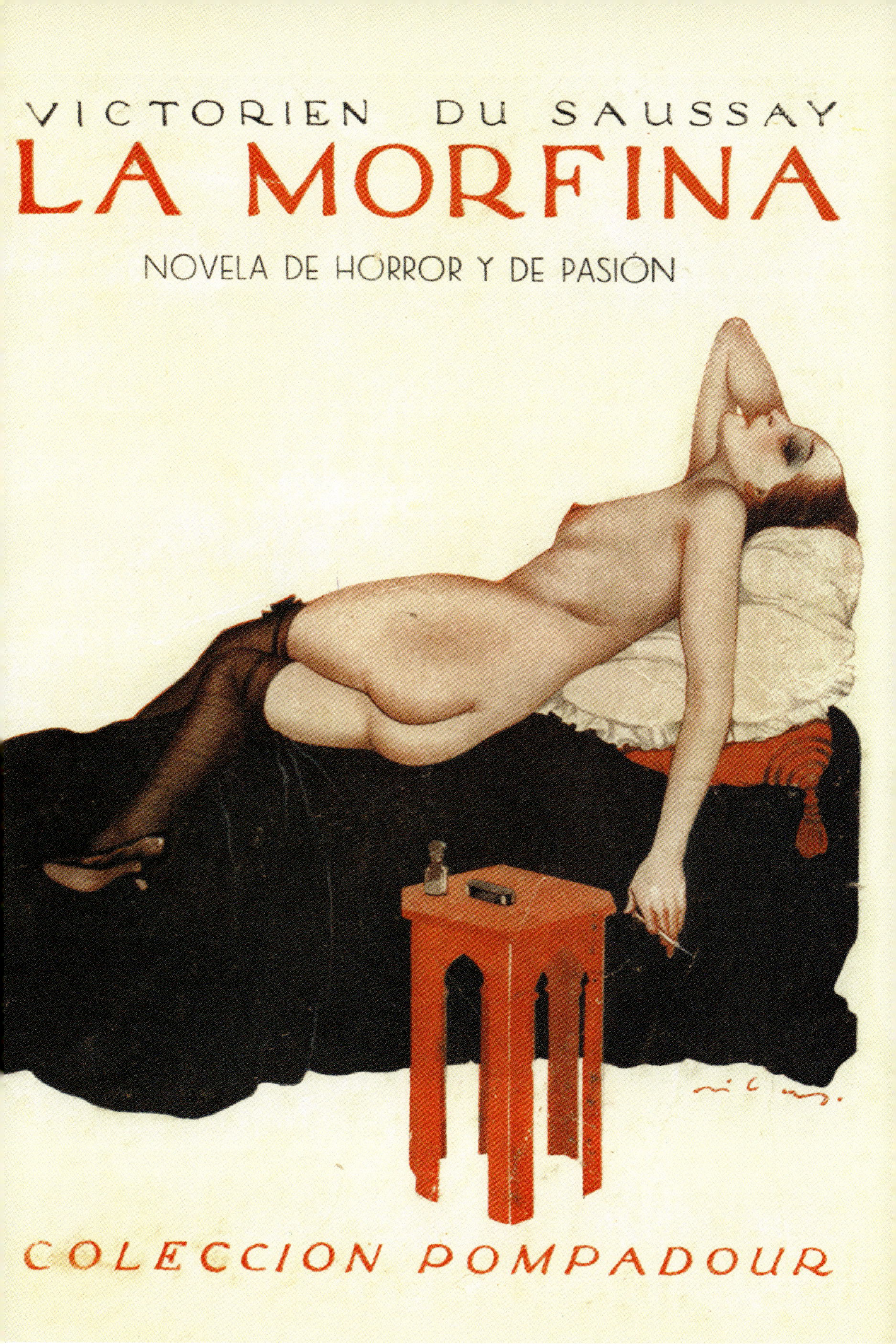
VICTORIEN DU SAUSSAY
LA MORFINA
NOVELA DE HORROR Y DE PASIÓN
COLECCION POMPADOUR

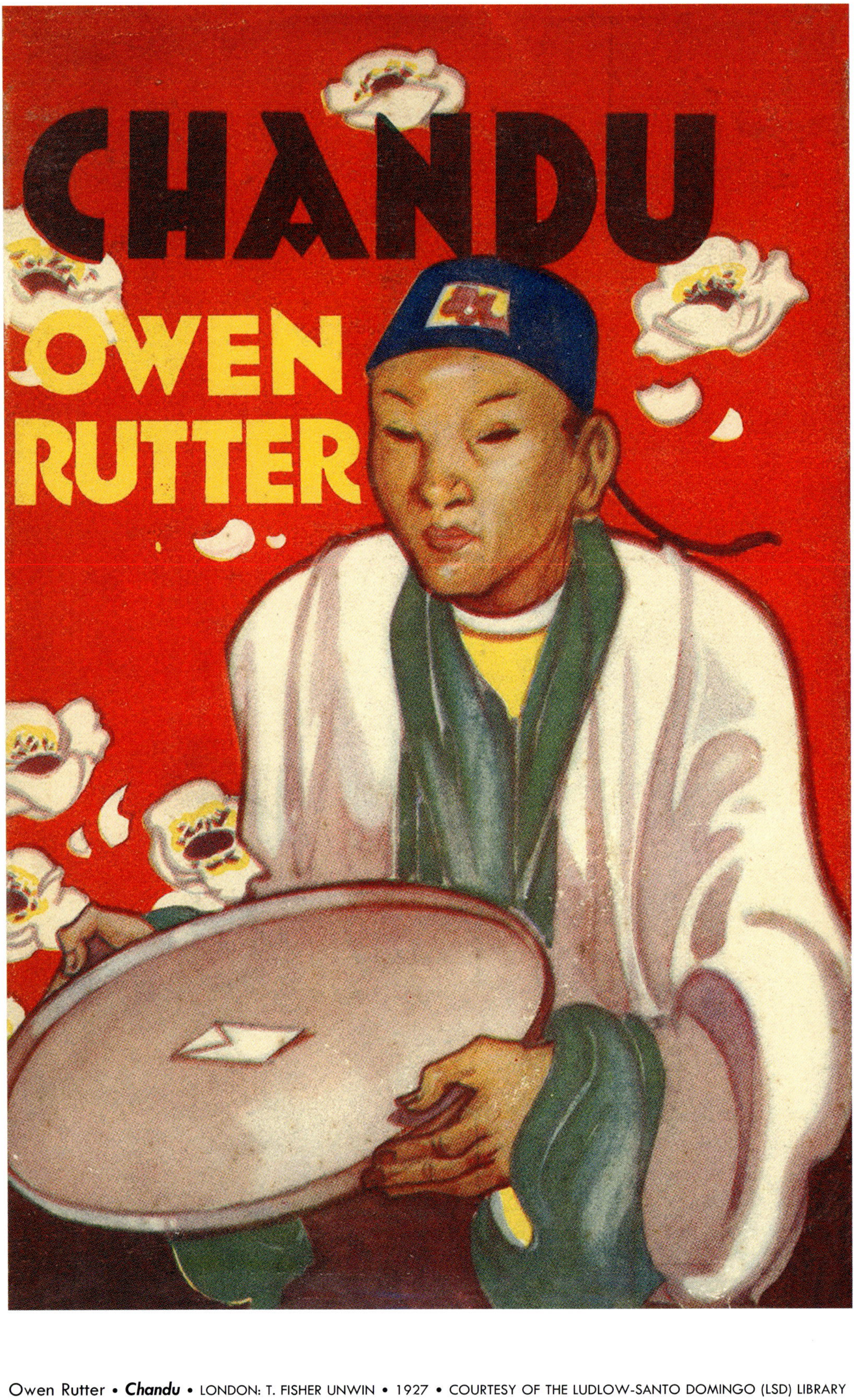

Owen Rutter • ***Chandu*** • LONDON: T. FISHER UNWIN • 1927 • COURTESY OF THE LUDLOW-SANTO DOMINGO (LSD) LIBRARY

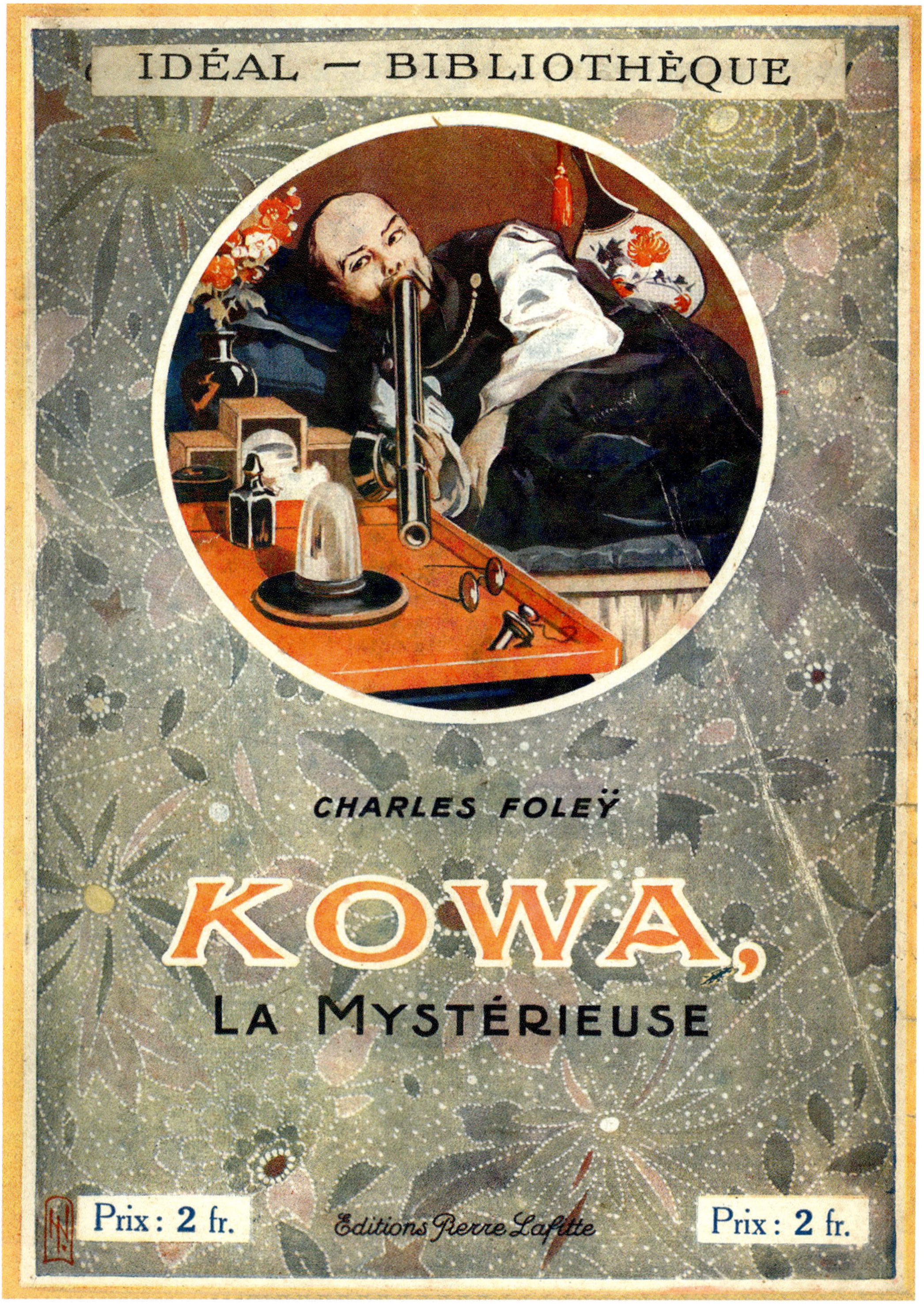

Charles Foleÿ • ***Kowa La Mystérieuse*** • PARIS: EDITIONS PIERRE LAFITTE • 1920
COURTESY OF THE LUDLOW-SANTO DOMINGO (LSD) LIBRARY

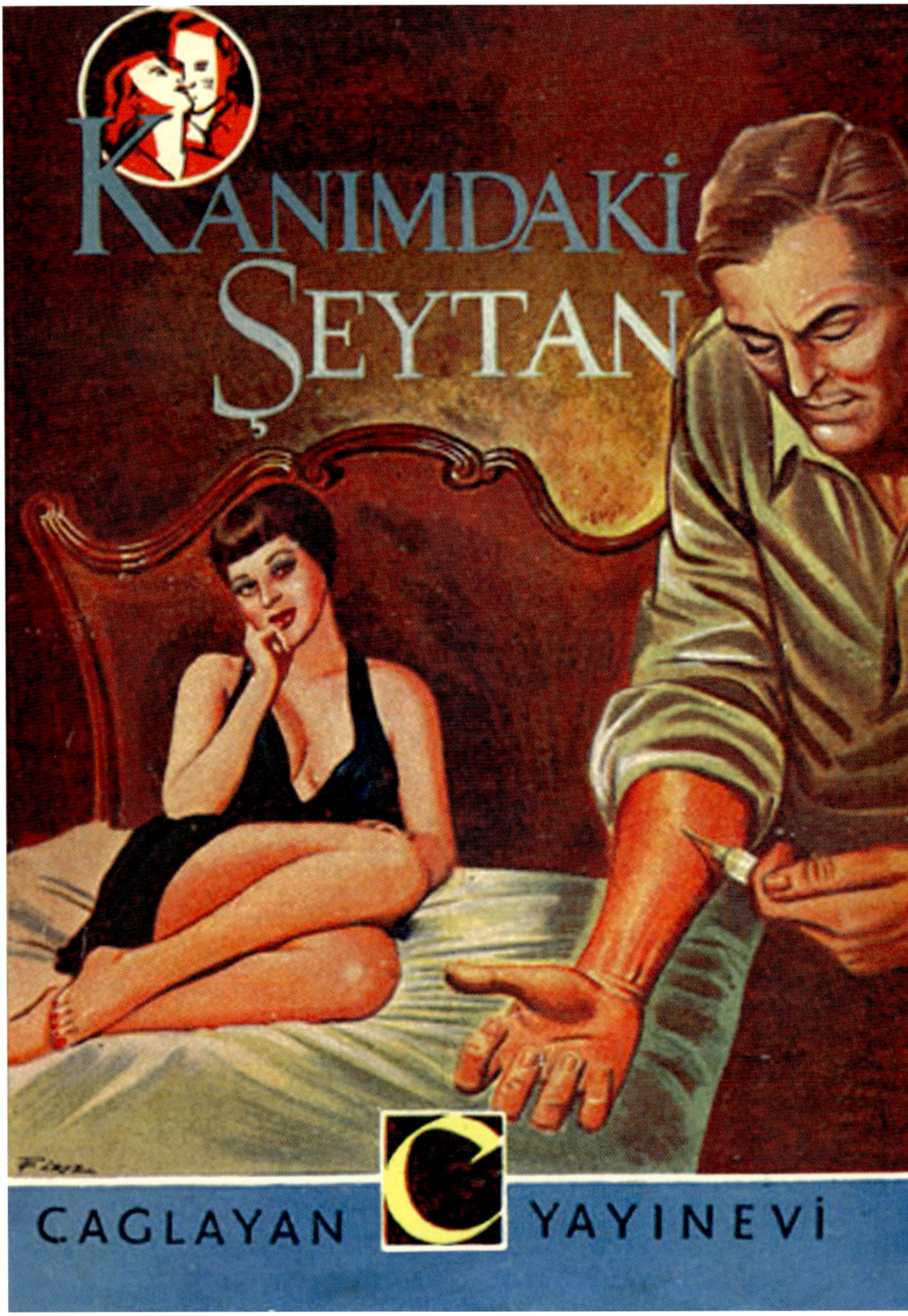

Kanimdaki Seytana • ISTANBUL • 1954 • COURTESY OF MIRIAM LINNA
QUITE POSSIBLY AN UNAUTHORIZED TURKISH EDITION OF BURROUGHS' *JUNKIE*

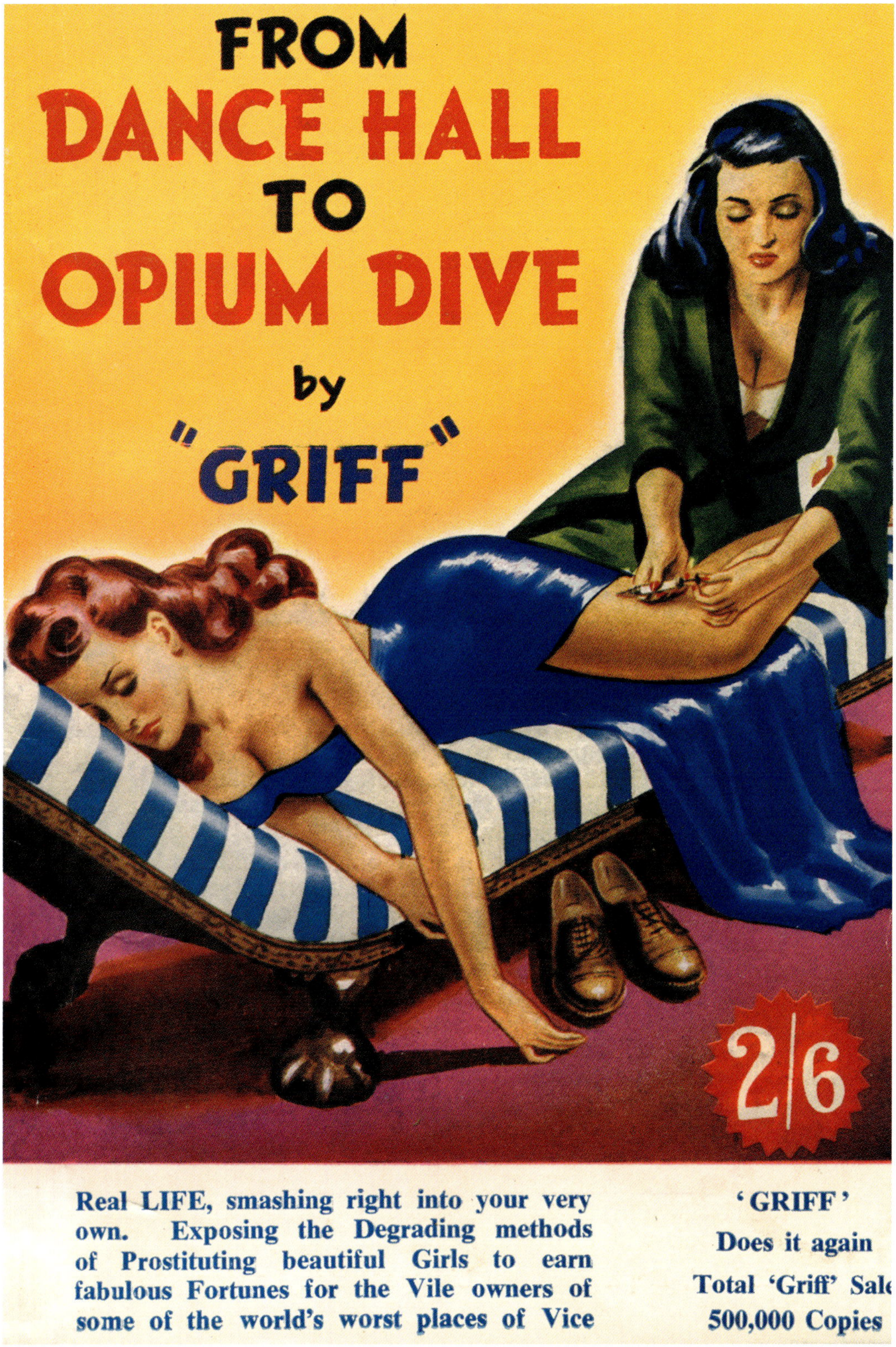

"Griff" [F. Dubrez Fawcett] • ***From Dance Hall to Opium Dive*** • LONDON: MODERN FICTION, N.D. • 1950s
PBO • COURTESY OF RONALD K. SIEGEL, PH.D.

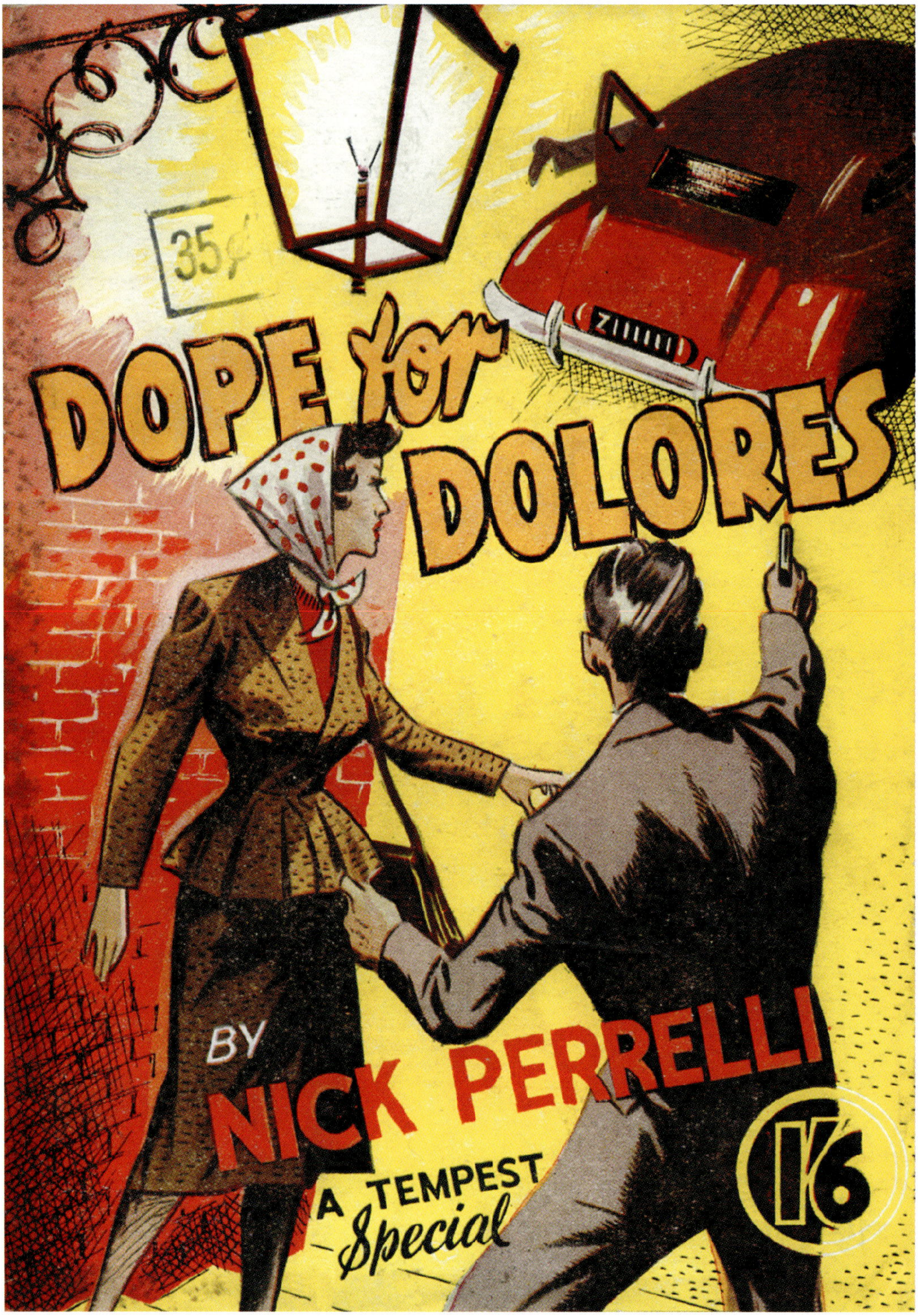

Nick Perrelli [Thomas H. Martin] • ***Dope For Dolores*** • LONDON: TEMPEST, N.D. • 1951 • PBO

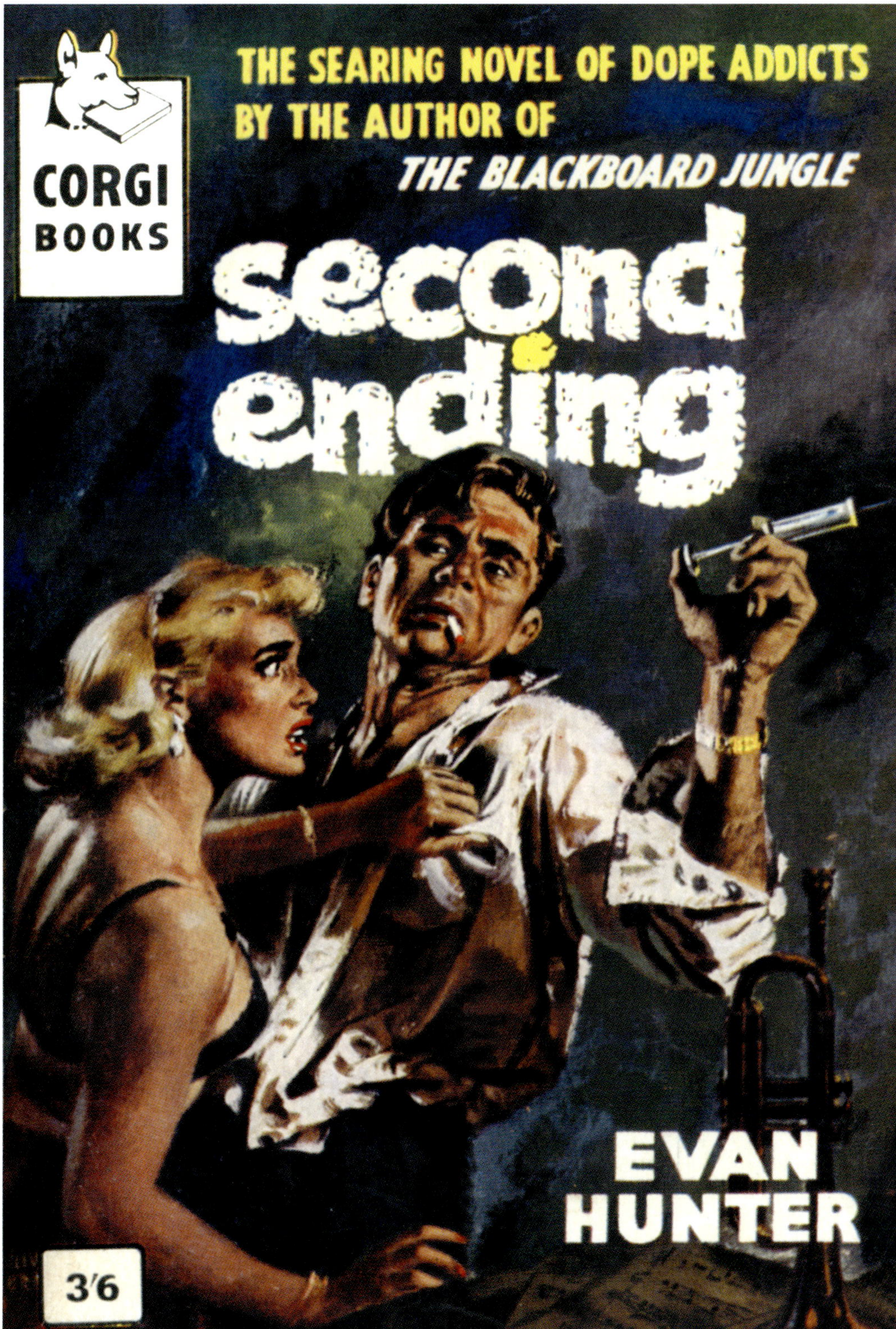

Evan Hunter [b. Salvador Lombino] • ***Second Ending*** • LONDON: CORGI 489 • 1957
FIRST U.K. EDITION OF *QUARTET IN "H"*

Without the mitigating influence of Helbrant's *Narcotics Agent*, British censors took offense and action against this edition of *Junkie*, ordering all copies destroyed. Few remain, and this is one of the scarcest, most desirable drug paperbacks, copies rarely coming into the marketplace. After a ten-year dry spell, a copy emerged and sold in 2002 for $5,000.

William Lee [William Burroughs] • ***Junkie: Confessions Of An Unredeemed Drug Addict***
LONDON: DIGIT • 1954 • COVER BY AL ROSSI • FIRST U.K. EDITION

(FOLLOWING SPREAD, LEFT PAGE) BACK COVER

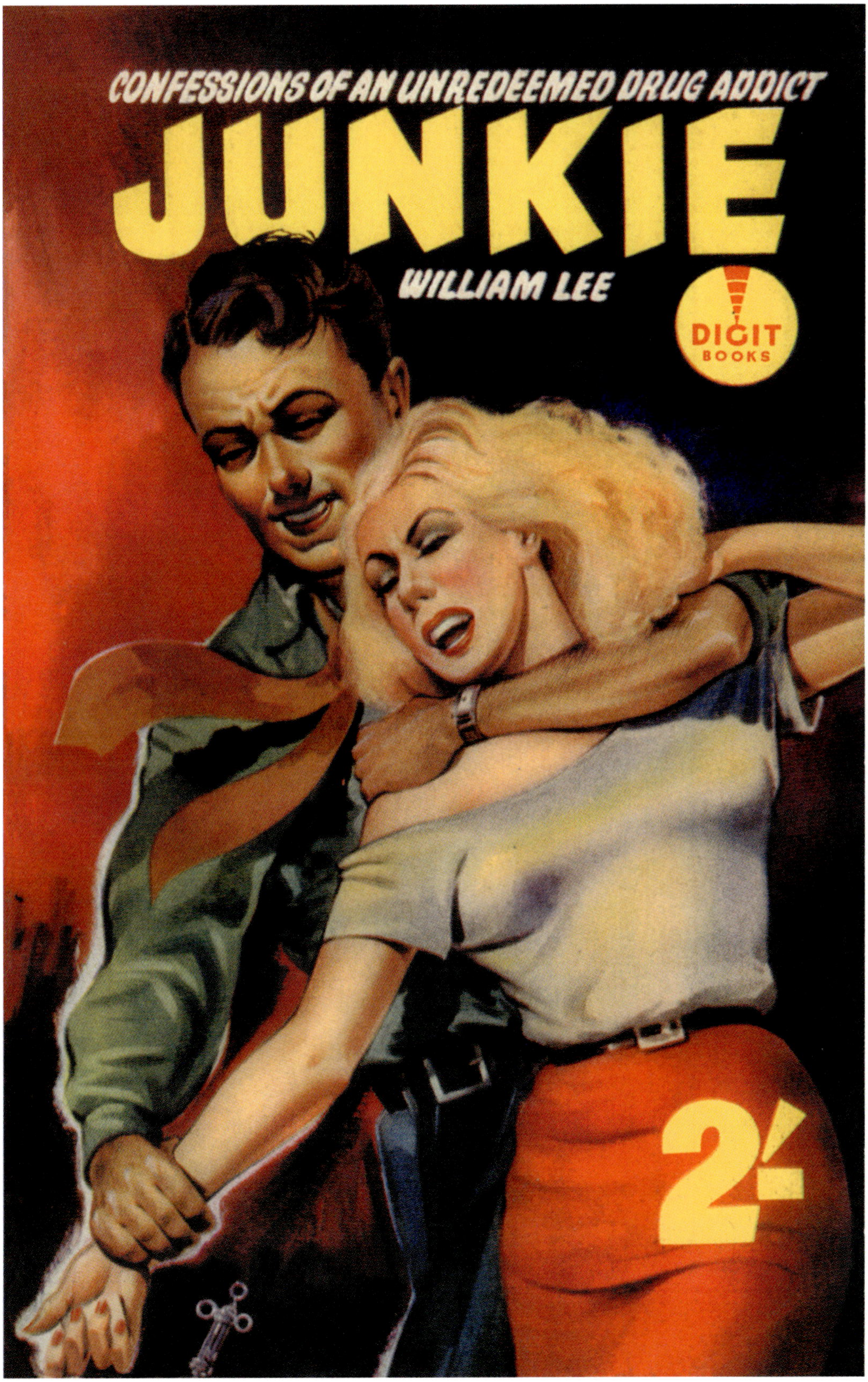
CONFESSIONS OF AN UNREDEEMED DRUG ADDICT
JUNKIE
WILLIAM LEE
DIGIT
BOOKS
2/-

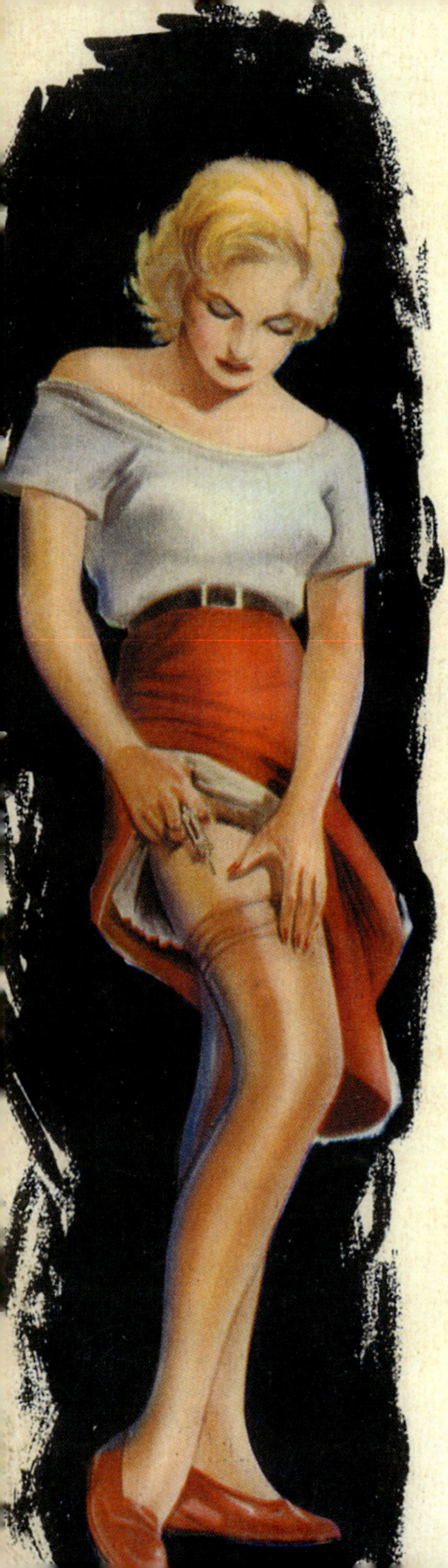

JUNKIE

THE CONFESSIONS OF AN UNREDEEMED DRUG ADDICT

WILLIAM LEE

NEVER BEFORE HAS THE FINGER OF LIGHT SHONE SO GLARINGLY ON THE WASTELAND OF THE DRUG ADDICT.....

JUNKIE IS PITILESSLY FACTUAL AND HARD-BOILED. IT STRIPS DOWN THE ADDICT WITHOUT SHAME OR SELF-PITY IN ALL HIS NAKEDNESS.....

DIGIT BOOKS

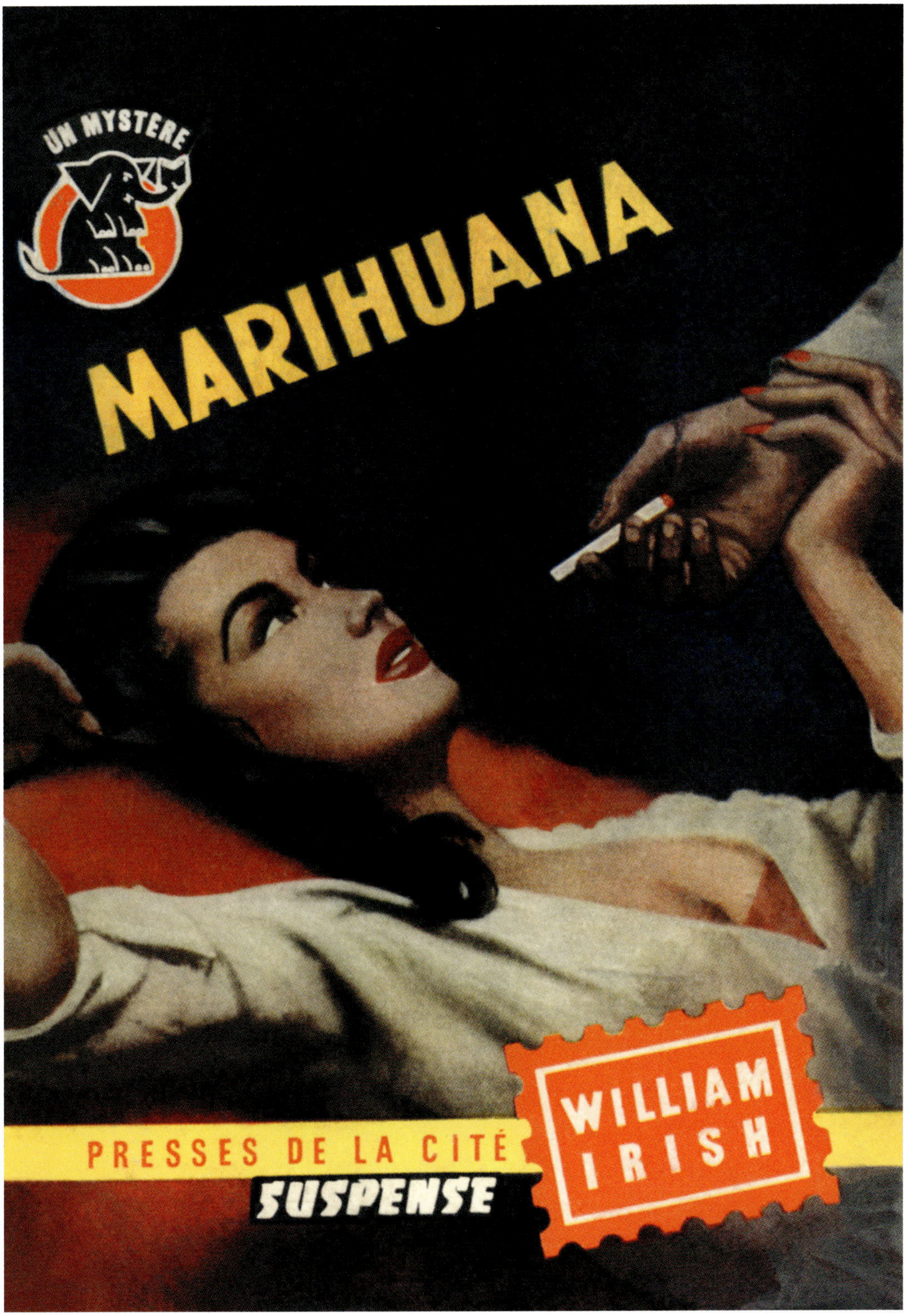

William Irish [Cornell Hopley Woolrich] • ***Marihuana*** • PARIS: PRESSES DE LA CITÉ • CA. 1952
FIRST EDITION IN FRENCH

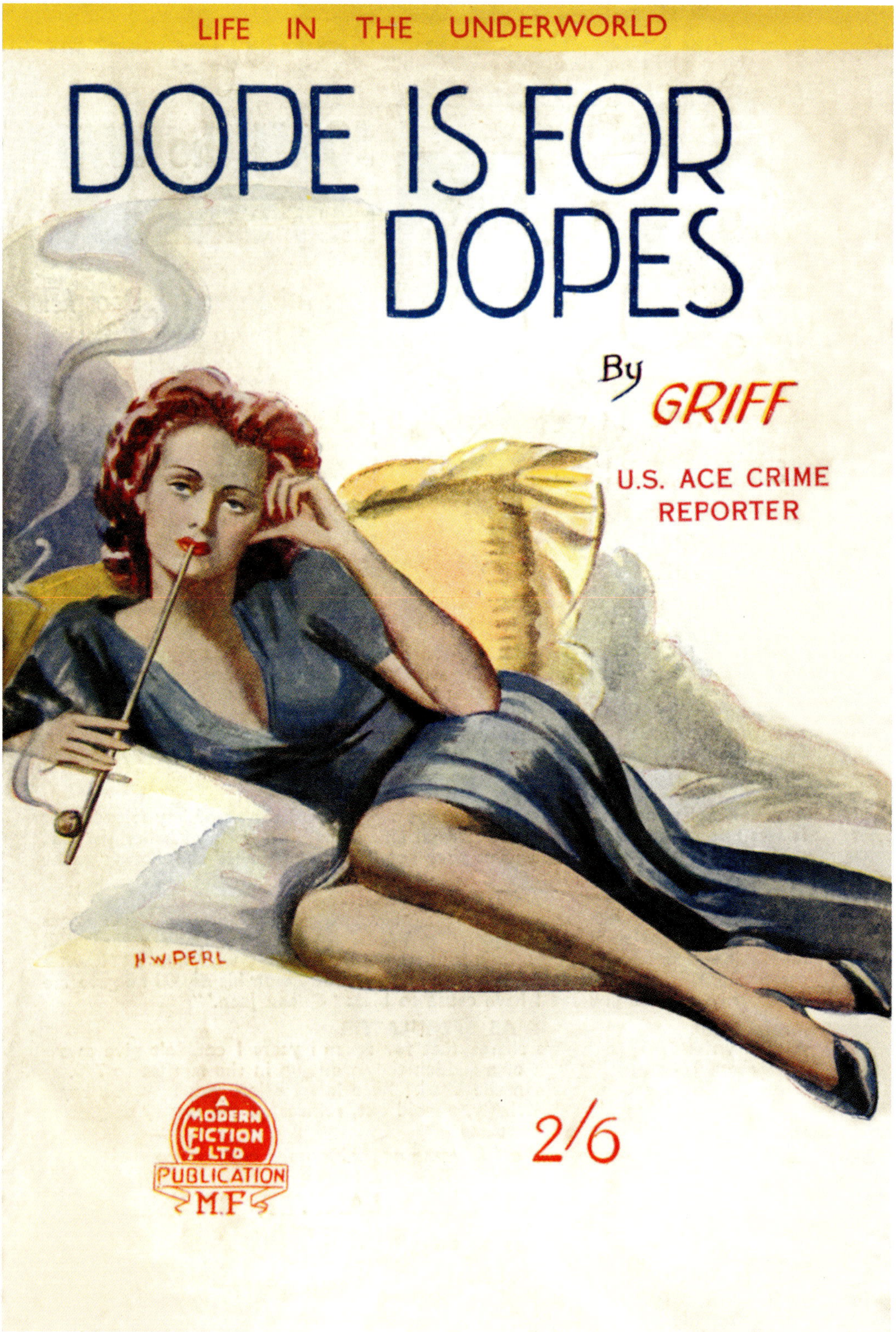

Griff [Ernest L. McKeag] • ***Dope Is for Dopes*** • LONDON: MODERN FICTION LTD., N.D. • 1949
COVER BY H.W. PERL • PBO

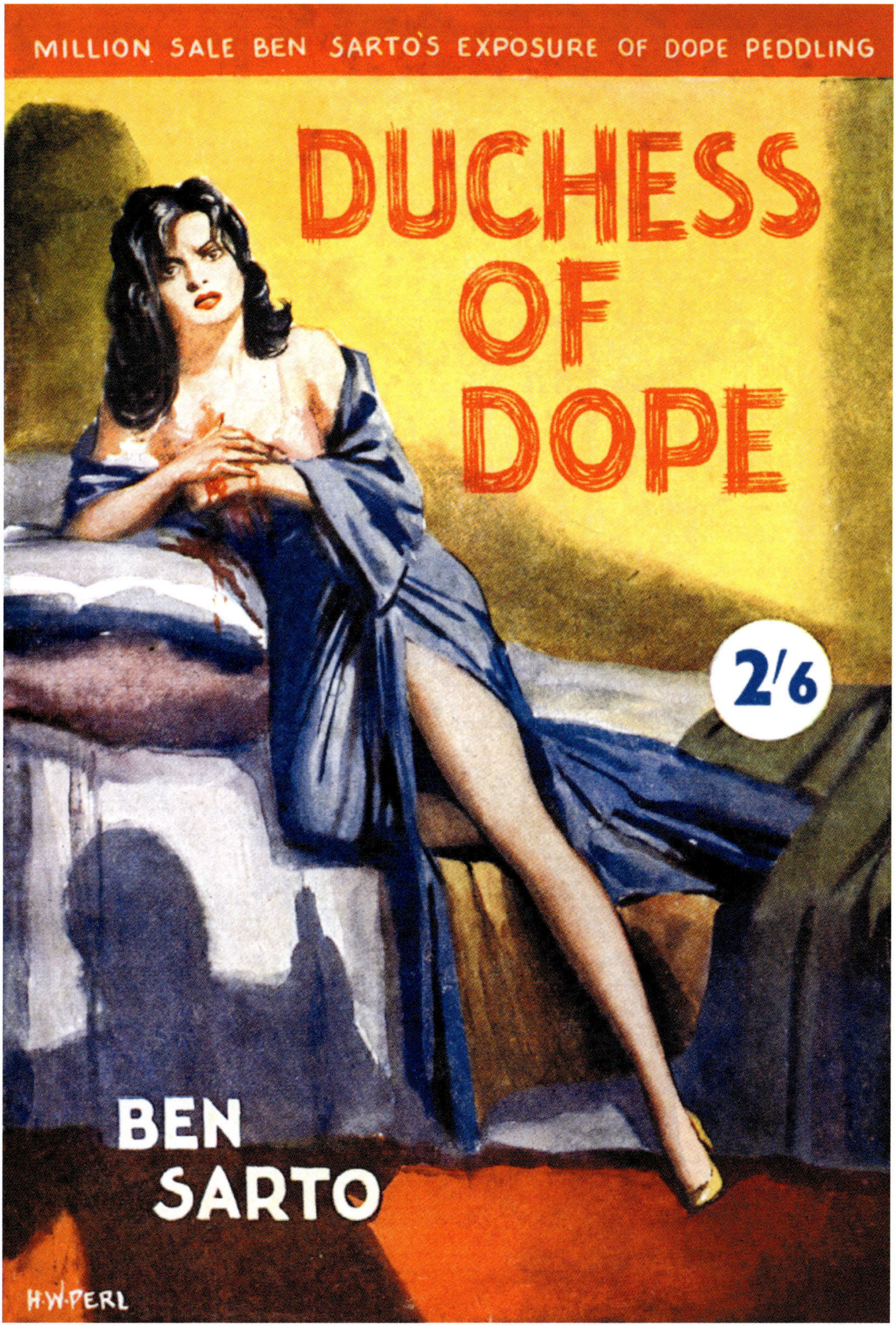

Ben Sarno [F. Dubrez Fawcett] • ***Duchess of Dope*** • LONDON: MODERN FICTION, LTD., N.D. • 1951
COVER BY H.W. PERL • PBO

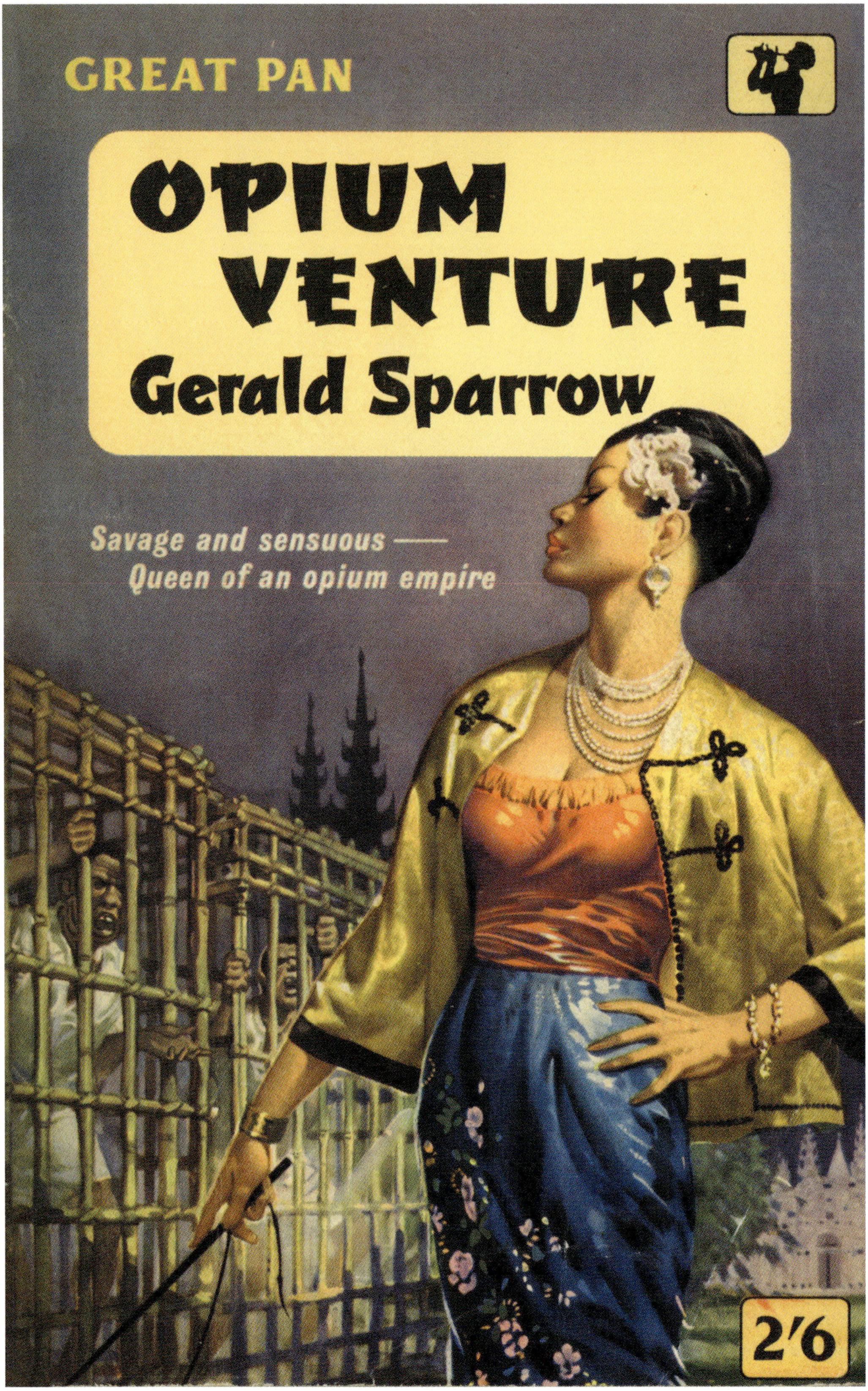

Gerald Sparrow • ***Opium Venture*** • LONDON: PAN • 1960 • REPRINT

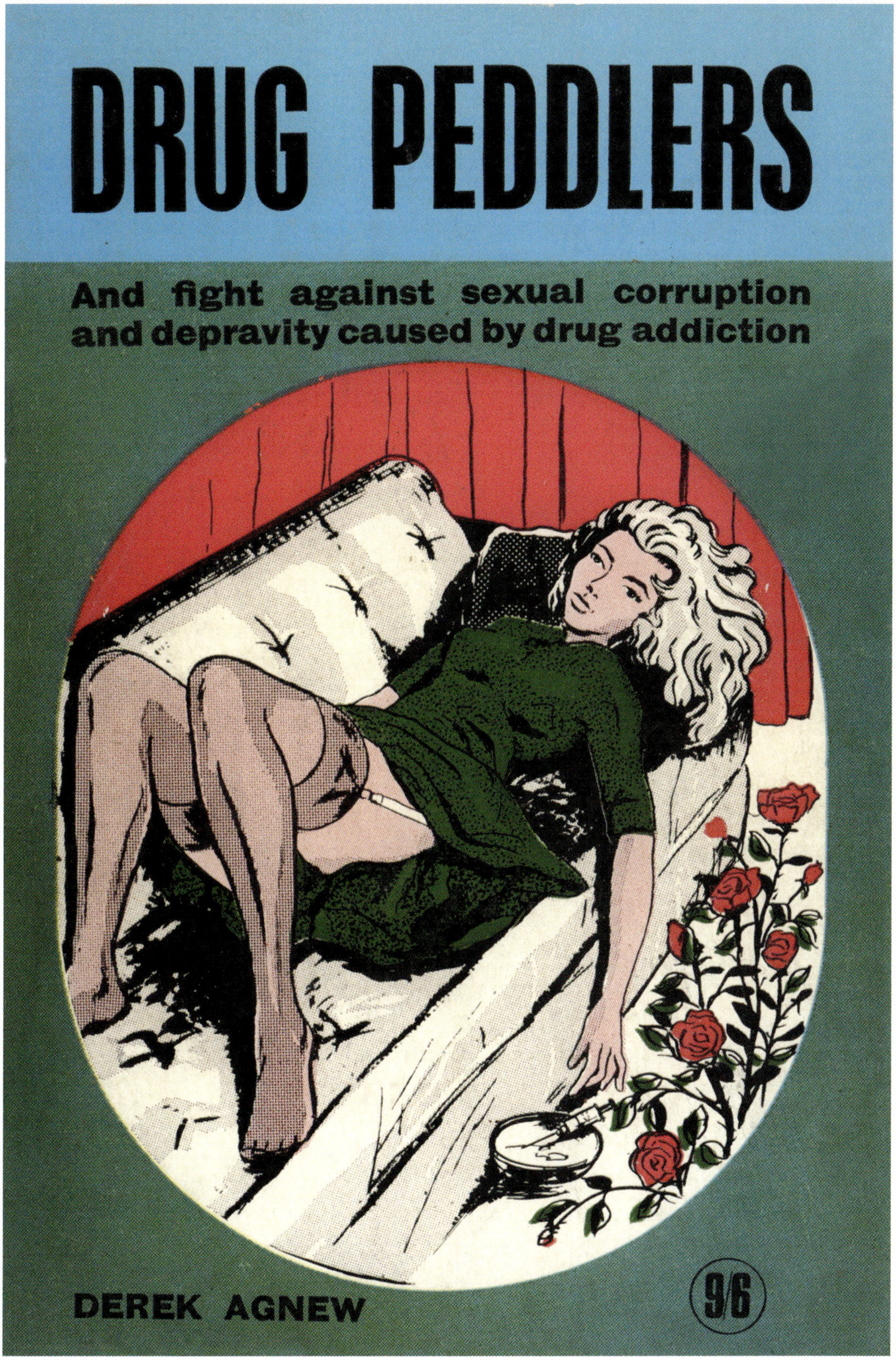

Derek Agnew • ***The Drug Peddlers: And [sic] Fight Against Sexual Corruption and Depravity Caused By Drug Addiction*** • LONDON: K&G PUBLICATIONS • 1967 • FIRST U.K. EDITION

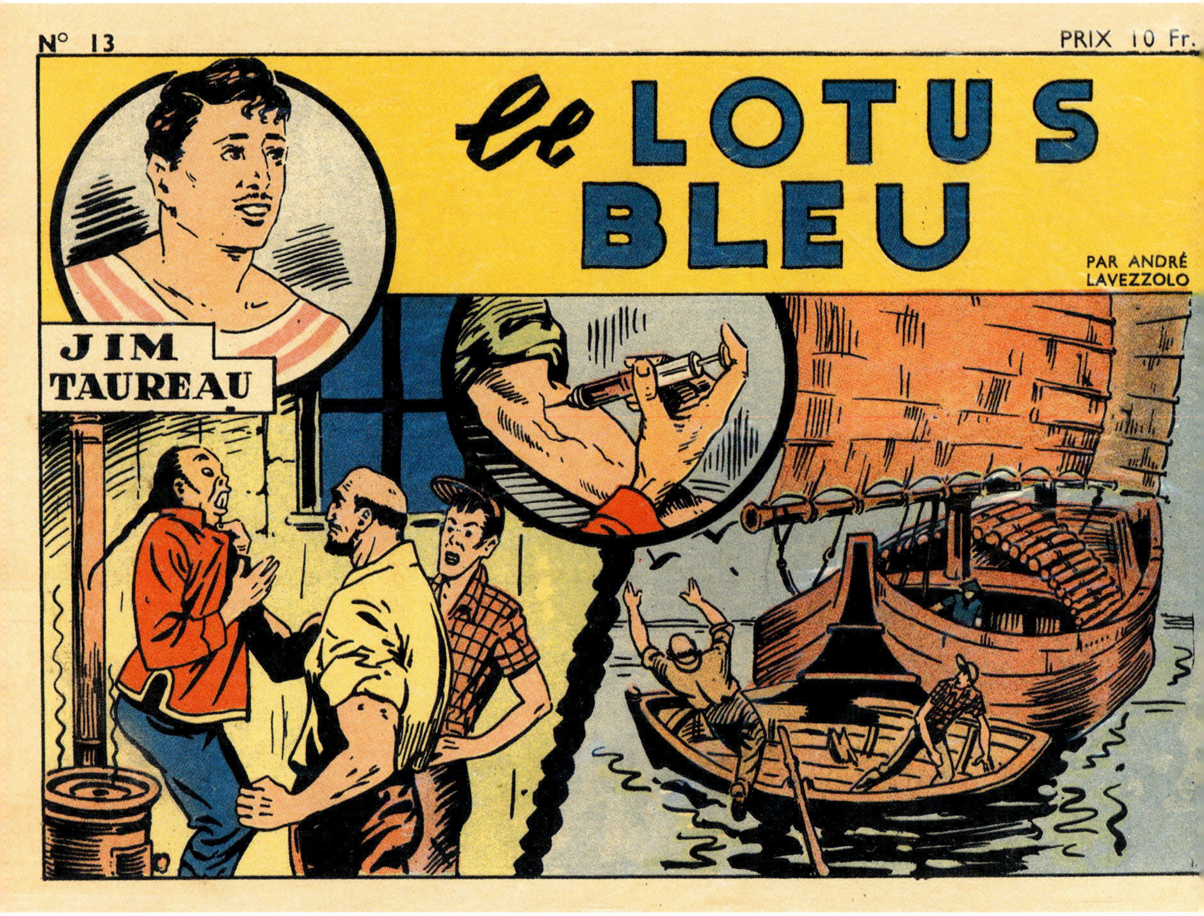

André Lavezzalo • ***Le Lotus Bleu De Jim Taureau*** • PARIS • 1947
COURTESY OF THE LUDLOW-SANTO DOMINGO (LSD) LIBRARY

Nick Carter Weekly No. 136: An Anarchist Plot • UNE FUMERIE D'OPIUM • FRENCH EDITION
NEW YORK: STREET & SMITH • CA. 1905 • COURTESY OF THE LUDLOW-SANTO DOMINGO (LSD) LIBRARY

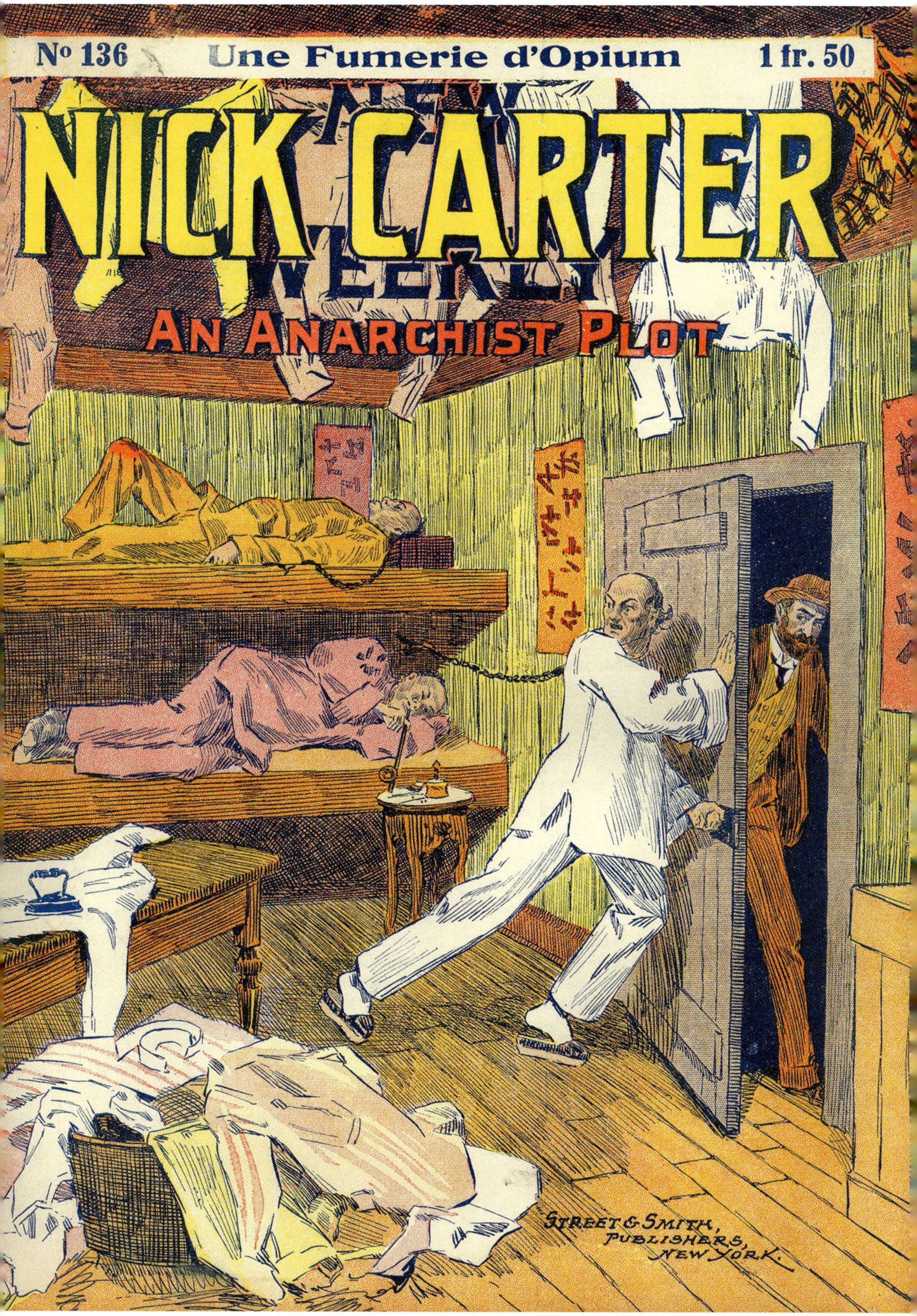
No 136
Une Fumerie d'Opium
1 fr. 50
NICK CARTER
AN ANARCHIST PLOT
STREET & SMITH,
PUBLISHERS,
NEW YORK.

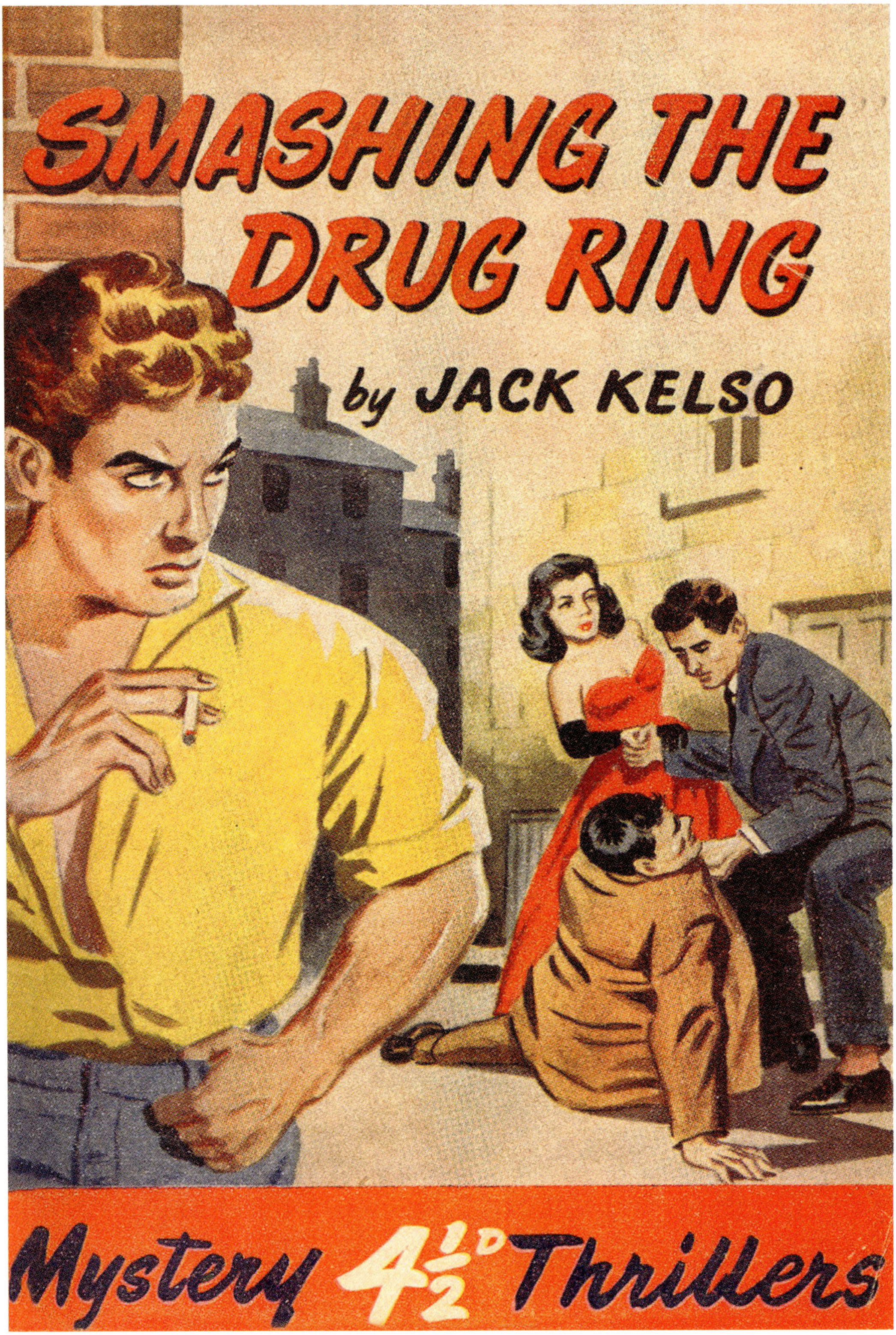

Jack Kelso (Frederick T. Foden) • ***Smashing the Drug Ring*** • U.K., N.P., N.D. • 1946
COURTESY OF THE LUDLOW-SANTO DOMINGO (LSD) LIBRARY

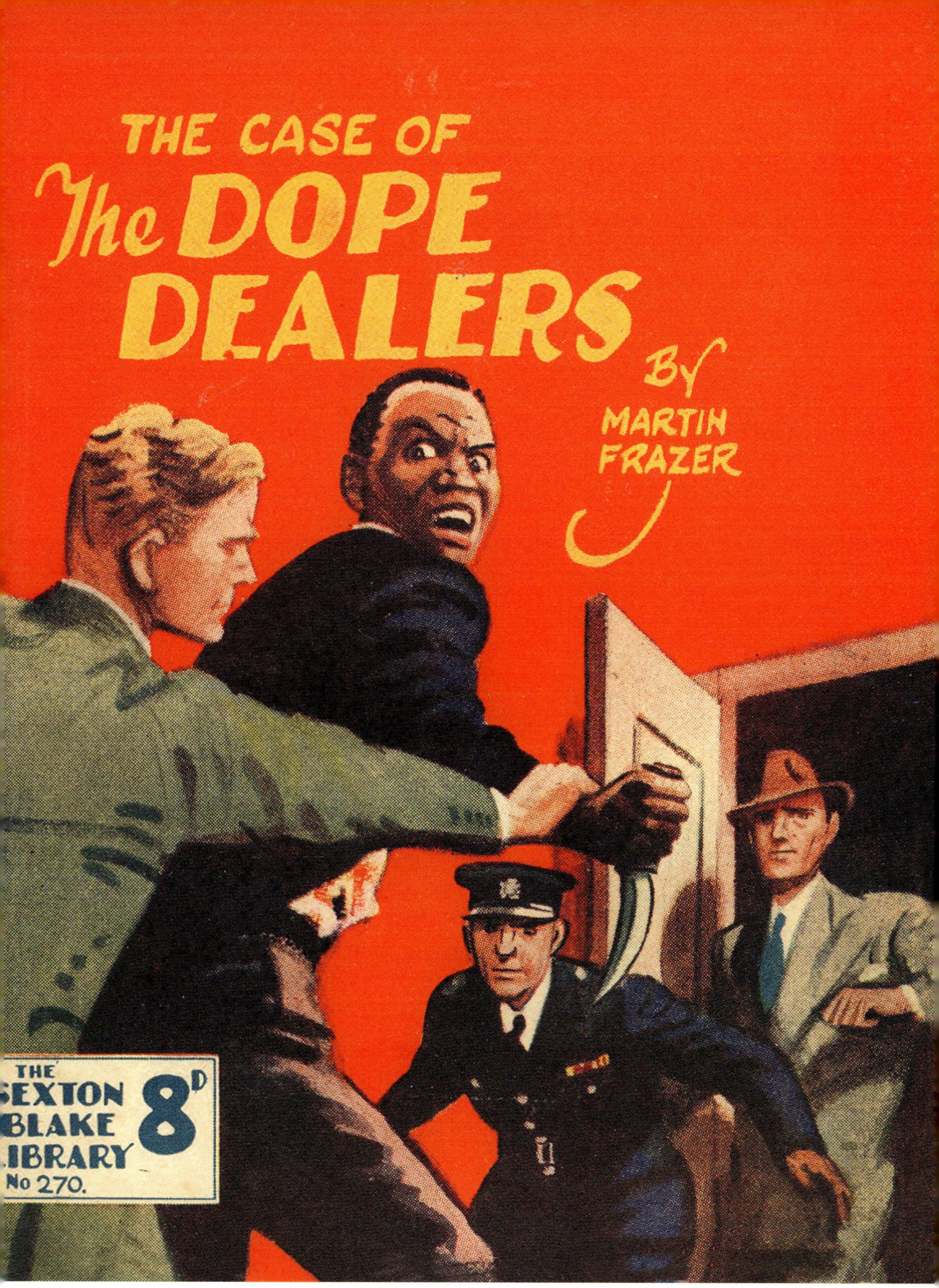

Martin Frazer [Percy A. Clarke] • ***The Case of the Dope Dealers*** • LONDON: SEXTON BLAKE LIBRARY NO. 270, N.D. 1952 • COURTESY OF THE LUDLOW-SANTO DOMINGO (LSD) LIBRARY

"From the reeking slums of a big city, from the twilight world of escape-hungry 'junkies,' comes this novel of tormented adolescents — neglected by society, victimized by ruthless dope peddlers."

Hal Ellson • ***Reefer Boy*** • LONDON: PEDIGREE BOOKS • 1955 • FIRST U.K. EDITION OF ELLSON'S *THE GOLDEN SPIKE*

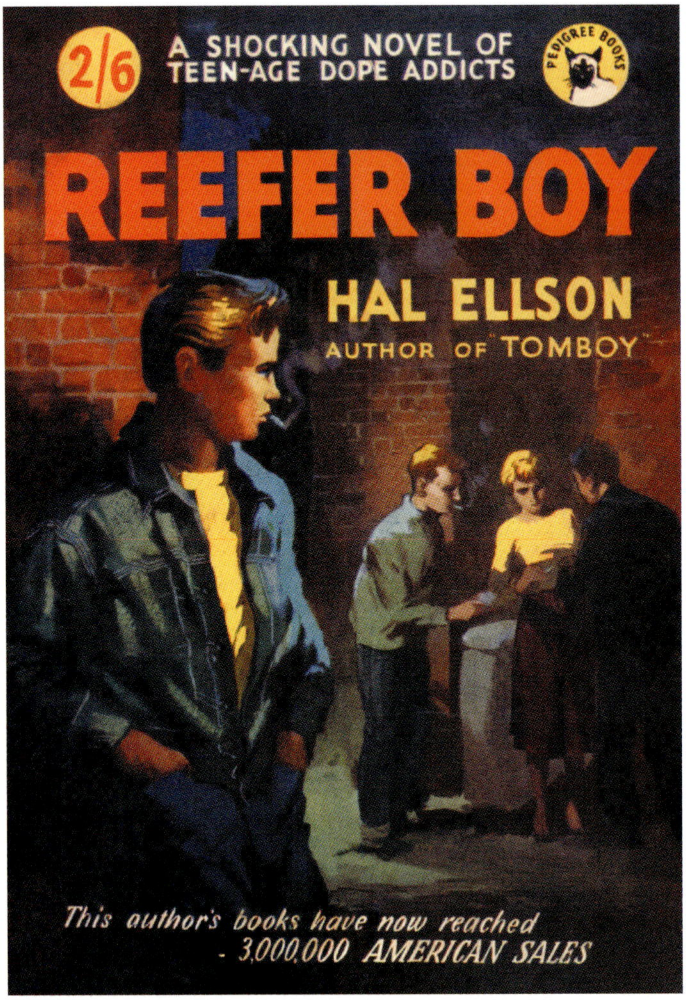

Thorpe's autobiographical classic of British drug addiction during the 1950s, *Viper* exposes the vividly sordid drug scene of London's Soho district and its bohemian underground.

Curiously, the title refers not to heroin addiction but to marijuana smokers, the word adapted from the the reptilian hiss that is manifest when inhaling on a skinny joint. The word was part of the jazz underground hipster slang prevalent in the U.S. as as early as the 1920s, and was immortalized in the song "If You're A Viper" (R. Howard, H. Malcolm, H. Moren) which jazz pianist and singer Fats Waller recorded to popular success.

"I dreamed about a reefer five foot long

Mighty Mezz but not too strong

You'll be high but not for long,

If you're a viper."

Note the reference to Mezz Mezzrow and the association of a well-rolled joint with his name.

Raymond Thorp • ***Viper*** • LONDON: WDL BOOKS • 1960 • REPRINT

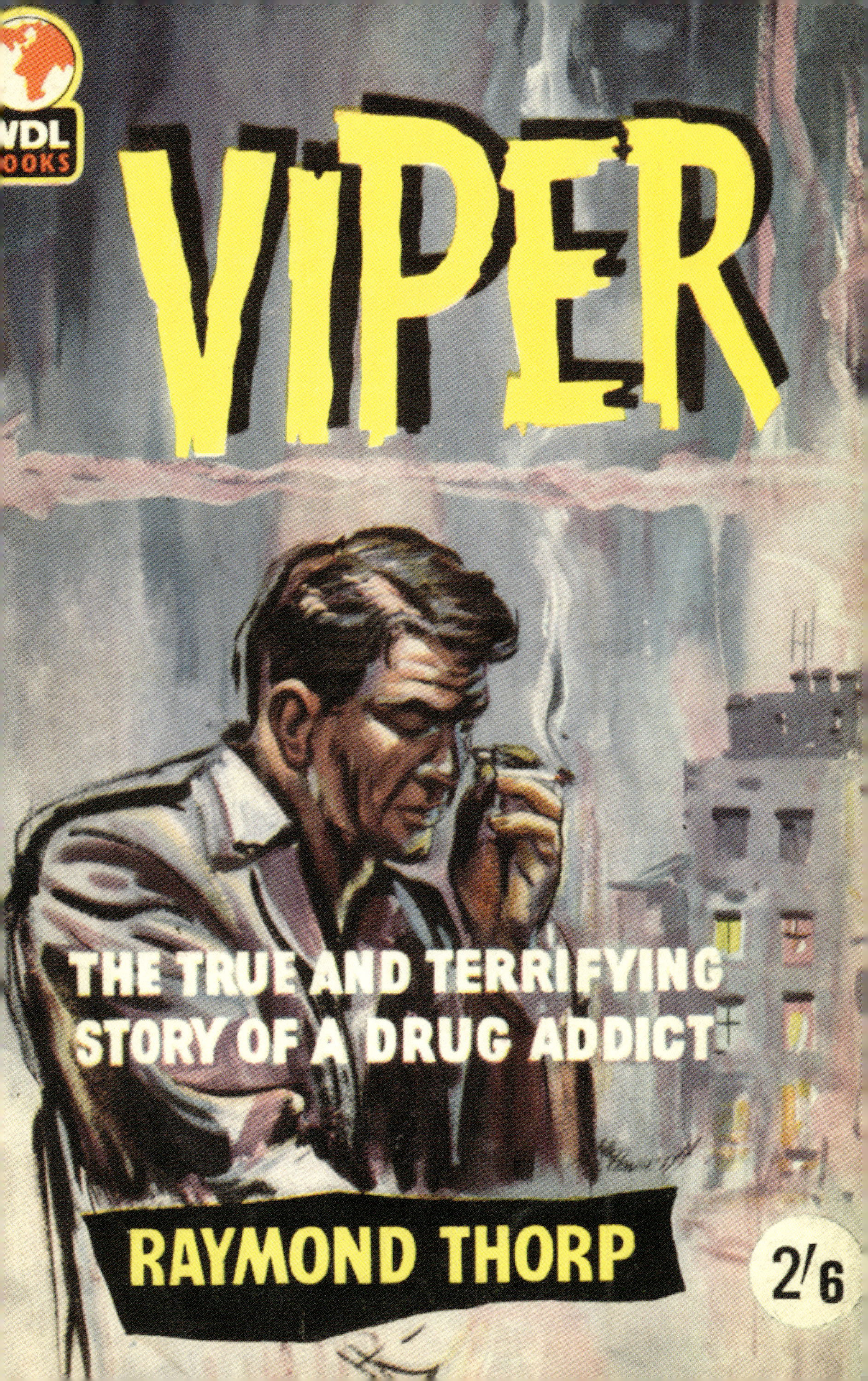
WDL
BOOKS
VIPER
THE TRUE AND TERRIFYING
STORY OF A DRUG ADDICT
RAYMOND THORP
2/6

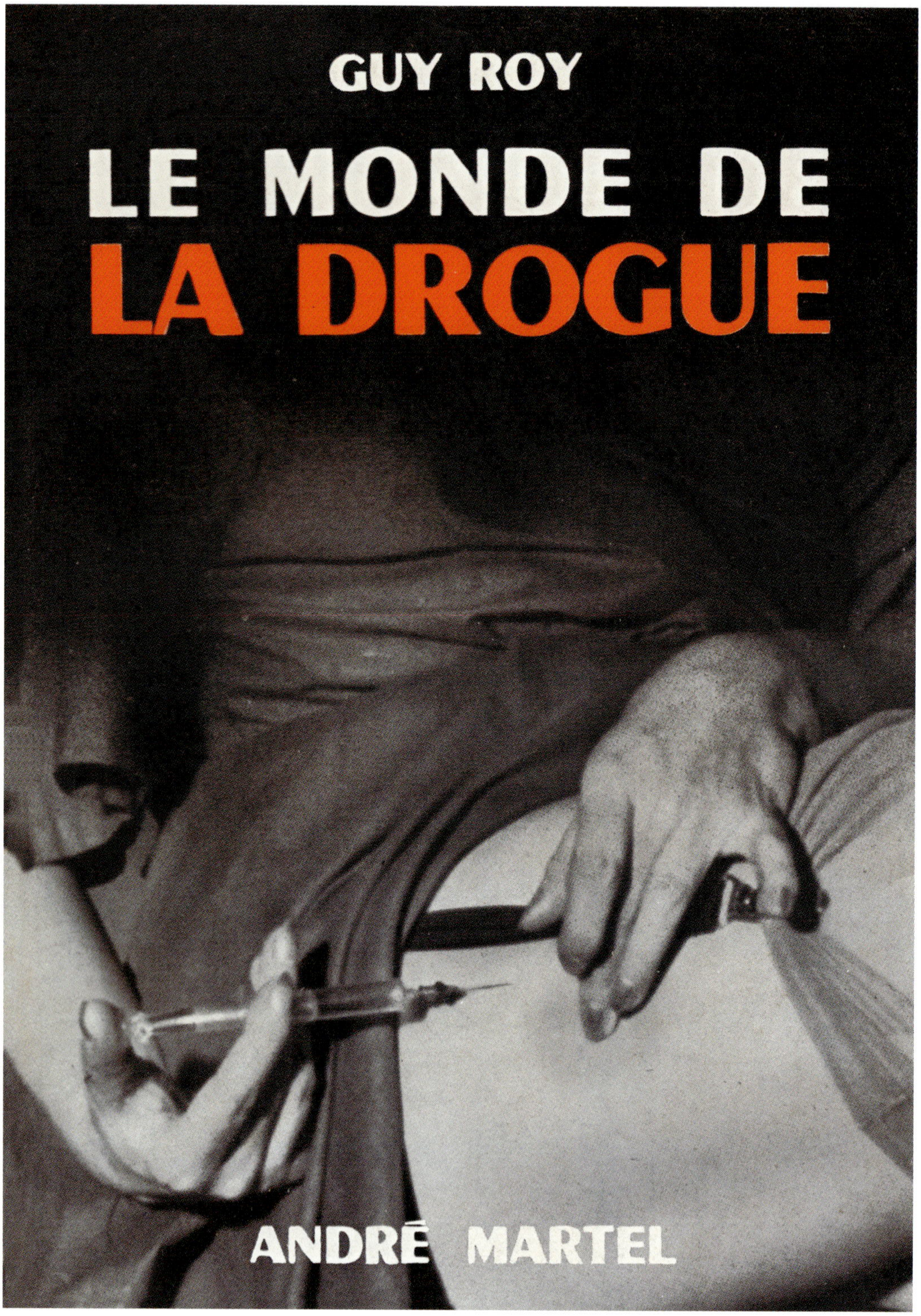

Guy Roy • ***Le Monde De La Drogue*** • GIVORS (RHONE): ANDRE MARTEL • 1955 • COURTESY OF WILLIAM DAILEY

L'Herbe Bleu: Journal Intime d'une Jeune Droguée • PARIS: PRESSES POCKET • CA.1968 • PBO

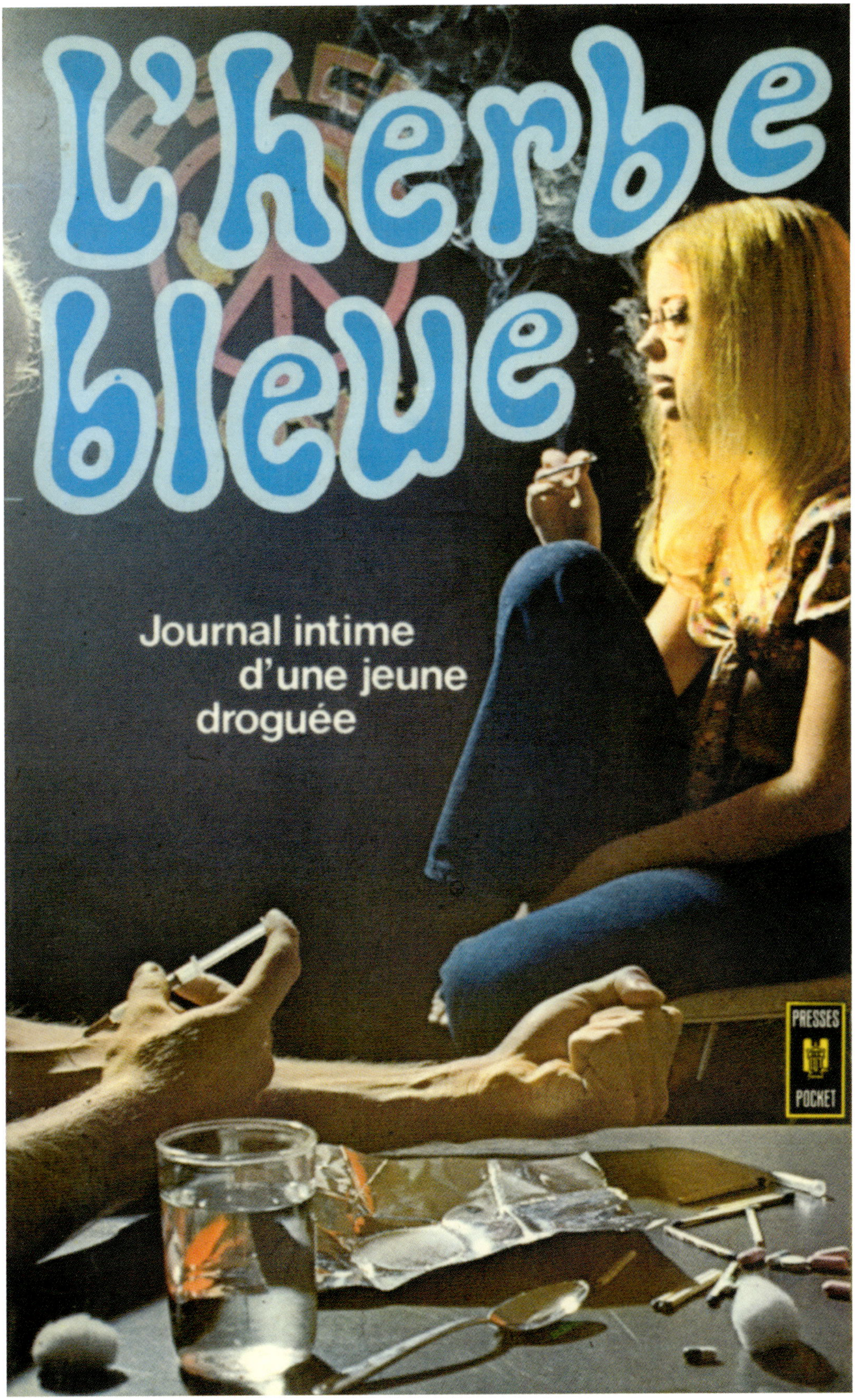
L'herbe bleue
Journal intime
d'une jeune
droguée
PRESSES
POCKET

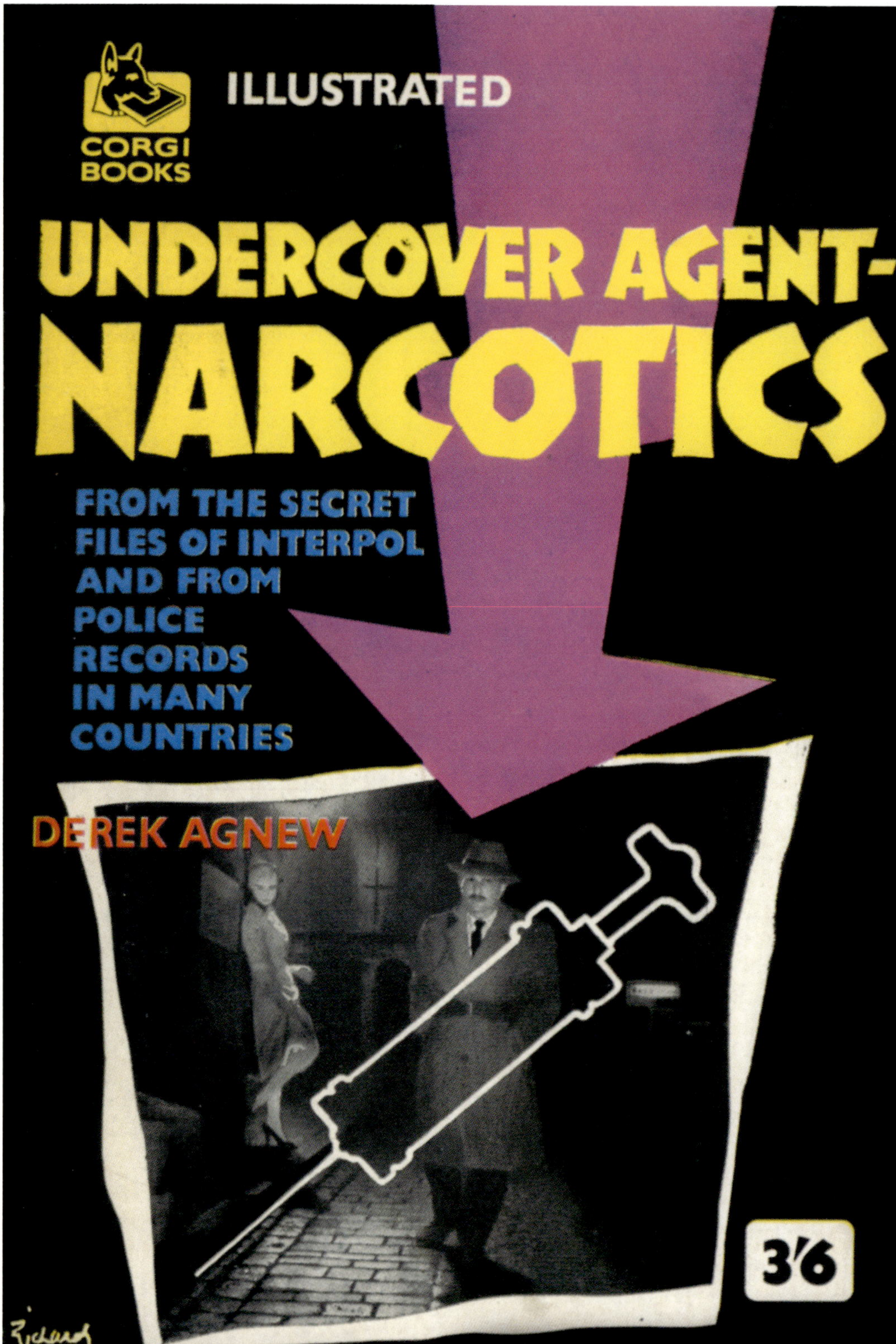

Derek Agnew • ***Undercover Agent — Narcotics*** • LONDON: CORGI 965 • 1959 • COVER BY ZACHERY • PBO

Richard Sapir and Warren Murphy • ***L'Implacable: L'Héroïne de la Mafia*** • PARIS: PLON 1977 • FIRST EDITION IN FRENCH OF *MAFIA FIX*

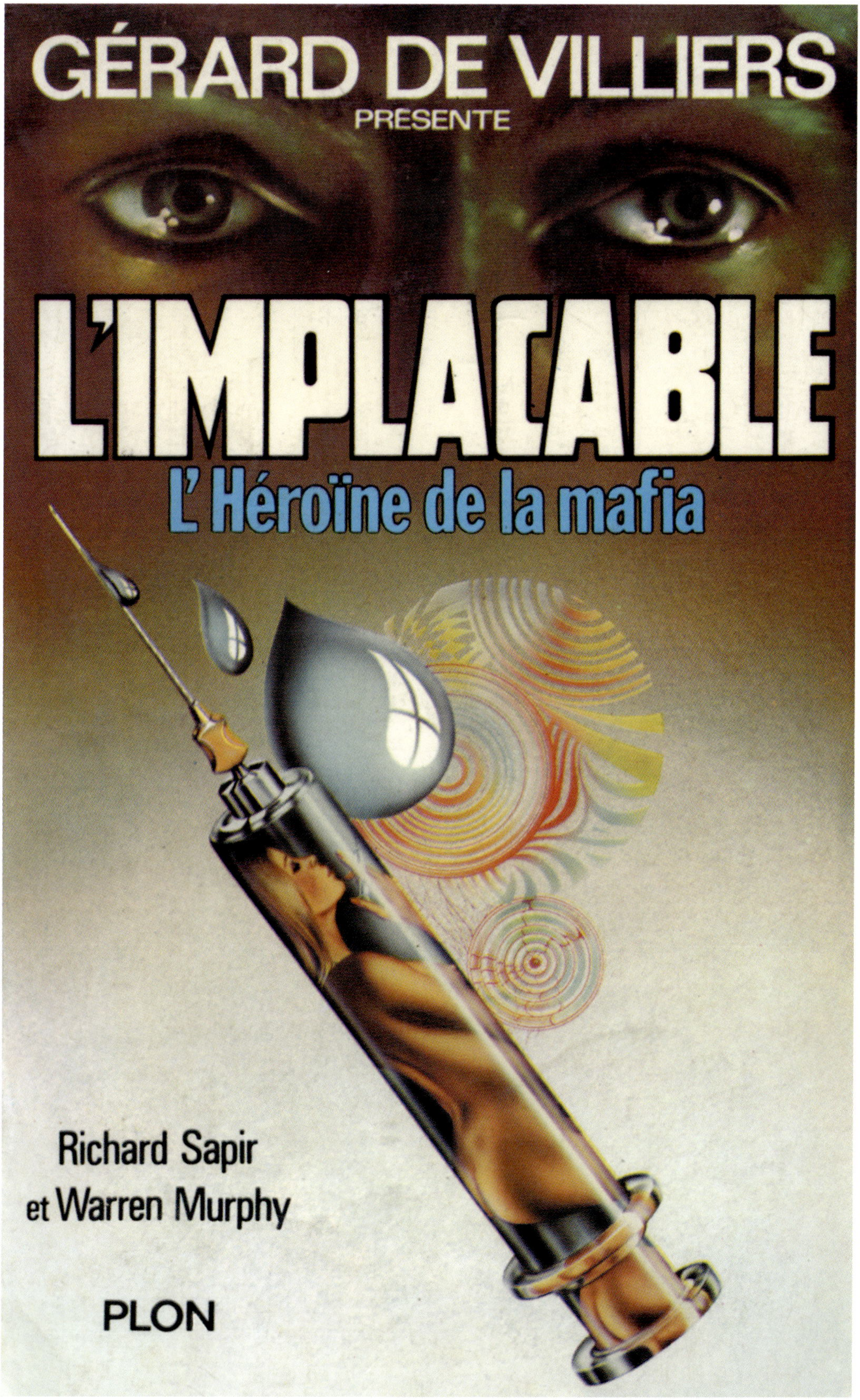
GÉRARD DE VILLIERS
PRÉSENTE
L'IMPLACABLE
L'Héroïne de la mafia
Richard Sapir
et Warren Murphy
PLON

ACKNOWLEDGEMENTS

Having sold the vast majority of my collection some time ago under the SJG Books For Bread program, I am deeply indebted to the following collectors and dealers who unselfishly devoted much time and effort providing me with images of books in their possession: **Doug Aanes**, **Bruce Brenner**, **Tony Jacobs**, and **Miriam Linna**. Messrs. Brenner and Aanes were particularly and enormously generous (and patient), and were extremely kind to share their unpublished drug paperbacks checklist with me. Unless indicated otherwise, the images within these pages are from their collections.

Brian Kirby continues to be a key source of insights and friendship, as does **Earl Kemp**. **Sharon Rudahl** and **William Kalinich** were kind to speak to me of their books, as was the late **Marsha Alexander**.

I owe a debt of gratitide to **Ronald K. Siegel, Ph.D.** for a key suggestion to the text, allowing me to scan images of scarce books within his vast and exceedingly fine collection of drug literature, and for ongoing friendship and discussion. **Michael Aldrich, Ph.D.** has my thanks for his encouragement and scans. **Beverly Potter** of **Ronin Press** was kind to answer a few questions. Mille grazie to **Ralph Sipper** who turned me on to the rarest (and most expensive) of them all and provided a scan of it. **Steve Holland** of the U.K. has been absolutely key in providing information on British paperback publishers and authors.

A warm thank you to the grand doyenne of paperback dealers, **Rose Idlet** of **Black Ace Books** for lending a helping hand.

Staff members of the **Los Angeles Central Library** were most helpful — and non-judgmental — with the many requests I made of them.

Very special thanks to **Mr. Julio Santo Domingo** of the **Ludlow-Santo Domingo (LSD) Library** in Geneva, Switzerland for images from the library's collection, and to library staff members **Natacha Antonini**, **Beatrice Rodriguez**, and the angelic, indefatigable **Flavia Aulieri** for their direct assistance, patience and forbearance.

Michael Horowitz and **William Dailey** were guiding spirits on this project. Mentors to me in this field of study, my professional association and friendship with these two gentlemen over the years has been quite rewarding and their support has been incalculable.

As captain of the *Dope Menace* pep squad, **Judith D. Henry** has been my pillar of support. Her love and faith kept me going during the anxiety attacks. Her feedback throughout the length of the project was invaluable.

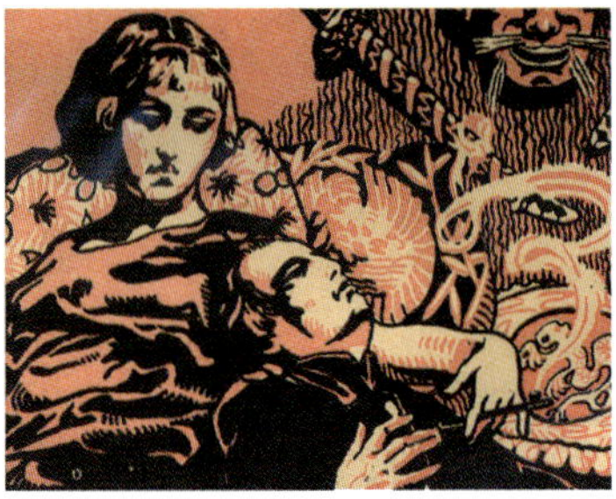

AUTHOR'S NOTE

This book does not pretend to include all drug paperbacks issued during the period under review, for reasons that will become clear within the text. There may be titles that to the hardcore collector are conspicuously absent. One such is *The Dealer* by Malcolm Spade [Tony Cohan], an excellent title originally planned for release as an Essex House book but which was ultimately issued as Brandon House Library Edition 6123 in 1970 in plain green wrappers with gilt decoration, shortly after Brian Kirby left Milton Luros' pulp porn organization. The author apologizes to those who feel that their favorites have been left out. Selection of the books included was entirely mine though some I wished to include were not available for scanning at press time.

REFERENCES

BACKGROUND MATERIAL VOLUMES NOT CITED IN THE TEXT:

Courtwright, D.T. *Dark Paradise. Opiate Addiction in America Before 1940.* Cambridge: Harvard University Press, 1982.

Courtwright, David, et al. *Addicts Who Survived: An Oral History of Narcotic Use in America,* 1923-1965. Knoxville: University of Tennessee Press, 1989.

Dailey, William. *Collections of a Bookseller. The Professional Rare Bookseller.* Journal of the Antiquarian Booksellers Association of America. No. 7, 1984, pp.8-11.

Holroyd, Graham. *Paperback Prices and Checklist.* Chattanooga: iGuide, 2003.

Kearney, Patrick J. *A Bibliography of the Olympia Press.* London: Black Spring Press, 1987.

Kearney, Patrick J. *A Bibliography of the New York Olympia Press.* Santa Rosa: Privately Printed, 1988.

Lovisi, Gary. *The Sexy Digests. A Survey, Checklist and Value Guide to the Sexy Exploitation Pin-Up Digest Paperbacks of the 1950s.* Brooklyn, Gryphon Books, 2001.

Perceau, Louis. *Bibliographie du Roman érotique au XIXe siècle.* Donnant une description complète de tous les romans, nouvelles, et autres ouvrages en prose, publiés sous le manteau en français, de 1800 à nos jours… Paris: Fourdrinier, 1930.

Pia, Pascal. *La Livres de L'Enfer Du XVI Siecle A Nos Jours.* Paris: Coulet & Faure, 1978.

Pressman, Jeffrey Lee. *Drugs, Counterculture & the Beat Generation in the Mass-Market Paperback: Two Hundred High (and low) Spots.* Books Are Everything, Vol. 5, No. 1, March 1992.

St Jorre, John de. *Venus Bound: The Erotic Voyage of the Olympia Press and Its Writers.* New York: Random House: 1994.

Wagner, Geoffrey. *Parade of Pleasure.* London: Verschoyle, 1954.

Warren, Jon. *Official Price Guide Paperbacks First Edition.* New York: House of Collectibles, 1991.

Wertham, Fredric. *Seduction of the Innocent.* New York: Holt, Rinehart, 1954.

ILLUSTRATION FROM COVER OF ***Le Royaume De L'Oubli*** *(Le Roman de l'Opium)*
PARIS: LA RENAISSANCE DU LIVRE, N.D. • CA. 1910 • COURTESY OF THE LUDLOW-SANTO DOMINGO (LSD) LIBRARY

"With long, meticulous fingers she prepared us each a pipe, cooking the little capsule over the flame and then, as the bubble appeared in it and swelled, slipping it with a deft twist of finger and thumb on to the tiny orifice beside the pipe, at the stem. For the bowl of an opium pipe is nothing but a smoke-filled reservoir. And from each pipe two or three lungfuls of smoke are obtainable, and the capsule is exhausted... I took the pipe from her hand, holding it near the flame. The first lungful began a beating in my head as if my skull were thin as a drum. Then it slowed, and slid through my body...the room about me seemed possessed of another dimension, seemed deeper, as if under the sea. A wall loomed up, and then as I turned my eyes, another, and then people, the two women, each on their couch gazing dreamily before them."

FROM ***Rogue Women*** • Nicholas Cutter (pseud.) • PARIS: OLYMPIA PRESS • 1955
REPRINTED IN PAPERBACK BY VARIOUS U.S. PUBLISHERS DURING THE 1960s.